How to Do It

Lovemaking in accord with advice from popular Renaissance how-to manuals on the best way to conceive a boy: heads are covered to keep essential fluids hot for their voyage to the genital area; he is on top to maximize sperm retention; the couple gaze lovingly into each other's eyes, thereby bringing their bodily humors into calm balance.

RUDOLPH M. BELL

How to Do It

Guides to Good Living for
Renaissance Italians

THE

UNIVERSITY OF

CHICAGO

PRESS

*

Chicago & London

Rudolph M. Bell is professor of history at Rutgers University. He is the author of *Fate and Honor, Family and Village: Demographic and Cultural Change in Rural Italy since 1800; Holy Anorexia;* and, with Donald Weinstein, *Saints and Society: The Two Worlds of Western Christendom, 1000–1700*—all published by the University of Chicago Press.

The University of Chicago Press, Chicago 60637
The University of Chicago Press, Ltd., London
© 1999 by Rudolph M. Bell
All rights reserved. Published 1999
08 07 06 05 04 03 02 01 00 99   1 2 3 4 5

ISBN: 0-226-04210-3 (cloth)

Library of Congress Cataloging-in-Publication Data

Bell, Rudolph M.
    How to do it : guides to good living for Renaissance Italians / Rudolph M. Bell.
        p. cm.
    Includes bibliographical references and index.
    ISBN 0-226-04210-3 (cloth : alk. paper)
    1. Family—Italy—History—16th century. 2. Marriage—Italy—History—16th century. 3. Conduct of life—Early works to 1800. 4. Life skills—Italy—Handbooks, manuals, etc. 5. Life skills—Italy—Early works to 1800. I. Title.
HQ629.B45   1999
646.7'00945'09031—dc21   98-35105
                                                                              CIP

For Gabriela and Luca Giovannetti,
joyful grandchildren

CONTENTS

ILLUSTRATIONS

The above illustrations were obtained with the assistance of Charles Greifenstein, curator of archives and manuscripts, from the Historical Services Division of the Library of the College of Physicians of Philadelphia. Figure 3.1, originally found in Jacopo Berengario's 1521 treatise, is reproduced from the copy in L. R. Lind's Chicago, 1959 edition of Berengario's work. All the other figures are from Girolamo Mercurio, *La commare* (Venice, 1601).

The frontispiece, reproduced courtesy of the Pierpont Morgan Library/Art Resource NY is an anonymous sixteenth-century Lombard drawing, *Couple in Bed*, taken from Leonardo da Vinci's *Treatise on Art Theory;* from a sketchbook, c. 1560–1580.

ACKNOWLEDGMENTS

More than a decade has passed since I began reading sixteenth-century Italian advice manuals seriously, and no doubt several people I now thank may have forgotten the project. More worrisome is that I may fail to remember a helping hand or two, for which I apologize. My memory is not all it once was, several generations of computers have come and gone, along with the bytes they contained, and my handwritten notes are scattered over two continents.

Cristina Ciccaglione, with her profound knowledge of how to find catalogued, uncatalogued, and miscatalogued materials at the Biblioteca Nazionale Centrale in Rome, got me started. In Rome I received more-conventional yet still courteous and helpful support at the Alessandrina Library and the Biblioteca Vaticana. At the University of Rome, Sofia Boesch Gajano, Claudio Schiavoni, and Eugenio Sonnino provided hospitality and a wealth of good advice.

In Florence, my home-away-from-home was the Biblioteca Nazionale Centrale, especially the rare book and consultation rooms, with their dedicated personnel. At the University of Florence, Sergio Bertelli, Mario Materassi, and Michele Ranchetti assisted me and my work in various ways.

I also am grateful for the professionalism of librarians at the Marucelliana and Riccardiana in Florence, at the British Library in London, and at the Folger Shakespeare Library, the Library of the College of Physicians of Philadelphia, the New York Public Library, and the libraries of Columbia, Harvard, Princeton, and Stanford Universities in the United States.

Back at my Rutgers University Alexander Library home, Joseph Consoli has been a mainstay and the entire entourage, starting at the top with Maryann Gaunt, has always been friendly and efficient. Also at Rutgers, Deans Tilden G. Edelstein, Richard L. McCormick, and Richard F. Foley, along with departmental chairs Ziva Galili and John Whiteclay Chambers II, provided friendship, financial support, and flexibility in allowing me time for research. The Study Abroad Program headed by Seth Gopin, for which I served as resident director in Florence during 1986–87 and 1994–95, and in England during 1995–96, put me where I needed to be. The students for whom I was responsible in those years all were wonderfully responsible themselves, which allowed me to spend some time on sixteenth-century matters. One of them, Carol Videtti, did outstanding work as my research assistant in 1986–87. Fellow Florence program directors Cristina Ancillotti and Jules Maidoff provided forums for presenting work-in-progress.

In the writing, two colleagues at Rutgers have been generous well beyond the call of duty in sharing their expertise: Jack Cargill on Greco-Roman sources and William Connell on humanism and the Italian Renaissance more generally. Other colleagues to whom I am grateful for coming to the rescue in one way or another are Andrea Baldi, Mia Bay, Alastair Bellany, John J. Giannotti, Guido Guarino, Donald Kelley, John Lenaghan, Jennifer Morgan, Karl Morrison, Philip Pauly, James W. Reed, Stephen Reinert, Traian Stoianovich, and Laura White.

Several professional friends made time to read an earlier version of what is now this book and offered extensive comments, which I hope I have put to good use. Ziva Galili, Martha Howell, Jennifer Jones, David Oshinsky, and Bonnie Smith—I thank you all profusely and wholeheartedly!

This is the fourth book I've done with Doug Mitchell as my editor at the University of Chicago Press. On each occasion I have thoroughly enjoyed working with him. The two anonymous reader reports he obtained were very helpful, especially the one that provided ten pages of detailed corrections. Ann Donahue edited the manuscript with splendid capacity and patience.

My family not only has put up with me for many years but also assisted directly in the work. They came along to Europe for extended stays, variously sacrificing career, friends, and normalcy. Laura Tomici Bell helped graciously, insightfully, and repeatedly with reading and analyzing texts. My daughter Alessia made cogent comments on several chapters and compiled an outstanding bibliography of advice manuals published over several centuries, which helped me to understand how-to books as a definable genre. My daughter Tara labored diligently printing out thousands of microfilm frames, and later she answered my innumerable dumb questions about pregnancy and nursing; more than that, she and her husband Steve let me try out some recommendations from sixteenth-century advice manuals on their children, to whom I dedicate this book.

CHAPTER

· *I* ·

Readers

Our parents may well have consulted an advice manual telling them how to conceive us, along with information on choosing the right moment for our conception. The same little book probably had a chapter about how to influence the likelihood that we would be a boy or a girl, followed by sections telling our mothers how to care for us in the womb, what to expect each month, and how to cope with a variety of physical discomforts and emotional swings. Once hospitals decided to allow fathers into the delivery room, guidebooks followed telling Dad how to be helpful. At our crib side surely there was a copy of Dr. Benjamin Spock, neatly indexed to find the solution to any problem. Parents and children gained relief in learning that everyone went through "the terrible twos." Further along, some of us may have been raised on the more fearsome teachings of Larry Christenson, J. Richard Fugate, and their fellow fundamentalists to use the hickory stick regularly and with vigor. Later came Dr. Seuss, and for the slower learners, books on how to teach Johnny to read.

Adolescence brought a new avalanche of printed wisdom. We were told how to combat acne, how to behave on a first date, how to be asked to the prom, when to kiss, what tongue kissing is, whether one can get pregnant from heavy petting, how to lose weight, and how to style our hair. There followed a range of books on which college to choose, which career to prepare for, how to find a rich husband, or perhaps a loving one, the traits of a good wife, and coping with exam stress, homework, loneliness, conflict with parents, sexual orientation, and just plain growing up.

As adults our dependence on advice manuals continues. They easily outsell every other sort of book by such a margin that best-seller lists often separate them to allow other works of nonfiction a place. Is any home without them? They tell us how to cook, how to repair our automobiles, how to fix a leaking faucet, how to paint the porch, how to travel on a low budget, how to heal our minor aches and pains, how to make a killing in the stock market, how to pay less tax, how to buy a home or a car, and how to commit suicide with minimum discomfort. Nor is the advice manual limited to purely practical, verifiable concerns. Indeed, the biggest sellers give us handy guidelines on how to be happy, how to get to heaven, how to achieve orgasm, how to be successful, how to get through menopause, how to cope with old age, and how to die with dignity.

When I sat down to write this paragraph (October 27, 1996), the number one best-seller according to the *New York Times Book Review* was a book titled *The Rules: Time-Tested Secrets for Capturing the Heart of Mr. Right* (eight hundred thousand copies in print so far). Television personalities like Oprah Winfrey and Jay Leno joked about *The Rules,* while some feminists feared that the book actually set back their efforts; but other people were paying $250 an hour for telephone consultations with the authors and forming self-help organizations to support sisters having trouble sticking to its precepts. Could it be that five centuries ago printed advice like this little best-seller shaped people's behavior in any way? The same *Book Review* showed that a close runner-up to *The Rules* had been on the best-seller list for 109 straight weeks: *Chicken Soup for the Soul,* a "collection of stories meant to open the heart and rekindle the spirit," according to the blurb. Also in this issue was a page-length ad from a respected university press devoted entirely to advice manuals, including a book on how to live and die with cancer, another on alopecia areata, and a third on HIV; the list closed with a book titled *The Prostate: A Guide for Men and the Women Who Love Them.* Another ad, occupying a full page, touted a three-volume video set that moves from guiding couples to "better" sex, on to "advanced" sex, and finally to "making sex fun"; it carried all the respectability of an "institute" mailing address and of course the fine name of the *New York Times* itself. Buyers were assured, nonetheless, that these goods, plus a giveaway on sexual creativity, would arrive in plain packaging. All in all, a pretty typical late-twentieth-century week for the advice-manual genre, except maybe for being a little sparse on how to get to heaven.

Among the many forms of literature that surround us, the advice manual seems to be of little historical importance. We look always for the latest and freshest, with the new twist or the new secret revealed. Keeping up with the most recent fad is everything. Today's miracle drug is Prozac, the au courant illness is anorexia nervosa (or was that last year's rage?), the latest panacea is safe sex, or perhaps it is a Mediterranean diet, low cholesterol, Viagra, trekking, or loving Jesus. Name the problem and there is a book telling you how to solve it; the goal, and there is a book on how to reach it; the desire, and there is a book on how to fulfill it.

The ephemeral quality of the advice manual, along with its notorious intellectual shallowness, may account for the relative lack of scholarly interest in this genre. The advice our grandparents took seriously may seem quaintly antiquarian to us, at best a humorous compote of misinformation laced with harmless backwardness. Serious works meant to guide our lives, and we may count everything from Plato to the Bible among these, have a lasting quality, a philosophical underpinning that separates them from recyclable how-to-do-it manuals.

Classic books are bound in cloth, printed with care on high-quality paper, purchased by serious libraries, and assigned for reading by college students in inexpensive editions. If we lend one to a friend, we want it back to be displayed on our coffee table, passed on to our children, inventoried, and admired. The advice manual leads a very different existence. A cookbook may stay around for a few years, but it is likely to get burned on a hot stove or suffer gravy stains; a medical "encyclopedia" may last a lifetime, but you would not pass along such outdated misinformation to your children's household. The rest lead an even more transitory existence: cheap acidic paper that turns yellow-brown, brittle spines, no library willing to accept them as a donation, no neighbor interested in buying them at a yard sale. The very eagerness with which we devour an advice manual on first read, or insistently share it with our partner, is matched only by our total indifference to it soon after. Even the most popular books on how to get to heaven lose their inspirational power on rereading. And how many of us actually reconsult a sex manual if we fail to achieve the promised results on our first or second try?

Under the category of "popular-advice manual" I intend to include books that vary considerably among themselves in content, style, and purpose. Let me provide a few examples from contemporary American bookstore shelves before turning to sixteenth-century Italy. As I revise this paragraph on October 12, 1997, *The Rules* no longer appears on the *New York Times Book Review* best-seller list, and if you're looking for Christmas stocking stuffers as joke gifts, you'll find dozens of copies on the bargain-book table at your local shopping mall. In my judgment *The Rules* fits nicely at the ephemeral, shallow end of the advice-manual spectrum. At the opposite extreme, I would place Dr. Spock's recommendations on baby care; they have had a much better shelf life, and their author brought impeccable scholarly credentials to his endeavor. Still, one may wonder why the advice has needed revision six times ("FULLY REVISED and updated for the 1990s" is the blurb on the 1992 edition) since it was first published in 1946 as *The Common Sense Book of Baby and Child Care.* Moreover, "common sense" no longer appears in the latest edition's title, just one of many puzzles I leave to your judgment. Apart from a new edition's value as a marketing technique, have the times changed so much—the babies, the parents, psychology, medical knowledge, everything?

Without answering that one, let's complicate things by thinking as well about why Dale Carnegie's *How to Win Friends and Influence People,* a thirty-million-copy best-seller (running behind Spock's fifty million but still a clear winner among advice manuals), has been translated into thirty languages and reprinted hundreds of times but never revised since its original appearance in 1936. A look at the Carnegie Internet site shows that the book continues to hold a central place in the experiences of millions of graduates worldwide of Dale Carnegie courses in effective speaking, stress management, business success, and human relations. It is an advice manual many people invest in seriously, one we might place somewhere between ephemera like *The Rules* and quality advice from Dr. Spock. As a quick refresher, here are Carnegie's "seven rules for making your home life happier."[1]

Rule 1: Don't nag.
Rule 2: Don't try to make your partner over.
Rule 3: Don't criticize.
Rule 4: Give honest appreciation.
Rule 5: Pay little attentions.
Rule 6: Be courteous.
Rule 7: Read a good book on the sexual side of marriage.

Some may snicker at the homeyness of this advice, while others may see nuggets of eternal wisdom. So be it. Our provisional advice-manual spectrum shall extend from the short-lived and shallow to the classic and erudite, so long as these books manifest a conscious effort to reach out to the self-help, how-to needs of sixteenth-century Italian families. My preference, when in doubt about definitions and boundaries, will be to err on the side of inclusiveness since you, the reader, can more easily pass over my discussion of a work you find extraneous than you can recover something I exclude entirely.

Now, with our flexible sense of what an advice manual might contain,

I invite you to leave the present behind and join me in an excursion through several dozen self-help books from sixteenth-century Italy, including some with rules for making your home life happier expressed with an aplomb to match Dale Carnegie's folksy maxims. My focus will be on advice concerning how to be a manly man or a womanly woman. Excluded entirely from our literary journey will be dozens of interesting sixteenth-century cookbooks and farmers' almanacs, as well as most advice manuals having no bearing on questions of relations between the sexes. Someday I would like to try a few of Bartolomeo Scappi's recipes; after all, he was chef to Pope Pius V, so the culinary delights must have been exquisite. The life of the gentleman farmer also beckons, perhaps when I retire. However, by limiting ourselves to a narrower range of advice manuals—those dealing with interactions among men, women, and their children—I hope to make the present work a coherent whole.

Occasionally the authors we encounter will be familiar names, such as the theologian Desiderius Erasmus and the Greek biographer Plutarch (both appearing in vernacular translations), and a few titles, such as *The Courtier*, still evoke considerable interest among literary critics. But our main concern with these "elite" items will be with how publishers transformed them into popular-advice manuals to be sold in less expensive editions with indexes, tables of contents, and capsule summaries added to facilitate quick consultation. The print medium tended to transgress presumed boundaries between high and low culture. Moreover, as we shall see, not everything written by classic theologians and biographers was particularly classic. Most authors and titles we shall engage, on the other hand, have been ignored or forgotten for centuries, although quite a few went through multiple editions in their day. We shall uncover almanacs telling farmers how to govern their wives, books telling priests how to use the confessional to guide their parishioners toward proper behavior, vernacular medical advice, herbals, books of secrets, and even literary spoofs done in the style of a how-to book.

Historians quite rightly have emphasized the critical importance of the printed word in the spread of Protestantism and in the development of enlightened scientific method. Much also has been made of Rome's censorship of the printing press, this being after all the moment when the Index of Prohibited Books was introduced, when printers were condemned to prison and their presses smashed. These truths notwithstanding, I shall treat Roman Catholic advice manuals as competitors for display space and sales against books presenting different views. This approach is in keeping with how Catholic Reformation leaders understood themselves. They knew they could not entirely suppress the spread of pernicious ideas through the printed book, although they certainly tried. So, influential prelates actively adopted the enemy's tactics and published with a vengeance. At the high end, the well-known Jesuit Antonio Possevino provided a list of ideologically correct books, the *Bibliotheca selecta qua agitur de ratione studiorum in historia, in disciplinis, in salute omnium procuranda,* first printed in 1593, which encompasses a total cultural program for the young scholar. But even this work underwent transformations typical of the advice manual, including major editorial changes clearly aimed at making it more accessible. Subsequent editions featured a more manageable quarto or octavo format, included extensive Italian translations for readers who did not know Latin, and added condensations (crib notes, we would call them) of the recommended books.[2] Possevino's selections are very studious indeed, nothing like the lowbrow popular manuals for parish priests and their flock that I shall be exploring, but rest assured that the same Catholic authorities supported both ways of influencing the faithful.

The church specifically courted female readers. Recent findings from a team of scholars led by Gabriella Zarri documented persuasively the conscious, massive efforts of Catholic reformers to control, shape, prescribe, reward, and inspire good Christian behavior among virgins, matrons, and widows of all conditions through books. The trusted traditions of convent discipline found their way into vernacular plays, poems, elementary readers, household guides, confessionals, pastorals, inspirational biographies, and hagiographies meant to be read by ladies, whether they resided in a convent or a secular home. Zarri's team recovered and individually listed 2,626 vernacular books/pamphlets addressed to female concerns and printed in Italy between 1471 and 1700. Among these, over 1,000 works had appeared by 1600, the cutoff date for my own study. Indeed, publication of prescriptive Christian literature for women actually peaked in the last quarter of the sixteenth century, both in absolute number of titles and in the percentage of them addressed primarily to laywomen. The advice manual, then, was just one genre in an array of Italian books for women.[3]

Several of the texts we shall examine first circulated in handwritten copies during the fourteenth and fifteenth centuries, products of what historian Elizabeth Eisenstein called a scribal culture.[4] Indeed, the later Middle Ages saw a great interest in giving advice on proper ways to raise a family. Churchmen led the way in writing explicitly didactic works, for example, the twelfth-century epistle by St. Bernard on governing the family *(Bernardus de cura rei famuliaris),*[5] and lay humanists were not far behind. Among the most elegant and detailed secular works in this genre was Leon Battista Alberti's *I libri della famiglia,* a book that today is still widely read and quoted. Many of these handwritten manuscripts kindled the interest of early publishers who chose to make copies or translations of them more widely available in the new medium of the printed book, as happened with St. Bernard's epistle, although it apparently was not a best-seller. But other handwritten works, including Alberti's *I libri,* remained on the shelves of monastic libraries or in the studies of elite scholars.

Literary taste was no less fickle then than it often seems to be today, and I am at a loss to explain why some manuscripts were not translated or printed. While Alberti's *I libri* went unpublished in the sixteenth century, the classic he so freely adapted (plagiarized?), Xenophon's *Economicus,* appeared in a 1540 Italian translation by Alessandro Piccolomini. Moreover, another of Alberti's works, *Hecatomphila,* a little tract of twenty-seven leaves that proclaims it will first teach young male neophytes the art of making love and then in part 2 will offer advice to women on how to end a relationship that has soured, was a huge success in the world of sixteenth-century print but is virtually unknown today. Why? For sure, we may hazard a guess that those manuscripts that did not make it to printed editions were judged by the printers themselves (who were what today we would understand as publishers) to be money-losing propositions, items that not enough people would buy at a given price. But what went into the decision-making process is not easy to reconstruct. It seems to me that at the high end of the market, publishers were concerned primarily with quality. They were willing to print items with very narrow, prestige-oriented markets because they could get away with charging a huge price from wealthy aristocrats for whom cost was a secondary concern. Once the target audience shifted to commercial and professional classes, however, sales potential mattered more, and items that would become of great interest to literary scholars in later centuries simply did not justify a printed edition. Dusting off Alberti's advice on seduction and on ending an unwanted relationship—all in a few little pages—had the feel of commercial success, as did a fresh translation of the quick-paced economic precepts of a wise ancient Greek like Xenophon. On the other hand, *I libri della famiglia,* a lengthy and wandering philosophical treatise on family governance by a Florentine patrician better known for his studies of architecture, just had too little market potential.

Take as another example the merchant Paolo da Certaldo's *Libro di buoni costumi* (Book of Good Ways), a delightful collection of aphorisms written around 1350 or 1360, in a vigorous Tuscan spoken dialect, surely a work known to Florence's educated men. It waited until the twentieth century to find a publisher! Whatever influence it may have had in the sixteenth century would have been limited to repetition of its little treasures in other works that succeeded commercially. Since my purpose is to capture for modern readers the range of printed advice available in sixteenth-century Italy, I reluctantly exclude most earlier works from the scribal culture, such as those by Paolo da Certaldo and Leon Battista Alberti, that did not find sufficient favor to enter the print domain at that time.[6]

Although my intent is to let the original texts speak for themselves, there are two major themes I shall highlight. The first is variety—the confusion of authorities made possible when so many printing presses, some quite transitory, emerged in so many places, setting forth with considerable freedom whatever truth or nonsense an author wished. What had been the controlled territory of a sovereign or of the church—the ability to communicate an idea or a directive—became a free-for-all with few rules. Plagiarism flourished, copyright protection ended at local borders, and printers flouted laws dealing with slander or libel. As early as 1540, preambles to legislation in Venice, where book publishing became a major contributor to the economy, lamented that the art of printing had sunk so low as to bring disgrace upon the city: "Economy, competition, greed, and cheap workmanship" affected the "whole literary world of Italy. . . . Venetian printer-publishers were in the habit of ignoring literary proprietorship altogether, and were accustomed to print any work they pleased, even in direct opposition to the wishes of the author." Laws threatened to confiscate and burn cheap, pirated editions, but no such thing seems to have happened. Even the push for guilds to regulate printers and booksellers had limited impact; censorship was important more for a few spectacular prosecutions than for its success in restricting the circulation of ideas.[7]

The second major theme in my work is how the printed word allowed authorities, or writers merely claiming to be authorities, to enter the intimate recesses of private life. A preacher like Bernardino da Siena once had filled the piazza with his thundering denunciations of improper sexual behavior by married couples, but public modesty meant that he and his clerical brothers could not instruct the faithful—orally and in explicit detail—about exactly what kinds of kissing and touching were evil. The printed book opened this avenue of communication, directly in manuals meant to be read by good Catholics before bedtime, as well as through inexpensive, vernacular confessionals for priests now helped by having before their individual eyes pocket-sized books containing appropriately delicate but precise words for interrogating the faithful.

The range of advice was wide indeed and by no means limited to sex. What to look for in a good midwife, secret salves for alleviating a baby's teething pains, how hard to push a child to read, what to do about a boorish husband or a flirtatious wife—all this and much more might be found in how-to manuals. Some purveyors of this popular wisdom trumpeted their noble titles or clerical offices, while others touted with equal vigor their independence of any pedigree, license, or official standing. Chaos reigned as access to print undermined authority, notwithstanding prodigious efforts by church and state to the contrary. Only after several centuries did power holders and gatekeepers of taste regain the upper hand in creating a hierarchy of trust in the printed word. Some of us may look for an "imprimatur," while others are faithful to the *New York Times*, because it claims to contain "all the news that is fit to print." Academics and administrators who determine tenure for college professors look for books published by university presses. And now that the Internet is poised to challenge print culture in ways that harken back five hundred years to print's supplantation of the world of scribes, anarchy once again threatens the norms of information retrieval and dissemination. Politicians join moralists and engineers to impose standards on what may reside in and be retrieved from the Internet; companies such as CyberPatrol and NetNanny promise to separate the wheat from the chaff, while protecting the innocent from pornography and violence.

The locale for my study of early-printed-advice manuals is the Italian peninsula, mostly for practical reasons. I have been studying the Italian historical scene for many years, so its contours are familiar to me. Moreover, the books and pamphlets under scrutiny usually were printed on cheap paper, bound poorly if at all. Copies often exist only in specialized libraries in Italy. I had the pleasure of working in Rome and Florence from mid-1985 until mid-1987, and again during much of 1994 and 1995, and was able to recover for my readers a wide range of popular literature without too many restrictions from the keepers of rare books. A similar potpourri of materials surely exists in various languages in different parts of Europe; more than a decade ago, Steven Ozment brought to scholarly attention some popular German-language materials, and very recently Suzanne Hull completed a fine study of English books telling housewives how to behave.[8] Yet more remains to be explored worldwide.

Closely related to the advice manual, especially in its pulpier manifes-

tations, is the "book of secrets." The brilliant and thorough recent study
by William Eamon, *Science and the Secrets of Nature,* explores this genre,
which consistently aims to tell "how to" rather than to explain "why."
These books, which often went through numerous printings, were very
popular with sixteenth-century readers. For unabashed hype and ample
doses of quackery, their contents rival anything on the self-help market
today. When the "books of secrets" examined by Eamon concern relations between the sexes, I freely recross some of his terrain. Although I
think many of my readers would also enjoy reading Eamon's book, I do
not want to make his work a prerequisite for my narrative.[9]

At the other, quality end of our self-defined advice-manual spectrum,
one might place pastoral literature from moralizing clerics like Girolamo
Savonarola and the dialogues of humanist philosophers such as Francesco Barbaro, both to be visited in the pages that follow. Many of these
works offer advice on gender relations, especially the proper behavior of
women, and Ruth Kelso, in her magisterial study *Doctrine for the Lady
of the Renaissance,* decades ago focused on these materials with an extraordinarily accomplished eye. This is another book the reader would
find useful, but once again I shall not make it a prerequisite.[10]

How to Do It begins with conception and features a series of manuals
aimed at married couples that tell them how God and the medical experts
think they should behave in bed. Without exception, these little books
have as their primary purpose the imparting of knowledge concerning
conception, but along the way they tell us much else about human relations and the art of lovemaking. The next chapter collects advice on pregnancy, mostly from vernacular medical texts intended for both midwives
and their patients, concluding as these manuals often do with childbirth
itself.

Our journey continues through the years of child rearing, beginning
with breast-feeding and related aspects of infant care, continuing with
the discipline of young children, and then turning to their education and
the problems of adolescence. This division bears a striking resemblance
to modern, Eriksonian-like approaches to understanding the life cycle,
but I can assure readers that these ways of thinking are abundantly
clear in the texts themselves and were not simply imposed by me as a
twentieth-century historian.[11]

The next set of advice manuals concerns whether to marry and how
to choose a spouse, more often a wife than a husband. Here I do include
a fair range of openly misogynous texts that purport to be advice manuals
but in fact seem to aim at providing perverse enjoyment for unmarried

men, many of them undoubtedly clerics. These books portray in especially clear fashion the battle of the sexes and masculine claims of superiority. There are a significant number of texts that take the opposite view,
arguing that women are equal or superior to men, but these works generally do not take the form of an advice manual. From there we turn to
more practical recommendations on how husbands and wives should
treat each other, and finally to prescriptions about proper behavior during widowhood.

Throughout this journey the emphasis is on what we can see in the
texts. For many pages we shall be browsing at a quite leisurely pace,
soaking things in rather than instantly analyzing, more to capture and
enjoy what is said than to impose modern interpretations and patterns.
Roger Chartier's injunction that, "the history of reading must be radically
distinguished from a history of what is read" is persuasive but not more
valid than his acknowledgment that, "to read is always to read something."[12] My book tries above all else to capture that "something." Sec-
ondarily, I focus on how these books may have been read, and for what
purposes, by the sixteenth-century people for whom they were written.[13]
That brings up two essential questions: Who bought these advice manuals? And who read them?

Most research on early print and literacy has concentrated on erudite
people, tracing carefully the appearance in the sixteenth century of
printed Latin translations of Greek works, the expansion of university
education to include an ever widening range of secular concerns, and
the development of a generally accepted version of Tuscan as the language we know as written Italian. We are extremely fortunate, therefore,
that one of the great living scholars on these matters, Paul F. Grendler,
also took time to dip into the hurly-burly of popular print on the Italian
peninsula. He tells us that popular books were instantly recognizable to
sixteenth-century people, by their size and print font rather than by the
covers, as we recognize such books today, because most often they did
not even have covers.[14] Venice was a great market for all kinds of books,
as visitors from throughout Europe arrived by ship to purchase them with
the same eagerness that today's tourists go there to buy Murano glass.[15]
One bibliophile lamented that the enormous number of books in print
made it difficult to find the individual ones of real interest.[16] We know
that there were at least thirteen hundred printer/editors (publishers) in
sixteenth-century Italy, with something over a third of them based in
Venice, but we cannot determine how many works each establishment
published, nor do we know with certainty for how long many of them

were in existence. The average print run was probably about a thousand copies, although proven best-sellers commanded runs of four thousand copies or more. Altogether, business was brisk.[17]

Books were not cheap relative to today's prices, but then again neither was anything else. Bread, theater tickets, travel, and books all have gone way down in real price over the centuries. From Grendler we learn that in 1500, the Venetian printer Aldus Manutius had copies of his five-volume set of Greek Aristotle on sale for eleven ducats, somewhere between 10 and 20 percent of the annual take-home salary of a university professor who might want to buy such a magnificent item. Competition was fierce, however, forcing printers to put out books aimed at an ever broader public.[18] Prices declined steadily over the next century, with popular texts printed on cheap paper in octavo or smaller sizes always costing only a tiny fraction of what a fabulous set of Greek volumes could command. Transposing now from Grendler's figures for ordinary books (octavos or duodecimos of 150 to 400 pages, typical all along the advice-manual spectrum), a fully employed master mason, who typically earned about a hundred ducats per year in the second half of the sixteenth century, could have bought a book for anywhere from 6 to 40 soldi. At 124 soldi to the ducat—and assuming a forty-hour work week—this means he would have had to spend the earnings from between two and thirteen hours of work to buy a book—high, yet not outrageous or unreachable.[19] Today, a skilled mason might labor for less than an hour to make a similar purchase, but even in the sixteenth century, working people could acquire books. The next question is, could a master mason read?

In a city such as Venice in the late fifteen hundreds, Grendler estimates that about one in every three adult males was literate. Approximately half these men could not read Latin, so a text in Italian automatically had double the potential audience of one in Latin. Among adult women, he estimates that 13 percent were able to read, but very few of these knew any Latin. Readers of Italian in the entire adult population, therefore, outnumbered readers of Latin by something approaching three to one. Literacy varied enormously by educational opportunities linked to social and economic conditions. Virtually all male clerics could read both Italian and Latin; nuns were widely literate in Italian but in most cases their Latin was limited to what they had memorized. Lawyers, physicians, professors, civil servants, and educated noble men usually could read both Latin and Italian. The bourgeoisie, including merchants, master artisans, and many established shopkeepers (both husbands and nearly half their wives/widows) read Italian. Outside the city walls, substantial landowners certainly were literate and people at the top rung of the peasantry probably could read. Looking toward the lower end of society's hierarchy, Grendler reasonably assumes that almost no servants or slaves could read, nor could the bulk of soldiers, sailors, retainers to nobles and merchants, and the peasantry. Many, perhaps most, petty shopkeepers and artisans below the level of master craftsmen could not read, but definitely there were literate people in these groups; uncertainties about overall rates of literacy refer primarily to people in these categories.[20]

In some ways the exact overall rate of literacy—33 percent of adult men and 13 percent of adult women—in sixteenth-century Venice matters less than the distribution by social category. Estimates of literacy in urban France in the seventeenth century run as high as 90 percent of the bourgeoisie, and that level seems about right for Italian cities as well. Venice teemed with galley rowers, street hawkers, fishmongers, prostitutes, soldiers, and marginal people, none of whom bought books of any kind or read them. A city such as Florence may have counted fewer persons from the lower classes in its midst, thereby giving it a higher overall rate of literacy, and certainly Florence considered itself to be a preeminent center of Renaissance humanism. Yet the very intellectual snobbery rampant among elites who knew Latin may have made for a less lively market in popular books among that group.[21]

I accept as both sensible and practical Grendler's definition of a "popular" book as "one within the intellectual grasp of ordinary readers of little learning and lower social status. This is the first and fundamental meaning of popular." Printer-publishers—who were in business to make at least a little money—must have been able to sell "popular" books to someone, indeed to quite a few people, since we know that prices dropped rapidly while the cost of production remained relatively unchanged.[22]

The printing press may even have influenced Sanzio Raffaello, whose 1504 painting *Madonna and Child with Book* graces the cover of *How to Do It*. In sharp contrast to a 1483 rendition of the same subject by Sandro Botticelli, wherein a symbol-laden infant totally ignores the hefty manuscript tome propped on a nearby table, Raffaello shows mother and child absorbed in looking at a handheld volume of the duodecimo size that was coming to dominate the popular-book market. Whether that object was a printed book, I cannot say, and surely it was a Psalter, not a how-to manual. Nonetheless, the image of Mary reading to her baby—a chubby, naked boy balanced firmly on her lap, surrounded by no accouterments foretelling his destiny and separating him from all other babies—fully supports what sixteenth-century-advice manuals recommended to all Italian Renaissance mothers.

Authors who opted to write in Italian knew exactly why they made that choice.[23] A wonderful example comes from the end of the sixteenth century—Girolamo Mercurio's *La commare* (The Midwife). Critics assailed the first edition, published in Venice in 1596, for putting into vernacular Italian so much of the secret, titillating, just plain immodest details of female anatomy and the birth process—made more shocking by being expressed in the prose of a Dominican monk. Friar Scipione, as he was known for years while making his rounds as a self-appointed public health officer throughout vast stretches of the Po Valley (well outside the confines of his convent, which did not want him anyway), shot back in the 1601 edition, the first of over a dozen reprints, translations, and updates that followed regularly for more than a century thereafter. His defense, actually quite an offense, starts as follows:

> My goal was to be useful, seeing how often the birth process was made more dangerous for mother and child because of the scant knowledge of midwives and other assistants—since it is extremely rare that a physician is called on these matters. I was determined to give light to instructions for the midwife so she would be better able to do her job. And I did this by choice after making a thorough search of the literature and finding that no one had written a book in the vernacular on this subject. . . . So to those who say it was an error to write in the vernacular, I respond that your arrogance does not justify this judgment. I think I did well because my Midwife does not comprehend Latin fables and the way I've written it the father of the household and others also can read it and provide important help at a critical moment.
>
> Moreover, I wrote in the vernacular because I wanted to, and I'm entitled to since I've also written in Latin on other occasions. I was born free, so I can do as I please! I would not have to answer for it if I chose to write in German or in Arabic. If [Francesco] Panigarola can penetrate the major mysteries of theology in the vernacular, and [Alessandro] Piccolomini can explore all of philosophy, and [Pietro Andrea] Mattioli virtually all the secrets of simple medicine, and [Juan de] Valverde all of anatomy, then how come I can't gather a few twaddles of the midwife? Where there is room for Queen Sacred Theology and for Princess Philosophy, surely there is a place for Mrs. Medicine dressed as a midwife, with her crude skirt and coarse Roman dialect understood by everyone, the very one I received in my crib from my wet nurse and at home from my mother. . . . I don't write in Tuscan because I'm Roman and if you prefer Tuscan, then go read [Giovanni] Boccaccio and [Pietro] Bembo and if you don't like my book for some other reason, do me a favor and don't read it. For as much as you don't want to read it there will be others who like it all the more.[24]

This lively, even feisty spirit, characterizes much of Mercurio's very practical treatise for the midwife and those who might assist at childbirth. He was thoroughly familiar with other advice manuals available to Italian readers; indeed, he was a friend of Lucrezia Marinella (who preferred a feminine ending to her surname), the poet, staunch defender of the superiority of women over men, and daughter of the physician Giovanni Marinello who authored *Delle medicine partenenti all' infermità delle donne* (Medicine Pertinent to the Infirmities of Women), another volume we shall examine carefully in the chapters that follow. Mercurio meant to be useful to people who could not read Latin but who would be better at their job or understand more fully what was happening to them with his little book at hand. In addition to the usual table of contents, he provided an alphabetized list of "notable things," running to some ten pages, beginning with "Abortion, what is it and what causes it," and ending with "Worms, in children and their cure"—just the sort of index that would be useful if a medical problem arose at home.

Drawing conservative, necessarily tentative conclusions about the readers of advice manuals, we may say that clergy surely could have read them, although in some cases they may have declined to do so because of the subject matter. Intellectuals also could have read them, although they probably did not keep such pulp prominently displayed when fellow elites called at their studios. The remainder of the well-to-do, joined as often as not by their wives, in town and in the countryside—lawyers, doctors, merchants, master craftsmen, substantial landowners, and rich peasants, along with eager and talented artisans—could read them. Finally and less cautiously, the sales pitches contained in defenses of the vernacular, such as Mercurio's, suggest to me that practical how-to manuals, especially the less expensive editions, may have been purchased even by people who owned few other books.

I also believe that what literate people read in advice manuals tended to be frequently repeated by them to their less literate friends, neighbors, and customers, either through reading aloud or through an oral summary—perhaps a special home remedy for menstrual cramps, a way to deal with childish misbehavior, or a technique for making sure your next child is a boy. I can neither prove that such wisdom was repeated in the sixteenth century nor provide an estimate about the extent of such repetition, but at some point even historians who are taught to document everything in long footnotes may appeal to arguments of common sense.[25] When I encounter written advice in a sixteenth-century popular book telling country housewives to take responsibility for gathering eggs, selling them at the market, and keeping honest track of the amount of money earned while not bothering their husbands daily with such trivia, then I conclude that the advice was not meant for a duchess with lots of servants. I surmise that the housewife either read this advice by herself or else her husband read it to her, whether in a scolding tone I cannot say. I also believe that the housewife told this information to her sister, her daughter, her daughter-in-law, and her neighbors. It is even possible that she told it back to her husband if he accused her of not turning over the full amount he expected to receive from her sale of eggs.

Finally, there is evidence to suggest that many people who could not sign their names to a document nonetheless could read. A little pamphlet, first published in 1524, by the Venetian teacher Giovanni Antonio Tagliente, proclaims that it will reveal the secrets of reading to artisans and to women of all ages. A modern scholar calls the pamphlet a "do-it-yourself one-on-one effort to foster adult literacy," one clearly aimed at the rapidly expanding market for how-to books. Tagliente's preface guarantees success in only two months with lessons of one hour each day, using a method that seems classic yet highly contemporary. Just learn the letters of the alphabet—this shape is a *B* and that is a *D*—and then put consonants with vowels to make syllables. Say the syllables out loud and you get words—really quite simple in a phonetic language such as Italian. Skip the rules, since there is no need for grammar in the everyday world of commerce and in the plain sense of advice manuals. A master teacher of calligraphy, Tagliente was hugely successful in the new medium of print; his manuals on reading, handwriting, composing love letters, bookkeeping, and embroidering patterns went through dozens of editions. He envisioned a public hungry for practical literacy—for secrets about how to strike it rich or how to end a love affair turned sour. He intended to meet the demand and bring literacy into the homes, shops, and taverns of Venice and the world. It hardly matters whether he was a mercenary or purely the altruist he claimed to be. He was not a charlatan, and the method he taught in fact works, at least if I remember properly the rhymes of Dr. Seuss's *Cat in the Hat.*

Maybe it took more than two months to learn to read, and certainly not everyone who started Tagliente's correspondence course stayed to the end, but I do believe there were a considerable number of not-so-illiterate sixteenth-century Italians sounding out their syllables as they consulted a how-to manual offering practical wisdom and easy solutions to life's challenges.[26] It is time to look over their shoulders and read along with them.

CHAPTER

· *2* ·

Conception

The only legitimate reason for sexual intercourse is conception, so that man may provide the seed and woman the soil, which are jointly essential for procreation. Failure to conceive a child, especially a son, means that the couple's bodily humors are not properly balanced, causing his seed to maturate poorly or not at all in her soil. According to the Greco-Roman theory of bodily humors accepted by all sixteenth-century people, men are hotter and drier, women cooler and wetter. The four humors are associated with fluids generated in specific organs, each of which corresponds directly with a natural element, as follows:

HUMOR	FLUID	ORGAN	NATURAL ELEMENT
Dry	Blood	Heart	Earth
Wet	Black bile	Spleen	Water
Hot	Bile	Liver	Fire
Cold	Phlegm	Brain	Air

Both internal and external factors affect how the four humors interact in any individual, which in turn determines his or her temperament. The internal factors, usually gendered, are present from birth, for example, the tendency of naturally hotter boys to be livelier and normally wetter girls to be languid. But dysfunctions in the internal organs, exacerbated primarily by environmental circumstances, may cause the body's natural balance of humors to go astray. Regulation and adjustment of these humors are central to human well-being, the basis of every physician's efforts to heal the sick. The doctor first determines what his patient's balance should be, then he measures what it is at the moment, and finally he prescribes a regimen for getting things back to normal—usually involving changes in lifestyle and diet, along with the ingestion or application of herbal medicines.

The legacy of Greco-Roman bodily humors theory remains with us—in classifications of type A versus type B personalities, gender-differentiated recommendations for intake of vitamins and minerals, programs for physical exercise, prescriptions for moderation as the key to well-being, and arguably even in the assertions of sociobiologists like Richard Dawkins, Desmond Morris, Sarah Blaffer Hrdy, and Edward O. Wilson. Moreover, in the sixteenth century, when surgery was more dangerous than most illnesses and when synthetic pharmaceuticals did not exist, holistic medicine was the approach of necessity, not choice.

Aristotelian biology provided the foundations for popular-medical books, which therefore inevitably conveyed hostility to women and denigration of their inferiority. Recommendations were heavily biased in favor of enhancing the hot, dry qualities associated with men and regularly abandoned the theoretical need for balancing the humors in favor of prescriptions for what these theories held to be more appropriate for men. Nonetheless, division over the Aristotelian view that only men produce seed (monogenesis) versus the very different Galenic assertion that distinct male and female seeds had to be unified (duogenesis) allowed some leeway for medical popularizers with access to a printing press. Many readers of these books were women, presumably wives who wished to conceive and had not done so, and their authors show far more compassion than Aristotle ever did. Indeed, some of them poke fun at the great master, teasing him for his legendary hostility toward his own wife![1]

The manuals offered nothing new, their presentations being no more accurate (and in some cases a bit more garbled and contradictory) than the original treatises of Hippocrates, Aristotle, and Galen written two thousand years earlier and repeated many, many times over the centuries.[2] Yet to dismiss these admittedly derivative works on such grounds, or simply to ignore them, would be to overlook a fundamental aspect of their originality. They were written in Italian, not in the classical Latin used routinely by physicians for teaching and for professional communication until the end of the eighteenth century. They aimed to please as they instructed, listing problems and providing solutions without expending much ink on abstract lessons in anatomy or chemistry.

Scholars of religious history stress the significance of Martin Luther's decision to make the Bible available in a language laypersons could read. Protestant printing transformed the mystical parish priest into the learned congregational minister and in some sects liberated the faithful to be their own ministers. Analogously, within the fields of personal health and human relations, the authors we shall be consulting—some of whom were highly respected elite members of the medical profession—equally understood the political and cultural significance of what they were doing by writing in Italian. They say so in their opening dedications (for example, "to genteel and honest women") and in the ways they arrange and convey their materials. Their readers were to become participants in treating their own ailments, thereby taking from the physician a good deal of his magical preeminence. Shared information and a common language undermined elitist authority and diffused power.[3]

Boy or Girl

A sixteenth-century Tuscan couple anxious to influence the likelihood that their next child would be a boy could have turned for help to a new book by Lorenzo Gioberti titled, *De gli errori popolari* (On Popular Errors), a work written and first published in France. It had been translated into Italian (actually, good Tuscan, according to the translator) in 1592, from the 1578 French original written by noted court physician Laurent Joubert, to whom I will refer by the Italianized Gioberti, who held a professorship in medicine and philosophy at the University of Montpellier. Previously Gioberti had written several medical treatises in Latin, as well as a youthful work on the nature of laughter.[4] That such a scholar would aim for a broad audience literate in the vernacular rather than write in Latin for fellow elites deserves a moment of our attention. Why did Gioberti choose to write in French when he decided to denounce popular errors about medicine? Did he hope to earn extra money, achieve wider fame, or improve the people's medical care? Perhaps all three motives pushed him toward the increasingly frequent choice of educated writers to publish in the vernacular as the sixteenth century progressed.

His book is well known today, at least at second hand, because historian Natalie Davis featured it in two of the influential essays collected in her *Society and Culture in Early Modern France*. She makes the sensible assertion that Joubert's outrage about the stupidity of popular medical lore increased as he saw vernacular books of secrets and instant remedies roll off the presses encouraging people to medicate themselves. He must have decided to join the fray by helping to improve the people's ability to cure their own ills, while accepting the need to call a physician if matters got complicated. But his good intentions backfired; he ran into a torrent of criticism for using dirty words, for revealing professional secrets, and for telling people how to determine virginity in a prospective bride—all especially unseemly in a book dedicated to Princess Marguerite de France (Marguerite de Valois, 1553–1615, daughter of Henry II and Catherine de' Medici)! The midwives of France who could read were not at all pleased about his disparagement of them, nor is there much evidence that the people to whom he so vehemently described their idiocies changed their ways very much. All in all, we have a wonderful example here of how readers may make of a book what they want and need, which may differ substantially from the author's intentions. What was supposed to be a book denouncing popular errors became a volume for laypersons to use for lessons in sexology, with all the anatomical details specified by name.[5]

The controversy faded over time, and to the best of my knowledge the translation into good Tuscan caused no shock waves. The book was authoritative, foreign, and pleasant to read. It retained a remarkable undercurrent of respect for folk traditions even as it dismissed the more absurd notions of that era. The references to genitalia were less crude in Tuscan, the language of Boccaccio after all, than they apparently had been in French. Prospective parents, some of whom already may have tried to conceive a son by following the "secret" remedies that sold everywhere, could turn to Gioberti with confidence that they were getting higher quality advice, yet nothing beyond their easy comprehension. We must remain open about what our Tuscan couple would have made of the book's first fifty-five pages, in which Gioberti offers a lengthy defense against charges that physicians fail to cure people, do not visit them enough, and are more interested in making money than in healing the sick. His intent probably was to encourage using the services of regular physicians along with those of midwives, rather than to push aside midwifery completely. Still, he is very defensive about what physicians do and fail to do, writing with an arrogance that strikes a modern reader as perversely humorous but which his contemporary audience may have found off-putting, especially the midwives among them.

Diligent reading would have brought our Tuscan couple to thirty pages directly on the problem at hand, namely, how to conceive a son. Gioberti accepts the Aristotelian view that only men produce seeds, without mentioning Aristotle or the dispute about female seed. These seeds are neither male nor female, he explains. The uterine environment, especially in the critical first few hours after the seed is planted, determines whether the child will be male. If the soil is dry and warm, the child will be a boy, whereas a wet and cool host produces a girl. God made the male more excellent and perfect; for this reason drier soil produces boys, just as every farmer knows that soggy soil rots the seeds, yielding weak plants. Practical recommendations segue into analogies with nature. Blood builds up gradually during the menstrual cycle, making the uterus increasingly wet as the cycle proceeds. To conceive a boy, therefore, you should have intercourse right after menstruation. Conception that occurs shortly before menstruation produces a girl.[6]

Gioberti turns next to the popular belief that somehow the man is responsible for the child's sex, based on tales about women who have only daughters with one husband but upon becoming widows and remarrying, give birth to a string of boys. He dismisses this slur against fathers without male heirs by reminding us that every farmer knows you need to rotate crops, that some things grow better in one environment than another. If his advice on the timing of intercourse does not produce the promised result, then the continued absence of male heirs means there is an inauspicious relationship between the semen and the uterine environment. As with so many recommendations found in these advice manuals, it is anyone's guess whether sixteenth-century authors and readers took matters to their logical conclusion, which in this instance would seem to justify casting aside a wife who does not produce male heirs.

Continuing with timing strategies, the physician advises that intercourse in the morning is more likely to produce a male child. The seeds themselves are drier, livelier, and firmer at this time. Semen is produced from blood in the testicles, and blood is renewed with eating. It takes several hours for the body to convert food to blood and thence to semen, so intercourse right after a big meal, with food still in the stomach, cannot be the best occasion for strong semen. Gioberti refuses to divide the twenty-four-hour clock into an exact recommendation on timing, because semen, like other fruits, ripens at varying intervals. Still, he writes, when you see an athletic looking, tomboyish girl on the street, you know that if her parents had waited just an hour longer to have intercourse, she would have been a boy. If you see an effeminate young man passing by, you know that turning back the clock ever so slightly on his conception might have made him a her.[7]

Then there is the matter of uterine environment. It is well known, says Gioberti, that agricultural laborers and city workers have more children than elite people, that they more often have boys even though their economic circumstances make the issue of male heirs less pressing, and that their babies are more robust than those of the rich. All this is explained by timing. Wealthy people have money to eat huge meals; then, right after gorging themselves, they flop into bed, lingering over sexual intercourse. For men, as noted above, the semen is no good at this point.

Moreover, digestion is interrupted, leading to gout, colic, kidney problems, apoplexy, paralysis, tremors, and a shortened life span. Workers, on the other hand, exhausted after a day of hard labor, eat a meager supper, go to bed, and immediately fall asleep. When the husband awakes after a few hours of rest, his semen is strong and dry; natural body heat drives him, not the dissolution of wine; he is refreshed and alert; the act of intercourse is accomplished quickly and cheerfully. Moreover, the wife's uterine environment does not get overly wet since soon she must arise to stoke the fire, do household chores, and take care of her children, rather than lolling around under the sheets as rich women are wont to do.[8]

While I hope this initial peek at the eminent Professor Gioberti's book has allowed for at least a chuckle, it also opens a more serious window on sixteenth-century culture. The "popular error" Gioberti attacks in his advice on timing of intercourse is the belief that the man is at fault if he fails to produce sons, a fitting object for ribald stories and cuckold jokes. In shifting the blame to women and their wet uterine soil, however, Gioberti invariably denounces "errors" that in fact are to be found directly in Hippocrates, Aristotle, Galen, and others. That people over the centuries had adopted Greco-Roman scientific beliefs as their own, perhaps adding a few humorous variations along the way, reflects an essential indivisibility of high and low culture—for medical beliefs and practices as for so many other areas of human activity. Gioberti's warning about the consequences—conception of a female or an otherwise weakened child—for besotted husbands who flop into bed and demand sex from their wives, whatever its biological basis, carries a social message of some import. Did Tuscan husbands who wanted a son curb their wine consumption after reading Gioberti? Did their wives use this knowledge—now in print from a French expert, even if it only said what wives had known for centuries about disgustingly drunk husbands—to refuse sex? I cannot answer these questions, of course, but at least they may be asked.

Also worthy of brief speculation is Gioberti's outright hostility toward rich people, or at least toward their presumed behavior. Did he intend to offend them, perhaps to browbeat them into better comportment? Do his praises of the sturdy farmer and the diligent worker betray the nostalgic longing of a university professor for the simple life, or has he unwittingly accepted the validity of folk wisdom? He means to attack supposed superstitions but in fact he ridicules precisely what physicians learned from the Latin and Greek texts accessible to them but not to readers of his vernacular book. How ironic.

Appeals to the logic of nature and agricultural rhythms are not limited to seed/soil analogies. Another author, the Tuscan physician and agronomist Francesco Tommasi, clearly writing from a Catholic Reformation vantage point, although for a lay audience not interested in specific biblical exegesis, explains that sheep and other animals with exposed genitals have long been known to sire stronger offspring who are more frequently male, if mating occurs while the prevailing winds are the drier *tramontana* or *bora* or northerly. He reasons that the same should be true for human beings and specifically advises couples to avoid sexual intercourse when wetter southern or African winds are blowing strong.[9] The same arguments, which may be traced back to Aristotle, are found in more authoritative medical texts such as that of Savonarola, to which we now turn.

[Giovanni] Michele Savonarola, born around 1385 to a family of wealthy wool merchants, studied medicine in his native city at the world-renowned University of Padua under the most celebrated teachers of his day, including Galeazzo da Santa Sofia. From them he learned to appreciate the contributions of Arab scholars to medical knowledge, especially Avicenna, thereby enriching and tempering his understanding of both Greek science and Christian teaching related to bodily health. He received his degree in medicine in 1413, took up a teaching post at his alma mater, and quickly became a revered master himself. He transferred to Ferrara in 1440, serving as court physician to Niccolò III d'Este and for a time also continuing to teach. From his early years until his death in 1466 or 1468, Savonarola wrote profusely, initially on medical subjects and in later life on the moral austerity he came to embrace. During his last years, he devoted much attention to the education of his grandson Girolamo, who carried the asceticism imbibed from grandfather Michele to new heights of spirituality, eventually suffering a martyr's death in Florence's Piazza Signoria in 1498.[10]

Many of his writings, both Latin and Italian, were printed several times during the century following his death, both in Latin and Italian. Indeed, the chapter on female genitalia in his *Practica maior* (1479, the first of numerous printings) is a founding gynecological text. His advice on a healthful diet first appeared in Italian even before 1500, and editions, updates, revisions, and expansions continued for a century. Our focus at the moment, however, is on a curious work printed only in the twentieth century. I make an exception and include it in our journey because Savonarola wrote directly in Italian, addressing specifically the concerns of women in his adopted city of Ferrara. The title itself comes down to us in Latin, *Ad mulieres ferrarienses de regimine pregnantium et noviter natorum usque ad septennium* (To Ferrara Women on Care during Pregnancy and of Newborns to their Seventh Year), but the work itself is in a lively

Padovan dialect laced with wonderful asides, homey metaphors, and a sense of humor appropriate for a book meant to be read by laypersons. Much of the advice, especially on diet and herbals, is repeated in his printed books. Moreover, authors such as Giovanni Marinello simply copied Savonarola's pregnancy guide in their own printed books. Therefore, in the years before the appearance in 1596, of Mercurio's *La commare*, whether in the plagiarized and somewhat garbled printed version of Marinello, as part of Savonarola's widely available vernacular books on food and good health, or for a more restricted audience in the hand-written *Ad mulieres ferrarienses*, he provided the best source of information in Italian for midwives and their patients.[11]

He had little use for the female-soil theory espoused by Gioberti. Instead, Savonarola asserted that the heat of the father's seed determined whether the baby was a boy. The right testicle produces hotter sperm than the left because it is closer to the liver, from which the spermatic veins carry semen to the testicles. When breeders want a cow to produce a bull calf, they tie the bull's left testicle; readers who want a male child should do the same. Despite his emphasis on the father's role in determining a child's sex, Savonarola posits that the right side of the wife's uterus is warmer and more likely to aid in producing a male child. Therefore, the couple should organize their sex to see that his semen gets to her right side. However, coition (with his left testicle in a tourniquet) should not be delayed so long that his sperm loses its potency. Once emission occurs, the wife should turn on her right side and stay that way for one hour, with her buttocks elevated as high as possible and her thighs pressed tightly together. If she can manage to engage in intercourse while staying on her right side, perhaps by putting a cushion to prop up her left flank, that would be even better. All this has to be done with great care, the doctor warns. Many experts say that male seed from the left testicle that finds its way to the right side of the uterus results in a *"viragine,"* that is, a female with male characteristics; conversely, seed from the right testicle implanted on the woman's left results in a *"femineo"* or a male with female characteristics.

If you want a male child, look first to making sure your seed is hot. Eat food that is easy to digest, hot not cold; drink good wine, warm, agreeable to the stomach. "And listen carefully, you women of Ferrara and you men, know that your *corbinèlo* [once a very popular table wine in the Venetian region, deep in color] and similar things that are hard to digest impede impregnation with a male child, because indigestion makes the seed cold and useless. For similar reasons, avoid tinctures, herbs, fruit, fish, crustaceans and other cold and moist foods; eating them will turn your seed female."[12]

Giovanni Marinello did more than anyone to make Savonarola's ideas on conception and pregnancy available in print, even though he never acknowledged by name the author from whom he copied so freely. In 1563, nearly a century after the master's death and about fifty years after Savonarola's book in the vernacular on dietary recommendations had been published, Marinello appeared in print with his *Delle medicine partenenti all' infermità delle donne* (Medicine Pertinent to the Infirmities of Women). Part 1 proposes remedies for problems that might break the bonds of marriage, everything from hatred for one another to bed-wetting. Part 2 concentrates on overcoming sterility, with lengthy sections devoted to male impotence and lack of sexual desire. The third and last part of the book, which altogether runs to 329 leaves (actually more, since some of them are misnumbered), provides advice on care during pregnancy and childbirth.

Born in Modena, Marinello spent most of his life in Venice as a dilettante physician and philosopher. The year before *Delle medicine partenenti all' infermità delle donne* appeared, he published a comprehensive book on female beauty and adornment containing, among hundreds of recommendations, more than two dozen recipes for making dyes to bleach hair blond. Taken together, these two books and their many subsequent editions made him a leading figure in the field of Italian-language advice manuals for women. Both books achieved French translations, and the beauty guide appeared in German as well. Marinello also published a commentary in Latin on Hippocrates and a collection of Savonarola's Latin medical texts. A flair for writing apparently ran in the family; in 1600, his accomplished daughter Lucrezia published a polemical book in the *querelle des femmes* genre titled, *La nobiltà et l'eccellenza delle donne co' diffetti e mancamenti de gli uomini* (The Nobility and Excellence of Women, with the Defects and Shortcomings of Men).[13]

Marinello's veritable encyclopedia of women's infirmities provides a list of eight sex-determining factors, all conveyed with the unspoken assumption that a boy is what every couple wants. The first determinate is sperm heat, with higher temperatures needed to conceive a boy. The second is sperm quantity, more of which is required for a boy. The third factor is less absolute. Marinello leans toward Aristotle's view that only men have seed, the hotter the better if you want a boy. But he is not dogmatic about this; in his desire to reach a large audience, the old debate about duogenesis probably meant less to Marinello than the appearance in Italian of widely read books such as Lodovico Domenichi's plagiarism, *La nobiltà delle donne* (On the Nobility of Women), of the renowned occult philosopher Heinricus Cornelius Agrippa von Nettesheim's work of a similar name, wherein we find the following conclusion: "Thus, just as it would be nonsense to say that rennet contributes more to the making of cheese than milk does, so only dullards say that woman is less of a cause than man in generation."[14] Domenichi must be read very cautiously, in the context of a panoply of writings that includes several misogynous tracts; even the above quotation is ambivalent about whether the uterus provides seed or soil. Nonetheless, the belief that women play an essential role in procreation, vaguely equal to that of men, had become common in popular literature, certainly by midcentury.[15] Marinello grudgingly concedes that in case he is wrong and female seed is essential, a third determinant in having a male child is that the mother's sperm should be pure and clean—well after her menses.

The fourth and fifth determinants are that the father's semen should come from his right testicle and go to the right side of the mother's uterus. This should be accomplished by tying his left testicle during intercourse as she shifts to her right hip. The sixth is that the mother's sperm, if she has any, should be hot so it does not diminish the heat of his sperm. The seventh is that northerly winds should be blowing, which explains why Germans have more sons, whereas eastern and southern peoples have more daughters. The eighth is that the parents should be young, because semen cools down over the years. Copying directly from Savonarola, Marinello repeats the theory about right-left mismatches between testicle and uterus to explain boys who behave like girls and vice versa. Finally, he provides advice useful in sizing up a prospective husband: robust men with reddish complexions and a right testicle larger than the left are the likeliest to produce male children.

Marinello then offers recommendations on monthly rhythm. The first five days after menses are most propitious for a boy, the fifth to eighth for a girl, the eighth to the eleventh again for a boy, and from the eleventh to the next menses for a hermaphrodite. All this has to do with the relative purity of menstrual fluid, which is cleanest right after menses. Why the flip-flop occurs between days five to eight and eight to eleven is not understood even by eminent physicians, Marinello tells us, and apparently he feels that readers need no further explanation for the deterioration after day eleven, as he moves on to more useful and knowable matters.[16]

Both husband and wife must have bodily humors not so hot and dry that they soak up the warmth and moisture of spermatic and menstrual fluids, resulting either in sterility or in female children. The same diets, suppositories, unctions, baths, and fumigations recommended elsewhere to overcome sterility also work to favor male offspring; therefore, Marinello finds no need to repeat them here, except that he cannot resist reminding readers to drink tea heated in wine spiced with spearmint and peony seeds, and to use suppositories of balsam and peony seeds, anything that heats up the blood.[17]

In sum, the man who will have healthy boys is strong of body himself, with hard and bulging muscles, hot sperm, large testicles, spermatic veins, and an ardent sexual appetite that does not diminish after intercourse. He feels his right testicle enlarging during the preliminaries, whatever they are, and he ejaculates quickly. The woman who will have boys has a rosy complexion and a pretty visage; her body is neither heavy nor flabby; her menstrual blood is neither too watery nor too thick; the mouth of her uterus is right up against her vagina so his sperm immediately gets to where it should without cooling off; she has a good appetite, good circulation, good sense, and good movement; she is neither constipated nor does she have diarrhea; her eyes are white not yellowish; and she is young.[18]

Frequency of Intercourse

And what if a married couple desired children but could not conceive? As we might expect, an abundance of advice poured forth from sixteenth-century printing presses telling people how to increase the likelihood of pregnancy. In the same work by Gioberti that tells how timing of intercourse affects whether the child will be a boy, we find the logic of bodily humors applied to the problem of getting pregnant. Advice manuals unite in warning against the belief that more must be better, and Gioberti explains why. Two conditions are essential for conception: first, that the seeds are abundant, and second, that they are fully formed and mature, hard and full of spirit, ready to sprout. Frequent intercourse results in semen that is too weak and sparse for procreation. Savonarola thinks five days of abstinence is about right, maybe a little less for choleric types, a bit longer for melancholy men. Gioberti, on the other hand, recommends building up semen strength for at least two or three weeks. That is why conception is especially likely after a husband returns from a long business trip or after abstention during the woman's childbirth and lactation. The seed is strong and abundant; the soil is rested and enriched after a period of lying fallow.[19]

Numerous authors who approve moderately frequent sexual intercourse to maintain balance among the male humors nevertheless warn against overuse of this particular body restorative. Generally these texts avoid a specific recommendation about how much is too much, but all are explicit on the dangers of excess. Castore Durante's *Il tesoro della sanità* (The Treasury of Good Health), a partial version of which he published in Latin two decades before completing the highly popular vernacular edition in 1586 (the first of many printings), draws shamelessly on medieval medical manuscripts without any acknowledgment. As if he has made an exciting new discovery, Durante encourages moderate use of sex for the following: to make men cheerful, fuel the natural internal fires, lighten the body, mitigate mental stress, invigorate the senses, and lift the spirits. But beware of excessive sexual intercourse, he advises, warning that it weakens the stomach, head, senses, nerves, and joints, hastening death itself.[20]

Other medical-advice manuals come to the same conclusion but give more credit to medieval predecessors and make some effort to separate new wisdom from old. Bartolomeo Boldo, for example, claims to have improved upon the classic advice of physician Michele Savonarola. Just as stallions become more agile and swift after they mount the mares, so also a man who engages moderately in sexual intercourse becomes much more cheerful, sleeps more soundly, eats more heartily, and is more virtuous after sex; headaches disappear, sadness becomes happiness, and many other good results follow. Excessive intercourse, however, damages the eyes and all the five senses, causes headaches, nervousness, chest pains, kidney problems, backaches and sore legs; facial paleness ensues, along with rapid aging and even early death. Other problems are loss of memory, tremors, aches in the extremities, especially the legs, along with kidney and bladder problems.[21]

Ugo Benzi's (1376–1439) *Regole* on health and food appeared in Italian as early as 1481, in Milan, and was reprinted on several occasions over the next decades. By the time we come to an edition of 899 pages published in Turin in 1620, the work has acquired the "enrichments" of moral and natural discourses by Lodovico Bertaldi and a lengthy treatise by Baldasar Pisanelli, including a commentary on Galen. This book belongs at the quality, expensive end of our advice-manual spectrum, a compendium to last a lifetime. All three authors concur that immoderate and superfluous intercourse, especially right after eating, causes much harm, whereas moderate use of sex contributes to good health.[22] Michele Mercati, in a brief text largely about how to avoid the plague, is more skeptical. Sexual intercourse is pernicious, and it has been known since the time of Hippocrates that eunuchs do not get *podagre* (arthritis or rheumatism of the feet) nor do young men until they start to engage in sex. Mercati reminds readers of his little pamphlet that even the ancients such as Galen, who by sixteenth-century Christian standards had a reputation for unrestrained licentiousness, held that sex worsens arthritis.[23]

Giovanni Marinello's advice manual complicates frequency calculations by adding seasonality as a relevant variable. Sex is least harmful in spring and winter but should be used sparingly in the summer and even less often in autumn, he tells his readers, without explaining why this is so. As to hours of the day, for conceiving a child the best time to get together is when digestion is not complete, right before going to sleep at night. The other positive window, in this case to get rid of excess-sperm buildup, although it is not especially good for conception, commences two to three hours after the midday meal and continues until right before supper. Although Marinello does not bother to tell readers how his recommendations relate to the four bodily humors—hot or cold and wet or dry—and his conclusions about time of day are in direct contradiction to several manuals we have considered, he is nevertheless clearly in the same Greco-Roman scientific tradition as Gioberti, Savonarola, and the others.

He continues with a little chapter addressed to couples who get so carried away with sex that they find themselves weakened in body and spirit, which he believes is true of a majority of newlyweds. Symptoms to watch out for are general weakness, loss of vision or memory, pallid complexion, yellow or brown spots, and flaky skin. Remedies are at hand: drinks and plasters to improve the digestion, ointments and unctions to rub on the genitals to put the brakes on their fury, chicken soup and sweet wine to restore the body, and plenty of rest. Once restored to health, couples should just be more moderate.[24]

Literary tracts in popular garb also might offer advice about frequency and timing of intercourse. From "Grappa," a nom de plume that appears in many misogynous works, we get a spoof on the dominant cultural norm about the conjugal debt, which is the obligation of husband and wife to have sexual intercourse with each other upon demand by either spouse. Translated in the bacchanalian spirit of the original, it advises husbands as follows:

> Let's not even mention wives who constantly ask for payments on the conjugal debt and threaten an appeal to Justice, where everyone gets their due. We're talking about women who want to grind night and day, all the time, who in the end unwittingly lead us to acquire the virtue of temperance. We're talking about women who want to forge two nails with one bang of the hammer and make eight or ten

miles a night, encouraging us to feel like manly studs. But surely we
would acquire even more strength by learning instead to put up with
their constant complaining.[25]

On a more sober note, the churchly Francesco Tommasi warns that
too much sex weakens husbands and makes wives lustful; it actually reduces the likelihood of conception, causes loss of appetite, shortens life
span, destroys natural virtues, makes bones brittle, and brings on senility.
To know this is true, just look at the licentious young skirt chasers in
the piazza who already are half-witted, shortsighted, and weak in the
knees. In a little book we shall turn to more fully in a short while, Brother
Cherubino da Siena urges wives not to indulge their husbands' requests
to prepare spicy foods and special drinks aimed at improving sexual performance. Nor were such admonitions confined to Christian texts. No
less an authority than Plutarch, in his instructions to brides and grooms,
advised that just as poisoning the waters makes for an abundant but ined-
ible catch of fish, so also a wife who uses love potions and magical spells
to enhance her husband's sexual prowess finds herself in bed with a dull-
witted, degenerate fool. The same wisdom is repeated in Francesco Barbaro's fifteenth-century tract on wifely duties, embellished only with the
gibe that in some parts of Tuscany people still fish this way.[26]

Churchmen knew all the classic precepts, humorous literary tracts, and
popular jokes about lusty women. Nevertheless, they usually assumed
that the wife would be the partner wishing to refuse to pay the conjugal
debt. Their advice allowed only very limited circumstances under which
a married woman might say no. The original justification for teachings
on payment of the conjugal debt did not make gender distinctions. St.
Paul in his letter to the Corinthians, it is true, begins by saying it would
be better for a man not to touch a woman and makes no mention of
whether women would be better off not touching men. Male lust, then,
required marriage as a cure or at least a social container. For the institution of marriage to function in this way, each partner had to have un-
restricted access to the other's body. Paul states unequivocally that a
husband owes conjugal rights to his wife, and likewise a wife to her husband. He goes on to use the language of ownership, writing that a wife
does not have authority over her body, her husband does; and he does
not own his body but rather it belongs to her. Thus emerged the idea of
sexual access to one's spouse as a right, like a repossession: "Do not
deprive one another except perhaps by agreement for a set time, to devote
yourselves to prayer, and then come together again, so that Satan may
not tempt you because of your lack of self-control," he added (1 Cor.
7:5).[27] Centuries of analysis about the conjugal debt by church leaders

did not always adhere to the potentially egalitarian spirit of Paul's initial admonitions. Not surprisingly, the assumptions of theologians like St. Augustine, Jean Gerson, and Bishop Antoninus of Florence about the greater strength of male sexual urges found expression in more popular, vernacular manuals as well.

From the Spanish Jesuit Bartolomé de Medina (Bartolomeo in the Italian editions), we have a *Breve instruttione de' confessori* (Brief Instructions for Confessors) telling confessors how to administer the sacrament of penance and pious laypersons how to prepare themselves for it. The work was first published in Spanish in 1579, and was followed by Italian translations on at least four occasions over the next two decades. The quick, authoritative style leaves little room for ambiguity or examination of conscience. There are six justifications for saying no to sex, all of which assume implicitly or explicitly that he is doing the asking and she the declining. A bride might refuse if her marriage had not yet been consummated and she decided to become a nun. Any wife might refuse if her life or health were in danger, or if her husband were to commit adultery. A request for sex in a sacred or a public place might be denied, along with a suggestion of any sexual behavior likely to result in spilling seed outside the vagina. Finally, she might say no if he had made a vow of chastity and was experiencing a lapse. While this list may seem restrictive—leaving no room for simply not being in the mood—the provisions about health and spilling seed may have given wives substantial opportunity to exercise religious justification for controlling or refusing access to their bodies by their husbands.[28]

Saints' lives offered additional support for pestered wives. There is the wonderful even if apocryphal report on how St. Hedwige of Bavaria (d. 1243) found ingenious ways of paying the conjugal debt in the tiniest possible installments. Married at the age of twelve, or maybe sixteen, to the future Duke Henry of Silesia, she took no pleasure in the sexual act but knew well her obligation to provide for heirs. Whenever Hedwige thought she was pregnant, she refrained from sexual intercourse on these biblically supported grounds. Whenever she felt she might be menstruating, she did the same, also allowed. She waited as long as possible after childbirth to reenter the church for purification before resuming payments on the conjugal debt. She celebrated Lent, saints' feast days, Advent, and other religious holidays in continence. Hedwige's biographer tells us that at other times she managed to avoid sex for six or eight weeks even without the excuse of pregnancy or a holiday. After more than two decades of rationing sex to her husband with these subterfuges, following the birth of their seventh child when she was thirty-five years old, she persuaded him to end the need for evasion by solemnizing a mutual vow of complete continence before the local bishop![29] Thereafter they lived apart, with the duke kept busy fending off Mongol invaders and Hedwige occupied with scourging her body by wearing a hair shirt and walking barefoot to church over ice and snow. After her canonization in 1267, the Vatican extended veneration of St. Hedwige to all of Christendom in 1706, with her desire for continence always featured in the retelling, each October 16, of her life on earth. How many less famous wives abhorred sex we cannot know. What we do know is that *The Catechism of the Council of Trent* explicitly instructed pastors to teach their married parishioners about the virtues of religious continence. Couples should abstain from demanding payments on the conjugal debt in order to devote themselves to prayer. They should particularly avoid sexual intercourse for at least three days prior to receiving the Holy Eucharist and frequently during the fast season of Lent.[30]

Advice from writers influenced by the Catholic Reformation increasingly went beyond lists of sins and prohibitions, delving into the intimate recesses of private life. Tommasi thought it important, both for conception and for marital relations generally, that husbands talk with their wives after intercourse. Style is more important than frequency, he wrote. The couple should be friendly toward each other, not merely engage in a physical relationship. Even when clerics were citing rules, their advice might backfire. What does it tell us about the power of the written word and about human behavior that Friar Bartolomeo de Medina warned married couples not to read dishonest books together, because this so often leads to putting the semen where it doesn't belong?[31]

In 1583, the Dominican friar Cherubino da Firenze published a self-help confessional of seventy-one pages. Although it looks much like a traditional medieval penitential in its listing and dictionary-like definitions of sins, my reading suggests that, more so than similar handwritten works from earlier centuries, which may have been aimed at clerics and meant for use in monastic schools rather than private homes, it consciously addresses laymen and laywomen. Along with the definitions comes a stream of practical advice on how to behave properly. The section on sins committed by married people opens with a warning that those who are not married should skip this part, because it is none of their business and can only lead to temptations. For married folks there follows a list of conditions that would render a marriage sinful or even unlawful (consanguinity, bigamy, and the like), followed by the usual warnings about ejaculation outside the proper place. But then the pamphlet drifts into questions of intent. Ejaculation outside the vase is a sin only if you do it voluntarily, whether to avoid pregnancy or for some other reason. Sex with the woman on top or with the couple in a lateral position is sinful unless excused for a physical disability. It is equally sinful for either the husband or the wife to engage in sexual intercourse while fantasizing about someone else as a partner. Both the husband and the wife should be cheerful and positive in responding to requests for sexual intercourse. To say no out of anger, annoyance, excessive piety, or false dignity is a grave sin. If one or the other really just does not feel in the mood, then he or she should ask the partner to withdraw the request but be ready to pay if this fails. Still, a double standard prevails. Brother Cherubino closes this section of his book with words meant clearly to be read directly by married women: "Note that you, wife, must never agree to be used by your husband in a manner that would be sinful, like being on top or in other ways. Indeed, if your husband asks you to do those kinds of things, do not obey him because they are contrary to God's commandments." Seek the advice of your confessor and if he says that such-and-such a position or act is sinful, then you must refuse, and if you fail to convince your husband and give in to his wishes, then the guilt is yours.[32]

Positions during Intercourse

Readers will not be surprised to learn that the most salacious advice manual printed in Italy in the sixteenth century concerned sexual acrobatics. *I modi* (The Ways) introduced readers to sixteen techniques for achieving new heights of lovemaking pleasure, each illustrated with an explicitly erotic woodcut image by the artist Giulio Romano. First published in 1524, the book instantly became the talk of the town in Rome, especially among the many high prelates who kept mistresses, some of whom may have posed for the engravings. All too soon, however, the stodgy Pope Clement VII found out about the publication and suppressed further sale and circulation. He ordered all copies burned, imprisoned the engraver, prohibited any form of distribution, and made republication punishable by death. Some fearless entrepreneur nonetheless put out a second edition in 1527, adding sixteen sonnets by Pietro Aretino, each containing many words and ideas that would receive an instant NC-17 rating in our own culture. Several counterfeit versions followed over the next few decades, as human imagination and talent increased the number of positions and sonnets to twenty, then even to thirty-one. Buyers clearly treasured their copies, passing them on to generations of artists and writers in France, Germany, and Italy who found inspiration for their own endeavors.[33] While *I modi* is a work of fundamental importance in understanding Renaissance eroticism, it was never meant to be a popular how-to manual; for more practical, albeit prosaic, advice, I shall focus instead on authors whose books could lie open on the kitchen table without causing scandal.

There was little dispute among writers about the physical basis for differences in how husbands and wives took pleasure in the sexual act, nor about how these differences related to positions during intercourse. Savonarola summarized the medical consensus as follows: men reach a more intensive, short-lived orgasm, whereas women have a more extensive, long-lasting orgasm. This is because the tip of the penis has so much less surface area than the longer, larger neck of the uterus. As we might expect, Savonarola confidently states that the male orgasm is more acute and more perfect, but at least he is of the view that each sex is capable of orgasm and, as we shall see below, should achieve it.[34]

Other writers were more afraid of female sexuality. Friar Bartolomeo de Medina adhered to traditional Catholic tenets, warning that intercourse with the woman on top was not only sinful but inhibited conception. Bernardo Trotto, in a series of fictional dialogues drawn from antiquity and from the Bible, urged a wife not to offer herself to her husband like a whore but to wait for him to initiate sex; be childlike and innocent, not aggressive like an adulteress. This is why the god of love is always painted as a young boy, explains Trotto, freely crossing gender to emphasize his central point. Bartolomeo Boldo, the physician from Brescia who published a heavily revised version of Savonarola's fifteenth-century advice on good living—whether he was speaking for himself or for the old master is unclear—added that sex while standing would lead to debilitation of the legs and feet.[35]

However, it was Savonarola himself who wrote openly and positively of the importance of foreplay in increasing the likelihood of conception. Husband and wife should touch each other, especially he should rub his finger on the area between her clitoris and vagina since this is the external zone where she gets the greatest pleasure, and it is near the neck of her uterus. He should prolong the sexual act by touching her breasts and caressing her nipples, lingering at her mouth and making sure to arouse the area below her navel, simulating intercourse but not actually doing it. All this will make her achieve orgasm (*spermatizare* in the original text), which is essential for conception.[36] Still, some women are more ready than others, in other words more hot; therefore, the man must engage in foreplay prudently, in a measured way. You even find women who have no need of these preliminaries, who reach fruition without them. If a man engages in foreplay with a woman who is warm by nature—apt to sow her grain quickly while still cold—then he risks losing his own erection (*cussì perderebbe l'opera suoa* is the delightfully delicate wording of the original). The eminent, dignified Dr. Savonarola then says that if writing such things means being accused of crudeness, he will bear the criticism patiently, because this advice is given for a good moral end.

He continues. The husband must not delay actual intercourse so long that he loses his heat. In entering her, the man, having aroused his wife, must consider her emotions. He began to increase her craving with actions akin to stuttering but now it's time to shout. The husband should force himself to shoot all his seed at one time, not in driblets, nor should he continue to stroke in and out, as is commonly done for enjoyment. Instead, he should stay fixed in the hole so that air does not get in and corrupt the seed. The doctor fears that some readers may find these rules amusing, and he concedes that they are; however, he perseveres, clearly crossing the imaginary divide between medical text and advice manual.

The wife should now raise her thighs, and her husband lift himself off her. Then she should hold her thighs, legs, and feet tightly together so that his sperm will descend deeper into her uterus and be retained, with no air entering. For better retention she should apply to her vagina a pomade of cotton soaked in musk, gum of lada leaves, and any of several spices—unless she has an abomination of such odors. Then she should try to sleep, keeping her uterus warm and maximizing the generative possibilities of the impregnation. Savonarola's contemporary, the Florentine Matteo Palmieri, adds the very practical advice that the wife should watch out to avoid sneezing, which could cause the semen to squirt back out of her womb.[37]

As we might expect, authors adhering to traditional church teachings were less supportive than Dr. Savonarola of the value of sexual foreplay. From among the many manuals in circulation, our Tuscan couple might have chosen to read Brother Cherubino da Siena's now classic *Regole della vita matrimoniale* (Rules of Married Life). Indeed, based upon the many advice manuals for priests and confessors I have read, my hunch is that, especially after the Council of Trent charged the clergy with instructing Catholics more clearly, closely, and fully on how to live their faith, many local priests may have loaned out or given copies of books such as *Regole della vita matrimoniale* to young couples about to wed. It was a good way to convey the church's detailed rulings on how married couples should behave in bed without getting into clinical details that would have been very unbecoming for conversation between a priest and his parishioners.[38]

Brother Cherubino da Siena (also known as Cherubino da Spoleto and no relation to Cherubino da Firenze) dictated his work in the latter half of the fifteenth century, making it a product of the scribal culture's waning years. His little volume became a big success in the new print culture, with some twenty-one printings before 1500, either alone or bound together with his "Rules for Spiritual Life." Although this *Regola* for celibate people probably outsold the book for married folks, there is no reason to doubt the nineteenth-century litterateur Carlo Negroni's assertion that this early manual of marital advice enjoyed considerable popularity in sixteenth-century Italy. Its style is colloquial, with the familiar *tu* form often used to cajole, admonish, and threaten husbands, and especially wives, to behave themselves with decency and modesty. The manual is given over largely to questions of sexual behavior, devoting more pages to these matters than to all other aspects of married life combined.[39]

Brother Cherubino's little book shares the Christian assumption that the object of marriage is procreation, and often his particular exhortations refer back to this tradition. More interesting is his emphasis, hardly unique but very revealing, about popular images of gender, on how men and women must rise above their animal instincts and cultivate their higher intellect. To encourage the faithful toward this goal, he reasons with his male readers, whereas he exhorts and shames their wives. A husband's first duty is to instruct his wife, by reading to her this work and similar writings. Second, he must correct and castigate her, and last, he must provide for her maintenance. The good wife (addressed as *tu, figliuola mia*) must fear her husband and do nothing to displease him or make him jealous. Her second duty is to attend to all the housework (a clear indication here that the intended audience lacks servants and is not aristocratic or patrician); last, if she sees her husband slipping into some sinful activity, she should sweetly and pleasingly try to talk him into better ways.[40]

A long chapter follows that begins by addressing both husband and wife in familiar fashion, urging them to observe three mutual obligations: cordiality, living under one roof, and fulfilling the conjugal debt. Brother Cherubino moves rapidly through the first two obligations before turning in the last two-thirds of his book to its main subject, detailed advice on proper sexual behavior. Hardly a fit topic for public discourse, it was ideally suited to written culture. Brother Cherubino rather easily, perhaps even with some delight, overcomes his reservations about dealing with such a topic and joins the legion of saintly, celibate men who have instructed the faithful on good sex. Virtually everything he has to say may be found in earlier writings. The novelty is the medium, not the message. What educated clerics always could have known, and what modern scholars have documented thoroughly, became accessible to ordinary Christian men and women.[41]

A wife's body belongs to her husband, and his to her. Thus, either may initiate, and must not be denied, a legitimate request to engage in sexual intercourse. Four rules govern whether such a request is legitimate: intention, timing, place, and mode. The intent to conceive a child is unquestionably legitimate no matter what other motives may be involved, but Brother Cherubino adds three additional good intentions. The first is asking for payment of the conjugal debt. The nearest analogy would be the right of a banker to call for immediate payment on a demand loan, one with an infinite principal. The borrower may ask nicely for a delay or simply to skip a payment, but the legal obligation is clear; a good banker collects what is owed. Another legitimate intention is to ward off one's own temptation to fornicate with someone else or engage in other sinful behavior. Finally, a spouse may demand sexual intercourse in order to keep her or his partner from sinful thoughts and actions: "I tell you, little daughter of mine, if you think your husband is chasing after other women . . . have sex with him. That certainly is not sinful, but highly meritorious."[42]

The second rule concerns timing. It requires married couples to abstain from sexual activity during prescribed times of the year: Sundays and other feast days of holy obligation, all of Lent and vigils of feast days, and around the time communion is received. Brother Cherubino tells his readers that the church fathers are not in complete agreement about the number of days of sexual abstinence appropriate when receiving communion; some say at least eight days, others less. He urges a practice of three days before and three days after communion, adding a special plea to husbands: "If your wife wants to receive communion three or four or ten times each year, help her along, comfort her, do this favor for the service of God. . . . Leave her alone at least three days before and three days after communion; in this way you will share in the good she is doing." In addition to these fixed times of abstinence, the demand of the conjugal debt is not legitimate during pregnancy, after childbirth until the mother enters the church for purification, during breast-feeding, during menstruation, and from the time a marriage contract is arranged until its official blessing by a priest.[43]

The rule concerning place brings Brother Cherubino to comment not only on such obvious matters as no sexual activity in churches (just one of the sins of Abelard and Heloise), open fields, and public squares but also to explain prohibitions on oral sex and anal intercourse. Here he does not address husbands at all but instead pleads with wives, reminding them of the scandalous behavior recounted to San Bernardino da Siena by a woman married for six years who remained a virgin because her sodomite husband used her only like a man: "And if because you do not consent to this horrible evil your husband tears you apart, cheer up and tell him you wish to become a martyr and truly to go to your eternal life. And if already you have fallen into this sin . . . go to confession, otherwise the devil will carry you off."[44]

Finally the cleric comes to the rule of modality, excusing himself for entering upon such a delicate question by invoking the precedents of such angelic virgins as Thomas Aquinas and St. Bonaventure and pointing out that unless his readers know right from wrong, they will not be able to make a good confession. He warns first against excessive frequency, telling husbands that just as a bull who defeats an adversary for the right to a cow and then copulates with the animal is so weakened that he loses his next battle with the same opponent, so also does sexual intercourse drain natural male vigor. Many are the husbands who have become insane or blind as a result of too much sexual activity. Ten bloodlettings sap male vitality far less than one coition. Frequent intercourse leads to early death—better to take a hint from the continent elephant or the sterile mule. Sex empties a man of virtue and spiritual vitality, rendering his offspring weak, sickly, and short-lived. Notwithstanding this logic, Brother Cherubino refuses to give advice about how much is too much, citing but not fully approving Boethius's recommendation of once a month and repeating San Bernardino's suggestion to sleep in separate beds while conceding that sexual needs vary considerably from one person to another.[45]

The discussion of frequency is addressed entirely to husbands, but the friar's next topic—situation—presumes that wives control the circumstances and need his advice. During sexual intercourse the woman should face the sky, her husband the earth. Other positions tend to inhibit conception and, moreover, they lead to libidinous, sinful urges. Inverted and lateral situations may be legitimate if necessitated by a physical handicap, but what excuse can there be for standing or sitting? Similarly, the chest and belly of the husband must touch the same parts of his wife's body. If in the past you have fallen into situational sins, warns the friar, then go to confession and in the future watch out not to do it again. While engaging in intercourse, husband and wife should look at each other face to face like friends, not like enemies, beasts, or dogs: "Oh beast, aren't you ashamed of yourself? And you, ribald wife, aren't you ashamed of consenting to him?" Sexual activity should not involve the eyes, nose, ears, mouth, tongue, or any other part of the body that is in no way necessary for procreation. Yes, a wife may look at her husband's private parts if he is ill, but to do so for excitement is a sin: "Never allow yourself, you woman, to be seen in the nude by your husband." Soaps and perfumes are fine for removing bad odors but evil if meant to arouse. Kissing is permissable but not with the tongue and only mouth-to-mouth: "*Oimè*! The devil knows how to do so much between husband and wife. He makes them touch and kiss not only the honest parts but the dishonest ones as well. Even just to think about it, I am overwhelmed by horror, fright and bewilderment. . . . You call this holy matrimony?"[46]

The friar then returns to more familiar themes. Husbands must ejaculate only into the appropriate vessel; wives must do nothing to inhibit conception or to induce abortion. Adultery by either partner cancels the right of the guilty party to claim the conjugal debt but does not remove the obligation to pay upon request. And, of course, sexual intercourse is prohibited among couples whose marriage is juridically invalid because of consanguinity, bigamy, murder of the partner's former spouse, or a prior vow of chastity.[47]

Setting

Finally, a couple wishing to conceive a son should set the right mood and atmosphere for their lovemaking. According to Marinello's popular *Delle medicine partenenti all' infermità delle donne,* the room in which the couple plan to have intercourse should be sprayed with pleasing, warming odors like musk of deer or civet cat, aloe, and amber. There should be masculine paintings on the walls, causing the couple's minds to be imprinted with virility. Gaze at pictures of valorous men while having sex, and that is what you will conceive. This explains why bastards often look like the adulterous wife's husband. She has been so afraid of him while doing it with someone else that her husband's likeness finds its way to the illegitimate offspring. Both partners should come to bed with a happy spirit; fear of pregnancy results in conceiving a girl. Finally, the woman should stay on her right side as much as possible both during sex and afterwards.

In Mercurio's *La commare,* readers might find yet more amazing information. In a chapter on how mental power can produce a baby similar to whatever the lovers are imagining, the friar repeats a section from Eliodoro's *History of Ethiopia,* which tells how King Idaspe and Queen Persina, both black, conceived their daughter Cariclia, beautiful and pure white, solely because the queen and her husband were having intercourse at noon in a room filled with paintings of white men and women. In particular, the queen was so taken with images of Andromeda and Perseus on the ceiling that she gave birth to a girl who looked like Andromeda. All this was confirmed to be possible according to the gymnosophists, who were the wisest men in that country. Mercurio, however, thinks this may be a fable, and he finds much more likely the story told by Aristotle of a woman in the Morea, married to a white man, who from an adulterous liaison with a black man gave birth to a white daughter. Even though the daughter, later married to a white man and not an adulteress, gave birth to a black son, it did not occur to Mercurio any more than it had to Aristotle that some kind of dominant/recessive generational traits might have been passed along here. Both saw the case as evidence of the power of imagination to affect even skin color.

Also more reasonable in Mercurio's judgment is Hippocrates' defense of a woman suspected of adultery because she gave birth to a child who did not look like her husband. The Greek master pointed out that in the room where she and her husband had engaged in sexual intercourse, there was a painting with features very similar to the baby's and that the woman may very well have had her gaze fixed on this picture. Other reports from Quintilian and more recently from the great legal scholar Andrea Alciato (1492–1550) tell of similar happenings, including white couples giving birth to black children. Nor is the power of imagination limited to human beings. Mercurio clinches his argument about the power of imagination with a citation of St. Augustine in book 10, chapter 30, of *The City of God,* reporting that the biblical Jacob did the same thing with sheep, placing white reeds in front of the drinking water of gray sheep so they begot white lambs and then mixing in green reeds to produce varietal flocks.[48]

Returning to Aristotle and following him more closely, Mercurio goes on to explain how even though only men have "seed," still a child may look like its mother or even relatives several generations back on its mother's side. This is all due to imagination. Either during pregnancy, a matter we shall return to, or during intercourse at the moment of conception, the mother might have focused so intently on one of her ancestors that the child became similar—replete with a limp or blind or crippled. Little wonder, then, that a wise father may produce a son who is stupid.

Mercurio closes with an arrow aimed at his intellectual, elitist de-tractors—one that might pierce a male college professor even today. Scholars tend toward melancholy, he writes, and melancholy is the carnal sister to insanity. This insanity may be so greatly despised by his partner that while having sex with him, her mind desires more a happy idiot than a child who is intelligent but gloomy. As to the scholarly father, he is so immersed in his studies that he pays no attention to what's happening during sex. By contrast, one encounters the father who is a dullard but of lively temperament. He delights greatly his woman in the delectations of Venus, and this gives rise to such pleasure in her that she wants a bright child and her imagination succeeds in making this happen.[49]

Male Impotence

Among the popular errors lambasted by Lorenzo Gioberti is the notion that if a couple is childless, the wife must need treatment. Once again, however, Gioberti was paying more attention to Latin medical books than to the lowbrow wisdom conveyed in numerous advice manuals, which are filled with remedies for men experiencing performance doubts and failures. From an anonymous *Thesoro di secreti naturali* (Treasury of Natural Secrets), comes a quick do-it-yourself test: to know whether he or she is the sterile one, place barley seeds in two pots and have him urinate in one and she in the other. Put the pots in a humid place and after ten days see which pot produces—the one that failed points to the sterile person. If the husband is sterile, take testicles of an old rooster, being careful to dry them slowly in the shade, and serve them in chicken soup. Dr. Marinello proposes a somewhat more complex experiment, involving placing seven seeds each of wheat, barley, and beans into his-and-hers pots, keeping the pots totally dry except that the man and woman urinate into their respective pots each morning; then see what comes up in eight or ten days. Both these tests are elaborations of diag-nostic procedures going back at least to Galen.[50]

Even the most distinguished authors addressed problems of impo-tence, for example, Charles Estienne (1504–64?), who advised that red chickpeas are very good for men who feel "too tired" for sexual inter-course. This bit of wisdom is buried in a handsome quarto book of over five hundred pages that must have been meant for gentlemen farmers who paid close attention to their estate. It came to Italian readers in 1581, through a translation by Cavalier Ercole Cato of the French original, complete with a detailed index for looking up just about any need that might arise on the estate. Over a hundred pages each are devoted to sections on general management, the vegetable garden, and trees. Other chapters advise how and when to hunt rabbits, deer, wild boar, wolves, birds, and foxes. A particularly interesting section for our purposes tells the female farmworker how to cope with small family medical problems without having to consult a physician, while not allowing things to get seriously wrong.

This section once again raises for us the question of how these advice manuals were used. Surely a female farmworker was not able to purchase such a large and splendid volume, most of which concerned things unrelated to anything in her daily life. Most likely she could not read anyway. So why the section on home remedies? I can only suggest that resident owners of large estates took an interest in making sure that the families who labored for them were reasonably well cared for. Their motives may have been selfish, with an eye more to maximizing the work time of their dependents than to good health for its own sake, but the fact remains that these rural elites probably could read a book like this one and then pass along its wisdom to their rural workers. Knowledge not widely available in the scribal culture of the fifteenth century became more accessible with the spread of print. Estienne's family was among the leading publishers in all of Europe, and he personally was an enormously prolific author who also wrote a formidable Latin treatise on dissection of the human body, which makes it all the more significant that he would choose in any way to direct his attention to the medical needs of female farmworkers.[51] My judgment is that he knew very well the potential market and how best to serve and exploit it. Let us return to surveying the range of information found in his advice book for gentleman farmers.

If the initial desire for sex is there and you are not simply too tired, yet somehow your penis is just "sleeping," continues Estienne, rub it with an ointment extracted from the oils of crushed grains of myrtle, juniper, lentisk leaves, terebinth, and ivy. In other places Estienne may be using the ploy of reverse advice, as when he tells the reader that scallions do not suppress sexual desire but in fact only incite a person to be more libidinous.[52]

Men with sexual performance problems who had less money to spend on books could have turned to Dr. Leonardo Fioravanti. More than any other author we shall consider, he was made possible by the printing press. Born in Bologna in 1517, he was a physician who scorned the pretensions of his fellow practitioners, wandered around southern Italy working miraculous cures, and trumpeted his successes with abandon in a series of highly popular books. The preface to the 1572 edition of his *Dello specchio di scientia universale* (The Mirror of Universal Science), originally published in 1564, proclaims that it is a book of great use-fulness, sure to delight all readers, and lists all his earlier publications. Avid fans might turn to his *Capricci medicinali* (Medicinal Caprices, 1561), *La cirugia* (On Surgery, 1561), or *Compendio de i secreti rationali* (Compendium of Rational Secrets, 1564); to a more specific set of cure-alls like *Del regimento della peste* (Controlling the Plague, 1565); or per-haps to something as general as *Il tesoro della vita humana* (The Treasury of Human Life, 1570). Editions and translations into French, English, and German rolled off the presses for the next century, offering hundreds of quick, easy, surefire cures for toothaches, potions to stay eternally young, beauty creams, gibberish prayers more effective than a "Hail Mary," and secrets for turning copper into silver.

Fioravanti championed himself as a man of the people, ever ready to expose the frauds committed by educated elites upon the masses they purposely kept in ignorance. Now that everyone willing to make a little effort could afford to buy books and learn the truth for themselves, the mysteries of medicine could be unveiled. Curing illness requires less for-mal schooling and more experience in following essential principles. Whatever is inside the body making it sick has to be gotten rid of, by one means or another: vomiting, bloodletting, excising, urinating, sweating, defecating, or exhaling. The only other possibility is that the bodily hu-mors are out of balance, in which case the obvious need is to restore things to order: cool what is too hot, heat what is too cold, wet the dry, and dry the wet—what could be simpler? With only a dozen medici-nals—bearing names such as "magnificent liquor," "angelic electuary," "mistral patch," and "fifth essence of anise," with each one costing any-where from twelve soldi to one ducat per ounce—the secret ingredients of which were to be found in one or another of his books, Fioravanti guaranteed that his elixirs, oils, syrups, and electuaries could cure almost anything. One must say "almost," because the doctor proclaims he is so honest that he lists hopeless conditions openly in his books. Thus, a doomed patient who reads very carefully will not waste money on failure. The hopeless cases cannot have been numerous, however, since the "fifth essence" could resuscitate the dead. Two skeptical physicians from Rome disputed Fioravanti's claims on that one, but he happily informs readers that he was proved right and honest when they both died within a year.

Anatomy was anathema to Fioravanti; he railed against it as contrary to nature and useless in curing anyone of anything. It would be better to spend time learning how to farm and raise herbs. He had a sense of humor, and in chapter 78 of his *Il tesoro della vita humana* he gives away his best secret for free: live like the chickens who get up at dawn, eat when they are hungry, stay happy, and go early to bed. Just follow this philosophy and you will live to old age without need of doctors. "And this is the best remedy in the world that has ever been written."

This doctor/charlatan/writer is someone we shall return to several times in the chapters that follow, for his advice covered many topics, but for now we merely note his solution for male impotence. Normally there is nothing a man does more willingly than engage in sexual intercourse, writes Fioravanti, but if for some reason a husband cannot keep an erection, then cook up twenty chestnuts, about four ounces of pistachios and pine nuts, stir in some ragwort, cinnamon, cubebs, and sugar, and boil it down into an elixir. Drink this and go to it.[53]

Not to be outdone by the men, Mrs. Isabella Cortese published a pocket-sized encyclopedia, a sextodecimo volume of wide-ranging advice on matters of interest to men and women alike. We know absolutely nothing about her beyond what little she tells us in her book as she laments that her study of alchemy over thirty years had left her nearly penniless, threatening her very life. The effort proved completely fruitless, for the works of the famous philosophers (as she termed these alchemists)—Geber (eighth century? Arab chemist), Raimondo (Ramon Lull, 1235–1315), and Arnaldo (Arnald of Villanova, ca. 1235–1311)—are complete gibberish, filled with fables and crazy recipes that only make you lose time and money. Then by the grace of God, she discovered good and true secrets on her own, and these have restored her wealth, honor, and health. Out of compassion for humanity, she now prays that everyone will stop wasting time with the philosophers' books and instead follow her little manual: "Don't leave out or add anything but do as I say and write, following my commandments." Among her ten commandments, the first injunction is never to work with "grand masters." Others follow: deny you have any expertise in alchemy; allow no one into your workplace; teach no one else because a secret revealed loses its efficacy; retain a faithful assistant always at your side. Interspersed with these rules are warnings to use only the best receptacles and ingredients, the right temperatures and doses. Finally, when you succeed, be sure to thank God and give charitably to the poor.

Cortese called her book *I secreti della signora Isabella Cortese* (The Secrets of Mrs. Isabella Cortese), and I think she purposely put female authorship right in her title. Perhaps she was really a he, maybe a monk with time to spare and a very good sense of what working people without servants might want to know, but that does not really matter. I suspect that she and her publisher must have thought female authorship would increase sales of this antiestablishment, anti-elite tract. Perhaps they were right since the book went through at least seven printings between 1561 and 1677. The 1584 edition that I was able to examine closely contains 206 pages, and is divided into four parts *(libri)*. The first gives 28 health cures and the second 75 household cleaners; the third provides 80 more remedies and mixtures for one thing or another, and the last part soars onward with 221 guaranteed potions for every need. There are lists of ingredients for mixtures to shine brass, glue metals together, or remove stains from leather and cloth; others are wonderful for bleaching hair, skin, and clothing; there are soaps and toiletries for people and for animals, including one to put a star on the nose of a white horse; there is a fabulous toothpaste, best in the world it says, made from a white wine base that polishes the teeth and restores the gums, and a facial cream that will make you look like a fifteen year old. So why wouldn't there be a quick fix to "straighten out the [male] member"? Testicles of quail, oil from the inner bark of storax and from the elder tree, large-winged ants, musk and amber from the Orient—just mix these together and apply as needed.[54]

At the opposite end of the spectrum from Mrs. Cortese's humble encyclopedia is the huge herbal—two volumes measuring thirteen by ten inches, each three inches thick in the edition I used, weighing a grand total of nineteen pounds two ounces—by Pietro Andrea Mattioli (1500–77). Either might have been consulted by sixteenth-century people on the problem of achieving an erection and each offered assurances of a cure, but here the similarities between the two books end. Mattioli served as physician to the court of Prince Ferdinand, Archduke of Austria, and his lavishly illustrated book—published in Czech, French, German, Italian, Latin, and Spanish—made him the foremost pharmacologist and herbalist of the Renaissance. His *Discorsi* (Discourses) translated and updated the influential work of Pedanius Dioscorides of Anazarba, *Treatise on Materia Medica*. Initially written in the first or second century C.E., this work contained descriptions of all the supposed virtues of remedies then used to treat illness.[55] Professionals in the sixteenth century who wished to consult Dioscorides had many ways of doing so, including Mattioli's own Latin editions. Yet Mattioli decided to reach out to a wider audience by bringing the old master to readers of Italian. To the herbals of Dioscorides he added lengthy lists of his own remedies, thereby creating an entirely new encyclopedia of pharmacology, one containing hundreds of color illustrations.

He did more. The inclusion of detailed, multiple indexes enhanced a book to be consulted again and again as need dictated, one that quickly and authoritatively offered solutions to problems as they arose. Like the herbals, popular-advice manuals were meant to be used, not to be read for pleasure, and indexes greatly facilitated such usage. What Mattioli did for the lavish book of herbs soon found imitators among less costly tomes offering home remedies. His first index lists alphabetically every herb, plant, tree, and other living thing included in the book, giving for each a page and line reference and identifying whether the information is from Dioscorides, Mattioli, or both. This index alone runs to forty pages and contains about four thousand entries. A second index, covering another seventy pages, provides entries by illness, listing for each the herbs and plants that will provide a cure. The arrangement of this functional index is literally from head to toe, so whereas in Mrs. Cortese's tract you would have to browse through hundreds of secrets in little apparent order to find your way to directions for having an erect penis, in Dr. Mattioli's book you just go to *"membra virili,"* which is found about where it should be, below the stomach and above the knee, and then to the subheading *"A provocare il coito,"* to find a list of all the relevant medicinals. Other indexes cover beauty aids and purges; there is even a glossary of technical medical terms and specifically Tuscan usages that may not be familiar to all readers.

Who were the customers for these fabulous volumes? Certainly not individual householders, unless they were quite wealthy and wanted an item that even today would make an elegant coffee-table book. Perhaps not all that many trained physicians, who could have done just as well with a less expensive Latin edition, one that omitted the color illustrations. The consensus among historians of medicine seems sensible enough; herb dealers were the primary purchasers of books of herbals. Merchants, both wholesale and retail, in the booming business of buying and selling medicinals, spices, chemicals, and drugs of all sorts now had at their disposition an authoritative manual showing what each plant or animal looked like, with commentaries from one past and one present renowned scientist on the properties of each item, and with a cross-indexing system geared to quick and efficient sales of merchandise. No wonder it went through numerous editions in many languages and brought such fame to its author.[56]

I suggest that Mattioli's volume did so well in the vernacular because people could read for themselves or to each other the touts about each plant, working either from what ailed the buyer or from what product the seller happened to have on the shelf. With this magnificent tome propped on the proprietor's counter and opened to the appropriate page, the seller could read aloud by pointing a finger, syllable by syllable, at claims of wondrous healing properties. Even a not-so-literate customer could hear the words and at the same time see if the plant in the illustration looked like the merchandise being offered. Perhaps a few buyers first had studied a page or two from Mrs. Cortese's *Secreti* in the privacy of their homes and now were ready to compare her antiestablishment medicine against expert advice, but this is only speculation on my part.

An attractive, although potentially dangerous, feature of Mattioli's lists of remedies is that one seemingly could try them all, either sequentially or simultaneously, with no particular worries about synergism and little concern for quantity. The problem of sexual arousal in men, explicitly of achieving an erection (from the *membra virili* section mentioned above), elicits the following list of helpful items from Dioscorides: costmary drunk with honeyed wine, saffron, linen seeds ground with apple and pepper, cooked turnips, large amounts of dame rocket, roots of dragon arum roasted or boiled with wine, roots of asphodel mixed in foods, nasturtium eaten whole or as a powder to mix and drink, seeds of leek in a drink, cooked scallions, minced garlic eaten with coriander, seeds of nettle drunk with wine, roots of gallium in watered wine, juice of mint, roots of strongly flavored carrots, anise, roots of ragwort, either drunk or eaten, horminium drunk in wine, upper roots of gladiola eaten or better yet drunk, kidneys of saltwater lizard.

And if these do not work, or even if they do, or just as insurance, or perhaps to do a bit of one-upmanship on the old master, Mattioli adds fifteen regimens of his own: things to be ingested include galangal, ash-tree seeds with pistachio, pine nuts, and sugar, Indian nuts, cuttlefish cooked with nuts and garlic, a doe's genitals powdered and drunk in a raw egg, half an ounce of cloves drunk with milk, beans cooked in cow's milk with long pepper and galangal, wild-carrot seeds drunk with wine, boiled pumpkin seeds fried in butter with long pepper, roots of red-grape vines cooked under the hearth ashes and seasoned with salt and pepper; rubs for the genitals include nutmeg and mixtures of deer musk and caster oil, civet musk and caster oil, or pistachio, mustard, and benzoin seeds.

There are also listings for items that suppress sexual desire, either for the chaste or perhaps for sexually active men anxious to keep up their carnal appetites by avoiding debilitating foods. Other compotes and rubs promise to enhance sperm production, overcome continuous erections, reduce nocturnal emissions, and cure seminal dribbling in both men and women.[57]

Another book printed in large and elegant editions in the sixteenth century, undoubtedly in direct competition with Mattioli's, was Castore

Durante's *Herbario nuovo* (New Herbarium). The organization of this early medical encyclopedia, also clearly too extravagant for the ordinary household and certainly aimed at herb dealers, is essentially the same as Mattioli's, with indexes by product and potential usage. Most of its five hundred pages are arranged as a dictionary from *A* to *Z* listing every herb by its Latin and vernacular names, with drawings and commentary on where each is grown and on its qualities and virtues. The latter part of the book switches from this "What is it?" approach to a "What is the problem?" format, complete with a quick and easy cross-reference system. In this latter section, for example, there are 26 entries (herbs and their preparations or mixtures) for curing syphilis, 24 for melancholy, 19 for breast aches, 160 to provoke menstruation, 37 to restrict menstruation, 4 to counter human bites, 58 for easier parturition, 7 for sexual frigidity in women, and 86 for various uterine problems. Much of the book is taken unabashedly and without acknowledgment from medieval texts that surely would have been known to the specialist, but they are all presented as the new wisdom of this Umbrian physician who went on to become a professor at the University of Rome and an advisor to Pope Sixtus V.[58]

Just enough is included of recent imports from India to excite any imagination. Betel, we are told, grows only in India; it has no fruit or flowers, but its leaves, to be chewed, excite the passions of Venus. Indian women chew it before they go on the funeral pyre after their husbands die, and it confounds the intellect if you chew it and drink wine at the same time. The doctor dismisses sexual stimulants that have been around Italy for a long time, such as truffles. He states that these tubers are composed more of earth than water and lack any taste. Eating them generates melancholy and a bad mood more than any other food; they upset the stomach and are hard to digest. Moreover, they cause tooth decay, paralysis, and apoplexy. They are even worse if you eat them at night, despite what people think about them awakening the sexual appetite when sprinkled with pepper. Moderns like myself who relish a plate of *pasta al tartufo bianco* may have to reconsider.[59]

With equal zest and a tone of unassailable authority, Durante's pages recommend the following for increased sperm production and quicker ejaculation: chickpeas, wild carrots, pine nuts, ragwort, flax seeds mixed with pepper and honey, flowers of clove, arugula, saffron, mint, cultivated asparagus, gladiolas, anise, cubebs, ginger, gallium, lentisk leaves, and beans. If your problem is the opposite, and you want to delay coming to a climax, try instead cannabis, betony, prickly or wall lettuce, or wild mint. As with Mattioli, any and all of these seemingly may be tried individually or in any combination.[60]

For sixteenth-century readers willing to forego entirely the wisdom of the ancients on a topic so important as how to achieve an erect penis and perform good sex, there was the alternative of virtually exclusive reliance on exotic medicine. Translated from the original Spanish into Italian, and therefore surely intended for a lay audience, was the work of Christovan da Costa (ca. 1540–99; Christoforo Acosta in the Italian edition), a physician and surgeon who specialized in drugs imported from India. The Italian version covers a total of sixty-seven products, each considered in a separate chapter of half a page or so. There is no index by medical problem, so my assumption is that the book was used primarily by herb dealers to tout the wonders of products on their shelves, rather than by physicians looking up cures for the sick. Shopkeepers would have had to flip to the appropriate chapter, absorb the wisdom contained therein, and be ready for customers to arrive. Reading aloud Acosta's hype may have been an effective sales pitch. The report on opium is worth summarizing with some care, so that present-day readers may flavor the wonderful mix of psychological and physical advice, both embedded in casually assumed cultural attitudes.

Opium is widely used in India by licentious youths, reports Dr. Acosta. The world's medics all know that opium produces impotence, but the imagination of plebeian peoples allows them to draw potency from impotency, and they linger much longer in the sexual act if it is performed under the influence of opium. Mental excitement enhances the bodily force of ejaculation, hastening completion of the "dishonest act" by rushing semen from the brain to the testicles and thence to the penis. In opium users with clouded heads, however, the aid of mental excitement is not there, so they take a long time to ejaculate. "Moreover, because opium is cold and closes the passage by which semen travels from the brain to the genitals, the result is that the two lovers reach orgasm simultaneously. But their [Indian] idea is not this, nor do they reason in this way; they only care about the effective results."[61] How sixteenth-century-Italian herbalists and their clients may have reasoned all this out I leave to your imagination. Certainly many twentieth-century plebeians believe that opium makes for good sex.

Although the title of Marinello's book, *Delle medicine partenenti all' infermità delle donne*, promises advice only on the infirmities of women, readers got a bonus as the popular physician devotes a thick chapter to the causes, signs, and cures of male impotence. Indeed, he begins by excusing the chapter's length with a special plea about the subject's importance, continuing in an unusually discursive fashion to explain the complexities of a problem that involves the correct functions of three body parts: humidity produced in the head must be thrust into the genitals by a lively spirit, which originates in the heart; this happens only if sexual desire, emanating from the liver, is strong. From this it follows that if impotence seems to be a failure of imagination or due to conflicting thoughts, then the problem is in the head. Loss of erection stems from the heart. Lack of sexual desire usually turns out to be a liver defect.[62]

A total approach, Marinello continues, must consider the virtues, instruments, and materials the man possesses. As to the virtues, sexual desire will be weak in men with competing concerns, such as students and clerics (which according to Marinello is a good thing), but also in merchants so worried about their business dealings that they lose their sexual ardor, which is by no means good. A different manifestation of the male impotence problem is when desire is initially there during foreplay but then some image or specter renders him unable to continue. Diabolic influences may be at work, and these we shall consider shortly. Other causes for failures of virtue may be that the man is too thin or has poor digestion.

As to the instruments, if the penis and the testicles do not receive enough humidity from above, they cannot be expected to perform, so the functioning of all bodily systems must be monitored carefully. Excessive coldness or dryness may render the man impotent, as will a case in which the testicles are too small to hold sufficient sperm or so large that the sperm gets lost. A penis that is too short to reach the mouth of the uterus cannot do the job, a particular problem if a fat stomach gets in the way on either side. If his penis is too long, there is danger that the sperm will get cold on its journey and lose force. The only solution is to choose a tall bride since her long uterine passage will wrap tightly around the lengthy penile road to keep the sperm warm on its travels.[63] The risk of losing vital heat on a long journey is made worse if the man has a cold, dry complexion. Before you laugh about this excess-cold advice, Marinello adds, consider that mendicant friars walk barefoot to help cool the sexual ardors, and it works! Most animals do not produce eggs in January or in July, which also proves that too much heat or too much cold leads to impotence.[64]

Good regulation of daily habits is essential. Don't eat to such excess that you suffocate or extinguish body heat nor consume food and drink that are too cold or that dry out the bodily fluids. Avoid immoderate exercise and hot baths or steam baths. Sleep neither too much nor too little. Don't eat so sparsely that you become constipated. Be cheerful and do not fall into dwelling on fear, shame, and similar thoughts. If the sperm is plentiful but watery and cold, nourish the body to warm up its humors. If the sperm is scarce and descends with difficulty, increase bodily humidity with food and drink; also, take more baths. If you feel a general aversion to food and suffer digestive problems, the problem is with your liver or kidneys. If lack of appetite is only about meat, the heart is the source of your impotence. If you are generally lethargic and in a stupor, your brain is too wet and cold to send good sperm down to the genitals.[65]

Some problems are natural and cannot be remedied. Boys, old men, big drinkers, gluttons, men with long penises, and those who devote too much attention to carnal desires all cannot generate children, or if by chance they do procreate, their offspring are monstrous or ugly.[66] Assuming the reader/patient is not in one of the above categories; that he has correctly figured out whether his impotence stems from his head, his heart, or his liver; and that he has determined whether the difficulty is too much or too little humidity and too much or too little heat, then Dr. Marinello is ready with fourteen pages of concoctions to drink or eat or rub or plaster on his body.

Since we have already come across many of the specific herbal mixtures and food suggestions found in these pages, let us skip over them and look instead at the way Marinello interlaces his recipes with advice on behavior. The patient now sipping on spiced goat's milk, for example, should also talk frequently with women about amorous matters, telling off-color jokes and kidding around with them, thinking about sex and letting the drive arise. He should drink really good wine with his midday meal but cut it with a bit of water, and later in the day he should not drink wine that is acidic. If his penis is flaccid or paralyzed, there are several good ointments to rub on the genitals; he should do this frequently and also take lots of warm baths, taking care not to linger so long that the warmth from the ointment is used up. Ogling young women and swapping stories with them about pertinent things can do wonders in curing this problem or anything else that makes a man feel weak. Then there are ointments to be used during sexual intercourse, sure to "delight the lady and consequently get her to love you more" and "give her a great experience she will really appreciate." Some of these strike me as particularly unappealing, as, for example, the advice for a rub sure to bring her desire to new heights: find ninety of those little grubs that stay in the sow thistle plant during the summer, or from any other plants that give off milk, and throw them in a liter of old olive oil; leave this mix in the sun for seven days before rubbing it on your loins and between your backside and penis.[67]

In advice manuals ranging from elegant herbals to cheap pamphlets of secrets, the man suffering sexual-performance failures comes across, perhaps unwittingly, as ever ready to blame someone else. Proposed herbal cures aim to stimulate desire or overcome inhibitions resulting from excessive cares, too much work, or boredom with life's realities. The approach generally is to alter emotional states rather than to remove physical barriers to sexual potency. Externalization of the problem of impotence was especially manifest in men who believed themselves to be victims of black magic. Some husbands in this frame of mind turned to an exorcist for relief, perhaps one who had consulted a self-help book such as Girolamo Menghi's *Compendio dell' arte essorcistica* (Compendium of the Arts of Exorcism). Menghi (ca. 1529–1609/10), a Franciscan friar who according to his epitaph was the sixteenth century's greatest exorcist, in this book sought a much wider audience than the monastery could provide. Certainly his lengthy and approving account of a pious laywoman's accomplishments as an exorcist run counter to Catholic Reformation trends, and the subtitle of his book is suggestive indeed: "A Work No Less Useful to Exorcists than Delightful to Readers, Newly Brought Forth for General Benefit." He hit the mark, with an impressive twelve editions published in three different cities between 1576 and 1605.[68]

The friar includes in his advice manual for exorcists (and perhaps for curiosity seekers generally) a chapter on how the devil and his assistants can inhibit the carnal act, even between husband and wife. Men can be bewitched either internally or externally, he tell us, citing distinction 34 of book 4 of the sentences of Peter Lombard. Internally, the evil spirits may directly attack the penis, rendering it flaccid, or alternatively they may close the seminal canals. Externally, they accomplish the same results by working on a man's imagination, especially by having him eat herbs and other things that are not efficacious in themselves but that lead him to think he is impotent. In other cases, the devil interposes his own body between the man and the woman. No less an authority than St. Bonaventure records that the devil sometimes interposes his body when the man attempts to have intercourse with one women but not with another, thereby creating all sorts of internal doubts and confusion.

Stories of impotent men and their eventual cures fill out the friar's text. Just as we had to read Dr. Christoforo Acosta's report about Indian lovers' use of opium with at least some openness to inverted or deeper meanings, so also we may assume that neither Menghi nor his readers were completely innocent about the mental games being described.

> There was a great Count in the Diocese of Argentina who took as his wife a woman no less noble than he; but after a sumptuous wedding feast for three years he was unable to consummate the marriage, always impeded in his attempts by an evil spirit. One day he had to go on business to Mexico City, where he met by chance his former concubine, who instantly spied the devil's familiar perched on his shoulder. Out of regard for their old relationship she asked him how things were going. He responded breezily that everything was splendid, but she knew otherwise, so she invited him for a private supper, when she again pressed him. Again he did not tell the truth, saying that he had three male children after his three years of marriage. She did not dispute what she knew could not be true but instead began to curse the evil woman who had come to her three years ago offering to make her lover impotent with his new wife by placing a vase of magic herbs in his family well. His former lover was delighted that the old witch had been a liar, because she never had wished him ill. Upon his return home the Count drained the household well and sure enough he found at the bottom a vase filled with strange herbs, which he burned immediately. Instantly his potency returned!

Other stories tell of advice to skip prayers and make the sign of the cross before going to bed; or of drinking secret potions and then in the middle of the night hearing violent thunderstorms, winds, and earthquakes; or of hearing human voices in the room shrieking, crying, and shouting, and of seeing thousands of weird persons tearing out each other's eyes and hair, punching and kicking one another, and tearing at their clothes for half an hour or more. One impotent husband subjected to this treatment, after the evil spirits finally left the room, quickly felt a certain warmth in his loins, at least enough to pay the conjugal debt, and years later his wife said that after the terror of that evening with the spirits, he was never afraid of sex again.[69]

Another 150 pages along in this thick book, Menghi returns to the subject of male impotence, apologizes for having already provided some "remedies" in the earlier section of the volume that was supposed to deal with "diagnosis," and proceeds to list the five ways in which the devil renders men impotent. The first is by interposing himself physically between the couple. The second is by rendering the man hot after one woman but cold versus another, usually by means of the occult application of herbs. The third is by playing on the imaginations of the partners, rendering one hateful toward the other or else filling them with self-doubts. The fourth and fifth, which he reminds readers were covered earlier, involve physical measures to render the penis flaccid or to prevent seminal fluid from reaching the testicles or being ejaculated.

The impotent man must first determine precisely into which of these five traps the devil has cast him. Then he must be certain that he is in God's grace; the cures about to be offered do not work for problems of performance occurring outside marriage. He must start with a contrite heart and a humble spirit and then make a thorough confession, followed by much prayer and fasting. After this essential beginning, the exorcist may recommend the following: a pilgrimage, more confession and deeper contrition for past sins, making the sign of the cross repeatedly and ritual prayer, plus continued legitimate and sober exorcisms. If none of these cures works, then the afflicted husband should be told to bear his misery patiently for the love of God, who must have some good reason for permitting this infirmity to continue as a way of increasing His grace and glory.[70]

As husbands grew older, they often had to cope with waning sexual appetite. Medical tracts such as Marinello's vigorously warned against too much sex for senior citizens. Frequent sex is fine for strapping youths, he writes, but mature men should be more moderate. Oldsters should do it less and really old-timers not at all. Certainly a man should desist if he develops any signs of tremors, chills, heart palpitations, loss of appetite, or digestive problems. Older women also should be careful. Friar Mercurio cites a proverb that circulated in his beloved Roman countryside saying that for a woman who is no longer young, every indulgence in the pleasures of Venus digs another spadeful of earth in her grave. And if she should become pregnant, she cuts a ridiculous figure and very likely will give birth to a child who is sickly or does not survive at all.[71]

A huge popular literature, in a tradition highlighted by Boccaccio's saucy tales but filled with lesser talents as well, speaks to the common wisdom that older men married to younger women are probably cuckolds, especially if the wife gives birth to a son. Against this folk wisdom, the popular-medical-advice manual could offer little comfort. Indeed, sixteenth-century writers reached new heights in satirizing physicians. Lodovico Dolce tells of the lovely young Giulia, married to the old, ugly, and sterile Carlo, who goes to his doctor for help. The medic is much attracted to Giulia and impregnates her himself, and when Carlo catches him between the sheets, his physician duly informs the old man that this was the only cure that would work, so why waste time on ineffective potions.[72]

Writers such as Professor Gioberti in his treatise *Errori popolari* struggled mightily to find hope for older husbands. A young wife is good, he claims against all common wisdom, because in keeping with his theories about how uterine soil determines the outcome of a unisex seed, at least the environment will be warm and fresh. Thus, it can do more to nurture an admittedly weak seed, perhaps even cook it up as a son. Although older men may be physically weaker, they are more rational, less impetuous, and better able to abstain from sex long enough to build up semen strength—ideally with a forty-day Lenten fast or at least during the fourth quarter of the moon and for periods of religious fast. No less an authority than Aristotle thought men could generate until age seventy, and Gioberti thinks some can go longer. Against all the cuckold jokes, there is the counter folk wisdom that as long as a man can lift a *quarto di crusca* (a sack of grain husks) by himself, he can still father a child. Gioberti, apparently not wishing his urban readers to miss the point, assures them that even a frail person can lift a sack of grain husks. He then takes up a theme we have seen before: clean living counts far more than chronological years. The hard worker in the countryside always is healthier than a rich idler in the city.

> The farmer who lives always in the open air, working hard at a steady pace but not to the point of exhaustion, who always eats and sleeps at the same hour, having his mind at ease and at peace, without excessive cares and passions, conserves a healthy mind and body much longer, so that at the age of sixty, even seventy, he is more robust and ready than a forty-year-old city dweller. He tires less easily, can run further, sees without eyeglasses, probably has all his teeth, eats with gusto and digests even the fattiest foods, does not have a chronic cough, nor intestinal problems, nor other aches and pains. What doubt can there be that such a man could still make babies?[73]

Finally, an impotent layman, perhaps having exhausted the remedies of exorcism, good diet, and herbal medicine, might set on the task of studying some anatomy. In a volume published in Venice in 1564, Dr. Prospero Borgarucci, a renowned professor of anatomy at the University of Padua, promises that by reading its five books "everyone may learn the order and the true way to understand anatomy and know all the infirmities that by diverse accidents may come upon our bodies." An added feature is that each body part is named in twelve languages, thus making the volume more widely useful. Anatomy had been studied and written about for centuries, of course, but always in the scholarly languages of Arabic, Greek, or Latin; and the information, therefore, was not easily accessible to Italian laypersons. Just who Borgarucci hoped would buy his book cannot be stated with certainty. Clearly he did not intend to restrict his audience to other physicians and surgeons, because in that case he would have written in Latin and much of the book's introductory material would have been superfluous. Perhaps his experience as a teacher led him to realize that some of his students did not understand Latin all that well and needed a vernacular primer. My judgment is that he also aimed to reach curious laypersons with various aches and pains who wanted to participate a bit more thoroughly in understanding why their bodies suffered some stress or malady. The modern Italian historian of medicine Luigi Firpo concludes that all of Borgarucci's works "remained faithful to this popularizing character, which also must have been inspired by a desire to achieve a diffusion not restricted to men of science." The worst fears of elite physicians who hid their knowledge in the mysteries of Latin were coming true—poor people and women were taking up self-doctoring, a reclamation effort aided and abetted by the printing press![74]

Since the problem at hand is inadequate male sexual performance, the right place to start is Borgarucci's chapter 22, which deals with the virile member and its functions. Here we learn that historically there has been much dispute about whether the member is composed of nerve, membrane, ligament, muscle, or cartilage, but this is easy to resolve with a little thought. It can't be nerve because then the penis would be connected to the brain or the spinal cord and it can't be membrane because a quick look and touch tells you that is wrong. It might be muscle or cartilage in beasts but not in humans because it does not have the color and action of muscle or cartilage, so it must be fatty ligament. It has two functions: excretion of urine and ejaculation of semen during intercourse deep into the uterus. To do these things it has to be able to straighten out, lower itself, tuck itself in, get hard, become soft, swell up, or thin out as "we need it to do." It originates at the pubic bone and has its roots in four muscles (not two or three as some mistaken experts say). Two of these are located at the end of the intestine, known as the sphincter, and push urine into the canal. There is only one canal for both urine and sperm, Borgarucci insists, and those who hold that there are two distinct canals are simply wrong. The other two muscles are located at the pubic bone, and it is these that give great pleasure during lovemaking because they maintain the penis straight "as long as necessary for what we're doing." The popularizing anatomist then sides with his colleagues who believe there are arteries going from the base of the penis to the tip through which the hot spirits of sexual desire flow to keep the penis erect, rather than the spirits being confined only to the seminal canal. He also supports the disputed view that all the arteries and veins are connected in a single circulatory system and that there are nerves extending to the tip of the penis. Now that the reader is clear about anatomical realities, Borgarucci confidently asserts, he should be able to judge among proposed remedies for whatever ails him.[75]

Finally, we look at a case in which popular diffusion of medical knowledge became degradation, the work of Giuseppe Liceti (d. 1599). The title of his 1598 sextodecimo book trumpets him as a surgeon from Genoa who promises to reveal everything about the excellence and use of the genitals, how semen is produced, how and why offspring resemble their parents, how monstrosities are born, and other matters—all told in ways both useful and delightful to read. Further along, the inner title page guarantees readers a result for every chapter, a counterpunch for each blow, and as many solutions as there are arguments. The facing page explains that Liceti will write in the vernacular, even though his superiors have warned him about the indecency of explaining these subjects except in Latin, because this book is partially a defense of his earlier treatise (1590), also duly censored for being written in Italian. He assures readers he will not use obscene words, conveying things only in honest ways. However, in both works, but more unabashedly in the latter, the veneer of being an advice manual intended to convey ancient wisdom to the common man quickly fades away to reveal the book's true character: misogynous satire and light pornography. Aristotle, pre-Freudian castration complex, and sperm envy abound in this woman-bashing diatribe that I believe potential sixteenth-century readers would have known contained no practical advice.[76]

Infertility in Women

Popular manuals offering advice to men contain a wealth of insights into how sixteenth-century people understood the emotional, mental, and psychological issues involved in cases of sexual impotence.[77] While an equivalent depth of concern with mental states is not to be found in tracts on female sterility, at least a few authors should be noted for their understanding that infertility among wives might be a complex problem, one requiring attention to emotional needs no less than to purely physical matters. Gioberti specifically urges that the husband wishing to see his wife become pregnant should be tender with her after ejaculation, allowing her gently to fall asleep if she can, or if not, then at least the couple should both stay awake a while in bed, acting playfully and talking happily with each other. He also warns women against trying so many different remedies simultaneously that one works against another. Better to go slowly, first determining whether the uterine environment is too cold for germination or too humid; then try a single appropriate medicine for a while. Otherwise, the woman's "poor body is so altered and messed up by a chaos of medicines and her spirit so agitated by false hopes and fears, desires and disappointments, that the seed cannot possibly reach a secure harbor." For the most part, declares Gioberti, herbal baths and douches are a waste of time.[78]

However, even an author as generally sympathetic to women as Gioberti shares in propagating misogynous views about female sexual desire. Many women are lascivious, insatiable, and licentious, he thunders, so full of sperm that, as the saying goes, they are "hot as a bitch," and were it not for some token of self-respect, they would run after the men and take them by force. These women on fire can never get pregnant; they would need a lot more than sperm to extinguish or at least moderate their uterine temperature. Very frequent intercourse just overheats them even faster.[79]

Any humor we moderns may find in Gioberti's tirades surely was not what he intended, but such is hardly the case with Ortensio Lando's spoof of the popular-advice manual. In *Paradossi* (Paradoxes), he lauds the virtues of a sterile wife, who will be humble and ready to obey her husband. The mother, by contrast, becomes proud and bold, parading around like the absolute *"signora della casa."* Before a wife has children, she is afraid to ask her husband for so much as a new dress, but the moment she gives birth she becomes commandeering, so that her husband's only peace is to go out of the house. The advantages of a sterile wife are many: no listening to screaming from labor pains, no crying from the crib and interrupted sleep, no arguments about wet nurses, and no deaths in childbirth. Who wants children anyway? All they do is grow up to murder, steal, fight, and end up in jail. Finally, in the case of an arranged marriage that the husband does not like, sterility may be the way out of it.[80]

For those couples who did want a child, more practical advice could be found in manuals such as Savonarola's tract addressed to the wives of Ferrara. In keeping with bodily humors theory and with Avicenna's advice not to heat up what is already hot or moisten further what is already wet, the starting point is determining whether the uterus is hot or cold. One sign of a hot uterus is if the woman feels warm all over. Paucity of menstrual blood is another indicator, especially if the blood is bright red or yellowish. Other symptoms of excess heat are pains in the liver area, ulcers on the womb, very wet labia, and thick pubic hair. Finally, urine coloration and pulse rate should be considered since the organs are interconnected. A cold uterus is likely if menstrual cycles occur only every two or three months, or if menstrual flow lasts seven or eight days. Eating cold, fatty foods, drinking cold water, and frequent sexual intercourse may all result in a cold uterus. Once its temperature is determined, Savonarola, like dozens of other experts, is ready with a vast range of concoctions to steam, fumigate, wash, flush, and otherwise alter the uterine environment.[81]

A more florid treatment comes from Marinello's book on female infirmities. The husband whose seed falls into an overly warm uterus has no more chance of success than a farmer sowing in the Ethiopian desert. At the other extreme, a wife with a cold uterus condemns her husband to the fate of an agriculturist who throws seed on the ice-covered high Alps between Italy and Germany—in less than an hour the effort is completely wasted. This sort of wet/dry, hot/cold balancing act is perfect for Marinello's barrage of advice on diets, baths, douches, and flushes, which goes on for many pages, mostly copied mercilessly from others or repeated with uninhibited self-praise from his best-selling *Gli ornamenti delle donne,* the subtitle of which proclaims itself to be "useful and necessary to every genteel person and wherein is recounted how with the right arts women can appear charming and beautiful." The regimens often require treatments lasting ten days or more, accompanied by recommendations of chastity for the duration. Then, before the couple resumes having sexual intercourse, the man should rub his legs and penis with various aromatic oils; for her there are vaginal suppositories to insert.

Even if temperature and humidity are correct, the uterine neck may be too wide to close properly over the seed or too narrow to allow the seed to reach the best soil. Any growths, hemorrhoids, or lesions on the mouth of the vagina will inhibit conception. Nor can much be expected of a wife who is too fat or too thin; troubles with menses or problems in urination also impede conception. All these defects may be treated with herbals and diets, which Marinello describes at great length. Thirty pages are devoted to tightening the mouth of the uterus, making it less lubricated, hardening it, and reducing flatulence.

Then there are more subtle qualities about a marital relationship. Marinello says that the primary reason a wife does not get pregnant is because her husband does not truly love her and in fact hates her. Beyond that, if the man ejaculates before the woman reaches a climax, her soil cannot possibly be ready. Couples who ardently desire children should try having him tie a string lightly around his testicles so that his sperm cannot be released. Then leave things to the wife who, when she feels she is nearing orgasm can untie the knot, letting his seed implant itself on her ready soil.

Another of Marinello's instructions sounds somewhat like the Rubin or tubal insufflation test still used today by gynecologists to check for blocked fallopian tubes. Have the woman sit on a chair with a caned seat covered with cloth and under the seat set a coal grill to cook up some perfumes, like gum of lada leaves, storax, musk, amber, or aloe; if she feels the perfume rise from below right up to her nostrils, then know well that the fault for the sterility is not hers. But if this test seems too complicated, just place a piece of garlic in the woman's vagina; if after a while the odor of garlic emanates from her nostrils, know well that she is not impeding conception. This test actually comes straight from Hippocrates, but as usual Marinello does not buttress his advice with classical citations.[82]

Consideration of blocked uterine passages may well have led couples to go beyond general treatments like Marinello's to consult instead a book such as Borgarucci's anatomical guide for laypersons. Readers learned that the information given about men also held for women, the biggest difference being that in females the parts are closed inside their bodies. The uterus is equivalent to the scrotum and the penis corresponds to the uterine neck. Women, like us men, have two testicles that are located at the upper corners of the uterus and are smaller than their male counterparts. These are connected by veins that bring sperm into the uterus; in accordance with lunar time, other arteries bring menstrual blood to the uterus. Female genitalia are located internally because that is where conception and generation take place, and nature in its perfection puts things where they belong. Borgarucci also agrees with the opinion that because women lead lives of leisure and are therefore more humid, having these organs on the inside keeps them warmer, making for better conception. Then there is the more manifestly misogynous view, to which he gives full expression: women are conceited and haughty animals, quite untamable, so nature made their genitals equivalent to men's but kept them hidden so they would think themselves less perfect than the male and ultimately feel more humility and shame.[83]

Borgarucci does not tell his readers which experts shared his opinion about the haughtiness of women but one source surely was Juan Valverde, whose widely disseminated text on human anatomy, itself a plagiarized (Valverde claimed "corrected") version of Andreas Vesalius's *De humani corporis fabrica,* proclaims:

On my honor I would have preferred to leave out this chapter so
that women would not become even more vain than they already are
once they learn that they have testicles just like men. Moreover, these
[testicles] not only support the work of nourishing the baby in the
womb, just as with any seed planted in the ground, but they also are
fertile in themselves, just like the men's, and the women do not lack
a member [penis] either. But the force of history just would not let
me do otherwise [than to tell the truth].[84]

Valverde's book found its niche as a full-length vernacular crib sheet of
Vesalius for medical students with weak Latin skills, rather than as a
family-medical-advice manual. Nevertheless, its snide fear that women
would learn from its pages that they had testicles may be a tantalizing
clue suggesting that, once books made their way into the vernacular, their
readership could and probably did extend from the elite classes to laypersons, including women. If trained physicians were the sole conduits
of this information, then its existence in Latin already had let out the
truth. Therefore, Valverde may be suggesting that women somehow
would read the text themselves, or have it read to them in a language
they understood, perhaps by their sons or lovers!

Among the many publication abuses that abounded in sixteenth-
century Italy we find the attribution of a distinguished authorial name
to a book written by some obscure ghostwriter (a practice not so uncommon for politicians, sports heroes, and movie stars in our own day). This
happened to Gabriele Falloppio, a pioneer in the understanding of female anatomy, from whom we get the designation fallopian tubes. Under
his renowned name, one Pietro Angelo Agato, probably a pupil, published a veritable encyclopedia containing all sorts of advice on ointments, waters, and alchemy for cures of male and female genital illnesses.
My guess is that such works had a certain following, especially among
people looking for quick cure-alls; although we cannot be sure just how
widely these materials circulated, the fourteen printings listed in the
National Union Catalog between 1563 and 1676, by no less than thirteen
different Venetian printing firms, suggest a lively market.

Most curious is why publishers thought to combine an authoritative
name like Falloppio's with recipes so clearly in a knock-the-establishment
style. One sample entry provides the flavor of such advice. Whenever a
woman suffers from uterine problems, we learn on page 21, she should
use this remedy: mix equal parts of galangal, marjoram, and mushrooms,
reducing them to a fine powder. Put a sixteenth of an ounce of this mixture into a piece of very thin taffeta, twist it to resemble a button, insert

it into the vagina as far as possible, and leave it there undisturbed for twenty-four hours. You will see coming out of the uterus so much putrid water as to surprise you. Then mix a pound of nettle, oregano, fennel, cumin mallow, mint, anise, and coriander; grind them into a fine powder and put them in a cauldron containing thirty liters of good wine and boil for an hour. Have the woman spread her legs on top of the cauldron so as to allow the vapors to enter her vagina. Repeat the procedure for five days, morning and evening. Also spread hypericum oil over the genital area at bedtime for eight to ten days. This remedy works for all uterine problems, promises our mystery author with a pseudonym, so there is no need for careful diagnostics.[85]

Similar in content but radically different in sales approach is a little pamphlet titled *Secreti naturali et medicinali* (Natural and Medicinal Secrets) that hails itself as containing "familial exhortations on conserving good health." Devoid of an author, any dedication or claim of professional expertise, and even page numbers, it claims only the knowledge that comes from personal experience and a desire to share its wisdom for the benefit of humankind. It does not lack in confidence. For uterine pains of any kind, just take crushed dodder and boil it in white wine; drink half a glass in the morning and immediately after put a pair of old shoes on the fire and squat over the fumes so they enter your womb.[86]

Another place where sixteenth-century people might find advice on conception and genital illnesses is one we have consulted before, the agricultural almanac of Charles Estienne. In the section on home remedies a female farmworker should know, we learn that partridge eggs are good for rendering a sterile woman fecund. To make conception even more likely, drink juice of dog's mercury and put catmint in your bath; then, just before intercourse, rub balsam ointment on your vagina.[87]

Just as the Sienese herbalist Mattioli sets records for numbers of remedies offered to men suffering from impotence, so also he overwhelms the field with the quantity of his suggestions for female ailments. To save space and retain your patience, here I shall merely list the main problems, along with the numbers of remedies offered by ancient Dioscorides and modern Mattioli.[88]

PROBLEM	DIOSCORIDES	MATTIOLI
Overheated uterus	19	12
Delayed menstruation	116	32
Protracted menstruation	61	33
White discharge	0	22
Expelling the placenta	25	8
Inducing parturition	45	11
Easing labor pains	0	5

Provoking labor	0	10
Prohibiting conception	18	3
Overcoming sterility	3	7
Removing a dead fetus	5	8
Preventing miscarriage	2	6
Clearing afterbirth	6	3
Easing morning sickness in pregnancy	1	0
Inflamed uterus	14	3
Ulcerated vagina	5	4
Uterus that is too soft	12	4
Flatulent uterus	2	15
Extracting postpartum tumors	0	2
Cold uterus	0	10
Tightening the vagina (after birth)	0	2
Dilating the vagina (using penile ointment)	0	5
Fallen uterus	8	2
Uterine pains and cramps	11	19

Finally from Friar Mercurio, we have careful illustrations of instruments that might be used to apply some of the concoctions proposed by Marinello, pseudo-Falloppio, Estienne, Savonarola, Mattioli, and Mercurio himself, of course. Figure 2.1 shows a pessary designed so the odors will not rise up to the nose and so that air can pass easily through the openings. Figure 2.2 portrays a uterine fumigator, much more practical than trying to squat over a hot fire to absorb the fumes from old shoes, donkey's hooves, or whatever you're trying.

Menstruation

Both Lando's humorous praise of the sterile wife and the more serious advice of Savonarola, which might be used for purposes opposite to its stated intent, point to the reality that many couples did not want more children than they already had, or any at all for the time being if they were not married. Couples in these circumstances could find plenty to read telling them how to terminate an unwanted pregnancy. In popular-medical manuals of the sixteenth century, people turned to the section on menstruation. Here they found a general commentary on menstruation, some advice about the properties of menstrual blood, and specific recommendations on how to induce menstruation, widely understood to mean a woman was not pregnant. Indeed, advice manuals such as Marinello's warn explicitly that attempting to provoke menstruation during pregnancy is a serious sin because it means the fetus will die. Some of his remedies explicitly say they will provoke menstruation only if the woman is not pregnant, but others are notably silent about such promises.[89]

Iſtromento, nel quale ſi mettono gli odori, affine di iɴ..romettet
li nella natura della donna : perche non arriuino al na-
ſo, e l'aere ui poſſa entrare facilmente.

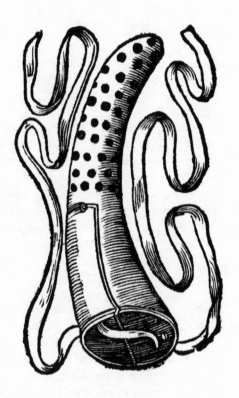

348

Iſtroᵢ

Figure 2.1. A vaginal pessary designed such that the air can pass easily through the vagina without letting odors rise up to the patient's nose.

Iſtromenti per fare i ſuffomigij alla matrice.

Del

Figure 2.2.   A uterine fumigator, surely safer than squatting over a hot fire to absorb the fumes from old shoes, a donkey's hooves, or whatever.

Advice on menstruation came within a context of Judeo-Christian taboos expressing male fears about the magical powers of female blood. According to the persuasive analysis of Italian feminist scholar Ida Magli, the story of Jesus' miraculous cure of a woman who had been hemorrhaging for twelve years (Matt. 9:20–22), in fact, should be understood as a conscious breaking by her and by him of the taboo against men being touched by a menstruating woman.[90] Over the centuries, however, most writers revered by the church had come to take a much harder line, expressed with utter clarity in the view provided by future Pope Innocent III (1198–1216) in his *De miseria humanae conditionis:* "It [menstrual blood] is said to be so detestable and impure, that, from contact therewith, fruits and grains are blighted, bushes dry up, grasses die, trees lose their fruits, and if dogs chance to eat of it they go mad."[91]

To counter popular phobias that flourished within such a sanctioned umbrella of hostility to women, maintained by scientists and churchmen alike, authors of differing views, for example, the physician Albertini Bottoni, had to go to great lengths in de-emphasizing the magical, sinful qualities of menstrual blood, urging readers (initially university-trained doctors since his book was written in Latin, with dissemination in Italian coming later) to pay attention only to medical properties. The enormously popular occult philosopher Henricus Cornelius Agrippa went even further, touting the wonders of menstrual blood as a cure for human madness, epilepsy, hydrophobia, and "many other similar pernicious illnesses."[92]

As we might expect, Michele Savonarola's tract addressed to the women of Ferrara, heavily influenced by his study of Greek, Roman, and Arabic authors who for all their hostility to women did not share a religiously based tradition about the uncleanness of menstrual blood, took a more realistic middle ground. In following Avicenna, Savonarola attempted to reconcile conflicting Aristotelian and Galenic views about whether female semen was necessary for procreation. Notwithstanding much contradictory citation of authorities, he ultimately sided with Galen's position that female semen was essential, not just the soil or the uterine environment in some general sense but actual seeds or semen found in menstrual blood. In the very first chapter of his vernacular treatise, he explains that the weight of medical opinion is that female sperm contributes in grand part to the formation of the body, just as dough does to bread, while male sperm plays little role in this physical formation.

Menstrual blood (or semen) consists of five levels. The purest, whitish in color, generates the reproductive organs; the next part, less pure, generates the new baby's fleshy, fatty parts; the third level nourishes the fetus in the uterus, while the fourth generates breast milk; the impure fifth part is expelled with the placenta. Even though Savonarola was not at all clear on how menstrual blood changed from one state to another, and granted that he emphasized the dangers of impure menstrual blood not used up in its earlier states, on balance his very influential work mitigated against religiously inspired fears about the evil powers of women's menstrual flows. His view is copied exactly, without acknowledgment of course, by such clearly popular writers as Giovanni Marinello.[93]

Gioberti also argues that menstrual blood is neither pernicious nor particularly disgusting, except for its crudeness. He explains that the blood is rich in nutrients. Girls, being more humid than boys, need this excess blood in their youth, but from about the age of ten, when more than half their growth is completed, they no longer require as much, so it gathers in the uterus to be expelled at regular intervals unless a fetus must be nourished. Gioberti also dismisses as a baseless superstition the belief (repeated by no less an authority than Savonarola) that a child conceived during menstruation will become a leper. This is not possible because, he reminds readers, the male seed cannot germinate during times of excess bodily humidity. Nonetheless, the injunction of Leviticus (15:19–24) should be obeyed; it is sinful to have intercourse if there is no chance of conception.[94]

Friar Mercurio, notwithstanding his Dominican training, rejects extreme commentaries—whether biblical or papal—about the dangers of menstrual blood. Menstrual blood must be good, he reasons, because God put it there. Everyone agrees that it nourishes the delicate fetus during the critical early stages of growth, so its essence must be pure even if sometimes it turns noxious due to buildup of bad bodily humors. Mercurio relishes answering his rhetorical questions about why women have so much more menstrual blood than female animals, a fact misogynists regularly used in their diatribes about the wickedness of Eve's descendants. The friar explains that menstrual blood in animals goes into the growth of their hooves, thick skins, and horns, whereas women have only thin nails on their fingers and toes. Moreover, women loll around and do less exercise than female animals, so more menstrual blood builds up; this also explains why active teenage girls sometimes do not menstruate until after age twenty. Finally, nature wants humans to be more perfect than animals; therefore, women expel more impure menstrual blood.[95]

While most vernacular texts, addressed as they were in significant part to female readers, are distinctly less phobic about menstrual blood than, say, church teachings or Aristotle, there are exceptions. Consider the sort of vitriolic comment found in the Sienese Pietro Andrea Mattioli's *Discorsi*, the work that established him as the Renaissance's premier pharmacologist. In the closing section, in a paragraph labeled as being about drinking bull's blood, he drifts off quite unexpectedly into a warning to men against drinking or eating menstrual blood, especially if it comes from a choleric woman or one with a rosy complexion or one who is bold or hot-blooded. Lunacy is certain to ensue, and the man will become a simple-minded fool. Mattioli then tells readers that an evil woman sometimes will secretly slip a little menstrual blood into what she is preparing for her husband or for any other man she despises. If you are the victim of such treachery, the only remedy is to drink one *dramma* (about four grams) of pearl dust in water of balm gentle, take baths in tepid water, and have sex with young girls *(usar carnalmente con giovani fanciulle)*, spending lots of time conversing with them and lingering around them! The only caution about this advice is that the underage sex should be done "only if it is possible to avoid injury to our laws." Readers may recall that I judged this elegant book to be aimed at buyers and sellers of medicinal herbs rather than at the general public, so what is the point of such blatantly misogynous advice? Perhaps it was only meant as a joke—rather a crude one—but it is entirely reasonable to see this advice to commit sexual abuse as a consistent, logical evocation of male power.[96]

Further evidence of menstrual phobias may be seen in Marinello's book on female medicine. In a discussion about setting a wedding date, he begins with the usual admonitions to follow church rules on the matter and also to consult the astrological signs; this done, he prescribes choosing a day when the bride will not be menstruating. A child conceived during menstruation may result in death during childbirth, he warns. A husband who engages in sex with a menstruating wife becomes older by ten years, physically weak, and simpleminded. His sex drive diminishes, and he develops aches and pains in his feet, eyes, brain, head, and above all his stomach. He hears ringing in his ears and runs high fevers, experiences tremors and weak nerves, sleeplessness, poor eyesight, baldness, backaches, kidney and bladder pains, bad breath, and foul body odor. The way to calculate the menstrual cycle is simple enough since it varies with the moon's cycles. Adolescent girls menstruate during the first quarter of the moon's cycle, women in their twenties during the second quarter, women in their thirties during the third quarter, and women beyond that age during the fourth quarter. Just remember the proverb: the new moon accompanies a young girl, the old is for the old.[97]

Given some of the spectacular claims made about menstrual blood, the remedies provided for inducing menstruation seem quite ordinary.

Fioravanti recommends boiling down a mixture of ivy and sage, borax, ribwort, parsley roots, sugar, saffron, and cinnamon. While taking this, do not wet your hands with cold water and everything should be fine. Charles Estienne attentively provides a good sample of items found in the ordinary home garden that can be used to bring on menstruation. Try marigolds or wild carrots, in fact any and all carrots, or caraway or common mallow or marshmallow; make a plaster of nettle and apply it to the navel, drink cloves ground up in white wine or pennyroyal cooked in white wine, eat coriander seeds (one for each day the menstrual cycle will last) or madder or distilled strawberries with the water and sugar they were cooked in or a distilled mix of iris, hyssop, and woodworm.[98]

Marinello notes at least briefly possible problems of physical obstruction before moving on to herbals. Check first to see if the mouth of the uterus is closed by excess fattiness or narrowness or by a growth of some sort, he advises. Consider the condition of other organs, especially whether the bladder is enlarged or something is wrong with the liver. Try to figure out if the menstrual blood is too thick or thin, if production is scarce or too much is retained. Where is the woman in her life cycle? Some experts think that women get hotter as they age; their desire for sex increases as their sperm production increases and, therefore, their menstrual flow also increases.[99] (As an aside, let me remind modern readers that earlier Marinello had declared himself in agreement with the male-seed-only experts, concentrating his advice on getting the female soil in the right condition. Here, nonetheless, he once again covers all possibilities, trying to accommodate those who accept the two-seed explanation of conception. Such eclecticism and self-contradiction are just part and parcel of the advice manual and seem in no way to discourage readers, then or now.)

Know the signs. If a woman does not menstruate because she is too hot, her skin will be flushed; she will be thirsty and dry mouthed, even feverish at times; her pulse will be rapid, her kidneys hot, and her urine strongly colored. She will be assaulted by carnal desires. On the other hand, if menstruation is impeded by coldness or by excessively thick menstrual blood, then her body will feel soft; she will sleep profoundly; her skin color will be white but her veins green; her urine will be copious, her stool phlegmatic; she will have cold sweats and a low pulse rate; she will rarely be thirsty and her appetite will be for cold foods. Once a diagnosis is reached, it is time to administer a cure, and Marinello's proposals go on for twenty-two leaves. My own candidate for least favorite concoction is the following, if only because finding all the ingredients is daunting:

Gather two handfuls of mugwort; and one each of pennyroyal, sweet flag, wild marjoram, melilot, bistort, savin, marjoram, elecampane, wall germander, verbascum, ground pine, betony and betony flowers, common centaury, rue, and bugloss. Throw in one handful each of the roots of fennel, celery, parsley, wild asparagus, saxifrage, dittany, sedge, wild blackberry, iris, and peony. Then add half an ounce each of seeds of juniper, lentisk, parsley, celery, fennel-flower, balsam-flower, costmary, elderberry, pyrethrum, cinnamon, cardamom, and sweet flag. Put everything into a very large pot filled with rainwater to soak for one day and night. Then boil until the water is half consumed and remove from the fire to cool until tepid. Mix everything with your hands, mashing and squeezing, extracting all the juices but discarding the pulp. Add enough sugar to make the liquid into a syrup. Then take an ounce of the syrup with an ounce of your best vinegar as a chaser. Just marvelous for tickling the humors and getting the menstrual flow going.

How could it not work? Or at least produce some effect in the patient? And if it did not, Marinello provides other ingredients to strengthen the medicine. Indeed, he closes this chapter with a listing of herbals divided into the weak, the moderate, and the truly powerful, giving encouragement, I would suppose, to do-it-yourself types to mix their own potions.[100]

Are You Pregnant?

We may well imagine the feelings of sixteenth-century wives, and their husbands, as they anxiously awaited the possibility that menses would not occur. If ever there was a moment to consult an advice manual and read carefully, this was it. Even texts intended for more sophisticated audiences, such as Palmieri's *Della vita civile,* took a moment out to describe the signs: about ten days from conception, look for complexion problems, sleeplessness, glassy eyes, and a full and upset stomach.[101] Other treatments are more detailed.

In a wonderfully candid opening to his chapter on signs of pregnancy, Michele Savonarola reaches out to a wider audience than medical practitioners alone, expressing his hope that readers will find what follows both useful and a pleasure to read. The first indication, he writes, is how the sex went. It bodes well if the wife has received her husband's semen with great avidity and if he has felt her vagina constrict around his penis, leaving the head dry. As the great Avicenna wrote, the woman will have felt a clear titillation in all her members as she reached orgasm simultaneously with her husband.

Time passes and she will not menstruate for two or three months, even though her health is otherwise excellent. A vaginal examination by the local midwife will show that the mouth of her uterus is firmly closed. Her labia will be unusually dry and her breasts will have begun to enlarge. The pregnant woman's body will begin to round out and she will have a little pain below her navel. Her urination will be both more frequent and more difficult, as the uterus presses on her bladder.

Behavioral changes will ensue, such as irritability and nauseousness. She will develop an abomination for sexual intercourse. There are many instances, Savonarola admits, when pregnant women somehow take heightened pleasure in sexual intercourse, but this is contrary to nature; even animals do not attempt to reimpregnate themselves. Often she will feel anxious, listless, and heavy of body and will suffer headaches—all caused by the retention of harmful vapors from her excess menstrual fluids. She may crave strange foods, and the whites of her eyes may turn yellowish. Her complexion will change, especially if she is carrying a girl since females use up less of her uterine heat. Her pulse may become faster and she may feel heart tremors.

Savonarola goes on to offer a series of self-tests that may be used to determine if a woman is pregnant. He cautions that sometimes even world-renowned physicians have been fooled, however, so one cannot rely on a single test result. That much said, he suggests ingestion of honey and rainwater; if the woman feels pains and pressures in her intestines, she is pregnant, because the filled uterus is not letting the flatulence caused by consuming this concoction to escape. Conversely, cotton laced with musk or a clove of garlic may be inserted as far into the vagina as possible; sniff at the nose and mouth to see if the smell rises unobstructed, which means no pregnancy.[102]

Uroscopy also should be weighed in the balance. If the urine is pale, starting as lemon colored but becoming whitish, then pregnancy is plausible. If the urine is dark, whether bright yellow or brownish or even red, then probably it has this color because the female spermatic materials in the uterus have not been impregnated and are being evacuated partly through the urinary tract. Particles floating upward and downward in the urine also mean that pregnancy is unlikely. Other experts, however, such as the French physician known in Italian as Gioberti, were very distrustful of urine analysis because their experience showed that many other things could cause changes in urine color and content, including such simple events as eating lots of vegetables like asparagus.[103]

Mercurio also attacks uroscopy, restraining none of his penchant for scathing verbiage: "As to the signs some people think they see in the urine, this is such a false lie that it belongs more to charlatans than to physicians because the moon has more to do with shrimp than with urine in showing whether a woman is pregnant." The real signs are that no sperm (his and hers) leaked out after intercourse, that on the next day the woman felt lively and agile as her uterus tightened around the sperm, that she suddenly developed an abomination for the carnal act and even for caresses from her husband, that her breasts enlarged, and that she has become fastidious about food.[104]

Marinello also warns that many midwives and physicians have been fooled by urine analysis, so other signs need to be considered. In addition to several of the tests given by Savonarola, which he states as if they are his own, Marinello adds a few new twists. If during intercourse a women feels pain beneath the navel and if she does not feel her sperm exiting, then she is probably pregnant. Very early in pregnancy she will feel bloated because of her retained menstrual blood, but then she will thin out again as the growing baby consumes these fluids. At this point her veins, especially in her breasts, will become yellow and green. According to some experts, one of the most efficacious signs are enlarged veins between the eyes and the nose, where tears start. The whites of her eyes may become yellow and the pupils smaller. In addition to cravings for strange foods, she may experience morning sickness and acidic burping.[105]

Eventually, however, all this testing and guessing become unnecessary because the woman should be able to feel her baby moving on its own, heavy, like a rock tilting from one side of her uterus to the other, fully alive![106]

CHAPTER

· *3* ·

Pregnancy and Childbirth

Sixteenth-century advice-manual readers like our imaginary Tuscan couple, if they had consulted Giovanni Marinello's *Delle medicine partenenti all' infermità delle donne* about conception, needed only to turn the page to learn all about pregnancy. "Praise God for the good news" is how Marinello begins. Immediately afterwards he provides rudimentary lessons on female anatomy and fetal development, his aim being to "please the gentlewomen who are anxious to know about these matters and also to instruct midwives on how things are with the creature in the womb."[1]

The healthy uterus normally opens and closes independent of a woman's will, letting sperm in and menstrual blood out. Now that she is pregnant, however, the uterus shuts itself so tightly that not even the point of a needle can pass through its mouth. Inside, the uterus embraces the sperm and just like any seed planted in good soil, the sperm's internal warmth allows it to expand, forming a protective coating around itself like the skin of an onion or the membrane of an egg. The uterus helps with its spirit or vapor or smoke, "whatever you want to call it," writes Marinello, seemingly exasperated when his male-seed-only theory causes him difficulty in explaining just how this early growth takes place. Anxious to please readers without getting bogged down in controversy, he moves on to subjects about which he feels more secure.

The spirit emanating from the sperm's heat in the uterus forms the essence of the soul, located at the sperm's center. This is the vital force that drives everything else. Then two critical things happen if the spirit (smoke or vapor) is strong: first, it stretches the spermatic material, allowing space to accommodate the limbs; second, it forms the "thing he has in front." Marinello is assuming the child is becoming a boy; otherwise, as we already know from Gioberti, if the spirit is warm enough to procreate but not quite hot enough to be a boy, the result is a girl. The formative substance *(la virtù formativa)* composed of menstrual blood is then driven upward by the spirit to form the brain, the heart, and the blood vessels. The menstrual blood has three essential parts at this point. The finest and most spirited (hot) forms the flesh of the heart; the second part, equally warm but less refined, forms the liver; the third part, by nature thick, cold, and phlegmatic but rendered dry as it is drawn upward, becomes the brain. Marinello reports that other experts believe that in the tiny sperm mass there are three distinct canals: in one, the heart forms during the first six days; in the second, menstrual blood left from the formation of the heart begets the liver; and in the third, menstrual blood, now whitish rather than red, forms the brain. After these three primary organs are in place, the umbilical cord develops, again from both menstrual blood and sperm, so that the air and spirit of the uterine soil form a rivulet called the navel and the umbilical, corresponding to the roots of any seed and composed of two veins and two arteries; these carry nourishment in and waste out between the baby's liver and the peritoneum and reticulum of the mother.

Thus nourished, the seed gradually takes human shape—in about thirty days, if a boy, or forty, if a girl. But the creature is still too small to move until about three months, if male, four months, if female. Why and exactly how males develop faster in the uterus and eventually come out sooner is a good question, at least according to Savonarola (upon whom Marinello is relying at this point, again without acknowledgment), who leaves the matter to those who like to speculate. Whatever the sex, its position in the womb is like Christ on the cross, feet down, arms outstretched, and head faced forward. There the baby stays, constantly taking nourishment through its navel, growing larger, and giving occasional kicks or elbows. When it feels that its house is getting too tight, the baby thrusts its feet against the uterine wall and does a somersault so that it faces backward with its head and shoulders pushed against the mouth of the uterus. Excess menstrual nourishment the baby did not use during the preceding months is coagulated together with its urination and kicked aside into the placenta. This movement results in the baby puncturing the sack of sweat and urine that lies between it and the uterine wall, which in turn lubricates the mouth of the uterus and readies everything for labor and delivery. This is how it works when everything is in order; further along Marinello provides advice about dealing with trouble spots along the way.[2]

Boy or Girl?

Reassured now about the routines of pregnancy, our Tuscan couple, like all parents-to-be, surely wondered about the baby's sex. Looking was and still is the primary way we speculate about whether a pregnant woman is carrying a boy or a girl. We evaluate the brightness of her face, notice the roundness of her belly, and formulate a guess on the baby's sex. Today, of course, we also study sonograms, surely more reliable than any of the visual clues discussed in sixteenth-century advice manuals; yet many parents-to-be in the late twentieth century, along with their friends and relatives, continue to take delight in speculating about whether the protrusion between the baby's legs in the image is just its finger or evidence that it really is a boy. Speculation is a lot of fun. While our evidence can be firmer now, our present-day predictions may mean much less than they did in the sixteenth century, when Italian people apparently gambled huge sums of money in lotteries to guess the sex, weight, and delivery date of the child. A Tuscan law of June 6, 1550, expressly prohibited betting on whether pregnant women, married or not, would give birth to a boy or a girl, a response to much fraud involving false registration of the newborn's sex by a corrupt city judge. In fact, one historian has suggested that infanticide was practiced in Florence, probably by married couples, and that the victims more often were girls, although a link to gambling would be purely speculative.[3]

Advice manuals had no hesitation about telling people how to guess a baby's sex, perhaps as information for placing winning bets or just to satisfy ordinary human curiosity. The *Thesoro di secreti naturali* revealed that carrying big, with more movement on the right side, meant a boy. The anonymous *Segreti bellissimi* (Beautiful Secrets), self-ascribed to one Carlo, aka *Il Franzolino*, said the same thing, adding that if the woman is especially cheerful, has a rosy complexion, and walks leading with her right foot, then it's a boy. Good coloring means a boy, he assures readers, as does more right-side movement. Look carefully and you will see also that her right breast grows more than the left, also that the right nipple turns darker first. If she is carrying a boy, then her milk is firmer, more wholesome, like pearls when you squirt a bit on a mirror. Not only will the mother-to-be of a son walk with her right foot first, she will also get up from a chair by leaning on her right arm; her right eye will be more mobile, moving better than her left. Both these pamphlets simply repeat tips found in classic Greek texts, although we may assume that many of their readers were unaware where this wisdom originated.[4]

Indications that the pregnancy may produce a girl are if the woman develops ulcers on her thighs and bruises on her feet. Or else try inserting roots of aristolochia (birthwort) in a honey-soaked wad of uncombed wool into her vagina, leaving it there from early morning until noon; then put it in your mouth. A sweet taste means a boy, sour a girl; if it tastes neither sweet nor sour, then the woman is not pregnant. More elegant texts, such as that of the humanist Matteo Palmieri, repeat similar guidance: weak feet, overall heaviness, and pallid complexion signify a girl.[5]

The French physician Gioberti is skeptical about much of this wisdom, candidly acknowledging its Greek scientific origin. Hippocrates was correct in saying that the mother-to-be of a son would have more color and be more cheerful, owing to the boy's greater heat, but he was wrong in stating that boys lean more to the right chambers of the uterus. The great master had examined too many ewes. In human females, there is only one uterus, in the middle of the woman's body, which gets filled up with babies of either sex, neither of whom leans particularly to the left or right. Gioberti also expresses doubt about signs of a boy such as early movement or the mother's increased appetite; indeed, he dismisses all the right-hand/side/breast theories as unreliable. He concedes that richer and whiter breast milk, as opposed to watery and pinkish, may indicate a boy, but he warns that it is easy to fake this result or to measure or see badly. Finally, Gioberti rails against what he dismisses as mere superstitions: put a parsley plant, root and all, on a pregnant woman's head, and the baby is the sex of the first name she says; put a drop of her milk or blood in water and if she carries a boy, it will float; if the woman has a nosebleed, she is carrying a girl—all nonsense says the expert doctor. As it happens, the parsley-plant prognostication technique comes directly from Galen, and nearly all the "popular errors" Gioberti condemns have similar classical antecedents—of which he was surely aware—so here again we see the fascinating mixes of folk and scientific cultural precepts that abound in early modern medicine.[6]

What one author dismisses as superstition, of course, another prescribes as scientific truth. Marinello begins his list by pontificating that to speculate about the occult is among the most ridiculous things human beings do. There is no point in resorting to magic to prognosticate whether a woman is carrying a boy or a girl since all you need do is look

for the proper signs. He then repeats all the right-side tests and preferences offered by other manuals, along with standard assertions about
liveliness and appetite. Finally, he concludes with an experiment he
claims to have gotten from the ancients (Hippocrates, no doubt). Make
bread with good flour and a little milk from the mother-to-be, and bake
it on the hot ashes; if the loaf stays together, it is a boy; otherwise it is
a girl. Readers who wish to try this, with or without breast milk, will find
that any decent cook can make a dough that stays together most of the
time by adjusting for the thickness of the milk, which makes me wonder
if Marinello was simply providing a test that would lead his readers to
happily expect a boy, which he assures us is the preferred choice. After
all, then as now, people consulting an advice manual wanted to feel good
about what they were reading.[7]

Perhaps the most satisfying treatment in sixteenth-century advice
manuals of the boy/girl question, certainly from a modern, politically
correct perspective, is found in Friar Mercurio's book for midwives. He
reviews all the literature starting with Aristotle and Galen, making it plain
that he is a two-seed thinker like Galen, thereby contradicting partially
what he wrote elsewhere about the role of imagination in controlling the
color, health, and sex of a child. Gently, for him at least, he rejects all
the ancient wisdom and that of the Arabs as well. The real reason why
you have a boy or a girl is to carry out God's will. Humans live together
and procreate primarily as married couples, so there must be about an
equal number of men and women. Sure, the individual conception will
be a boy if both the father's and mother's sperms are hotter, but nature
makes certain that about half the time the two sperms, or one of them
as the case may be, while not hot enough for making a boy, are the correct
temperature for a girl. Even though guesses about the sex of the baby
are wrong about as often as they are right, Mercurio dutifully provides
a list of all the signs to look for, warning readers not to count on any of
them.[8]

Maybe Twins?

Sometimes it happens, Marinello continues in his next chapter, that the
woman is carrying twins or even more babies. To discover why this occurs should prove both useful and delightful to hear.

One way is that the male sperm breaks apart on arrival in the uterus,
going into two or more of the uterine "cells"simultaneously and thereby

generating two or more babies. By "cells" Marinello does not mean anything like ova; instead, he is referring to accepted wisdom that the uterus is divided into seven compartments. Sperm deposited in any of the three cells on the right produces male offspring, while sperm in the three on the left results in girls. The cell in the middle, at the top of the uterus, is for hermaphrodites. This seven-part structure is the anatomical basis for all the advice on left/right positioning during sexual intercourse that we encountered earlier. If sperm reaches more than one cell, then more than one baby will form (another reason for Savonarola's advice that men avoid dribbling and instead squirt all their sperm in one concentrated dose). If multiple conception occurs, it is highly likely that at least one, and often all, of the babies will die in the uterus, or else one or more will be seriously defective or deformed in some way. If both members of a set of twins are of the same sex, they may survive, but if one is a boy and the other a girl, they will die. Marinello then writes that here is not the place to explain why this is so, it just is.

With the reader's indulgence, I want to digress a bit to consider an illustration (see figure 3.1) from a book published in 1521—four decades before Marinello's advice manual appeared—a Latin medical text by Berengario da Carpi, one clearly meant for physicians. It was the basic anatomy text used in Italian universities until Vesalius came along. The illustration employs a provocative style not to be missed and also provides an excellent example of how confusion and contradiction in scientific knowledge communicated in Latin might (or might not) be represented in vernacular advice manuals. As a trained physician, Marinello surely had read Berengario, but on balance he must have come to a different conclusion about the uterus; apparently he did not deem it necessary to confuse or inform his readers about scholarly differences of opinion. The drawing portrays a woman pointing to her uterus, which is lying at her right on a table after removal from her open abdominal cavity. All but the blind now can see that she has just one uterus. "*Tamen est purum mendatium dicere quod matrix habeat septem cellulas*" (It is a pure fabrication to say that her uterus has seven cells) is Berengario's triumphant comment. And to show her disdain for the past masters who wrote otherwise, the woman's left leg and foot firmly press closed the useless tomes of classical and medieval experts who held the contrary opinion. Among the books stomped on with such disdain is surely the famous *Anatomia* by Mondino dei Luzzi, which continued to dominate the text market used to train physicians for about two hundred years after its first printing in 1478, all the while applauding the necessity of doing careful anatomical work and yet still identifying seven compartments in the uterus. Thus,

Figure 3.1. The model points to her uterus, clearly just one, which is lying at her right on a table after removal from her open abdominal cavity. Now that the truth is displayed for all to see, she stomps triumphantly on the medical books claiming that a woman's uterus has seven compartments.

the contradiction in popular manuals over whether there is one uterine cavity or seven (Gioberti versus Marinello, respectively) owes its ancestry directly to scientific texts (Berengario da Carpi versus Mondino dei Luzzi). Once again, what may appear to be "popular" errors, and are even specifically denounced as such by our vernacular authors, turn out to be practices and "facts" embedded in the elite culture of university education and Greek classics.[9]

Returning now to Marinello, who probably would not have found this digression convincing or helpful, another way twins occur is that a woman is fertilized once and then a few days later she is superfertilized with a second fetus. (Surely Marinello got this idea by reading Hippocrates' treatise *De superfoetatione*, although he cites no authority.) This happens mostly with hairy, full-blooded women who have soft bodies, he tells us, with menstrual fluids in sufficient quantities to make both conceptions possible.

Weaker women also may become sequentially pregnant with twins resulting if after becoming pregnant, they linger so long in sexual intercourse that the mouth of their uterus, which is supposed to remain tightly shut, suddenly reopens and swallows up a second sperm. The time difference between the birth of the first baby and the second tells you the elapsed time between the first and second conception. This could be ten, fifteen, or more rarely even thirty or forty days, but all the experts agree that if a woman has a menstrual cycle after becoming pregnant, it is impossible for the fetus to become a healthy, normal child.

Finally, twins may occur because some internal spirit in the sperm causes it to blossom two or more times so that the uterus cannot do other than make one mouthful of bread and then right away another, just like fish take breaths in rapid succession.[10]

Due Date

Along with fretting, speculating, and maybe gambling about the baby's sex and whether there are twins in the womb, the human species also has no end of curiosity about exactly when the birth will occur. Most sixteenth-century advice manuals take a fairly relaxed position on this one. Lorenzo Gioberti, a typical example, explains that pregnancy is not exactly nine months but rather nine lunar cycles from the time of conception. Further variation occurs because, as in all of nature, not everything ripens at the same rate. Finally, people do not always count accurately, and even skilled arithmeticians may not know exactly when the clock started ticking, especially if like many couples, they have not followed the earlier advice about having sex infrequently to build up semen strength. All this said, Gioberti thinks anything from as brief as seven to as long as ten months is normal. From this he follows with the entirely sensible recommendation that after seven months, the mother-to-be should avoid excess strain and should not stray far from medical assistance. If the ninth month passes without her going into labor, there is no reason for alarm. Just give it a few more weeks.[11]

Missing entirely from Gioberti and from many other manuals is any treatment of the folk belief that delivering a full-sized baby at seven months means that the mother conceived the child nine months earlier and is covering up something, usually that nine months ago she was not married or that her husband was away on business or at war and she is an adulteress. You weigh the newborn, note its vigor, wink, do not contest the new mother calculations or otherwise cast doubt on her, but everyone knows the real story, or at least what cannot be true. The refreshing exception among our texts is Girolamo Mercurio's *La commare*, which minces no words. Nowhere is Mercurio's plain intent more evident than in his treatment of premature births. He repeats approvingly the opinions of Hippocrates and Aristotle about the survival chances of babies born after seven months, explaining why the seventh month may be less dangerous than the eighth. However, sophistry about whether a fetus can survive after five or six months, the friar leaves to others,[12] shifting to a more literary and even impish style, one appropriate for a vernacular, popular text.

> I leave these subtleties about births after five or six months to those who wish to pursue such matters, which in truth I do not believe could be accepted in a well-ordered Republic unless proven by repeated and carefully verified experience since they bear all the trappings and insignia of shamelessness. Unfortunately we all know, as Boccaccio has taught us, how many evasions lewd women are capable of so that their simple-minded husbands will see a lighthouse where there was only a flicker (*intendere lucciole per lanterne* is the robust play-on-words of the original). Without the benefit of this poppycock, we'd be rid of those brides who, already two or three months pregnant but under the safe-conduct pass provided by this doctrine, and having been with their husbands only five or six months, give birth as if everything is just sweetness and light!
>
> But as to me, such a dogma could never enter my head. So, if I were to take a wife, I would not want to sleep with her initially, be-

cause if she should present me with a son after five or six months, for sure I would think myself to be what in Latin is called a goat, or in the vernacular a cuckold.[13]

Miscarriage

The *Thesoro di secreti naturali* informs an expectant mother that the way to prevent miscarriage is to wear two emerald amulets, one strung around her neck, reaching the abdomen, and the other tied to her left arm. When the time for giving birth approaches, move the one on her arm to her thigh. Actually, this bit of advice—appearing in a humble, anonymous pamphlet—repeats what may be found in the authoritative writings of Dioscorides and with some variation in the works of St. Isidore of Seville, Trotula of Salerno, and Albert the Great.[14] More sophisticated, at least in physical appearance, printed advice manuals treat the danger of miscarriage with greater care and logic. Marinello warns against strong medicinals, even those that a woman has been accustomed to taking before finding herself pregnant. Bloodletting, commonly practiced in the sixteenth century to relieve all sorts of conditions, also is to be avoided, certainly in the later months of pregnancy when the large fetus needs all the nutrition its mother's body can provide. If the pregnancy commenced very near an approaching menstrual cycle, then a small bloodletting may be appropriate but otherwise not. Other sources of trouble in retaining the fetus include a cold uterus or one that is too hot, one that is too humid and therefore slippery, or one containing a variety of lesions, growths, and sores. Against any of these problems, the remedies are an array of potions, pessaries, plasters, ointments, and suppositories described in exacting detail as to amounts and frequency of use but more often than not with little discrimination about exactly what should work against which specific danger.

Then there are more generalized precautions against miscarriage, all of which merge medicine with magic, conveyed with approval by Dr. Marinello because their efficacy has been noted by both ancient and modern philosophers. If a woman carries a bit of clay around with her, she will not miscarry. (Sicilian women I talked with in the 1970s said they kept a lump of clay with them at all times during pregnancy. They explained that God made man from clay, so clay would protect and help form their babies too.) Marinello also writes that many gentlewomen place a diamond in their vagina to guard the little creature against harm. The next recommendation specifically proclaims that it is not for the rich alone: find the skin that a snake has shed in the fields, mix about four grams worth with some bread crumbs, and feed it to the pregnant woman. Another good one is dried blood from the fetus of a wild rabbit. Fresh water shrimp, dried and finely chopped and mixed in a drink, are wonderful for assuring that the pregnant woman will retain her baby. "Some of my friends swear under oath that they have seen the proof, that women who many times were unable to keep a baby in the womb succeeded after trying this one": take the skin that surrounds a chicken's cloaca and pull, clean, and then cook it on a coal fire and eat this for several days. Finally, as an afterthought, the ashes from burnt nut shells also help marvelously in keeping the fetus healthy.

If a thin, pale-complexioned woman loses her baby in the first month, then before her next pregnancy, you need to fatten her up, and she should have no trouble carrying to term. On the other hand, if miscarriages come in the second or third month, then the woman's uterus is failing to expand, thereby suffocating the baby. Before conceiving again, she needs to undergo treatment to soften up her uterus, starting with insertions of cooked apple laced with pulverized colloquintida and benzoin. She should eat plenty of garlic and other foods likely to fill the uterus with gas. Then, after her next menstrual cycle, she should be ready to go to bed with her husband.[15]

Moral issues might be involved in miscarriage, especially one occurring during the first three months. Even Michele Savonarola, who seldom invoked church teaching (at least until late in life, when he became deeply ascetic) and indeed actively contradicted it on matters such as the value of sexual foreplay, takes a stern line on maternal responsibility. Watch out woman (addressed as *frontosa*) that with your carelessness, you do not kill two souls, yours and your child's, because on the day of judgment God is going to ask you why you lost the baby; if it comes out that the fault was yours, then eternal punishment awaits you way beyond anything you received on earth.

During the first three months, when the fetus is tied only weakly to the uterus, any strong medicinals are dangerous and should be taken only with extreme caution. The last three months also are risky, because even though the ligaments to the uterus are now sturdy, the fetus is large and heavy. To understand the problem, just look at any fruit tree: in the spring, early blossoms may detach easily even in a gentle wind or rain; similarly, toward harvesttime, adverse weather may cause ripe fruits to break off and drop to the ground; but in the intervening months, the fruits resist all but the most severe storms. So it is with the baby in the womb.

Signs of a possible impending miscarriage in the early months are vaginal discharge or unusual labial wetness. Note whether your breasts, which had hardened with the formation of milk, become soft again, diminish in size, and leak. Do you feel sharp and continuous pain in your eyes? If such things occur, try pessaries brewed from various herbs in red wine, a topical ointment, plenty of rest, a more gentle diet than usual, and no sex. "Just give your husband to understand that you are sick." Violent coughing spells could cause the baby to be expelled from the uterus, so give up any idea of walking around in cold weather lightly dressed. Wash your hair in warm water, not cold. Take digestives derived from cardamom, nutmeg, musk, ginger, and stonecrop, in the morning and again at night. In his advice on selection of herbs, the renowned physician lists both specific choices for rich people and reasonable alternatives for the poor.[16]

The attention to economic circumstances in this section of Savonarola's manual, found even more frequently in Mercurio's work at the end of the sixteenth century, is another indication of how widely these books may have been read. It is noteworthy that "the poor" would have been addressed at all in a book. Did poor people read such treatises for themselves? Or did the neighborhood midwife read Savonarola, Marinello, or Mercurio and pass along her newly acquired wisdom to women of all conditions? I suspect more the latter than the former, but we cannot assume that people of modest means did not read.

Mercurio, the Dominican friar and country-circuit physician, reiterated almost exactly the dire warnings found in Savonarola about the punishments on Judgment Day that awaited mothers-to-be responsible in some way for aborting their potential offspring. He reserves particular venom for those who refuse to give up the small pleasures of life that may be dangerous to the growing fetus: riding in a carriage, dancing, eating and drinking immoderately. Still, Christian charity might allow some sympathy toward women who behaved selfishly but not with the explicit intention of killing their child. No mercy should be shown, however, to those infamous Megaras, those vile hags who cover the consequences of their insatiable desires and dishonest acts by willfully procuring an abortion. (Actually, it was Megara's husband, Heracles, who killed their children, but Mercurio either did not know the mythological details or did not consider them important enough to distract him from the main targets of his opprobrium.) And what about the souls of those physicians who give advice or assist in abortions? They would be struck down instantly by lightening were it not for God's pity for the poor earth that would have to swallow up these horrible monsters. Mercurio thunders on a bit on this topic, one we know arouses the deepest passions even in our own time, and then excuses himself before his real audience: "I made this digression longer than a physician should because I want my midwife to be fully aware of such an important matter. Please excuse the excess affection I have for these little creatures who taste death before life, who die before they are born, who are abandoned before they have a chance to gaze at this world, who are buried in the earth before their feet can kick the ground, who experience their mother as a murderer before they can know her as a nurturer."[17]

In contrast to the suspicions of medical men about female complicity in miscarriage, the assumption was universal that a pregnant woman could not be responsible for the death of a fetus retained in her womb. Indeed, the general concern in advice manuals is that women not endanger themselves by failing to recognize and accept signs that the creature has died and needs to be extracted. Savonarola lists nine indicators that the fetus might be dead, clearly in my judgment for the self-appraisal of a pregnant woman or at most the neighborhood midwife, rather than to inform other physicians. Above all, try to sense if the fetus moves or rolls in a lump, like a stone, rather than kicking or turning here and there. Other warning signals are a cold uterus, shrinking breasts, cloudy eyes, rigid ear lobes and nose tip, abdominal swelling, and halitosis. Try to hold your breath, lie down, and feel gently with your hand where the baby once stirred. If there is no movement after several tries, the baby is dead. Should the baby be dead, a fetid, strong humidity may emerge from the vagina, and the mother may have recently experienced an acute fever or other great infirmity.[18]

If the baby dies late in pregnancy, things are much more complicated. This is not women's work, advises Savonarola. You need to call a surgeon to come with tongs and other tools to pull the fetus out. It may be necessary to cut the dead baby into pieces to get it out, hardly a task for the midwife. Marinello urges the same, and directs the remainder of his chapter on this topic to an evidently male surgeon, assigning to the midwife and her assistant the task of holding down the patient, stuffing her with bread soaked in wine so as to keep up her spirits or else maybe to knock her out, and mopping her brow with cloths soaked in wine.[19]

Mercurio, on the other hand, had more confidence in the midwife's abilities or he may have realized that as a practical matter many women would be called on to perform the operation, whether because no surgeon was around, the time was short, or the expense was too great. Hippocrates had written a treatise on the subject, available to surgeons as *De partus immortui extractione,* but Mercurio was always keenly aware that his readers did not read Latin. So, wrote the doctor/friar, first the midwife should cover the patient's face to keep her from seeing such a terrifying procedure. Then, with the nail of her middle finger she should dig into the dead baby's abdominal skin and rip it away so she can pull out the intestines, which will ease the passage of the rest. Next she should try to get the dead creature to a headfirst position and use a hook (like the ones illustrated in the original book and reproduced here in figures 3.2 and 3.3) inserted into the eye or ear or under the chin to pull it out. If the fetus is feetfirst, she should just hook on as best she can, being very careful not to wound the mother. If the corpse is too large to get out in one piece, the midwife should latch onto it with her fingernails or use the tongs to hold it where it is, never letting it slip back further into the womb; she then should start cutting, limb by limb, whatever she can reach first.[20]

I do apologize to modern readers for this horrifying description, but I have included it so we can begin to appreciate how much was expected of the midwife and how perilous the circumstances of stillbirth were to mothers. Mercurio has no time to go into further detail on extraction of a dead fetus. Instead, he introduces an exciting new medical technique he has discovered in France—birth by cesarean section. At this point, he crosses the arbitrary line between an advice manual and a medical text, stating flatly that this operation should be performed only by a qualified surgeon. We shall skip over these chapters, therefore, except to note that Mercurio was truly among the avant-garde in recommending this procedure in Italy, which he even advocated as an anticipatory measure for women with a narrow pelvis, and that his practical advice on how to perform the surgery is fundamentally sound.[21]

Diet and Daily Activity

Serious illnesses in an expectant mother should be treated by a physician, warns Gioberti, since there are two lives at risk. As to more routine aches and pains, however, the message is clear: women should learn to put up with a certain amount of discomfort without complaint, accepting the sacrifices assigned them by nature. Even some of the popular errors this Montpellier physician rails against seem to him to be linked to the capricious, demanding ways of pregnant women. Don't believe the old saw that if you deny something to a pregnant woman, you will get a tumor above your eye, he tells his readers. Feel free to say no to frivolous requests. It is not true that when an expectant mother is hungry she should put her hands behind her back, because any part of her body she touches, such as her nose or her eye, will result in a mark on the baby at that very

A A Due iſtromenti, iquali ſeruono ne' parti·vitioſi per reſpinge-
re le creature dentro il ventre, affine di ridrizzarle per poter
le hauere facilmente.

B B Vncino buono per adoprare nell'hauere le creature morte at
taccandolo nelle concauita de gli occhi, bocca, ò mēto di eſſe.

C D Due tanaglie pure neceſſarie a cauare le creature morte dal
ventre della madre.

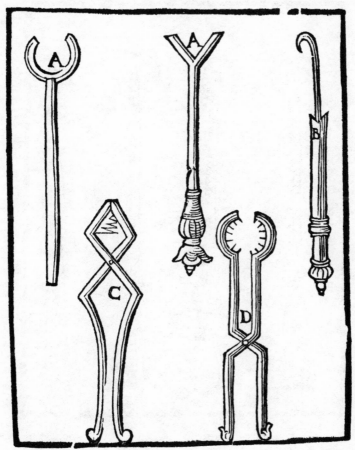

E E Due

Figure 3.2.   Instruments for the midwife: *A*, device to push the fetus back into the uterus so that it can be manually straightened for better delivery; *B*, hook to latch onto the eye, mouth, or chin of a dead fetus; *C–D*, pliers to extract a dead fetus.

E E Due altri vncini più gagliardi, che ſono neceſſarij per cauare
    la creatura morta in pezzi, affine di tenerla ſalda, acciò coſi
    tronca non torni dentro la Matrice,

F F Due vncini taglienti come raſori da vna banda, i quali ſeruo
    no per tagliare, e sbranare la creatura morta, eſſendo i raſori
    ordinarij pericoloſiſſimi per ferire la madre;

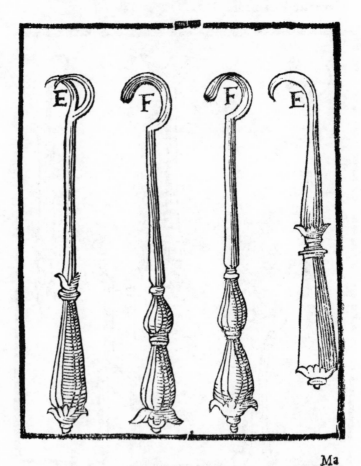

Ma

Figure 3.3. Instruments used for dismembering a dead fetus: *E*, hooks for removing pieces of the corpse while preventing the remainder from being retracted further into the uterus; *F*, hooks with razorlike edges to cut the dead fetus in pieces with less danger to the mother than using a straight razor.

spot. It is not true that the first food and drink the pregnant woman ingests goes directly to the fetus. Pregnant women should not give in to every food craving and hunger pang but instead should go about their business as normally and fully as possible.[22]

Sixteenth-century Italian mothers-to-be looking for more sympathetic, supportive advice might have turned instead to Savonarola, either to his specific treatise addressed to the women of Ferrara or else to the widely circulating printed editions of his general recommendations on diet. Because books on healthful living and good diet were best-sellers in the sixteenth century (as they are today), I want to summarize in some detail what the pregnant woman might have been told. She would have found in front of her many pages of regimens to counter the negative effects of pregnancy on appetite, both the cravings for strange foods and the frequent loss of appetite. Problems of flatulence, nausea, and morning sickness are real, according to Savonarola, owing to imbalances of bodily humors caused by retained menstrual fluids, and these too may respond to the home remedies proposed in great number. For heart palpitations or rapid pulse, first try drinking a little warm water and if that doesn't do the trick, then take only light medicines, perhaps a little powdered bugloss or some warm milk spiced with a bit of clove. If your stomach feels too hot, try a glass of cold water with a little marjoram, but if it feels too cold, then take the marjoram with some warm wine. Other suggestions follow for reducing menstrual spotting, overcoming constipation, and avoiding fainting spells and dizziness. All these remedies are bland in character, palliatives in Savonarola's view no less than in the reader's, possibly useful and certainly not harmful.[23]

The chapter on diet is addressed to pregnant women in a particularly direct, personal way. "You [*tu,* familiar form] understand me, woman reader [*frontosa,* feminine form]," eat three meals each day, trying to space them out with ample room for digestion between one and the next. Just how much time between meals I leave to your discretion, depending on how hungry you feel; an hour one way or the other doesn't matter much. Base your diet on eating the very finest bread, baked from flour ground from kernels of pure wheat if possible. In an aside Savonarola expresses sympathy for readers who are too poor to afford the best flour and have to mix in coarser grains, urging them to do what they can within their circumstances.

Moving along to meats, Savonarola starts with four-legged animals. Especially good for the pregnant woman are veal, beef, kid, milk-fed lamb, and young mutton. Pork from an animal younger than a year old is fine, but not beyond that age since the meat of a mature pig generates bad humors and is difficult to digest. Stay away from excessive salt and from salted meat products. Among the gamier meats, wild boar is best; you can eat hare in small quantities—it is better if roasted—even though it tends to make you urinate too much. Young roebuck is allowed, but eating the mature specimens will make you melancholic. Venison should be avoided completely because it is hard to digest and provokes melancholy. Most fowl is good for you, such as chicken, capon, pullet, young grouse, pheasant, partridge, and pigeon. Savonarola knows he is invoking an appetizing table and adds, "Oh, woman reader, who wouldn't want to get pregnant just to be held to a diet like this?" Duck and goose are acceptable only if you have a strong stomach, because these are not easy to digest, especially the old birds, even for people who are not pregnant. Avoid completely the crane and peacock, which are hard to digest and generate bad blood. A fat gray partridge or quail is excellent for the blood. "And you readers who happen to be rich and powerful, when you're pregnant seek out other delicacies that are good for your blood; go for the young, fat turtledoves and leave the old, skinny birds to others. Don't eat too many quails, and if you want to get even with your physician, assuming you have one, present him with a plate of them. Skip over the little creatures, which have no meat anyway, and indulge yourself with skylarks, thrushes, and blackbirds. Let all the aquatic fowl go their own way."

In accordance with prevailing beliefs about bodily humors, Savonarola recommends pregnant women avoid virtually all fish, because they have flesh that is cold and humid, which would contribute to making the expectant mother's blood phlegmatic, exactly the opposite of what she needs for her health and that of her baby. If you must eat fish, then roast or cook it in wine seasoned with cinnamon to counteract the frigidity and humidity. Eat only the best fish, such as sea bream, mackerel, cod, or eel. Savonarola's work is directed explicitly to the women of Ferrara, so they would have known exactly what he was writing about when he added, as an aside, that eels are especially abundant in the region and long have been known to be the best thing for clearing the bronchial passages, which in turn makes for a great singing voice. You wives who delight in singing can't very well be expected to give up eating eels everytime you are pregnant, so at least be sure to boil them first and then cook them in a good, spiced wine.

Crustaceans generally are better for you than scaly fish. Some think prawns are especially good for preventing miscarriage and, despite what Galen says to the contrary, shrimp also are fine. Be careful about oysters and clams, however, since for anyone they are hard to digest and will make you gassy, which is particularly bad when your enlarged uterus is pressing on your intestines in the last three months of pregnancy.

Fruits, like fish, are cold and humid; moreover, many of them are gassy, so generally you should avoid them altogether or eat them only in moderation. (The term "fruit" in the sixteenth century referred not only to things we classify as fruits but also to many varieties of nuts and vegetables such as squash, cucumbers, and turnips.) If you must eat fruits, then choose cooked over raw and ripe over immature. Those early hard green apples are especially bad. When you crave a piece of fruit, just think that the most noble and beautiful fruit in the world is the human creature in your womb, so surely you can resist the vituperative claims of your palate for a vile, ugly, bad piece of fruit that will harm what you carry inside yourself. Tubers are not good for you and neither are the seeds of fruits such as melons, squash, fennel, and cucumbers. Grains also cause problems. Although rice is tolerable, the larger grains and beans, especially red beans, provoke menstruation and are universally prohibited by physicians in recommended diets for pregnant women. Peas are not quite as bad as lima beans, especially if the peas have been allowed to dry out, but basically these things are not very good for you expectant mothers and should be eaten only in moderation, if at all. Certain green leaf vegetables, such as cabbage and rape, also should be avoided because they tend to provoke menstruation. Some of the noxious effects can be reduced by cooking your greens with plenty of meat fat, especially chicken fat. Lettuce is fine, even raw in a salad with some wine vinegar to stir the appetite. The local Po Valley varieties of endive and radicchio not only are entirely harmless but they are good for getting bodily fluids moving through the liver and blood flowing in the veins. Arugula eaten by itself will give you a wicked headache but loses its negative qualities in a mixed salad. Spinach remains your friend even during pregnancy, as long as you do not have a cold stomach. Some say that thyme can cause menstruation, but Savonarola does not agree. Still, just to be on the safe side use it only in moderation; the same goes for rue, marjoram, sage, and rosemary. Garlic, onions, leeks, and scallions are good for some digestive problems, but they all tend to provoke menstruation and bleeding hemorrhoids, so use them sparingly.

Milk products can cause stomachaches and a bloated feeling, especially the whey or ricotta from fresh milk, but if the milk is thoroughly boiled down so that it loses its watery properties, the remainder is less harmful. Eating ricotta can give you kidney stones; probably the huge popularity of this food in the Ferrara region explains why so many people have such stones. As to cheese, the best is one not too fresh but also not too aged, just in the middle. Avoid butter altogether and use virgin olive oil, which is much better for the stomach and does not interfere with appetite. Be on guard against honey, which is very gassy and likely to keep you up all night with sharp pains. Sugar is acceptable.

As to preparation, roasting is fine in the first three months, after which boiling is best because it reduces constipation. For the same reason, the pregnant woman should shift gradually to foods that are more humid or soupy, less of the dry and hard, to keep her uterus and lower abdomen light and lubricated. This is especially advised in the last ten to fifteen days before the expected due date, when a good regimen should include lots of warm baths, ointments concocted from almonds, chamomile, and chicken fat to rub on the genitals, and consumption of fatty foods, nothing that might cause constipation.

Finally, a word on wine and other beverages. The mother-to-be should drink wine that is subtle, aromatic, and well aged. "And if you say 'such wine is an aperitif' then I say mix it with a little water." Stay as far away as you can from white wine, woman reader, even though it's true that white wine looks better in your hand. In your ninth month, however, start drinking white wine, because it will open you up and facilitate childbirth. Sour wine and vinegar are acceptable for flavoring meat or fish, but be warned that the good they do in calming a hot stomach and stimulating appetite may be outweighed by the damage they cause by refrigerating your uterus. Cold water is not good at all—better to drink wine.

Having written at great length on a proper diet for expectant mothers, one that we moderns might find a bit high in alcohol and rich in proteins and fats but which seems to have worked for sixteenth-century Italians, Savonarola turns to a proper regimen of daily activities. In keeping with his analogy between fruit in the womb and the blossoms that become fruit on a tree, he urges great caution about exercise and other exertion. The most dangerous time is the first few months, when the fetus is only lightly attached by the veins that hold it to the uterine wall. The middle months are less problematic, but moderation again becomes critical in the last months, when the fetus is large, heavy, and nearly ripe. Still, too little exercise is also bad, especially in women who are naturally very humid, because failure to dissipate this humidity by strenuous body movement allows the fetid humors to multiply, eventually weakening the ligaments holding the fetus in place.

Some people think that frequenting thermal baths to rid the body of bad humors is good for pregnant women, but Savonarola cautions about the dangers of a miscarriage. In the ninth month, especially for first-time mothers who are young, he recommends bathing once a week at home.

Just heat up a big tub of ordinary water, not too hot, climb in, and soak yourself for a quarter of an hour or so to gently dilate the abdominal passages and prepare for an easier delivery, but don't stay in so long that the water becomes cold.

Get lots of rest. Although nothing should be done to excess, too much sleep is better than too little. Eat moderately. The gassy pains that come after eating too much are very harmful to the fetus. On the other hand, the growling movements that come from being hungry also are bad. Stay away from all strong medicines, especially laxatives. For constipation, eat prunes or take some cassia or manna. Absolutely do not let your physician tell you to perform an enema after the third month of pregnancy. Try not to get angry or give in to moments of fear or sadness, particularly in the early months. Avoid exposure to excessive hot or cold air, which in themselves can upset the balance of bodily humors. Cold air also can give you bronchitis and in a coughing fit you could lose the baby. Don't start washing your head so frequently that catarrh descends to your lungs. Above all, guard against getting cold feet and drinking chilled water, especially on an empty stomach.

Sexual intercourse is dangerous, especially in the first and second months of pregnancy when jostling the uterus can break the weak ligaments holding the fetus. "And you, male reader, in knocking on the door be careful that you don't move the fetus inordinately. It would be much better and more secure and praiseworthy that you just leave your wife at the foot of the bed; but if you must have her, at least do it with dexterity, with suave strokes and not too many of them, so that when the little morsel gets disturbed by such violent movements, it doesn't cause him to be like the lord of the manor who exits his castle. Exercise similar caution in the ninth month, when the ligaments are old and weak, that you don't cause the wine to flow from the barrel before its time."[24]

Not many households could have possessed for themselves a complete copy of Savonarola's advice for the women of Ferrara about pregnancy, since it was available only in handwritten form. But many could have owned Giovanni Marinello's printed book on the same subject, wherein most of the eighty leaves of book 3 of his *Delle medicine partenenti all' infermità delle donne* draw directly and shamelessly from the old master. For the most part, the recommendations in one are repeated in the other, and since we have just read an ample selection from Savonarola on questions of proper diet and daily activity for the mother-to-be, let us confine ourselves to observing the tone of this highly popular author's printed text.

Marinello stresses the need for the mother to supply a continuous source of heat to her baby in the womb, eating smaller amounts more often to keep the environment constant without letting the baby get too cool, thus providing steady nourishment, with what the mother eats more or less simultaneously converted to sustenance for the fetus. Wine is beneficial for the stomach and generates good spirits and heat. A light red is best, and if you mix it with water, then use water in which you have extinguished hot iron (what, I suppose, we would understand as a recommendation to take iron supplements). Sleep more so you feel properly rested and don't overexert your body with dancing, jumping, or running. No sex during the first two months of pregnancy. Try to overcome bouts of melancholy, fear, and wrath, for these are most harmful to the baby. Instead, laugh heartily and often. Whatever else you do, don't take long soaking baths to lose weight because this may cause you to miscarry. Do not listen to those physicians who want you to take herbs to relax the muscles, at least not until the fourth or fifth month when the baby is firmly tied in the uterus.

Loss of appetite, craving for strange foods, and mood swings occur frequently in pregnant women, due to the accumulation of menstrual blood not yet consumed by the fetus that then invades the stomach, causing all sorts of problems. The peak period of distress is about forty days after conception; you should not be alarmed even about desires to eat charcoal, earth, and equally disgusting things. You may need to spit a lot; the same imbalance of bodily fluids that causes you to experience nausea also accounts for feelings of fear, torpor, and helplessness. You may feel like something is biting at the mouth of your uterus. If the acidity builds up too much in your stomach, go ahead and induce vomiting by drinking some warm water. Indulge your appetite in anything that is not harmful and if you desire some food that may be out of season or otherwise hard to find, make an effort to locate it. Give yourself a treat. All this may last even until the fourth month, but it goes away eventually as the baby gets larger and uses up more of your menstrual blood. Problems such as vertigo, headaches, swollen feet, and clouded vision also are real—not simply the self-indulgent complaints of women (as Gioberti would have it). Unfortunately, strong medicines are dangerous to the fetus, so only milder remedies should be tried, pretty much the same ones recommended by Savonarola.[25]

Another book mothers-to-be and their families could have consulted was Friar Mercurio's *De gli errori popolari d'Italia* (On Popular Errors in Italy). Published in 1603, eight years after the first appearance of *La commare*, it was much less successful, at least to judge by translations and editions; I must add that it is also much less interesting to read. Parts of it are quite anti-Semitic, a few are misogynous, and many are tedious. The zest of the earlier work is largely absent, replaced by crankiness and suspicion. Mercurio seems to have lost entirely his eye for the comic and in some instances even his common sense. He writes that he produced the work in response to a kind invitation from the French physician and philosopher Laurent Joubert (our Lorenzo Gioberti in the Italian translation), who in the preface of his original work, *Erreurs populaires*, called for studious readers to send him their own collections of popular errors. However, the invitation was hardly personal or pressing, since Gioberti died ten years before the Italian translation appeared in 1592. As it turns out, Mercurio's collection of errors, superstitions, and stupidities among Italian people was not that different from what Gioberti had detected among Frenchmen and Frenchwomen, perhaps explaining why so much of Mercurio's new book is a rehash of his earlier *La commare* or else of Gioberti's *Errori popolari*. Still, shrewd observations on human behavior emerge for the patient reader.[26]

The first 68 pages cover errors against medicine; the next 111 expose errors against medics, followed by 84 on errors against sick people who are bedridden and 74 more on errors against sick people who are up and about. The fifth section, of more relevance here, takes up errors against pregnant women, while the sixth rails against errors in treating the illnesses of children. The final section takes over 100 pages to say how proper control of air, exercise, eating, drinking, evacuation, and pain can allow one to live a long healthy life without resort to medics or medicine, a recommendation that contradicts the sense of the first 400 pages but is in keeping with the antiestablishment style of best-selling authors like Fioravanti.

The section on pregnancy starts off dubiously with a title page that misspells Mercurio's name and then, in what amounts to a total dismissal of the impact of his own book eight years earlier, declares that midwives in Italy are completely ignorant *(ignorantissime)*. Not only do they know nothing about the art of curing their patients but they run to the doctor asking his advice and then misapply it, causing great danger to the mother and her unborn child. All this leads to a tirade against abortion, either willful or through negligence, but one that lacks the literary grace of his approach to the same subject in *La commare*. Next comes a reprimand against the bestial woman with child who wants four meals a day instead of her usual two; if her husband cannot convince her to give up such self-indulgence, he should find a confessor who can talk or scare some restraint into her. One should not give in to the demands of a pregnant woman out of fear that denial may cause the baby to be born with a mark signifying what she craved. Mercurio concedes that in book 1, chapter 20, of *La commare* he had recommended exactly the opposite, but now he advises that birthmarks result only if the unfulfilled desire is both ardent and of long duration, which women's flightiness makes them incapable of sustaining. You need proof? Just look at how few babies are born with such marks, considering that all pregnant women have foolish cravings.

Here and there the book offers more practical advice, often in a rather disparaging fashion. Do not stand in the doorway in your shirt sleeves; avoid going to the cellar or other places where the temperature drops suddenly. Bad air can rip through any skin lesions, go right to the womb, and harm the baby, so cover up and stay away from fresh air. Rich women face danger in winter even indoors, because they have thick carpets on the floor and keep the fires so hot that their blood boils and gets too thin to nourish the baby. Peasant women are also in danger because in their avarice to save a penny and conserve earnings from the last harvest, they leave the house so cold that their hearts freeze and cannot supply enough blood to the baby. Rich women are at risk if they take fast, bumpy carriage rides, poor women if they lift too many pails of water from the well. All women endanger the baby if they sleep until noon and nap after meals. As they say in the Po Valley, women should dust the furniture, sweep the floor, and do similar chores that don't require much force. Unfortunately, women by nature always rush to extremes, either lolling in bed all day or else staying up past midnight gossiping about trifling matters *(cianciare nelle questioni de lana caprina)*.

Two feelings, love and hate, are the tyrants that rule our hearts and minds. Love produces the passions of immoderate happiness, ardent desire, jealousy, cruelty, and finally melancholy. Hate gives rise to anger, contempt, rage, wrath, and melancholy. Succumbing to these passions hurts not only the mother but also the baby. The husband has much to contribute here, writes Mercurio—by staying home and giving up any extramarital affairs or flirtations, by not inviting relatives over who upset his wife, by speaking loving words to her on every possible occasion, and by overlooking her faults and not giving too much ear to her words said in anger, that is, changing the subject or joking and dismissing them as unimportant. Thin wives are especially liable to be choleric and are in need of these calming influences.

Advice to pregnant women who go about town is more hostile. The friar can overlook foolish ways if they are limited to the usual female indiscretions but not this business of going out to hear lewd comedies, join in festivals and dances, and witness spectacles. Just imagine what effect a scene that strikes terror in a courageous man, say the reenactment of a battle, must have on a pregnant woman and her baby. Or think of the birthmarks that may come if the mother suppresses her desire to start dancing. A good belly laugh at some ribald joke could be just enough to abort the baby or the booming of a cannon could frighten it to death. The mother-to-be who needs to go to the bathroom may hold it in, either because she is enjoying the show too much or else out of embarrassment, thereby damaging the little creature inside. Or she might slip and fall or get jostled in a crowd. Her carriage could lose a wheel or otherwise be unable to proceed, and she might have to walk a great distance to get safely home. While on foot, she could be trampled by a horse or assaulted by a highwayman. "Some readers may think all these restrictions make pregnancy into a punishment but I say that sterility is a punishment and pregnancy is a blessing." Finally, if you must go out in public, at least take precautions: at the festival do not go on the dance floor, at the theater do not sit in the balcony because it might come crashing down, stay near the door in case you need to go to the bathroom, keep your visits with friends short, use your pregnancy as an excuse to say you're not feeling well and cannot eat too much. Go back home!

Midwives

If a sixteenth-century Italian woman was well cared for during her pregnancy and properly attended at her delivery, the credit belonged largely to her midwife. The reader already may have concluded that even the most renowned physicians of that time, such as Marinello and Gioberti, sometimes did not know what they were writing about when it came to gynecology and obstetrics. One reason for all the confusion was their unquestioning adherence to Greco-Roman theories. Whatever intellectual efforts western medieval and Renaissance medical experts brought to reexamining the teachings of Hippocrates, Aristotle, and Galen were devoted more to reconciling pagan assumptions with Christian beliefs than with the anatomical realities before them. We may remind ourselves that sixteenth-century physicians seldom saw, much less examined, female genitalia. A physician's honesty *(onestà)*, to use the delicate phrasing of both Marinello and Mercurio, did not allow for direct examination of the organs uniformly referred to in sixteenth-century texts as the shameful parts *(parti vergognose)*. Let the midwife be diligent in carrying out the doctor's prescriptions, taking care to check for changes in minute detail on a daily basis. Since the physician out of "honesty" cannot see for himself, watch that he is not deceived by defective information or misapplications of his remedies.[27]

Friar Mercurio in the 1590s, recalled with pride that as a pupil in Giulio Cesare Aranzi's University of Bologna anatomy class, shortly after 1568, he had once examined the genitalia of a virginal corpse. This was a special occasion, for public anatomical dissections of corpses occurred only once or twice a year, given the difficulties of obtaining and preserving corpses of either sex, supplied mostly by public executioners. Master and student had observed the celebrated hymen, which they found to be just as beautiful and complete as depicted by Avicenna and other glorious lights of the profession. During his days in medical school, Mercurio also assisted in removing and measuring three uteruses. His next hands-on experience, however, came only in 1578, when Aranzi asked him to assist in removing a live fetus from the womb of a mother who had been killed in the ninth month of her pregnancy. Over the years he had assisted at three difficult births, most likely from a distance, without seeing or touching the patient. And that was it, or at least all that he felt necessary to report in establishing his credentials to write his book of advice for midwives, one that dominated the field for over a century after it appeared and was translated into several languages.[28] Marinello and Savonarola may have had even less direct experience, as each rested his authority entirely on book learning; although Gioberti warned midwives to seek professional medical assistance, he reported no practical training or work to bolster his reputation.

For most births, a physician was not called at all unless life-threatening complications ensued. Even when he was summoned, the doctor did not see his patient, examine her in any direct way, or apply any remedies or therapies himself. In the case of a dead fetus retained in the womb, a surgeon might be called in to cut the corpse into pieces so it could be extracted with less risk that the mother would bleed to death, but most physicians left that job to the less esteemed barber surgeons—several rungs down on the professional ladder—who also handled cesarean deliveries. Thus it was normal in a lifetime of practice for a physician never to see or examine the genital organs of a female patient, whether pregnant or not. If a physician was called, he would wait in an adjacent room, giving instructions to the midwife and her assistants, or possibly to the pregnant woman's husband, on what to do next as intermediaries scurried in and out with progress reports or news of setbacks. The scene, although profoundly tragic and obviously dangerous, had its comic strands. Notwithstanding the widely reported case of a Hamburg physician burned at the stake in 1522, for cross-dressing in order to practice as an obstetrician, Mercurio himself recommended exactly the same tactic. He advises the midwife who has done all she can and finds herself in difficulty to call in a doctor, without letting the patient know. "This should be easy to do if the room is dark and he is brought in without speaking, dressed as a woman and with his head thoroughly bandaged."[29]

During pregnancy it was the midwife who examined vaginal discharges, checked urine color and consistency, tested stool specimens, and heard the patient's complaints. It was she who made adjustments in the mother-to-be's diet and applied the plasters, pessaries, and suppositories recommended in books like those of Marinello and Mercurio. And as labor began, it was she who inserted progressively larger cylinders to increase dilation, timed the intervals between contractions, decided when to break the water, and in extreme cases judged whether to call for additional professional help. The reason for exclusive reliance on midwives, at least according to the only sources we have, which are those written by male physicians, was women's sense of modesty. Mercurio found it very strange and unfortunate that female patients, when asked if they had their menses or other discharges, often became embarrassed and said no even though the contrary was true, as if they were confessing to something shameful. He urged the good midwife to reason with her patients, telling them that they were not alone in such things, that the physician's wife and daughters from time to time had experienced the same problems, indeed that such things happened even to princesses![30]

Midwives had their pride too. Lorenzo Gioberti, the Montpellier medical expert and philosopher whose book *Errori Popolari* was our opening text, urged that a physician be called or at least informed of every impending birth. "The arrogance and presumptuous of some women who think they know better about all the maladies peculiar to women—like suffocation of the uterus, spontaneous abortion, and childbirth—than the most eminent physicians in the world, who for this reason do not deign to call the experts in until it is too late" cause all sorts of harm. They wait too long, until after having exhausted all their knowledge in dealing with a miscarriage or birth complications, they are faced with a high fever, bleeding, or other difficulties. The little home remedies used over the ages by midwives are fine in their place but are no substitute for professional expertise.[31]

Friar Mercurio was more sympathetic. He opens his chapter on the qualities and duties of a good midwife with the thoroughly uplifting statement that she is even more important to the pregnant woman than a good doctor. He helps only with advice, whereas she sustains the patient both with advice and with her hands.[32] In ancient times, Mercurio relates, the midwife had three distinct functions. The first was to determine whether a woman was pregnant, a matter of great legal importance if pregnancy preceded marriage or conception occurred during a husband's absence. The second was to assess, before the arrangement of a marriage contract, whether a prospective bride could conceive male children, including recommendations on what type of husband (hot, cold, wet, dry) offered the greatest likelihood of producing male offspring. The third was to assist at childbirth. (Although Mercurio believed only the third function remained to midwives in his day, I know from personal study of Italian villages in the twentieth century that midwives still are called upon to perform all three of their classic tasks, serving as matchmakers and nurses throughout life and even as home undertakers at death.)[33]

The good midwife should be very experienced, having delivered many a creature happily, but not so old that she has poor eyesight or weak, trembling hands because she may be called upon to use great strength in repositioning the baby in the womb. She also must be expert in judging accurately when birth will occur and in separating true labor pains from other aches. In this way she can get the woman to the bed or birthing chair and break the water just when it will help the baby by lubricating the vaginal canal for an easier delivery. Once the baby is due, she must stay with her patient day and night because time lost in calling the midwife can be critical. She also needs to be there to ascertain if the fetus is positioned badly, quickly using her hand to straighten it out; otherwise, there is great risk that the baby will die or that the mother will be killed by excessive pain. Her presence gives the patient a sense of comfort and overcomes a thousand problems that otherwise could arise.

The good midwife always has her assistant along, not only as a trainee in this crucial job but also so someone is there to prepare the oils, heated ointments, towels, scissors, and thread for cutting the umbilical cord. Not all women are up to these tasks and mistakes can lead to fatal hemorrhages.

The good midwife should be affable, lively, gracious, easy with a joke, courageous, and always ready to cheer up the mother-to-be with promises that it's going to be a boy for sure, that she will not feel much pain, and that she has every positive sign ever encountered in all the midwife's previous successful deliveries. "Even though these are little lies, they are said not for harm but for a good purpose, so I think there is no risk of sin in saying them, the more so since Plato in book 6 of the *Republic* says that a doctor may tell lies to console a sick person." (Actually, the nearest thing to this in the *Republic* is in book 3, 389b, not book 6; once again we see that Mercurio was no more careful about citing secular classics than he was about referencing Christian sources such as Augustine.)

The good midwife also must be pious and devout, being sure to remind the pregnant woman to make a thorough confession and receive communion well before her due date, given the manifest peril that goes with childbirth. Encourage her to seek the intercession of the saints, especially the Virgin Mary, who having given birth without sin or pain is especially ready to assist those condemned to great suffering. Urge her to order masses from local religious communities, to give alms, and to do other charitable works. Mercurio especially commends the practice popular throughout Lombardy of lending out holy reliquaries to be placed by the pregnant woman while she is in labor, less for a direct miraculous effect than for the impact this has on the woman's mind, focusing her attention on prayer for a healthy birth. It is clear that the friar is offering a competitive alternative to the non-Christian amulets still much in use throughout Italy.[34]

The above passages, all from *La commare*, clearly reflect a benign, supportive attitude toward midwives. A sharply different tone emerges in Mercurio's later work, *De gli errori popolari d'Italia*, possibly due to some personal experience but more likely to his desire to curry favor with fellow physicians who had criticized his earlier book. Gone is the laudatory description of a good midwife, replaced by strident warnings that fathers-to-be check carefully to determine whether she fears God or is a minister of the devil. They should investigate to be sure she is of good habits, not a ruffian or a whore. These women who have no fear of God take the placenta and the caul to have them blessed in diabolic ceremonies, saying masses over them and then selling the pieces to ignorant men who think they will be protected from injury and death as long as they carry them about. So anxious are they about preserving these bits for diabolic usage and profit that they ignore the health of the baby and its mother, endangering their very lives.[35]

Anatomy

The anatomical lesson provided by Giovanni Marinello that I used to open this chapter was meant for gentlewomen who wanted to know for themselves more about what would happen to their bodies during pregnancy. Without any doubt, Mercurio was aware, indeed he probably had a copy at hand, of what Marinello had written and just as certainly he found it inadequate as a guide for the practitioners who were the intended audience of *La commare*. He also had in front of him and plagiarized heavily from Frankfurt physician Eucharius Rösslin's *Der Schwan Frawen und Hebammen Rosegarten* (the first German-language book on obstetrics, published in 1513). Surely he was aware of the extensive Latin literature on female-reproductive anatomy and conception, including the writings attributed to Salerno physician Trotula.[36] Possibly he had seen a 1541 Spanish guide on childbirth and early child care.[37] But the Italian midwife did not read German, Latin, or Spanish, and she needed more details and specifics than Marinello provided, including illustrations to show her exactly what she would have to feel and manipulate with her hands.

I hope modern readers will find this anatomy lesson of interest, for it tells us exactly, in plain language, where medical knowledge stood in 1596. Mercurio was a highly competent popularizer, fully trained as a physician and with many years of practical experience as well. What he wrote for the midwife he took from the latest and most authoritative Latin texts, leaving out some details but accurately and more than amply conveying what a midwife or a mother-to-be would reasonably need to know. Much of what had been written just thirty years earlier by Marinello about the differential development of male and female fetuses is entirely absent from Mercurio, or else presented in a way that clarifies how very suspicious he has become about such theories. He devoted twenty pages specifically to this anatomy lesson for the midwife.

The uterus is an organ necessary for procreation composed of nerve material, which in some places is slightly more meaty than in others. It has nerves, veins, and arteries, arrayed in two membranes, one interior and the other exterior. The exterior one, which is tougher and thicker than the inner, arises from the peritoneum, binding the uterus to it. The interior one, the true substance of the uterus, becomes much enlarged in pregnant women. The uterus is divided into two parts: the *collo* (neck, vagina), which begins with the *natura* (vulva) and extends inward to the mouth (cervix) of the uterus, and the *fondo* or *cavità* (cavity, womb itself) connected to the neck by its mouth. During pregnancy the womb is like a blown-up bladder, but in women who are not with child, it is more like a new leather bag tied very tightly. The two horns of the uterus (fallopian tubes) extend from the top at oblique angles, being rough on the outside but smooth and red inside; from these horns extend the roots necessary to dilate and nourish the uterus. Figure 3.4 shows the location of the uterus and surrounding organs, while figure 3.5 displays details of the female genitalia, including the cavity, neck, vulva, and testicles.[38]

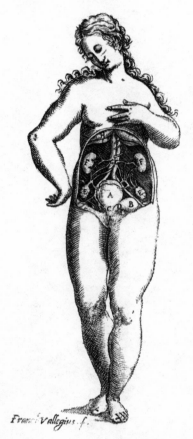

Franc. Vallegius f.

A Fondo della Matrice.
B Corpo della Veſſica.
C Collo della Matrice.
D Collo della ueſſica inneſtato
   nel collo'della Matrice.
E E Due teſticuli della Matrice.

F F Due reni, per i qualı paſſa
   l'orina.
G G Vaſi grandi della uena Ca-
   ua, e dell'Arteria grande.
H La parte del fegato detta gob
I La parte caua dell'iſteſſo. (ba.
          A A Matrice

Figure 3.4.   Female abdominal organs: *A*, the base of the uterus; *B*, the bladder; *C*, the neck of the uterus; *D*, the neck of the bladder grafted onto the uterus; *E*, the two testicles of the uterus; *F*, the two kidneys, where urine passes; *G*, principal artery and vein to the uterus; *H*, the hump of the liver; *I*, the hollow part of the liver.

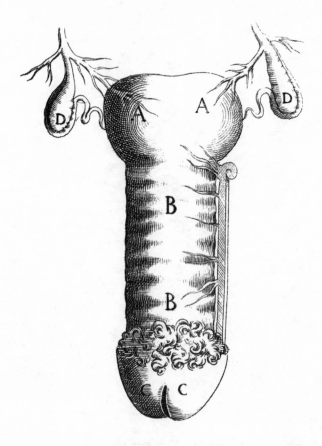

A A   Cauità , ò concauità nella parte di fuori della Matri-
ce,diuiſa da Galeno in due ſini.
B B   Collo della Matrice.
C C   Pudendo, ò natura della donna."
D D   Teſticoli della donna.

A A   Con-

Figure 3.5.   Female genitalia: *A*, the cavity, or concavity, of the outside of the uterus divided, according
to Galen, into two parts; *B*, the neck of the uterus; *C*, the pudendum or natura (vagina) of the woman;
D, the testicles of women. This is an adaptation by Mercurio of the well-known and much-discussed
drawing of the female uterus in Vesalius, *De Humani Corporis Fabrica* (1543).

With great self-righteousness and absolutely no acknowledgment of scholars such as Jacopo Berengario, whose illustration showing the woman with a single uterus standing triumphantly on the false books of the past we saw earlier, Mercurio fires away at his ignorant predecessors. From the above description, he writes, one can see clearly the falsity of that ridiculous opinion held for many centuries and repeated by learned men with such arrogance that their errors penetrated not only the books of philosophers but also of lawyers and theologians: that the womb has seven chambers, three on the right for generating boys, three on the left for girls, and one in the middle for hermaphrodites. This is a rotten lie, notwithstanding the writings of Nicolò Falucci, Gentile da Foligno, Sebastiano Manilio, and Albert the Great, all of whom are wrong because in truth the womb is nothing more than a sack or cavity. Galen and Hippocrates also are wrong in saying there are two sacks or cavities in the womb, the right for boys and the left for girls. They based their conclusions on examination of goats, animals that do indeed have two sacks; for humans, however, this is not true.

In the neck of the uterus, near the vulva, are two small meaty pieces, like the crests of a young rooster, called the *ninfe* (labia minora) or the hymen; in virgins, these are closed and when during sexual intercourse with a man they break apart, often with much bleeding, this is a sign of lost virginity. "I know that most modern experts say it is not true that all virgins have this hymen, some do and some don't, but I disagree, based on what I saw at school in Bologna [autopsy of a virgin], on what is disclosed by Lorenzo Gioberti in *Errori populari*, book 5 [chapter 4], about reports from numerous midwives experienced in these matters, and on what is written in the book of Deuteronomy, chapter 22." (Mercurio gets this citation right, as he is clearly referring to Deuteronomy 22:17.)

The neck of the uterus is made of spongy material, allowing it to expand when aroused by the appetites of Venus. Uterine volume varies even in women who are not pregnant, in accordance with their overall body size and with sexual activity: small and tight in virgins, more dilated in married women, huge in prostitutes, wrinkled in the elderly, relaxed in women who have borne children, and firmer in those who have not.

Enough on the interior because we need to talk about the testicles (ovaries). These are lodged on the sides of the womb, attached lightly to the peritoneum by seminal ducts. These testicles are much smaller overall than men's; they are long and narrow, unequal in size from the outside and composed of meaty granules resting in a membrane or skin of nerves and having seminal vases with distinct veins and arteries, just as one sees in men. Galen was right and Aristotle wrong; the semen of women, from these testicles, is actively essential to procreation.

After seven days, semen received in the womb coagulates and tightens, becoming frothy as it gets ready to receive a human form. Then mother nature prepares three little canals in which the brain, the heart, and the liver mature; immediately thereafter the umbilical cord develops from semen and menstrual blood. Once the purest part of the sperm forms the brain, heart, and liver, the remainder becomes the chest, head, arms, legs, and other parts necessary in a perfect body. The gross part of the sperm forms a veil or membrane, which physicians call the *secundine* (placenta). After the sixth or seventh day, until the ninth, wings sprout on either side of the creature's chest and the womb pulls it deeply inward, where until the fifteenth day, it is nourished on menstrual blood. From the fifteenth day until the twenty-seventh, the meat of the entire body is generated, as the three principal organs take on a clear shape. At this point the heart, brain, and liver begin to separate, and over the same nine days a certain fatty humidity forms the spinal cord and the nascent nerves that will become the instruments for moving the entire body. Then the head separates from the shoulders while the lateral and lower limbs extend to become a tiny but perfectly formed baby. The entire process takes about forty days, ranging from as few as thirty to as many as forty-five.[39]

In the womb, the creature holds its head upright, with its arms folded, elbows resting on hips, palms on knees; legs are crossed and tucked, soles against the buttocks; eyes rest above the knees, touching the outsides of the hands, nose resting between the knees. Figure 3.6 shows the classic fetal position—circular—the perfect mathematical figure, one that allows the creature to roam about freely without getting damaged by the mother's movements. Several experts have written that the creature, head up, faces the mother's spine, but this is a lie told by scholars with no anatomical experience who have relied on reading that erroneous little book of Eucherio Rodione (Frankfurt physician Eucharius Rösslin, author of the *Rosengarten* that Mercurio plagiarized so mercilessly).[40] It cannot be true that the fetus faces backwards because midwives all over Italy affirm that in about ninety out of a hundred cases, the baby is born head down, facing the ground (that is, the spine of the mother, even if she is using a birthing chair). The creature gets to this position by doing a somersault in the womb shortly before birth, using its feet to push against the uterine wall; if it had been facing the rear, therefore, after the somersault it would be facing the front, which is not so. It is also not

Frācis: Valſ

A A   Matrice aperta della donna grauida con la creatura
        dentro.
   B   Teſta della Creatura, come ſta dentro il corpo della
        madre, con i reſtanti del corpo.

B 3   *Delle*

Figure 3.6.   The uterus during pregnancy: *A*, the open uterus with the creature inside; *B*, the head of
the creature, showing how it stays in the mother's body, along with the remainder of its body.

true that girls are born facing the sky and boys facing the ground. Figure 3.7 shows the normal birth position for both boys and girls—facing the rear.

Before closing this chapter, it is necessary to inform the midwife how the creature is nourished inside its double membrane. She should know that the umbilical veins are like all other veins in the baby's liver; they spread throughout the womb like the roots of a tree, and together with their paired arteries receive nourishing blood provided by the mother. This is why pregnant women no longer menstruate except for a few thin ones with excess bile who have superfluous blood or for some other reason have spotting, about which more follows further along.[41]

Labor

By the time her labor pains actually began, the sixteenth-century-Italian mother-to-be who relied on an advice manual surely had committed the relevant information to memory. What was in the books she may have read, what she knew from experience, and what her relatives and neighbors told her all blended into some plan of action, however well or poorly developed. If her midwife was not already present, then someone was sent to fetch her immediately. If contractions had begun well before the anticipated due date, or if for whatever reason preparations were incomplete, then someone had to rush off for plenty of clean water, wood for the fire, and fresh towels. Emergency care for young siblings might have to be arranged, farm animals tended, and supper prepared. Husbands may not have been much help. Gioberti's *Errori popolari* ridicules the custom among rural husbands of leaving their caps with their expectant wives for good luck; much less does it recommend women wear this headgear while going into labor. The physician asserts this tradition is just another proof of how husbands do not want to stay around during the birth, because they are frightened by all the screaming and the blood, which makes them feel helpless. Moreover, midwives probably found them just as much of a nuisance in the sixteenth century as American hospitals did until as recently as the 1960s (in fact, still do, according to all the delivery assistants I've spoken with, but "you have to keep up with the times").[42]

Other superstitions caught the attention of Friar Mercurio, who dismisses them as the stupidities of young girls and old women. When labor begins, some people believe you should girdle the woman with a belt made of vervain leaves gathered before dawn on the feast day of St. John (June 24) or save one of the candles left from blessing the paschal candle

Sito del parto naturale, nel quale nafcono
cofi i mafchi, come le femine per lo più.

C *Del*

Figure 3.7.   Normal birth position, facing the mother's rear, for both boys and girls.

and light it at a mass said by a priest named John, who was born on a Saturday. All this is the work of the devil, and is especially ridiculous in a region such as Lombardy, where so many churches have powerful saints' relics that in fact are very efficacious if you just place them devotedly upon the woman in labor. Prayer to the Virgin Mary is what brings about an easy and successful labor, not walking around in your husband's shoes, putting his pants on your head, and other such ridiculous buffoonery. As to the one about heating up your husband's hat and putting it on your abdomen, if this actually works, its efficacy can only be from the heat, and not because it happens to be a hat that happens to be your husband's.[43]

Then what? According to Michele Savonarola, the woman starting labor should first sit on a chair with her legs extended so that the contractions get concentrated on her birth passage rather than diffusing throughout her abdomen and lower limbs. Do this for about an hour and then lie in bed to see if the baby knocks on the door. If not, climb onto a dresser or other high piece of furniture and jump to the floor, repeating this several times. If all this climbing and jumping becomes too tiring, get hold of a pair of stilts, stand on them on the points of your toes, kick your legs in the air and jump down to the ground landing on your heels. Then take very deep breaths and close your mouth and nose for as long as possible so the air descends to your abdomen. This breathing exercise should be continued once the baby is at the door.[44]

When delivery is imminent, the mother in labor must position herself properly. Advice manuals all agree that lying flat on a bed is the worst possible choice (despite how frequently this position is pictured in illustrations from the day), but with this exception the norm stated by Gioberti seems to hold widely: take whatever position makes you feel most comfortable—standing with help from someone, thoroughly propped up with firm pillows on a bed, seated in a chair open at the front, or on your knees with hands either forward on the floor or leaning backwards. Just be sure the placenta doesn't get in the way and strangle the baby. Sitting on a cauldron of hot water so steam lubricates the vaginal area is good, but use wood guards to prevent burning your legs. Avoid steaming up the area above the pubic bone, which will cause swelling of exactly what needs to be reduced for safe delivery.[45]

Savonarola prefers the birthing chair. Even though he is a physician, not a furniture maker, he cannot resist saying how he would build an ideal chair. It would be made of thick, strong wood, very heavy, with no tendency to sway; be the width of two bishop's feet, with a seat one and a half feet high; and be closed with boards on the sides. The front would be carved out in a curve to enable the baby to descend easily while the mother remains sitting. On either side would be sturdy arms for her to use as hand rests that are lower in the front. Behind her back, a cushion would be placed for comfort; when the contractions come, the cushion would be taken away, and she would push hard with her back directly against the boards so as to get maximum force in thrusting the baby forward. Mercurio agrees that a birthing chair is better than a bed, but he also recognizes that many of his readers, I suspect both midwives and their patients, could not afford such an expensive piece of furniture. For those pressed by poverty, he suggests the sturdy knees of another woman as a substitute for the chair.[46]

If the woman's water does not break spontaneously, Savonarola instructs the midwife to insert her hand before the baby's head enters the vaginal canal to pierce the membrane. This can be done using a round instrument with a cutting point, but it is better if the midwife probes with her oiled index finger, the nail of which should be long and sharp like those of harp players. Subsequently, perfumes and odors of nutmeg should be applied to the vagina to draw the womb downward, the assistant should hold the mother's legs wide apart, and the mother should scream loudly. The screaming exercise is good for getting the baby out. Savonarola adds that it may arouse the husband's compassion, so he'll put a nice capon marinated in spiced wine on the stove for his wife, who should recall what was said earlier about eating nutritiously yet sparingly while in labor, and who should drink none of that constipating red wine, just a subtle white.[47]

Further along in labor, get on your knees with your head on the floor and hands on the ground for support, knees touching your abdomen. The midwife should enlarge the vagina with her finger or a dowel, using warmed oils and fats. And, midwife, when you see the surrounding sack, know the baby is near; it's time to break the membrane if it has not already broken spontaneously. And if all the liquid dries up without the baby coming, you need to prepare plenty of egg, chicken fat, and oil of dill as an ointment to thoroughly grease the neck of the uterus.

It does happen that labor may go on for many, many hours, with the mother-to-be becoming exhausted, famished, and worn down with pain. Everyone must take courage and genuinely believe that without the mother's virtue and effort, things would be even worse. Eat lightly, poor woman, and do the best you can. Another day you won't lack for an egg. Give the woman in labor some spiced wine to smell and get her engaged in conversation. Try a warm bath, waist deep, tending toward really hot for maybe half an hour. If the surrounding air feels cold, light the fire, and if the mother gets too hot, fan her gently. Keep greasing her genitals and reminding her to breath deeply and close her nostrils. Next try a series of suppositories and flushes, maybe putting a plaster over the whole pubic region. Some authors say that holding a magnet in the left hand or tying a string of corals on the right wrist helps with parturition. These methods can be used by poor as well as by rich women. Keep trying.[48]

Even if the mother is fully dilated and pushing hard, there may be trouble with the baby's position. Savonarola is in accord with other writers we have cited (indeed, many of them copied from him) who believe that for most of its time in the womb, the creature is in a crouched position, facing forward. Then just before delivery, the baby does a somersault to be head down, facing the rear. At this point in his treatise, the renowned physician adds an aside that tells us worlds about the folksy relationship between advice-manual writers and their readers. The reason the baby faces backwards at birth is so that the first altar he will kiss upon entering the world is his mother's sex, in this way asking for and receiving pardon for sins committed in the womb. He continues: "Note well, you proud reader, how in the hour of my decrepit old age I now understand why when we were school children and wanted to insult each other we'd all shout 'ass kisser,' exactly what every one of us had done."[49]

The competent midwife must insert her hand to feel that everything is in place, if necessary straightening out the arms so they are tight at the baby's sides and twisting the body around to face backwards. More radical intervention may be necessary. If the baby is feet first, the midwife should insert her well-oiled hand and try to turn the feet upwards while bringing the head down. If this is not possible and feetfirst seems to be the only way to proceed, tie the feet together with a cord and give a good hard pull.[50] We moderns need to remind ourselves that forceps to grab onto a live baby would not be "invented" for another century, around 1720, after Mercurio's book. Moreover, once forceps came into widespread use, male surgeons made the argument that it was not appropriate for women to wield surgical instruments and therefore they should be excluded from the ranks of qualified assistants at birth.[51] Everywhere in Europe during the sixteenth and seventeenth centuries and in rural areas until the mid-twentieth century, women delivered babies using only their hands. The hands-on way babies were delivered in the absence of instruments is portrayed eloquently in figure 3.8.

If the baby is a boy, it will push harder, making things easier, but it's too late now to worry about that. Other difficulties may arise if the mother is young and has a narrow vaginal canal. First births tend to be tricky anyway, because mothers often are too timid about pushing hard;

B Sito neceſſarijſsimo in ogni parto uitioſo nel quale ſi debbono
collocare tutte le grauide , che difficilmente partori-
ſcono per quale ſi uoglia cauſa.

Del-

Figure 3.8. Recommended position for difficult parturitions, whatever their various causes. Even in these difficult cases, the delivery is "hands-on," without use of special instruments.

the ligaments holding the fetus in place have never been broken before and are tougher; dilation also tends to be insufficient. With any birth, complications may ensue if the womb is ulcerated or has growths that impede passage, if the placenta is too big and hard to break, or if immediately neighboring organs like the bladder or intestines are inflamed. Maybe labor has been triggered too soon, induced accidentally by the lifting of heavy objects or some similar activity. More subtle problems may make the birth difficult. Women suffering depression are likely to have trouble, as are those rich women who find all this very disgusting and take soporifics in an effort to faint away from life's unseemly realities![52]

The same felicitous mix of magic and medicine that marks Marinello's treatment of miscarriage also characterizes his recommendations for midwives on how to deliver the baby with least harm to child and mother. Several pages of practical advice tell how to turn a fetus that does not present itself headfirst and how to deal with twins, including a reasonable standard for instantly choosing which one to deliver first and therefore insure the best chance for survival. There follows with equal certainty the recommendation that tying an emerald around the woman in labor will make the baby come more quickly or, if this doesn't work, inserting a jasper in her vagina. If these fail, there is nothing better for getting the little creature to start moving out of the womb than fumigation with smoke from putting horse hooves on the fire (or ass hooves or salted fish will do). It has been shown to be very helpful to shove an apple, or something similar that will get the baby to come out, in her behind part. And if nothing else works, then call upon God and start saying prayers into the woman's right ear. Try something obvious like three Our Fathers or else this incantation used by women in Salerno with great success: *"bizamie, lamion, lamiad, azerai, vachina. Deus, Deus Sabaoth,"* followed by a more Christian "Hosanna in the Highest."[53] One little devotional book, a legend of the life of St. Margaret, proclaims on its title page that recitation of its verses will ease a woman's labor. Indeed, just placing the book on her abdomen may bring divine assistance during a hard birth.[54]

Mercurio devotes much of book 2 to detailed advice for the midwife on how to deal with problems arising because of the baby's womb position. There are separate chapters on each of the following: headfirst but neck twisted, arm in front of the head, two arms in front of the head, foot in front, two feet in front, feetfirst and arms above the head, feetfirst but knees bent, feet and hands together first, knees first, stomach first, buttocks first, side first, feetfirst twins, twins with one headfirst and the other feetfirst, twins with one alive and the other dead. My judgment, based on the way these chapters are arranged and on the illustrations, is that Mercurio never intended a midwife suddenly confronted with one of these positional problems to interrupt her work and start consulting his book. Rather, I think he meant to educate midwives through advance reading at home about the enormous range of difficulties they might face on the job, to give them the sense that they had seen it all before and would succeed.[55]

An entire chapter follows concerning what the good midwife must do if the mother-to-be is seriously overweight. Every sort of birthing chair is useless and will only cause her body fat to press on her womb, making it more difficult to get the baby out. Instead, have her kneel on the floor, arching her head backwards to touch the floor, with her lower legs tucked under her backside; then use cushions to raise her lower back as high as possible from the floor, letting the body fat roll harmlessly to her sides and leaving the vaginal tract clear and easily dilated for a successful delivery. An illustration from the original text, reproduced here as figure 3.9, makes it obvious why this might work. The midwife must then get on her knees to thoroughly oil the vaginal and anal passages as deeply as possible with an ointment made from madonna lily, chamomile, common mallow, marshmallow, fabaceous herbs, and linseed.

Turning now to problems related to age, if the mother's youth is making her timid, it's too late now to scold her about what she should not have done nine months ago. Just urge her to be courageous, assure her everything will be fine, and tell her she will have a bouncing boy. But if she is old and already leaning toward her grave, you'll need more than words. Try to restore her with some full-bodied wine; maybe break the usual rule to provide no food while in labor and give her some raw egg or boiled meat.[56]

Constipation is quite common and retained feces can add considerably to the difficulty of giving birth. Resolve this problem by feeding the patient soups made with diuretics such as common mallow, beets, borax, and dog's mercury. It may help to apply a local ointment of oil and fat. If the expectant mother runs a fever, this too can be alleviated easily with some barley soup spiced with borax, sorrel, betony, yellow lupine, chicory, and agrimony. Be on the lookout for sores, cancers, growths, and lesions in the womb, vagina, and urinary tract, and do be ready to call in a physician if something seems serious. Such growths or lesions may have started months earlier and been hidden by the pregnancy, so there is no time to lose in attending to them.[57]

Why is it, a woman might wonder, that labor should be so painful? In the Judeo-Christian tradition, of course, the answer is right in Genesis

A Sito, nelquale si debbono collocare le donne parturienti, che
sono molto grasse.

L 2   Del

Figure 3.9. Recommended position for parturition by obese women.

3:16, so it is no surprise that every advice manual on childbirth starts there. More interesting is that the manuals largely abandon their usual acceptance of the church's teachings and instead try to tell women how to ease the pain, apparently in an effort to thwart or at least ameliorate God's judgment. Even the Dominican friar Mercurio postpones the inevitable repetition of biblical condemnation until after a thorough discussion of other authorities on the matter. How can it be that humankind, conceived by the Greek philosophers to be a microcosm of the entire universe in all its perfection, able in the person of Moses to speak face-to-face with God, suffers more in giving birth than any other animal and risks death itself, something unknown in the births of other species? Mercurio's style is not Socratic dialogue, so when he poses a question of this sort and does not immediately explain it as God's will, we can be sure that he feels the need to muster additional evidence. He agrees with the philosophers who hold that human mothers are too weak and fragile to exert the strength and undergo the exhaustion inherent in all animal births. Therefore, they necessarily suffer more. He also accepts that the humors of women are colder and wetter than men's, making them weak and indolent, and that their habits tend toward a laziness and a fondness for leisure that would sap the strength of Hercules or Atlantis. However, Mercurio firmly rejects Aristotle's much repeated view that women are literally "monsters," that they are imperfect, incomplete versions of men. His disrespect is just delightful. "Maybe the great man was ranting on this way because he happened to be mad at his wife." To be absolutely certain his audience will get the message, Mercurio then inveighs against his contemporary Giovanni Camillo Maffei da Solofra for repeating much the same thing. Since man and woman are equally essential to procreation, he scolds, it is obvious that God must have intended to create both of them, so one cannot be a failed version of the other.[58]

The real cause of woman's suffering, the friar concludes, is not just her own frailty but also the baby's bodily characteristics. As Albert the Great had written much earlier (Mercurio once again provides a citation that is wrong), what distinguishes the human newborn from all other animals is the relatively huge size of its head. Since this large and rather firm head must pass through a twisted and narrow passage, extreme pain is inevitable for both the baby and the mother. Woman's travail is not God's punishment but rather the necessary price paid for human intelligence.[59]

A curious variation on justifications for suffering in childbirth comes from the French philosopher and physician Gioberti. He observes that women suffer less pain during their first birth; indeed, many do not have heavy labor pains at all. He ascribes this to the greater uterine strength of a young woman giving birth for the first time. Moreover, God wants to be sure women will be willing to have more children, so he sends less pain on the first one. While we are with Gioberti, we may note some of his related advice from the twenty-seven pages in book 4 on parturition. It is foolish ignorance and anatomically impossible that a woman's pubic bone widens to allow the baby out or that older women have more trouble in childbirth because their bones are harder and more resistant. All ointments, heat treatments, and massages intended to enlarge or soften the pubic bone are therefore a waste of time and effort. How the umbilical cord is tied does affect the baby's bladder, but forget about the tradition among midwives that you should tie the umbilical cord long for a boy, because this determines the length of his penis, and short for a girl, so that her vagina will not be too wide. It is idle superstition to think that if the baby is born with a full moon, the next one will be a boy, or if there is a new moon, the next will be a girl.[60]

It is also not true that you can tell how many more children a woman will have by counting the nodes in the umbilical cord. In disagreement with Gioberti on this tradition, however, we have the Venetian Marinello attesting to exactly the opposite. While delivering the first or second or even third child, the midwife should look closely at the umbilical cord for wrinkles or nodes, whatever you want to call them. If there are none, then no further pregnancies may be anticipated; if there is one or more, that is how many future births she will have. Indeed, the wise physician will be sure to ask the midwife how many nodes there were so that in the future he will seem especially competent in diagnosing whether his patient is pregnant.[61]

Other popular errors falsely ascribe magical significance to things that do no harm and maybe even some good, concedes Gioberti, so these he does not condemn as vehemently. Preparing oil of sweet almonds and cooking capon soup for the mother to eat right after birth offer no miracles, yet have other virtues. All that screaming during labor, which was great for relaxing the abdominal muscles, may have given the patient a sore throat, so a spoonful of almond oil could be soothing. If the labor lasted many hours, the mother may be hungry and in need of a nourishing bowl of soup. Be careful not to overfeed her, however, because it is not true that her womb is now empty and in need of refilling. Watch her evacuation carefully and adjust her diet accordingly. Amazing though it may seem, it is true that a woman who has just given birth can urinate milk *(possa pischiar del latte)*, but other abnormally colored discharges of any kind should be causes for concern.[62]

Postpartum Care

The midwife's job is not over with the actual birth, Savonarola reminds us. Immediately she must see to properly removing the placenta and putting the mother comfortably to bed. If the placenta has not spontaneously descended after the birth, it will cause the mother great pain in her head and stomach. She may even die. It is imperative to tie the placenta and pull it out entirely, using whatever force is necessary. If there are problems, begin by oiling the uterine passage; prepare some hellebore to wipe on her nose and mouth so she starts sneezing. And if that still doesn't work, roll a fat ball of soaked oakum into a wooden bowl, bandage it onto her navel, and start the sneezing routine over again. Should even these efforts fail, inject various perfumes and spices into her vagina (Marinello provides fourteen pages of mixtures that may work), try fumigation, and as a last resort—even though it will cause great pain—use your hand to rip it out. This must be done firmly but carefully, a little bit at a time, so you do not pull out the entire uterus with the placenta. When you get a piece out, tie it to the patient's foot so it won't slip back in, then insert your hand again and continue the job. According to Marinello, the midwife should use her left hand for this task, another item in the long list of prejudices concerning left-handedness that awaited advice-manual readers.[63]

Once the placenta is entirely removed, bathe the mother, starting with her feet, legs, hips, vagina, and everything up to her navel. Massage her lower body with oil of iris, dill, or lily; then bathe her from the waist up. Help her stand up, perhaps with a footstool, and put some pepper or hellebore under her nostrils to make her sneeze out any noxious substances in her respiratory system. If she is too weak for a tub bath, at least sponge her down thoroughly.[64]

A little residual menstrual blood is normal. Indeed, the uterus may be so inflamed and sore from the birth process that it closes prematurely, not allowing noxious substances to exit; in this case Marinello offers a range of herbal cures to be consumed, rubbed, inserted, or otherwise applied. But if there is excess or the discharge continues, warns Savonarola, it must be soaked up and the flow stopped. Try placing plasters saturated in vinegar on the womb and kidneys or else suppositories of spiced red wine. Some experts say a singularly effective suppository can be made from a slice of pork wrapped in a wad of uncombed, unwashed wool. Retained blood is usually due to the midwife's negligence, more likely if the child is a boy, because the midwife and her brigade tend to become overly solicitous of the baby; in this case the blood must be heated to provoke its flow. Plasters immersed in water of cyclamen are a great secret for this, and any herbalist in Ferrara can get you some. Treat a moderate fever with barley soup, but if the fever is high or persists for several days, go to the doctor.[65]

Savonarola continues his advice on postpartum care of the mother with a folksy joke about the stingy Florentine tavern keeper who always served minuscule amounts of wine for his customers until the clientele who passed through from Forlì outwitted him by pouring more and more frequently. "O companions, what are you doing?" he said, to which they replied, "You're in charge of how little, we of how often." "So it should be, women of mine, when our women who have given birth at first want to eat sparingly but frequently, of light foods that are easy to digest and very nutritious." Give her fresh eggs, capon, pullets, and chicken; for the rich ones, offer partridge, pheasant, and ptarmigan. Serve light, aromatic wines, not the heavy ones that make a person constipated; better the white wines or at most a rosé. You midwives have to be careful not to fall into the common way of feeding up your patient with a diet that is too fat; she'll end up with a fever and produce too much milk, causing her breasts to become painfully engorged and maybe develop abscesses. So, you midwives who have just helped the woman through a dangerous time, don't create new risks. And you, new mother, if you don't want your breasts to become like two barrels, listen to what we have to say.

But if you, good midwife, ask, "How shall I know the proper amounts to feed my patient?" then I respond that you should consider her age, strength, and constitution. The young need more food, as do the robust and those who are normally big eaters anyway. Follow a middle course. Think of the wise midwife as being the helmsman of a boat, now raising and now lowering her steering arm. For the first week, try four meals daily. After the first week, increase the intake, supplementing the morning eggs with meat to be chewed with her own teeth rather than as a puree, but not so much that she starts waddling like a duck. Still, there is more harm in too little food than in too much, and the harm of excess is more easily remedied.

Finally, the midwife could turn to the most satisfying part of her job: caring for the baby. There are hints in the advice manuals that some midwives may have enjoyed this aspect of their work a little too much, rushing to attend the baby while leaving the mother to hemorrhage until her life was at risk. Fathers and other relatives who assisted may have been no better. In any event, when the baby emerges, the midwife should hold him in her hands very gently, with due awareness of his tenderness, being careful not to damage any of his limbs. Then she must tie the umbilical cord with a strong string, for which purpose wool is much better than linen, twine, or cotton, because the wool curls naturally and can be tied tightly but gently so as not to cause the baby pain. Next she should take a scissors or a razor, cut the cord about four to six inches from the umbilical, and bandage it with linen soaked in warm oil. The bandage should be changed frequently, always soaked in warm oil, for about four to eight days, when the remaining cord should wither and fall away. Practices, presumably derived from ancient Sparta, such as placing the newborn baby on the cold floor while cutting the umbilical cord and immediately giving the infant a cold bath are uniformly and strongly condemned. The uterine environment was moist and warm, and these are exactly the conditions that now should be provided.[66]

The common tradition once the umbilical cord is cut is immediately to give the newborn a bath, but Savonarola does not think this is such a good idea, even in tepid water. The baby is tired from all the movement and exercise of getting through the uterus, so it may be better to place some moderately warm towels over the baby's body. Let him rest for a while, according to how difficult the birth trauma was, but certainly for one hour and generally for three, making sure he stays warm during this time. Now is also a good opportunity to return to care for the mother, seeing to it that she does not get cold and that she has no retained menses.

That done, go over to the baby, who by now should be tired. His body, covered with natural oil and fat, will be filled with air, acquired first in the womb and now through his porous, tender skin because of the relative coldness of his new surroundings. It is imperative to bathe him thoroughly so he is not only clean but his excess internal air and humors escape; only then can his skin toughen up a little to protect him. This is especially true of his first and second baths, for which the water should be made astringent with some salt and sage leaves. Venetians and all others fortunate enough to live near the sea already know the value of saltwater baths but for some readers this may be new information. Bathe him two or even three times daily if his fattiness requires. Do this when he awakens, keeping him in the basin until his skin starts to turn red. Hold the baby with one hand under his back and the other on his chest, not the abdomen, with the abdomen higher for the first bath but lower for the second. Be sure to raise his feet towards his mouth and wash carefully behind his sex, as it's called. Use your hand to keep the head raised and do not let water enter the ears, being especially careful to use your hands gently to feel and reshape the baby's members.

With great diligence, round out the baby's head since this is where the brain is housed, and it cannot be that a badly formed head does not damage the brain. And if you say, "I've seen lots of people with distorted heads who were very wise and learned," then I say, "sure, I believe you, but if they had had better-shaped skulls they would have been even wiser and more learned." Everyone knows that a carpenter with poorly sharpened tools will break the wood and that you can shave better with a well-honed razor than a dull one. The same is true for the brain; it reaches its true nobility in a well-formed cranium. So you say, "Teacher, instruct me on how to shape the head," and I respond, make the top as round as possible and then press in the sides, that is the temples, so that the back is larger than the front. When you're finished with the head, turn to the nose, making it larger or narrower as you think looks good. Next, press the baby's ears against its head. Then wipe the eyes with a wad of silk, very gently, or else with some soft linen. Avicenna suggests using a little oil for this because it cleanses and does not irritate or do any harm. Similarly, swab the nostrils with water and oil. Brush the palate with honey, spreading it with your pinky finger, the nail of which should be cut very short and smooth, just the opposite of the long, sharp nail on the index finger that every good midwife must have. Then use your pinky to spread the baby's sex so that nothing obstructs the urinary passage. Attend next to the limbs, distending the arms and crossing them to provide much needed exercise, since they have been cramped up in the womb for so long. Similarly, stretch the legs and bend them so the heels touch the buttocks. Press the lower abdomen to make urination easier. Check to see if one leg is longer than the other, in which case carefully and gently stretch the shorter one.[67]

Note well, female reader, how agile the midwife's hand must be to do these delicate tasks. Once a midwife is too old, her hands tremble and all her experience becomes useless; she'd be better off instructing someone else how to do the job. Not that a young girl should be elevated to the role of expert midwife, but just as every wise doctor trains an apprentice, so the midwife should teach another woman all she knows. Marinello agrees, saying plainly, if your midwife is not up to every aspect of the job, then find another one immediately.[68]

During the first month, bathing and stretching the baby should be done once or twice daily, and thereafter every eight or fifteen days. Some people think it is better to bathe the baby in wine. However, authorities including Avicenna, Rhazes, and Galen, as well as many of the ancients, prefer water because they think bathing in wine is too great a change for an infant. Those who favor the wine bath, generally in red wine, hold that it relaxes the limbs and combats the frigidity the baby feels on exiting the womb and being exposed to the air. Savonarola sides with the ancients, concluding that a wine bath is just too dangerous, in that vapors from the wine could do notable damage to the baby's brain. Looking to the future, Savonarola recommends bathing the baby as many as three times each month until the child is five years old. True enough, it is uncommon to bathe children so frequently, but it is a good idea, especially for poor people, since at least they will thereby have strong and pretty children, which is a grand inheritance in itself. As the saying goes, "Who is born beautiful is not born poor." So be aware, female reader, that if you do not want your children to remain little, follow the advice of Avicenna and Galen—bathe them often and let anyone who wishes trumpet against you.

Back to the midwife's duties. After giving the newborn its first bath, she should wrap the baby in warm swaddling cloths, fully extending the arms and hands toward the knees and even extending the baby's fingers. The cloth should be soft and plush, well-washed, with no roughness left in it. Follow the advice of the ancient philosophers and cover the head as well, although not too tightly, and ignore contrary opinions that would leave the head unwrapped. All this should be done with great dexterity. Watch out for left-handed midwives who as a consequence swaddle badly and leave the baby defective. You see this all over the Friuli region, especially among peasants and artisans who walk with a limp, whereas very few gentlemen and gentlewomen are lame; the reason is that the upper classes have better infant care. Other deformities, such as occur in the Puglie region where women give birth to monsters in the shape of animals like snakes, frogs, bats, or hawks, may be blamed on supernatural misfortunes, but this is not the case with deformities due to poor care. Always swaddle in a darkened room where the baby is not exposed to cold air. Keep the baby swaddled this way for eight days, until its limbs are strong; then transfer the infant to a cradle to be covered with a warm blanket.[69]

Some advice manuals end at this point, with the mother and her newborn baby ready to face the world, the midwife off to her next patient, and the father welcomed into the room to see his new offspring. More often, however, the manuals go on, generally in a new "book" or section, to offer advice on nursing and, in many cases, on early child rearing as well. It is to these matters that we turn in the next chapter.

CHAPTER

· *4* ·

Raising Your Child

Nursing: Who Should Do It?

Let us imagine that the sixteenth-century Tuscan couple I began by casting as forward-looking readers of Lorenzo Gioberti's *Errori Popolari* are
now the proud parents of a healthy boy. Perhaps they truly believe they
have benefited from its authoritative recommendations, so they eagerly
turn the page to find the answer to the urgent question of who should
nurse their son. Alas, they would have come upon a chapter more likely
than any other to provoke anxiety, self-doubt, and even tensions between
them. Like every other text I have read, from the most impressive Latin
medical treatise to the lowliest anonymous pamphlet, Gioberti told
mother not to put her child with a wet nurse but to breast-feed her
child. With the notable exception of Socrates, who advocated the Spartan
model (according to which women communally fed the city's infants
without each mother knowing her own offspring—itself part of a lengthy
defense of eugenic breeding that found little favor in Renaissance Italy),
Greco-Roman philosophers, Arab scholars, and Judeo-Christian moralists all advocated maternal breast-feeding if possible. Pliny the Elder,
Plutarch, Tacitus, and Aulus Gellius said so unequivocally. In Islamic
society, where use of wet nurses was widespread, elaborate taboos developed against marriage among milk kin, a sure indicator of the powerful
logic that a woman's milk carried the characteristics of her blood group.
Old Testament accounts of miraculous breast-feeding by grandmothers,
as well as numerous tales in saints' lives, tell of wet nursing as a charitable
act, never as a routine commercial activity or as public policy. Mary her-

self gave suck to the infant Jesus, a lesson for all of Christendom. Finally, the renowned physician Moses Maimonides reported to the Spanish community of Jews that husbands could compel their wives to breast-feed and that a mother could refuse her husband's command not to do so. In essence, Jewish customary law thus protected the right of either spouse to insist on maternal nurture.[1]

"Mom should do it" is what all the popular sixteenth-century books recommend, even though it seems that no amount of insistence and argument eliminated the widespread practice among their readers of hiring wet nurses.[2] In the previous two chapters, we saw that advice manuals about conception and pregnancy offered little or nothing beyond what could be found in the classic texts of Greco-Roman scholars such as Hippocrates, Aristotle, Galen, and Soranus, or else among Arab experts such as Avicenna and Averroës. The newness of popular-advice manuals lay not in the wisdom they contained but in how they presented information for a wide audience that did not read Greek, Latin, or Arabic. Not only is the language different but also the ways in which things are told, what is included and what is left out, how frequently things are repeated or embellished, whether ancient authorities are cited at all, whether contrary opinions are entertained, and the certainty with which cures are offered.

I assume that our typical Tuscan couple did not read Gioberti and say, "Oh, he got that from Plutarch or Quintilian," unless of course Gioberti chose to say so as a means of bolstering his own authority, which he sometimes did but more often did not. Historians of ideas and of medicine have devoted much attention to tracing links between classical and Renaissance thinking on many of the topics treated in popular manuals. Study of these connections certainly is worthwhile, but it bears repetition at the onset of this chapter on nursing and child care that my major aim is to capture the world of knowledge available to vernacular readers of popular books in sixteenth-century Italy. I eschew offering glosses on ancient texts that common people could not have read, and I consciously forego providing correctives from the perspectives of modern medicine and educational theory. In that some ancient texts, in fact much of Plutarch and Quintilian, were available as published Italian translations in the sixteenth century, our Tuscan couple could have read these classics, finding in them some of the "advice" contained in the pulp I am concentrating on; mostly, however, these translations were for schoolboys or their teachers. The texts themselves, whether in the original language or in translation, are not organized and indexed in the way of advice manuals intended for families to consult while coping with their daily lives.

Thus, I shall mention wisdom from the ancients in the present chapter on child rearing more frequently than I did in earlier chapters on conception and pregnancy, because the texts themselves were more readily available in the vernacular. Still, format and price meant that a Mercurio or a Gioberti probably reached many more households than Quintilian's *Institutio oratoria* or Plutarch's *Moralia*.[3] With these explanations in mind—or apologies, if that is what they amount to—let us see what the popular manuals have to say about breast-feeding.

First we consider the oft-repeated advice that mothers suckle their own children. Gioberti asserts that maternal milk affects the child positively, whereas nourishment from a stranger is not as good. This recommendation follows logically from the four-humors theory universally shared by Renaissance physicians. The mother's humor balance would be most similar to the baby's; in any event, the infant would have adjusted to his mother's hot/cold, wet/dry characteristics over the preceding nine months. Medical experts agreed that breast milk is converted from blood, in particular menstrual blood, so the baby thus continues to nourish on exactly what fed him in the womb. Nor is the balance of humors the baby's only benefit. Gioberti reminds readers that nursing creates a special bond between mother and child. If an infant is sent to a wet nurse, then the appropriate maternal bond does not develop and the child instead becomes attached to its nurse. Finally, with the milk an infant also imbibes the personality traits of the person who nurses him. While it may be that women who are stupid or prone to vice should not breast-feed, indeed they should not have children in the first place, all mothers of good character should pass this blessing onto their child.

Gioberti then turns to husbands, asking them to make some minimal sacrifices. Sure, you do not like your sleep disturbed by an infant wailing for nourishment, but this will pass. Many men tell their wives not to suckle only because they are afraid their breasts will balloon up, leaving them less tender and ready for sexual play. How selfish! Finally, the Montpellier physician warns that some men want to bring a wet nurse into the home, not out of concern for the child's health or his mother's beauty, but only to create an occasion for a little sex on the side with the new lodger. Were husbands supposed to read this passage to their wives as the couple decided whether to employ a nurse? I think not. Possibly this paragraph addressed midwives who would pass the wisdom on to their patients, although most of Gioberti's book attacks rather than instructs them. Whomever the immediate audience for his warning, it is there for us to ponder as we note that sexual exploitation by husbands

and fathers of their female domestic employees was not invented in contemporary America.[4]

Friar Mercurio bemoans the pompous, evil trend in Italy whereby even
artisans now want a wet nurse for their infants, a practice once reserved
for princesses because of their delicate constitutions. He is at his most
eloquent in this chapter, so I shall let him speak for himself. The newborn
nourished in his mother's womb for nine months suddenly is banished
from the house, like some traitor or rebel. Such behavior is more inhu-
mane than that of the fiercest tiger, who at least feeds her own young.
Not only tigers but even crocodiles, bears, and asps nurse their offspring.
How can a mother who succored the baby for nine months without
knowing if her womb held a boy, a girl, or a monstrosity, now, when she
sees a healthy boy, send him into exile? Does she think God gave her
breasts only to adorn her chest? Alas, sending the baby out to a wet nurse
is so widespread and has been going on so long that it is easier to deplore
the practice than to hope for its disappearance. Sometimes the newborn
is sent not to a neighbor but to a stranger, maybe to some barbarous
mountain dweller, not to a free person but to a servant, not to a chaste
person but to a prostitute, often unhealthy and maybe syphilitic. "Good
God what cruelty this is; I'll add in case it's not clear to the whole world
that an almost infinite number of people are infected with syphilis solely
from sucking milk." Moreover, a child who is bastardized *(imbastardirli)*
by being sent to a wet nurse never develops a deep bond of filial love
and lacks the affection that comes from sitting around the hearth together
with grandparents and great grandparents.

Then the Dominican friar (and practicing family doctor) adds a plea
that strikes a cord of romantic sentimentality even in our own day. There
is no recreation in the world that approaches the sweetness of little children; no theatrical comedy that equals their laughter, their tears, their
spontaneous gestures; no experience like watching them laugh and cry
at the same time for reasons that are as amazing as they are indecipher-
able. What joy to see them fly into a rage over nothing, seek a toy with
such diligence, throw away coins, run after an apple, listen to a witty
proposition and answer back; to observe their games, their gestures, their
exuberant movements; to hear them dispute with cats and dogs, build
houses, cook, play at being a grown man, an old man, a priest; to look
on as one minute they defend their mother against one-and-all and the
next wildly pummel her. Nothing could be more irresistible for a father
than to return home from the shop and see his beloved little son or
daughter at the top of the stairs waiting with such happiness and joy to

receive him, hug him, kiss him, and tell him many things. Every worldly care vanishes and immediately he begins to join in the child's antics. "Some people say it is not right for a serious man to be playing with children, but I say that maybe children these days have degenerated so much relative to their fathers" just because they lacked this fatherly attention in their early years. Mercurio then goes into a written soliloquy in which he contradicts this last assertion by listing several greats among the ancients whose children were something less than a chip off the old block. Still, he concludes confidently that mother's milk is best.[5]

Even in ephemeral books of guessing rhymes *(Indovinelli)*, which enjoyed enormous popularity in the sixteenth century, one finds little ditties on the joys of breast-feeding.

Ventre con ventre, & peloso, con peloso	Skin to skin and chest to chest
congiunti a carne cruda entro nel buco,	Joined as raw meat enters the mouth,
ad ambi rende un suave riposo	Giving to each a suave rest
[What Can It Be?]	
la Donna quando da la poppa	The woman when she gives her breast[6]

On a more serious note, Dr. Michele Savonarola reminds the women of Ferrara that breast-feeding your child means you will live much longer because you will not get pregnant again so soon. Every birth is like another big beating on your life, taking its toll with months of corrupted appetite, stomach pains, and backaches. Shifting to a different line of reasoning, the physician pleads, "You woman reader, I've known many matrons who did not want to suckle their child solely so as not to lose the beauty of their breasts and the chance to show them off from the balcony alongside those women who have kept theirs beautiful enough for display to admirers." But against these flatteries from the window, consider how much more your son will love you if you nurse him yourself, how much better he will be nourished than with the milk of a woman too poor to eat properly, how many tears, sleepless nights, and lengthy stays in dirty diapers he will suffer. Keep before your eyes the humble virgin mother of God and follow her example in caring for your son. And if you are rich and can afford a servant, nurse yourself but bring in a woman to help with the other tiring aspects of baby care.[7]

Even Matteo Palmieri, whose dialogue *Della vita civile* is addressed mostly to fathers responsible for raising sons to become good citizens, devotes several pages to maternal care of newborns. "Noble mothers who refuse to nurse their children deserve their hatred." Nature in all its perfection nourished the baby in the womb with his mother's blood, and now this blood has moved upward to her breasts. No other food can be as good, and if the substitute is too far removed from the mother's characteristics, then the child will become like a stranger, just as the white lamb suckled by a black sheep turns dark and the lamb given suck by a goat not only develops coarse, tough hair but sees its body desiccated, its voice and habits changed. No wonder a bad wet nurse can turn a good boy depraved and spoiled, with skin blemishes, hot blood, bouts of melancholy, acidity, and sleeplessness. Many a prospective wet nurse was drunk when she got pregnant, out to trap a man, dissolute and full of putrid body humors. Then she offers her breast to a noble, healthy infant with no fear of his father's wrath. What could be worse than to put a little one at the breast of a Saracen tartar, a barbarian, or a denizen of some other bestial, wild nation?[8]

Fellow humanist Francesco Barbaro, emphasizes a different aspect of nature's perfection by pointing out that while all other animals have nipples under their stomachs, women have them on their chests. This is designed so that as a mother feeds her child she can at the same time fondle him. Borrowing again without acknowledgment from Plutarch, he suggests that a noble woman should occasionally take the infants of her servants to her breast so that they will be more loving toward her own child.[9]

All this exhortation sometimes had little effect, however, so practical-advice manuals faced realities and instructed parents how to choose a good wet nurse. Savonarola begins by telling his readers she should be between thirty-two and thirty-five years of age. Milk may be more abundant in women in their early twenties, but the common view that younger women make the best wet nurses is wrong because their milk is too watery; therefore, a mature woman is preferable, even up to age forty. Examine carefully the milk's color to see if it has a healthful white consistency. The wet nurse should be muscular but not fat, with a sturdy neck, a broad chest, and moderately large breasts, not swollen with watery blood/milk, with no sores on her nipples. She should be of good dietary and personal habits, with a jolly disposition, not melancholic. Her lactation should have begun recently, perhaps four-to-six weeks earlier. It is better if she has given birth to a boy, because her menstrual blood, now turned into milk, will be warmer and purer. She must not be pregnant or prone to miscarriage because that means something is wrong with her nutrition. A well-behaved widow is the best choice. Then Savonarola adds in typically ironic style that you have about as much chance of finding all these qualities in a single person as you do of finding a white crow, but go ahead and try. And if while in your employ the wet nurse catches a contagious disease, get another one until she recovers or switch the baby to a diet without milk if he is old enough.[10]

Contrary to Savonarola's advice to select a wet nurse who has given birth most recently to a boy, Gioberti follows the rule of opposites. If your own child is a girl and, because you cannot breast-feed her yourself, you must find a wet nurse, then choose one who had a boy; but if you have an infant son to feed, then choose a nurse whose last child was a girl. He also believes that it is entirely possible for a woman to have milk even if she has never given birth, so ignore all the gossip saying that young girls who offer themselves as wet nurses must have abandoned their own child at some nearby monastery and are of dubious moral character.[11]

Whereas Savonarola's guidelines for choosing a wet nurse concentrate on physical qualities, and Gioberti adds obvious moral issues, all of which are found in Mercurio, the friar also raises several more subtle concerns. If you must use a wet nurse, have her come to your home to be sure she gets a good diet and your baby breathes healthful air, but see that her own children stay out of your house. By moving in with you, she also will be apart from her husband, so she won't get pregnant and ruin her milk. You, the mother, will have the joy of seeing your baby continually, hearing his cries, and attending to his needs while making sure that the nurse is diligent. See to it that she keeps the diapers sparkling white, also the swaddling bands and shirts for the baby, so he will not be offended by their bad odor or coarseness and start crying or fretting. She must be chaste because even if pregnancy does not follow, sexual intercourse burns up bodily heat needed for good digestion and the conversion of blood to milk. She should always be cheerful, even if that is not her nature, sing often to the baby, and caress him attentively. She should flee from the abuse committed by nearly all Italian wet nurses who while they are cuddling the baby, say things to him using words that are clipped, wrong, or distorted. (Baby talk may be what Mercurio is lambasting here or perhaps specifically Italian class-based dialects and speech patterns, but the general admonition about correct usage and pronunciation comes directly from Quintilian.) Instead, the nurse should always speak distinctly, using articulate words, so that the seeds she plants as his first teacher are good and true, with no improper usages to be unlearned later on.[12]

Above all she must be sober in food and drink. How wrong these wet nurses are nowadays who think they have some legal right to four meals daily instead of two, who go around day and night with a glass continuously at their lips. They tell you they need the extras to make lots of milk, but the truth is that when they eat too much, their stomachs cannot digest and turn food to blood/milk; therefore, what they eat and drink just becomes excrement, wasting whatever nourishment was there in the first place. If the day becomes very long, supplement the two regular meals with a bowl of soup or maybe a wine pudding but no more. The wet nurse should eat nothing salty, no garlic or onions, fruit only moderately and with meals, and no heavy wines that might make her drunk and so groggy that she smothers the child. She should take a nap in the daytime if her rest during the night has been broken, because sleep is essential to good digestion. Finally, she should force herself to evacuate regularly and get light exercise by sweeping the house, dusting the furniture, and doing the wash.

What of wet nurses who cared for the baby in their own homes? For the most part in this book, I try to let advice manuals speak for themselves, without getting myself and my readers heavily engaged in historical debates. At least briefly, however, it strikes me as worthwhile to make an exception here to explore something the manuals do not say. If a mother could not or would not suckle her own baby, then clearly the preference among writers of advice manuals was for bringing a wet nurse into the home. But surely some parents could not find such a person or else they wished to have their infant out of the house for one reason or another. What then? We do have Mercurio ranting about the evils of sending your child off to a mountain barbarian; from this diatribe we can assume that at least some parents did so. Further, I assume that Mercurio simply expected that such parents had little or nothing to do with the child until he or she returned two years later. But there is almost nothing in the many texts I have examined telling parents how to assure good care for a child placed nearby.[13] It seems strange that authors who wrote in such detail about how to select a wet nurse and supervise her if she lived in would be so silent about how parents should check on a child put out to nurse.

One issue is how frequently babies were sent away. The now classic assertions of historian J. B. Ross on the putting out of infants are clear:

> Birth in the parental bed, bath in the same room, and baptism in the parish church were followed almost at once by delivery into the hands of a *balia* [wet nurse], generally a peasant woman living at a distance, with whom the infant would presumably remain for about two years or until weaning was completed. Immediate separation from its mother, therefore, was the fate of the new-born child in the middle-class families of urban Italy in the period of our study [fourteenth to early sixteenth century]. It became wholly dependent for

food, care and affection upon a surrogate, and its return to its own mother was to a stranger in an alien home, to a person with whom no physical or emotional ties had ever been established.[14]

Although Ross provides no numbers, the title of her essay asserts that putting out infants to a distant wet nurse was the norm for middle-class children in urban, Renaissance Italy. She cites several authorities who seem to assume as much, including Francesco da Barberino and Paolo da Certaldo, but we have already noted that their works did not reach print until modern times, so their direct impact upon sixteenth-century, middle-class parents may have been limited.[15] Indeed, Francesco da Barberino's handwritten treatise was lost entirely—simply went missing—until the seventeenth century. Ross also cites Giovanni Rucellai as echoing authors who treat wet nursing as customary, but the text, another that did not make it to a publisher, says no such thing as far as I can tell.[16] Bernardino da Siena, who lamented the practice, admittedly had more influence and drew big crowds when he preached in city piazzas, but his sermons are no better as a guide on the frequency of putting out infants to wet nurses than they are on the ubiquity of sodomy.

Neither the Renaissance humanists nor the classical authorities cited by Ross assumed the parents would put the child out rather than have a wet nurse come into the parental home. This is crucial, because a long tradition of relying upon a wet nurse, as practiced among elites in classical Greece, meant she was a woman who entered service at the child's birth and continued as a caretaker until the child reached maturity, often as a revered member of the family. Another example that comes to mind from a very different cultural setting is the big plantation in the American South, both before and after the Civil War, where the black slave mammy and the infants in her care frequently developed relationships that both described as loving and long lasting, however ambiguous their affection may have been. Realities never matched the celluloid world of *Gone With the Wind,* but there is good evidence that most white women resolved, at least to their own satisfaction, any doubts about what traits their babes might imbibe along with milk from a black breast.[17] Urban, middle-class Renaissance Italians who brought in a wet nurse do not seem to have made her a permanent or beloved member of the family, so we should not paint too rosy a picture here. Still, the difference between having any sort of wet nurse in the house for whatever length of time and sending the infant away is profound, especially if what Ross writes about the child's becoming a total stranger to its mother is true.

Indeed, some of the very authors Ross cites in making her case about distant placement in fact explicitly advocate finding someone who at least

lives nearby when a child must be put out. None support distant placement or condone such practices even by implication. Ross draws four
examples of placing out from archival sources, but in none of them does
the text say that the placement was at a distance; in two, the parents first
used live-in wet nurses and only switched to a nonresident as a last resort.
Several examples are given of twins being provided for by keeping one at
home and sending the other out—hardly sufficient evidence to establish a
norm for middle-class children in urban Renaissance Italy. Ross then
recounts how the famous merchant Francesco Datini and his wife Margherita helped many of their business associates find wet nurses, a curious pastime for a childless couple, and reminds us of the undisputed fact
that when Francesco had to locate a nurse for his illegitimate daughter,
he did not look for a live-in arrangement—hardly amazing. Kindly husband and father that he must have been, Datini eventually brought the
girl into his home, presumably under the caring eyes of his barren wife,
but only when the child was six. There are a few other references, all
interesting individually but not forming any pattern delineating general
social patterns.[18] Even the song of Casentino wet nurses looking for work
that Ross quotes tells us nothing about who if anyone actually sang the
verses. Moreover, the words may have had a different meaning than she
ascribes if one considers the special relationship of Florence to its countryside and the firm belief, quite sensible, in fact, that mountain air was
just the thing to allow any person to escape the perils of a plague-infested
city.[19]

Not long after publication of Ross's essay, historian Christiane Klapisch-Zuber returned to some of the same materials, where she thought
she found more systematic evidence to support similar conclusions about
widespread use of wet nurses.[20] Whatever my reservations about her
quantitative assertions, I find her observations on the wet-nursing market
extremely interesting. She shows that economic arrangements for wet
nurses were controlled by pairs of men who made contracts and payments among themselves for services, one on behalf of his child and the
other for the milk of his wife. Since a husband was supposed to abstain
from sexual intercourse while his wife gave suck, and in view of what
we have observed earlier about the conjugal debt, maybe this is not as
chauvinistic as it initially sounds, although I doubt that wet nurses in the
Casentino countryside actually abstained from sexual intercourse unless
that was their choice; certainly their songs do not boast about this feature
of their work. Men made these arrangements to ingratiate themselves
with their betters, from whom they later hoped to obtain favors. Frequently, a countryside woman who had recently given birth would put

her own child out to nurse for about one florin per month and then her husband would collect two florins per month while she suckled some city-elite's infant. This all sounds terribly mercenary, although we modern Americans might reflect on child-care arrangements provided for career families by women of color who somehow must attend as well to their own children. The two-to-one profit margin, and the risk of poor care for the substitute mother's biological offspring, have not changed that much in five centuries.

I wonder about many aspects of these arrangements. How frequently did a wet nurse in the countryside, unsupervised as she was, sneak off to the villager caring for her own child and take him to her own breast? Or leave the city baby with a neighbor? Or substitute a little goat's milk? Or increase the supply of regular food so the baby needed less milk as he grew, well before the contract expired? Or organize a few women with milk into a Sparta-like arrangement to satisfy all the hungry mouths somehow? The notion that a mother could not produce enough to feed twins was accepted only by people who had never tried. My suspicion is that women in the Casentino region figured out that they could feed two babies at the same time, have sexual intercourse with their husbands or refuse as they pleased, and add to the family income all at the same time.

However these rural mothers coped, which we can never know with certainty, being sent to a wet nurse in the countryside may not have been unhealthful. Even in years when outbreaks of plague spared Florence, the city was not a good place for infants, and there was much truth to what everyone said about the salubrious air of the Tuscan hills. Mortality rates for children brought to the city's hospital for foundlings ran between 26 and 50 percent. Some of these infants were abandoned one evening only to have their mothers appear miraculously the next morning looking for work as paid wet nurses, knowing they would receive their own child back. But this charity/welfare system could do only so much to improve the odds of survival for poor babies. The rich did better. Among the 283 children (all of them well-to-do) sent to a wet nurse whom Klapisch-Zuber was able to track for a year or more, mortality was 15.8 percent for girls and 18.1 percent for boys. These percentages compare orphans from the very bottom of society against the most elite of all newborns. What the mortality rate was for middle-class infants who stayed in the city at their own mother's breast we simply do not know. Nonetheless, survival through the first year by more than five out of six babies, which is what Klapisch-Zuber's figures show for infants put out to nurse, seems quite good against known data for premodern Europe, so maybe Bernardino da Siena was wrong when he preached that babies nursed by their mothers were more likely to live.[21]

Apart from general innuendo about unloving, horrid, and selfish parents who did not even care for their own infants, neither Ross nor Klapisch-Zuber offered any specific suggestions on how putting out to nurse might have shaped the emotional development of Florentine children. One recent scholar is notably bolder. Hanna Pitkin interprets Niccolò Machiavelli's writings in fascinating ways by reading allusions to women and wet nurses in both his fiction and prose. A powerful paragraph goes as follows:

> Simply in terms of common sense, one would not be surprised to find children who have been reared in the wet-nurse pattern as practiced in Florence coming to resent women—at least large, older, powerful, "mother"-like women—and to regard them with deep suspicion, as changeable, unreliable, and treacherous. One would not be surprised to find a continuing later fear of dependence on (such) women and of anything resembling feminine nurturance; the unthinking, trusting bliss of the nursing infant was, after all, what put him into the mother's treacherous power.

But there is not a shred of evidence that the infant Niccolò was in fact sent to a wet nurse—no diary, no account book, no direct or indirect reference of any kind in any of his writings, nor in those of his father. Pitkin readily admits this total lack of evidence but continues her analysis anyway, based on the assumption that he must have been—because Klapisch-Zuber and Ross say this was the dominant pattern. Or, despite the hysteron proteron, perhaps his adult writings prove that his mother denied him suck.[22]

Yet more provocative is the recent assertion by sociologist Michael P. Carroll that the frustrating oral-erotic experiences resulting from sending Italian infants to wet nurses, which he extends from fourteenth-century Florence to all of Italy from 1500 to the present, "contributed significantly to a fixation at the oral stage." Further musings lead him to conclude that "the time has come to consider the possibility that the poor, exploited *balie* of Italy may have exerted as much of an influence on the outcome of the Reformation in Italy, and the shape of popular Catholicism in Italy, as Luther, Calvin, the Italian evangelicals, and De Rosa's reforming bishops together."[23]

One could go on with detailed criticisms of Ross's and Klapisch-Zuber's claims, along with the works that draw upon them, but that would not further my main point. Historians have painted a sweeping

canvas of medieval and Renaissance European children as neglected, un-
loved, and actively harmed by parents trapped in families formed for
business, not love—homes where little girls were especially unwanted
and maltreated. According to these historians, childhood came into its
own with the triumph of the bourgeois, nuclear family beginning in the
seventeenth century (made possible for an elite few by huge profits derived from European global expansion that fueled industrial capitalism,
I would note, although proponents of the bourgeois thesis would not
accept such crass linkages). These bourgeois families wholeheartedly
adopted maternal breast-feeding (true), wept copious tears when disease
robbed them of a beloved child (true), and reveled in sentimental tales
of childhood innocence (true). Eventually working-class families and
peasants came to adopt the same values, the very ones we hold today,
although poverty and a life of hard toil inevitably meant that the ideal
companionate family would not be achieved by all, or equally across class
lines. My skepticism about this idyllic picture of how the loving modern
family emerged progressively from the uncaring medieval household
need not detain us further.[24]

What I do want to suggest is that sixteenth-century advice manuals
overwhelmingly support the view that parents in those days loved their
children dearly and tried to raise them with individual, caring attention.
Evidence to portray an indifferent, unloving premodern European family
is often scanty, subject to different interpretations, and easily misunderstood when looked at through the prism of modern experience. It seems
to me highly unlikely that popular-advice manuals could have been popular at all if their message were totally out of line with ordinary people's
thinking on these matters. Boccaccio's horror at Florentines who failed
in their parental duties during the terrible days of the Black Death makes
no sense unless the norm was to cherish children. The proliferation of
paintings from the fourteenth century onward that depict Mary giving
suck to the infant Jesus could not have enhanced the religious devotion
of mothers who put children out to wet nurses. Nor, to take just one
additional literary example, can one explain the popularity of a sixteenth-
century translation of Plutarch's letter consoling his wife on the death
of their two-year-old daughter except in terms of a culture that wept over
such losses.[25] I would suggest, to get back to the specific starting point
of this digression, that the reason advice manuals do not give advice on
visiting infants put out to nurse is that very few infants were put out to
nurse, at least not by the middle-class people who bought these books.
Upon close examination, the assertion that putting out to wet nurses was
the norm simply does not hold up; it was not even a common practice

among the urban bourgeoisie and certainly not in the countryside. I think advice manuals did not treat the subject in any detail, because it was irrelevant for most of their readers. It is reassuring to me that modern historian Steven Ozment, who studied parallel popular materials from the German scene, came to the same conclusion.[26] What the authors of vernacular advice manuals invariably do provide are detailed instructions for an inexperienced mother on how to care for her infant on her own or else by closely supervising a live-in nurse.

Nursing: How to Do It

To feed your baby, hold him so his right side rests gently on your hip with his head looking upward, being sure that his limbs are not twisted or pressed too hard in some way against your body. During the first few days, when your own milk is not entirely pure, give your breasts to an older child to suck out and get someone else in to feed your own baby the best possible milk. Feed him many times each day, giving first one breast and then the other at the same feeding so he doesn't get tired pulling too long on just one as it drains. Later on you'll need to avoid overfeeding and three times daily will be enough; otherwise, you risk the baby getting worms or epilepsy. Against these dangers the best remedy is to give him a small amount of chicory syrup, not only when he first emerges from the womb after the sputum in his mouth is cleansed with a honeyed pinky finger, but also every morning for the next few months. Overfeeding also can cause the baby digestive problems, making him so irritable you won't be able to tell whether he is hungry or overstuffed.

At his morning feeding let him nurse for quite a while, alternating breasts so he gets the cream from each. After feeding, do not carry him around in your arms. Instead, place him gently in his crib, so as not to disturb the milk in his stomach. He should sleep for three or four hours. When he wakes up, check his diaper; if it is not soiled, then feed him less than you did at the start of the day. His evening feeding should be full and leisurely, like the morning one. Do not awaken him for a night feeding, although it is likely, especially in winter when the days are short, that he will let you know he needs one. Keep it brief and not too abundant. However many times you feed him, try to alternate between fuller and skimpier feedings in accordance with his bowel movements and not according to the amount of milk you feel in your breasts. Absolutely avoid that nasty habit found especially among the Italian nobility of stuffing moist bits of bread *(panatella)* in the baby's mouth while he is at the breast in the belief that this will fatten him up. Leave soaked bread for toothless old people, not for babies who become bloated rather than properly fattened with bread. Fruit juices are also not good; they can give the baby a high fever, internal bleeding, and worms leading to blindness. Wine and puddings cooked in wine are as wonderful for restoring the energies of old people as they are terrible for ruining the liver and blood of infants. Avoid them completely. Mother's milk is the best and only thing a baby needs.

In summertime, bathe the baby every day in tepid water and dry him well. Then put almond oil in your palm and spread it over all his limbs. But in wintertime, bathe him less often and skip the bath entirely or wash him only from the waist down if there is any danger he will get into a draft of cold air. Do not let too much light into the room. Baptize the baby as soon as possible, even if he is healthy. If the baby cries, maybe he needs something other than a feeding. Check if his diaper is dirty with urine or excrement, which not only annoys him but attracts fleas. Or maybe he is crying because he is sweating or because he is swaddled too tightly. Wean the baby by eighteen months if a girl and certainly no longer than two years even for boys. Going on until age three or four just makes the child an obese blockhead. All these suggestions come from Friar Mercurio, but the recommendations of Gioberti and Savonarola are similar.[27]

Gioberti is even more an advocate than Mercurio of what we would call demand feeding. In the initial few hours after birth, give the baby a little honey or sugar. Once regular maternal feeding begins, the infant should be given the breast whenever he wants it; do not follow a strict time frame. His diapers should be changed accordingly. Do not let the baby cry for a long time but pick him up and feed him. The Montpellier philosopher/physician then goes to some length in denouncing the old wives' tale that declares if you heat breast milk, it will dry up the source. Complete nonsense! (I believe he takes such a firm stance so mothers will understand that they can express milk for the baby and then be away temporarily while someone else feeds him in their absence.)[28]

Whatever one concludes about the implications of advice on heating breast milk, when taken together with recommendations in favor of demand feeding, a picture of infancy emerges that merits pausing over. The essential hue is plain enough: if a baby cries, there is some good reason for his wailing—he is hungry or wet or cold. Absent from these popular manuals is concern that the baby may become spoiled or willful. Later on, there will be advice about molding good character, and we shall be reading it closely just as I think sixteenth-century parents did, but for now the books tell us that the infant's nature is innocent. His (or her, for no differential or inferior treatment for little girls is suggested) demands are reasonable, entirely appropriate for survival and healthy growth. All this is said, or merely assumed, without any need to explain or defend the position at great length. That in itself is quite remarkable in a Catholic culture deeply imbued with St. Augustine's distrust of nature and his ultimate rejection of the innocence of babes. No doctrine of original sin impinges here to corrupt parental love for their newborns.[29]

Savonarola's advice, notwithstanding some differences in detail, also portrays a pure, wholly good infant who desires only what he actually requires, one whose needs should be satisfied without fear of catering to mere whims. If anything, it is the mother who pulls the baby to her breast at every cry more for her own peace of mind than for the baby's. A little crying between feedings is good exercise for the baby's lungs. Infants cannot need to be fed eight or ten times each day, writes Savonarola, as so many mothers do; three good feedings daily should be enough. Use a pacifier (quieta puti) instead, as often as the baby wants it. For the first day put a little honey on the baby's gums and tongue, also on your nipple; let him latch on, but do not actually feed the baby that day because your milk is much altered by the birth process. If you can find someone to feed your baby on the second day, that is better, but otherwise just start yourself. During these initial days, squeeze out the initial liquid in the mornings; it is too watery and not as nutritious for the baby as the milk that follows.

Examine your milk regularly and adjust your diet accordingly. Testing can be done simply enough by rubbing a few drops between your fingers to see if it runs watery or beads up too much. The milk should be of consistent texture, not frothy; the color should be white, not yellowish, greenish, reddish, or dark. It should smell sweet, not bitter, sour, tart, or salty. Abundance is not critical; indeed, you women who have lots of milk must be especially careful not to overfeed. Always remember that even maternal milk of poor quality is far better than not giving your own milk and switching to either a wet nurse or animal's milk. Do not overfeed, as this invariably causes indigestion; do not space feedings too far apart or too near so that your milk is either too stale or too fresh. Continue breast-feeding throughout the first year, or at least until some teeth come in, but after that you can wean if you are really tired of nursing. It would be better to continue for another year, however, especially for a son. Husbands and breast-feeding wives should sacrifice as much as possible the pleasures of Venus in the best interests of their baby's health because, even when no pregnancy ensues, sexual intercourse spoils milk and makes it smell bad.[30]

Gioberti adds the warning that contrary to popular opinion, a woman can become pregnant during lactation without first experiencing menstruation. This happens because a portion of her uterine blood is not transformed into milk and remains to nourish the new semen there (in accordance with the author's one seed in good soil theory). This is more likely as the child becomes older, eats other foods, and therefore does not consume enough milk.[31]

Some mothers and wet nurses faced the problem of too little milk or milk that was somehow not digestible; for this, as we can well imagine, the advice manuals have dozens of suggestions. The same authors who earlier gave us cures for infertility and for a variety of sexual-performance failures are ready on this problem as well. Here we may sample briefly only a few remedies. The student who published his *Secreti diversi* while claiming to be no less than the eminent Gabriele Falloppio suggests a variety of rubs to stimulate or diminish lactation. The agriculturist/publisher/humanist Charles Estienne, who devoted an entire chapter in his elite book to providing home remedies for the tenant farmer's wife to follow, advises drinking ass's milk to keep breasts firm and beautiful, while concoctions laced with fennel are sure to make for lots of milk.[32] In the numerous publications of Bologna's doctor/charlatan Leonardo Fioravanti, one finds remedies for engorged breasts that require common mallow, marshmallow, barley seeds, honey, flour of lentils, and sweet flag cooked in the whey of goat's milk, then ground with butter, pork fat, and wheat flour. Whether the patient was to rub this on, somehow ingest it, or perhaps both is not entirely clear to me.[33] Castore Durante's huge herbal book recommends seeds of amaranth dissolved in wine to produce abundant lactation and an ointment of ground pine to soften the breasts, while warning against parsley because it both increases sexual desire and dries up milk.[34] And then we have Mattioli, always with the longest list of remedies. To dry up the breasts, put hemlock or squash leaves on them. To make milk more plentiful, try powdered hooves of donkey or cow dissolved in herbal tea or a chickpea broth, or else cauliflower cooked with pepper and betony in a broth or pulverized thistle roots, fennel seeds, and long pepper in herbal tea. Or follow the ancient wisdom of Dioscorides for more abundant milk by eating or spicing your food with barley, fennel, mint, sow thistle, lettuce, basil, arugula, anemone, anise, dill, fennel flower, seeds of turkey oak, cooked clematis, or juice of white briony.[35]

For a more organized and complete approach, readers might turn to Mercurio. Book 3 of *La commare* devotes five chapters to telling the midwife how to treat her patient for each of five distinct lactation difficulties: insufficient milk, excess milk, poor-quality milk, coagulation of milk in the breasts, and cracked or sore nipples. The problem-oriented content and colloquial writing style definitely intend to educate a wide public. The friar is not trying to peddle some syrup or elixir like Fioravanti, nor does he offer miracle cures like pseudo-Falloppio or seek primarily to justify expensive and exotic herbs such as one finds in Mattioli, nor is his text even remotely a treatise for physicians. Monitoring of breastfeeding is woman's work, whether the mother, a wet nurse, or the midwife who calls to see how the baby is doing and offers follow-up advice throughout infancy. The enterprise will go better with this book at hand.

Too little milk may result from breasts unable to draw enough blood from the uterus, either because the mammary veins are too narrow or too dilated or because the blood has become drained of the heat needed for conversion to milk, due perhaps to body fever or else the pain and fatigue of giving birth. Purges, herbals, and ointments may help, but look first to correcting errors in the mother's daily routine. Lack of milk goes with being too hot and dry, so the woman needs to do things that make her wetter and colder. Keep her room humid by sprinkling it with water, vinegar, and leaves from cane, grapes, and grain. Let her sleep longer than usual because being awake dries out the body. Avoid exercise so strenuous that it heats her body; sexual intercourse is doubly bad because it also provokes menstruation and dries up the milk. She should not undergo bloodlettings and must eat moderately, always emphasizing quality: boiled chicken, capon, partridge, and veal. More milk comes with eating rice cooked with sheep's milk and sugar-coated almonds; for poor women, rice and milk cooked as for *polenta* are just fine. Butter and drinks made from barley also are good; too much wine is to be avoided, especially sweet and heavy varieties; skip the salted meats and fish. Broth and other simple liquids are excellent for abundant milk. Try a bowl of milk with some melon seeds and sugar before bedtime. If it is really necessary, in the morning give the woman a soup made with almonds, pistachios, and pine nuts in a capon broth seasoned with borax, endive, and melon seeds.

Mercurio goes on to advise that if lactation does not improve with these initial suggestions, then maybe it would be a good idea to consult a physician, since he knows the patient best and can judge how much purgation or ingestion is necessary to put the bodily humors in balance. But then he immediately adds that if the doctor does not want to come or if the patient does not wish to call him (probably for economic reasons, although the friar does not say), then further remedies to be administered by the midwife are at hand anyway. He recommends a variety of soups made mostly from leafy vegetables with a little chicken or veal, both to eat and to use as a wash for the breasts; put an agate around the patient's neck and massage her breasts, squeezing them hard after soaking your hands in warm white wine spiced with mint, rose, and violet petals. Dry the breasts and rub them with an ointment of white lily oil, musk, and crushed lada leaves. More herbal remedies follow.[36]

An excess of milk can be even more dangerous than a paucity, because if an infant overfills his stomach and cannot digest, the residual vapors go to his head, causing convulsions or epileptic fits. The underlying reason always will be too much blood being converted to milk, due to an excessively wet and cold body. In order to dry and heat the body, thereby reducing the milk supply, long walks are ideal, as well as lots of exercise, body rubs with rough towels, fasting, and abstaining from drink. Open windows in the room so as to get the dry northern winds circulating throughout. Eat roasted meats and salted fish; sprinkle saffron and cumin on your food. Best of all is a good bloodletting. (All of these remedies are merely the logical opposites of what to do if there is too little milk, except that Mercurio's logic does not go so far as to recommend plenty of sexual intercourse.) Until the supply of milk is properly reduced, put the baby with another woman or even give animal's milk. Some say you can rid yourself of excess milk by using a glass instrument (breast pump), but this is not a good idea because more disgorging just stimulates more milk. These days many mothers, especially among the rich and the aristocracy, choose not to breast-feed their children, so it is important to know how to prevent milk from coming into the breasts at all. For this there is an ointment followed by a plaster (with explicit directions for each), which will send blood already in the breasts back to the uterus, from which it will be expelled after about fifteen days.[37]

Problems with quality of milk are numerous and can be quite complex. As anyone today who has breast-fed knows, even mothers who do not hold firmly to bodily humors theory, eating onions, garlic, and spicy foods generally, or drinking heavy wines, quickly affects the milk. More subtle interactions and allergies also are possible, both in the mother's digestive system and the baby's. In the sixteenth century, when digestive problems were much harder to overcome and easily led to an infant's death, rapid diagnosis of what might be wrong with the milk was essential. There would have been no point in trying to improve the baby's digestion, since animal milk definitely was a worse alternative and nothing else was available, so everything focused on the mother or wet nurse. This was surely an area where an advice manual addressed to midwives had a dissemination far beyond the person who bought the book and could read it. At least that seems to be Mercurio's aim in casting aside occasionally dubious folk wisdom on this subject and replacing it with authority derived from the ancient physicians, now reduced to simple tests people could do for themselves. Take a sparkling white piece of cloth, wet it in the milk, and set it out to dry in the shade, he begins. If the dried cloth is yellowish, then the problem is intemperance, if dark, then melancholy, if spotted and bad smelling, then phlegmatic. Once the defect is diagnosed, change the diet and sleeping/exercise patterns in accordance with what has been written in the previous chapters about a deficient or excessive milk supply or in the next chapter on coagulation problems.[38]

Advice on treating coagulation presents some difficulty for Mercurio because the experts are not in total agreement on the causes. Everyone accepts that milk is composed of calcium, butter, and serum, and that if all three coagulate in the breast, they form something like a piece of cheese, known as *caseatione* (casein); conversely, if the calcium and butter dissolve but the serum remains, then little globules form, like chickpeas, and this is called *grumefattione*. Most physicians follow Hippocrates, who held that excessive coldness and wetness cause both conditions, but Avicenna, citing the findings of Aristotle and Galen that milk coagulates when heated, held that excessive bodily heat must be the cause of breast lumps. Since diametrically opposite recommendations on diet would follow from the two conflicting theories on cause, the friar is in a quandary. He escapes in a way that captures nicely why and for whom he is writing: "I already have protested that I do not wish to make my Midwife into a disputant but only to instruct her in the things necessary to do her job." This being the case, he chooses to give advice on a corrective diet based on the cold/wet theory adhered to by the majority of experts, even though the other side might be correct. The proper regimen is the same one prescribed for reducing milk supply, including the recommendation for bloodletting, repeated with just a few minor variations.

Now that this dilemma is out of the way, Mercurio cannot resist a wonderful aside meant to undermine classical authority generally and to tout new-age science: "Here it is appropriate to say that I do not know where Aristotle had his head when he affirmed in Book Seven, Chapter Eleven of his 'History of Animals' that a single hair swallowed by a woman could produce this illness (coagulation of breast milk), since as a Philosopher and a Physician he could have known that this is impossi-

ble, since food loses half its weight in the stomach upon first digestion
and then passes through very fine veins to the liver where a second digestion turns it into blood." More ridicule follows as Mercurio traces the
imaginary hair back up to the spongy breast before he concludes:

> In sum, it is fatal for great men to be led astray by little women who
> tell big lies *(piantare grande carote)*. Like we said above, the eminent
> Tertullian made a clown of himself writing about their moods and
> tastes, and Averroes told that stupidity about how a woman could
> get pregnant in the bathtub without knowing a man [from sperm
> emissions he had left while bathing on a prior occasion], and now our
> Aristotle gets shot down, like they say happened to Vessalio [Andreas
> Vesalius] by some Madame Gossip, when he says we should believe
> that a hair has more impact in our body than an armed man does
> at a spectacle.[39]

Even more clearly aimed at mothers themselves than Mercurio, who
directs his advice to midwives, is Savonarola's tract addressed to the
women of Ferrara. His chapter on treating inadequacy of milk supply
will be long and detailed, he apologizes, but since he "wishes always to
do good and to please the ladies," he hopes it will not be judged "prolix"
or "tedious," indeed that "reading it will prove to be a delight and very
fruitful." Most of the advice is on supervising closely the diet and daily
activities of a resident wet nurse, although the same recommendations
would apply to a mother who nursed her own child; nothing in the chapter could be applied to a wet nurse living at a distance. Fathers must not
complain about spending a bit more money on feeding the wet nurse a
healthful diet, one rich enough to make plenty of blood for milk conversion. Mothers must observe carefully the wet nurse's milk, adjusting her
diet to make her blood warmer and drier or cooler and wetter as appropriate, choosing foods and cooking methods similar to those we have
seen already in Mercurio (rehashed by all authors, from classical writers onward, and similar in the essentials to what may be found in late-
twentieth-century dietary recommendations for nursing mothers).

At the end of all this sensible advice about moderation in diet, Savonarola offers an aside he hopes will be a special delight for his readers; in
turn, I shall share it with you. The doctor knows on good authority that
along the Dalmatian coast in towns within the Venetian domain there
are women in league with the devil who use incantations to steal each
other's milk. They cast a spell that not only dries up completely their
victim's breasts but also transfers abundant lactation to themselves.

Then, if the deprived woman appeals to the magistrate or mayor, under threat of punishment, the witch restores her milk.[40]

Child Rearing: Physical Health

If we take seriously what sixteenth-century-Italian advice manuals have to say, then protecting children's health was of utmost concern to their parents. Evidence is abundant that girls as well as boys were cherished, well treated, and sometimes spoiled a bit. Even the oft-repeated recommendation to breast-feed boys for as long as two years while for girls eighteen months should be sufficient, however discriminatory that may sound to modern ears, followed logically from accepted views about their relative hot/cold, wet/dry balance of bodily humors. The wetter and colder girls needed to switch earlier to more solid, hot and dry foods, while boys could continue nursing until age two before incurring the danger of becoming blockheads, literally soft in the brain. What is not written also matters. Whereas diatribes against using a wet nurse undoubtedly mean that wet nurses in fact were employed, especially among elites, the absence of warnings that parents should take an active role in raising their sons and daughters suggests that abandonment or indifference were not frequent. Rather, mother and father needed advice, or at the very least writers of advice manuals thought they did, on how to channel parental concern into bringing up their children properly.

Savonarola sets the tone, both in regard to the folksiness of his recommendations and in their clearly benign, supportive intent. Look first to the air that surrounds the infant. Air that is either too warm or too cold can be dangerous, but cold air is always more to be feared because it quickly leads to fatal respiratory problems, aches, worms, and fevers. The cool fog that descends frequently in the Po Valley brings the added threat of excess humidity. Mothers should be especially careful to wash the baby's head using a very mild soap, dry him thoroughly, and wrap a towel around his head; if you let him go around with a wet head until it dries in the air, then much of the humidity will descend to his eyes and chest. Even if the sun is shining, first dry his head and then let him take in the warmth of the sun. If the day is cold, then heat up the towel before using it to dry his head. Bathing is very good for the baby's growth because it maintains the humidity his body needs and rids him of edema, so you should bathe him as often as three or four times each month, even until the age of six.

The infant's exercise should be moderate but regular. During the bath is one occasion for calisthenics. Another is around feeding time. After putting the baby in his cradle, rock him, but gently, so the milk in his stomach does not slosh around. Watch out for a wet nurse who swings the cradle impetuously or on a slippery floor or with her left hand so that the baby falls out and lands on one of his limbs and remains permanently crippled or deformed. Yet another good opportunity for healthful exertion is to let the baby cry a little while before giving him milk. Finally, with the baby in the wet nurse's arms, you should dangle something pleasing like a rose or a jewel to attract his attention and encourage him to move his eyes, head, neck, and shoulders. Gently raise and lower his arms, get him to laugh by tickling him a little, and maybe lift him onto his toes and blow on him to get his whole body moving. Only then give him the breast.

Let the baby sleep as much as he wants because rest is better for his body than being awake. Do not overfeed; each baby absorbs a different amount of nourishment, so it is not possible to write down how much is too much. You must use your own discretion. If the baby is constipated, try some barley sugar, honey, or beet sugar, or perhaps a spoonful of broth with honey or butter, or milk with sugar or broth with sugar. Never frighten the baby; sing a lively tune, but soothingly, to put him in good spirits. Until his teeth come in, there is no reason to nourish him with anything beyond milk, but if you must do so for whatever reason, then give him a thoroughly cooked piece of bread soaked in oil or almond milk or broth, with the least possible saffron. Infants have very few needs, so no other rules are necessary for proper care at this stage.

When the baby's first teeth come in, usually around eight or nine months, it is time to add to his diet so he gets more solid nutriments than milk alone can provide. Food should be well chewed and given at regular intervals, not frequently as with milk. "And look, you woman, if your teeth are rotten and you have bad breath, don't make the baby suffer by eating from your mouth but give the food to some healthy young person to chew." When you (or whoever) chew for the baby, first rinse your mouth with wine or water, then chew a mouthful and spit it out; then chew another mouthful to actually give the baby. This is because your mouth, especially in the morning before you have eaten yourself, is filled with harmful vapors rising from your stomach or with catarrh that has descended from your head. Next give the baby some bread soaked in honeyed water to help him grow, or else bread soaked in watered wine or maybe milk, or perhaps some rice thoroughly cooked in milk. Whatever you choose, the critical thing is that the food be humid, because humidity extends the body and helps growth, whereas dryness impacts everything. Dry bread alone is not really good; it's much better to imitate the ways of poor people who, having only stale and coarse bread, soak it for the baby in very watered-down wine.

Rich people err in giving the baby bread saturated in good wine, saying it will make his head strong and protect him against worms. Remember instead what the great Avicenna says, that giving robust wine to a child is like adding fire to fire in weak wood. Better to go without the wine, which can cause fevers and other complications. Stay with broth made from quality meats, prechewed bites of these cooked meats, and diluted wine. Don't overfeed because this can cause vomiting, overextension of the stomach, and a lifetime of gluttony.

To soothe the inflammations of early teething, rub a little hare's brain or butter of chicken fat on the gums morning and evening. When the baby begins to speak, you'll need to cleanse his tongue frequently with salt and honey. Also very good is to rub his neck and throat with oil and give him plenty of barley broth, both to drink and to rub on his gums. When the gums become less sore, which you'll know when he bites down on your finger, let him chew on a root of blue lily to heal the ulcerations.[41]

As the baby grows, really right through to age seven or so, continue to watch against drafts of air, just as when he was an infant. Gradually introduce more chewy meats but always of high quality, and the same goes for bread. Keep wines to a minimum, always diluted, and choose whites over heavy reds. Stay away from fruits and other foods that physicians advise are harmful to bodily balances. Serve modest portions and get the child used to four servings daily: breakfast, lunch, snack, and supper. Put him to bed at an early hour so he gets into the habit of rising early, because for sure a good riser is a good worker (*buono levadore è buono lavoradore* is the play on words in the original). But above all, if he wants to sleep more, let him, and do not force him to get out of bed.

When the baby is ready to take his first steps, put him at a bench, always with someone standing behind him, in case he starts to fall. Do not walk around holding him by the arms because a sudden movement could dislocate them. A circular table of wood is safer than a bench because you can follow him all around. As baby gets more sure of his little legs, hold the table a bit away so he can take a few steps but always with someone behind him to protect him from falling backwards. When he is surefooted at this, he is ready for the baby walker. Place it against a wall for support, toss a toy or an apple near him, and coax him to go get it and return to you, so that gradually you teach him to lead and follow. Beginning at around twenty to twenty-four months, let him play with other children, climbing on a log, running, playing catch with a ball, scampering freely to and fro. Once he is three years old, begin to restrain him with quiet times when you start to teach him moral lessons, about which more later. And, once again, follow the advice of Avicenna to bathe him frequently.[42]

Illnesses in children were very dangerous in the sixteenth century, resulting in death far more frequently than in our own day. Physicians knew the perils and wrote numerous treatises in Latin specifically on treatment of children's diseases. These works were meant for specialists, not for a popular audience, and so we shall not be examining them specifically, but it is important to note their existence as part of our overall understanding of how Italian parents at that time cared for their children. The most important of these medical texts include those of Paolo Bagellardo, first printed in 1472, which was followed by numerous later editions; Michelangelo Biondo, initially printed in 1539; Leonello Vittori, with editions throughout the sixteenth century; Ognibene Ferrari, for an illustrated text with many reprintings; Girolamo Mercuriale (not to be confused with Mercurio the author of *La commare*), for influential works both on children's diseases and on gymnastic exercise; and at the end of the century, Jacobus Trunconius. Although it should not be imagined that a distinct subdiscipline of pediatrics already existed, the book market makes clear that Italian physicians must have been called on frequently to cure children's illnesses. The doctors apparently did not approach these patients as "little adults" but instead consulted specialized, rather expensive texts advising them how to diagnose and treat sick children. Parents did not abandon their children, ignore them, or neglect to spend money on their care. The popular-advice manuals parents might have had at hand—the ones we are perusing in these pages—specifically warn readers about the difficulties of applying home remedies to children's ailments, quite the opposite of the confidence they exhibit in making recommendations about overcoming sexual dysfunctions and coping with the discomforts of pregnancy.[43]

Savonarola, who throughout his work displays great respect, even affection, for the women readers of Ferrara whom he takes as his audience, and who had no qualms about giving detailed advice on everything from techniques of sexual foreplay to brewing all sorts of herbal elixirs, plasters, and ointments, sounds the alarm loudly:

> Since I was more interested in satisfying women than men, I decided to provide cures for certain infirmities that occur in infants during breast-feeding and while in the arms of a nurse. After that, however, fathers should have greater care over children, using the

support of physicians, but this does not exclude entirely providing some remedies women can also use in giving succor to older children.

If one wanted to write about every infirmity that could occur, it would require translating all of medicine into the vernacular and that would not be useful for women, not even literate women, and would place on me the heavy burden of maybe causing more deaths than cures by putting medical knowledge into the hands of practitioners working without any fear, relying only on prescriptions without understanding the rules on when and how to apply them, like those quack doctors who do not fear God.[44]

From Friar Mercurio we get an equally complex warning. All over Italy, he laments, people think that doctors are not necessary for treating children's illnesses, just as they are not needed to attend to pregnant women. But this is not true. Children need doctors more than anyone else because they are filled with maladies even before they are old enough to say what is wrong and exactly where it hurts. While they cannot take various kinds of medicines as well as an adult, this does not mean you should give up, just as you do not abandon the study of theology or philosophy because it is hard. Even if the child does nothing but cry, the doctor still can feel for body temperature, check the pulse rate, and examine the stool. Even an infant who cannot be given medicine internally can be cured externally, either with body rubs or by altering his milk supply. The manna, prunes, syrups, and so forth that the nurse or mother ingests will pass through her blood to her milk and then to the baby, thereby healing him. This works to reduce high fever and also to treat chicken pox and dysentery. Renowned physicians such as Girolamo Mercuriale have proved that children's illnesses can be treated. Not getting medical attention for a sick child is dangerous even to the republic, which thereby risks losing a future senator or similarly distinguished citizen. And if the doctor concludes that the baby became sick because of some bad behavior by the wet nurse (such as drinking too much or eating spicy foods), or if she won't take the medicines ordered for the baby, then drive her away like the mortal enemy of an innocent creature that she is; and if you were to give her a beating on the way out, that would be indiscreet but quite necessary.

At one level, Mercurio's plea fits with the admonition typical in "popular-errors" books for readers to turn to professional physicians, in this case emphasizing the need for doctors in child rearing. But I think it also does more, especially if it is read in the context of his major earlier book, *La commare*. Years of practice as a roving public-health officer throughout the Po Valley had convinced Friar Scipione, as he was widely known, that parents were overly fatalistic about the possibility their sons and daughters would not survive. Man of God that he was, he offered detailed, folksy, doable household advice on how to thwart "God's will" with human intervention. Going to the doctor was a last resort, one Mercurio knew from experience that most folks did not even consider for their children. So, following an appeal on behalf of professionalism that he knew would fall on deaf (or impoverished) ears, he turned to his true mission, which was stated so eloquently in the passage quoted at length in my opening chapter: bringing medical knowledge to laypersons who might therefore better heal themselves.

One common practice in the Lombardy region that Mercurio cannot resist mentioning before closing out this chapter in his book on popular errors in Italy is to let the baby who has started to walk on his own go all about the house, falling hundreds of times every day on his head, forehead, and face. The cumulative damage weakens the baby's head, leaves him deformed, and sometimes kills him. He becomes susceptible to headaches, dizziness, and loss of memory. The friar recalls that during his boyhood in Rome, rich and poor parents alike protected their child with a kind of helmet made of cotton wrapped in sarcenet and wound in the form of a cross around the forehead, down to the eyebrows, and over the top of the head. Because it is light and open at the top, the baby does not sweat.[45]

For practical advice on home cures for children's maladies, Mercurio urges readers of his *De gli errori popolari d'Italia* to turn to his earlier work, *La commare*. Unlike the prolific Fioravanti, who repeatedly tells readers that they need to obtain all six of his books in order to be sure of curing themselves, Mercurio claims to be less interested in selling books than in saving oil and ink. Since he has nothing new to say on the subject, anything he repeats from the earlier work would be simply a copy, not a composition, because once you know from *La commare* what you should be doing, then all else is an "error," as anyone who reads the book will see with utmost clarity. So, we turn to the middle of book 3 of *La commare*, with its twenty-eight chapters on childhood illnesses that presumably can be cured at home without calling a doctor, or at least not at the outset. The person nominally still being addressed is the midwife, who indeed may have been called in locally, especially in rural areas, before the parents decided to take the baby on a distant journey to see a physician. In other instances we may assume that mothers and fathers used the advice to do what they could when their baby awoke in the night with a fever or a rash or crying inexplicably. The chapters are arranged to suit a layperson with little medical training, divided according to whether the condition's cause is internal or external (although chicken pox appears externally, the cause is internal). Within this division, the chapters start with afflictions of the entire body and then move from head to toe.

First the internal conditions: fevers, chicken pox, swollen body, shriveled body, suppurations, epilepsy, convulsions, paralysis and torpor, nightmares, sleeplessness, runny nose, congested nose, coughs, breathing difficulties, earaches, strep throat, tongue and lip sores and cracks, ulcerations under the tongue, teething pain, hiccups, vomiting, bedwetting, retained urine, urinary-tract stone, constipation, diarrhea, intestinal blockage, body aches, and worms.

And then come the external problems: cradle cap, lice, water on the brain, inflamed and red eyes, crossed eyes, cracked lips, scrofula, umbilical growth or inflammation, and distended large intestine.

In virtually every chapter, Mercurio warns readers that if symptoms persist or appear to be getting worse, or if matters seem very grave from the outset, then call for a doctor immediately. Also common to most chapters is treatment through the baby's milk supply rather than by direct ingestion of anything. Because all the sores, fevers, flows, and blockages listed according to where they break out are a result of some imbalance in the four bodily humors, the way to heal the child is to eliminate an excessive humor or supplement an inadequate one. Fevers are lowered by cooling the body, suppurations by reducing both heat and wetness. You dry out a swollen body or a bout of diarrhea, whereas you increase wetness for constipation or to flush out a urinary stone. To accomplish these changes, the mother or wet nurse adjusts her diet, and a few hours later the resulting alteration of her milk gets to the baby's body. To take just one example, Mercurio recommends complete abstention from wine by the nurturer when the baby has a fever; moreover, do not give him the breast every time he cries but instead slake his thirst with a dab of broth with vinegar and sugar on the tongue. Further relieve the fever with compresses on the abdomen.

Many people believe that certain conditions, like chicken pox, arise from bad menstrual blood retained by the baby after its birth. They think there is no way to cure this by altering the milk supply, so you should just let the disease run its course and avoid scratching and popping the pustules and causing permanent scars. But Mercurio explains in language he believes a midwife or mother will understand that the menstrual-blood explanation cannot be true because lower animals, who also are nourished in the uterus, do not get chicken pox, nor did the ancient Greeks. Moreover, some menstrual blood is very pure, not defective in any way, yet many children of mothers with good menstrual blood still get chicken pox, whereas other children of mothers with clearly impure blood do not get the disease. So what is Mercurio's explanation for the lay reader? He accepts the theory of Girolamo Mercuriale (one of the contemporary authors of Latin works on children's illnesses mentioned earlier) that around the time of Avicenna some sort of pox, initially probably carried in the air, became a hereditary condition that predisposed certain people to get the disease. Chicken pox arises not from residual menstrual blood but from subtle humors found in all blood, technically called "ichor." The blood of the ancient Greeks contained ichor, but because they had not been exposed to the original airborne pox, it is only since the time of Avicenna that the disease has spread, and now it has become ubiquitous. At first it was very difficult to cure, but like all diseases that originate in the celestial constellations, over the centuries its potency has abated. Now people do not even bother to call a doctor to cure the disease. It is to be expected that syphilis will follow a similar course. (This highly rational explanation, some of it not so alien to our modern sensibilities, is all the more remarkable for the inclusion of a possible application to syphilis, which elsewhere is seen as a scourge of God to punish licentious sexual behavior.)

Even if there is no cure for chicken pox and the disease is rarely fatal, mothers should take care to keep the baby covered without creating a danger of suffocation, lessen the baby's food intake, have pure water at hand for the baby to sip, and wash the baby's eyes frequently so no pox form there and cause blindness. Separate washes are given for the rich, which include dunking a piece of gold in the flush, and for the poor, who can make do with breast milk and rose water. If the baby scratches too much, make him soft mittens and pin his covered hands to his sides. There is some dispute about whether you should prick the heads of the pustules when they turn white, but if you do so, which Mercurio thinks is all right, be sure to use a pin of gold or silver; otherwise, just let them dry out on their own. Rubbing the dried sores with human fat, or much better with human sperm taken from the father or carefully from the mother, does wonders.

Shriveling of the baby's body may be caused by a witch's spell, and this requires parents to seek the aid of an exorcist or a blessing from the church. But more likely the baby has worms or his milk supply lacks nutrition because his mother or wet nurse has lost too much of her vital force by engaging frequently in the pleasures of Venus. Once again, moderate the mother's habits or diet and things will improve. So also for nightmares, sleeplessness, and sudden tremors or fears—all are caused by a disturbed stomach. Earaches take too long to be cured by diet and must be treated immediately with drops of almond oil, dill, or chamomile. Have the baby sleep on the bad ear so the pressure is relieved; keep him out of rain and wind. Mothers should not put plasters on cradle cap and other such skin eruptions because doing so just keeps the bad, imbalanced humors inside the baby; let them out. To straighten the gaze of a baby with a crossed or lazy eye, which was caused in the first instance by carelessly letting too much light shine on one side of the infant so that his eye turned the other way, beam a light across his crib so it lands on the hand you want him to look away from.

Although the above paragraphs condense and select from more than fifty pages of detailed advice, I hope readers have a reasonable sense of what the recommendations are like. I find them to be practical, reasonable, caring, protective without becoming overprotective, direct and easy to follow, not at all fatalistic, and with no hint that suffering is somehow good for the soul or a necessary part of growing up. A few references are made to classical authors such as Hippocrates, Aristotle, and Avicenna, but these strike me as meant to impress the reader without causing any confusion. They are never ponderous or remotely erudite—just a dash here and there that I think would have allowed parents or a midwife to feel comfortable about following these recommendations instead of whatever competing folk wisdom may have held sway in town or village. It does not surprise me at all that Friar Mercurio's advice manual for the humble midwife was translated into several languages and republished more than a dozen times during the next century.[46]

Child Rearing: Good Character

Michele Savonarola begins the final segment of his advice for the women of Ferrara on an uncharacteristically pessimistic note. He who had been so sure in telling readers how to conceive a boy, ease the pains of labor, or eat the right foods to produce healthful milk, and who had even found time for little asides and a few jokes, suddenly becomes a complainer. Everything is happening sooner nowadays, he laments. Three-year-old children are as astute as five- or six-year-old children used to be; those who are five behave like children of seven or eight once did. Life spans seem to be getting shorter. Not all that many people even reach the age of seventy, whereas in the old days lots of folks lived to a hundred or more. Back in biblical times they really grew old; Adam was 930 when he died, Noah 700, and Methuselah 900. (I suppose Savonarola was writing this from memory, since the Bible [Gen. 5:27, 9:28] actually says that Noah lived for 950 years and Methuselah for 969.) What accounts for this decline in longevity? One reason is the conjunction of the stars, but Savonarola says that would take too long to explain. He will write instead about human failings.

First of all, men and women today pamper their stomachs much more than in ancient times. According to Galen, our ancestors ate chestnuts and other coarse foods that made their bodily humors, as well as their spirits, compact and strong. When they were sick, they were able to take really powerful medicines, like hellebore, euphorbia, and mezereon, in large quantities. Our bodies are weak because we eat delicate foods that are liquid and subtle and easily dissolved. A gust of wind blows us to the ground and we get exhausted with any exercise. That is why the air seems to be stronger than in the past, and movements of the constellations have more effect than they once did. "You delicate gentleman and you delicate lady, with your lifestyle you will die much sooner than peasants and burghers." If you want your children to live a long life, get them accustomed to coarse foods, but do so gradually *(puoco a puoco)*, because they are already so fragile at birth that they cannot withstand much.

> Oh woman reader, think, if this first explanation seems pertinent, how much more you will appreciate my next caution: young men and women should stop having sex. Woman, I want you to know that in ancient times, more precisely not even two hundred years ago, men did not marry before the age of twenty-five and women were at least eighteen. Nature being what it is, sexual intercourse did not debilitate either partner, in fact it made them stronger and they had healthier babies because each had strong seeds.

Today our youth marry before their time. The nutriments that should go to strengthening their limbs are dissipated on superfluities; they remain feeble and their weak seeds produce frail offspring who die early.

With this opening judgment before the reader, Savonarola shifts to the main subject of this part of his treatise—proper moral upbringing for children. He invokes none of the Christian authorities but instead cites his Islamic medical hero Avicenna, who says that fathers must always act so as to improve the comportment of their children. This can only be done by exercising great prudence and by encouragement so as to gain the child's honest desire to please—not by forcing him against his will and not by making him angry or fearful: "Force and scare tactics result in habitual anger and fear which offend the child's total complexion because of the heat that flows from anger and the melancholy that accompanies fear and sadness. The health of the child's body and mind consists in the moderation of his ways."[47]

Once again I want to pause a moment here to consider some implications of Savonarola's approach to child rearing, one found in most of the texts considered in the remainder of this chapter. My colleague Philip Greven wrote an important book several years ago titled *Spare the Child*, in which he documents in all its horrors the practice in Christian culture of beating and whipping children, along with the excuses for doing so. Greven's condemnation of such treatment is uncompromising, and his assessment of the consequences in our own times merits close attention. It is a book I recommend heartily to all parents, one that I gave my own daughter when her first child was born. Greven analyzes how passages in the Bible have been used to justify inflicting the lash upon children, and he explores how in America today fundamentalist preachers quote from Scripture as they take their places among the most prominent advocates of corporal punishment.

Sixteenth-century Italians living during the Catholic Reformation obviously also knew something of the Bible, and so it might be expected that advice manuals from this time would recommend great firmness and even physical beating as a means of making children behave. They do not. Indeed, as we shall see, even the authoritative *Catechism of the Council of Trent* condemns excessive harshness toward children. The very essence of the Judeo-Christian justification for physical beating, which is to break the child's will, is precisely what the Italian manuals say must not be done. They tell readers how best to strengthen the child's will so that he may choose on his own to do what is right. Greven never intended to comment on sixteenth-century Italy, so of course I am not suggesting that his findings are incorrect. Indeed, I believe they are devastatingly accurate for the American culture he focuses on. What interests me instead is how one might explain the presence of such a reflective, even lenient style of rearing children in an Italian society that surely is part of western Christianity.[48]

Renaissance scholars long have known that humanist educators recommended tolerance in rearing children, so I am telling them nothing new here. That the same permissiveness should infuse the popular manuals, albeit with some interesting modifications, does not surprise us either, since we already have seen that manual writers copied each other and the classical texts all the time. The explanation by modern Renaissance scholars for all this leniency among humanist theorists is that they adopted entirely the writings of Plutarch and Quintilian, which espouse the same ideas.[49] But that strikes me as invoking an uncaused cause. In the panoply of writings available to humanists, as to experts on child rearing in all times and places, one can always cite advocates of beating children and others who advise exactly the opposite. In the Bible, for example, it is easy enough to find both disciplinary methods supported with equal vigor and conviction. My judgment is that even if Quintilian had not been rediscovered and if Plutarch's essay on education had been denounced then as a false or pseudo-Plutarch (as experts now believe), Renaissance humanists might have expressed themselves a bit differently but would nevertheless have written tracts supporting benign methods of raising children. I cannot prove such a "what if" hypothesis, and I do not intend to try. For me it will be sufficient to provide a few insights on sixteenth-century Italian pedagogy, so you readers can ponder the big questions for yourselves. It also must be admitted that the injunctions we are about to read against breaking children's wills should be taken as evidence that some parents and teachers must have been doing exactly what the advice manuals told them not to do, so I am certainly not arguing that Italian Renaissance children did not get spanked or hit hard on occasion. What I can report is that the manuals do not offer justifications for beating children, which definitely cannot be said of what many parents read in twentieth-century America.[50]

As an example of an archetypal text, let us look briefly at Maffeo Vegio's treatise in praise of liberal education, written in 1444. Although an obscure and anonymous Italian version appeared later, along with a misattributed French translation, it is the Latin printings, beginning in 1491, that most probably influenced the vernacular authors we are considering in depth. A modern scholar convincingly hails the work as "the most systematic and complete of all the Renaissance treatises on education." Maybe it was appropriate that later writers copied so unabashedly from Vegio, because in his own time he had borrowed heavily from Pier Paolo Vergerio's *De ingenuis moribus,* from Guarino da Verona's Latin translation of pseudo-Plutarch's *De liberis educandis,* as well as from newly discovered complete editions of Quintilian and of Cicero's *De oratore.* Although Vegio makes extensive use of Augustine's writings and absolutely reveres the saint's rearing by his holy mother, St. Monica, the humanist does not accept mainstream Christianity's dark view of human nature; what he actually prescribes leans mostly on secular Greco-Roman, not Christian, sources.

What might have confounded less eclectic theologians, Vegio solved easily. He acknowledges numerous biblical injunctions to discipline children severely, even including quotations from the apocryphal book of Ecclesiasticus (30:1, 8–12) and from Proverbs (13:24, 29:15) that tell parents to bow down their child's neck and beat his sides and warn that a willful child shall bring shame upon his mother. Against these harsh words, Vegio sets the authority of St. Paul's letters to the Ephesians (6:4) and to the Colossians (3:21) advising fathers not to discourage children by provoking them to anger. Making the right choices among manifestly conflicting biblical authorities requires parents to consider carefully their baby's disposition. The Old Testament maxims are fine for Jews, a hardheaded and stiff-necked race according to Vegio, but for Christians the New Testament shows the way. Shifting to less anti-Semitic appeals, the humanist reasons that if man can tame dogs, elephants, and even lions, then surely he can tame a child using skill and wisdom. What is needed is not excessive indulgence on the mother's part but steady encouragement, reward, and example from mother, father, and then teacher. The individuality of each soul, itself a staple of medieval theology, is entirely in harmony with classical precepts on child rearing, blended by Vegio into an optimistic mixture of physical, mental, and moral teaching to raise God's perfect creation into a noble citizen.[51]

A century after Vegio wrote his treatise, readers of Italian would have had available to them the translation published in 1545 of Desiderius Erasmus's famous essay "A Declamation on the Subject of Early Liberal Education for Children." The ideas therein are entirely consonant with the advice of Quintilian, Plutarch, Vegio, and every Italian Renaissance humanist who addressed the topic at all, especially the impassioned plea against using force to beat children into submission. What is noteworthy for our purposes is that a text written in the international language of Latin, theoretically addressed to a learned audience that had no need of a vernacular version, should so quickly have been translated after its original appearance in 1529, first into French (1537), then Italian, and even English (1551). It is literally an advice manual, taking the form of a prescriptive letter addressed to Prince William, Duke of Cleves. According to Erasmus himself, however, "the method of education it describes is especially appropriate for children of rulers," and therefore I make no claim that it was a practical-advice manual for the middle class. Yet I do believe that, while we cannot know how many proud parents thought their child worthy of an education befitting a prince, that number was not zero. A copy of Erasmus on child rearing in a vernacular language, not hugely expensive by my best estimate but not cheap either, strikes me as something that well-to-do Renaissance Italians might have wanted to possess. Apparently a publisher agreed and invested in it. Moreover, Erasmus's *Colloquies* were widely read to grammar-school boys, earning them the vociferous condemnation of high prelates as early as 1537.

Thus, the full might of Erasmus's eloquence was there in defense of children and in support of their tender, nurtured upbringing.[52]

What we are finding in Italian Renaissance advice manuals on rearing children remains consistent in both erudite texts and those aimed at a wider audience. This unitary, coherent approach to child rearing begins with advocacy of demand feeding for infants, continues with portrayals of the innocent babe in no danger of becoming spoiled, and carries forward with pages on how to encourage the child to choose good behavior rather than how to punish him for being bad. As in my assessment that wet nursing was a much less common practice than some historians have concluded, so also now, as a result of my reading texts encouraging a loving approach to children—one that nurtured their individual development and did not fear willfulness—I find myself wholeheartedly in agreement with Steven Ozment and the judgment he reached after exploring popular German sources: "Neither belief in original sin nor the experience of high infant mortality inhibited a positive and caring attitude toward the children of Reformation Europe. Such negative associations appear to reflect the logic of a modern mind far more than they do the experience of people in the sixteenth century."[53]

Now let us forego further historiographical digression and return to history, picking up again with Michele Savonarola. When your infant begins to talk and understand what you are saying, usually during his second year, you should encourage his speaking ability by saying things like "My little son . . . ," and filling in his name; simultaneously show him some treat, saying that if he repeats what you just said, he may have it. Women are especially good at doing this. But do not make him afraid of failure or continue at this so long that he becomes melancholic or pusillanimous. Do not let him become languid and lazy but let him run around and play.

Once he has mastered some words, usually between ages two and three, you want to encourage good speech and begin his moral upbringing. Do this by being reverent mothers and fathers, and also insisting upon this in all your relatives, according to their closeness; above all, get on your knees to call piously for help from Jesus and Mary. Say the Hail Mary and the Our Father everyday, and teach him to make the sign of the cross—all things that a Christian matron does so well.

When children reach the age of five, they should start with a teacher for instruction in good habits and in reading, not at those schools where they are cooped up all day but at one that sends them outside to play and exercise. See that the teacher lets them come home for an hour or more at midday, at least until they are fourteen, and that his method uses few blows and many rewards. The teacher should not behave bizarrely but in the old prudent ways, so that the children will have great respect for his age and wisdom. Reverential awe for the teacher should never come solely from fear of getting beaten.

As to spiritual growth, fathers and mothers should take their child to church to check the almanac for what ceremonies are taking place in honor of God. Similarly they should attend prayer services and vespers so that as an adult, the child will return to observe what is already familiar. Find a competent confessor with whom the child can develop a harmonious relationship. Above all, teach the child not to curse; watch out for the company of children who have gone astray or are spoiled. After your child masters the Hail Mary and the Our Father, teach him the Creed, which is the basis of our salvation. Savonarola then adopts a more Augustinian position, although with no citation of that authority, and warns that virtue is not natural but must be acquired through discipline and good habits. The parental role, therefore, is critical in providing nutritious soil for growing the seed they have planted on this earth.

"At the risk of repeating myself," the doctor/moralist continues, find a teacher who cares more about children than about money. "You understand me, man, you too must be diligent and stay away from prostitutes and gambling, wasting more money on them than you would have spent on a good teacher."

As the child grows older, there is more room for punishment. Continue to form good character with encouragement and praise, but now add abjuration, reprehension, fear, and blows, mixing one and the other in good measure, going from shame to praise, and using one as a brake on the other. Remember that he is still young. Do not do as some fathers who push their child to exhaustion, such that he excels over his classmates now but in the process lacks the ability to succeed in the future on his own. Leave time for play. Check daily on what he is doing and examine his homework. Make sure your child's efforts are his own; absolutely do not deal with those mercenaries who work for a price and sell crib notes. "Oh beastly and blind male reader, tie this last bit of advice to your finger, remembering the old saying that the eye of a master fattens his horse."

Father and teacher above all must see to it that the boy exercises his memory, which is the mother of the muses, that is, of the sciences, which rest in its arms. Keep the child away from too much idle talk and from temper tantrums. Encourage him to be benevolent and courteous to others, keeping his hands to himself, not idling on the street and making fun of priests, and above all not telling lies.

You, fathers and mothers of devilish and wicked habits, how can you expect to raise your children properly? Leaving such a bad, vituperative heredity is going to be your downfall. Let it be your own moderation that beats, punishes, and warns your children. Support them with good words and do not turn instantly to spankings. By observing these rules, you will be a good father of good children.

"So, my Ferrarese matron, to whom my little book is addressed, you should read and study what is here. Don't be afraid of the effort, which will prove most useful to you and your little ones. Maybe you say 'who could possibly observe so many rules?' And I answer that these are posted as a complete guide for the rearing of children. Fathers and mothers should be like a mirror so that when their children inspect themselves in it they will know better their own errors and amend these more easily."

Savonarola closes this section, and his entire treatise, with a special appeal to people of humble circumstances:

> All of what has been said here truly can be followed; moreover, poor people can raise their children in the same way, with good habits, making them studious and strong so they grow in virtue. Virtue exalts a man. Those who at present or in the past have found themselves in base conditions or born of vile parents by their own virtue can become rich, counting themselves among exalted doctors, cavaliers, great captains, cardinals and popes. . . . So, you poor who have no goods to leave your children, see that they are virtuous and friends of God.[54]

Matteo Palmieri's *Della vita civile* conveys an equally benign, flexible, folksy approach to child rearing. When the baby is two, we are told, he should play freely with his little friends and engage in all sorts of frivolities. Father should use proper speech and be well mannered with the baby, not indulging him so much that he becomes spoiled and accustomed to softness. What a wicked tongue those parents must have who laugh when a child says a dirty word, who shower him with hugs and kisses when he blasphemes, and who teach him to give the raised-index-finger-insult sign to his own mother. How awful to talk and joke about our own vices in front of our children, to go on about gluttonous encounters with our friends, and to sing lascivious love songs and tell off-color stories. The cautious father should be talking about good, honest things. He should check that the baby's collection of womanish fairy tales contains only those with a moral purpose, the ones that teach him to fear evil and love good—like the one about the hairy, horned ogre waiting in hell while the good boys and girls go to paradise and dance with the angels.

As the child gets older, he should begin to leave the family nest, little by little strengthening his memory skills and eagerness to learn and being introduced to Christian precepts. There is no agreement on a set age at which formal instruction should begin. Some say to wait until age seven because otherwise the mental fatigue is too great, but Palmieri favors the view that an earlier, perhaps less formal start is better, calibrated to the child's predilections and abilities. Try fun things like using fruits or pastry puffs cut in the shapes of different letters, saying this twisted one is an *S* and the round one an *O;* when the baby repeats the correct letter, he gets to eat it. This may seem silly, Palmieri admits, but by starting early, when the boy reaches age seven, he will know what would have been expected of him from ages seven to nine, and by age nine, what is expected of an eleven year old, and so forth. Still, every child learns at a different rate. Do not waste precious time and inquisitiveness, but don't push too hard either.[55]

Next we look at a very official pronouncement, *The Catechism of the Council of Trent.* The eminent Roman Catholic prelates who assembled at Trent and struggled to revitalize their church in response to the challenges of Protestantism went far beyond esoteric theological issues and into the innermost recesses of family life. On the matter of raising children, they chose as their guiding text a single sentence from Paul's letter to the Colossians (3:21): "Fathers, provoke not your children to anger, lest they be discouraged." The words are entirely unambiguous, and nothing in the sentences preceding or following them modifies their injunction. Nonetheless, churchmen apparently felt the need to add some further advice in fulfilling their mission of being good spiritual teachers.

The danger of harshness, they explain, is that you will break your child's spirit, rendering him of abject mind, afraid of everything. Reprove your children as appropriate, but do not avenge yourself upon them. Of course children sometimes commit faults that require reproach and chastisement; when they do, parents must not be overly indulgent and forego correction, for children often have been ruined by parents who are too lenient. Finally, parents should "not enter into preposterous designs; for there are very many whose sole thought and concern it is to leave their children wealth, riches, an ample and splendid patrimony; who encourage them not to piety and religion or to the pursuit of honorable and virtuous things but to avarice and to the increase of patrimony; and who, provided their children be rich and wealthy, are regardless of those qualities that would ensure their reputation and salvation."[56] If the assembled clergy at Trent had had in front of them a copy of Savonarola's advice to the matrons of Ferrara, they could hardly have restated his argument more accurately, although their text admittedly has less style and verve. In fact, they could have had before them any of dozens of Italian Renaissance texts on child rearing—such as those of Vegio, Palmieri, or even Pope Pius II (Enea Silvio Piccolomini)—for it was commonly accepted that parents should not break a child's will or spirit, that they should not strike in anger or revenge, that they themselves with their worldliness and greed were the biggest cause of children going astray, and that they should teach primarily by example, not by proscription.[57]

Not content with the proselytizing being done throughout Catholic Europe by the new catechism, and perhaps suspicious of the rather generous tendencies of Renaissance humanist tracts, the powerful future saint Charles Borromeo, archbishop of Milan, asked fellow Cardinal Silvio Antoniano to write a book on Christian education.[58] He specifically requested a treatise that would enlighten the upper class in society while reaching out to the masses. In 1584, after some complaining by Borromeo about how long the task was taking, Antoniano published a substantial work, judged by one scholar to be the Catholic Reformation's most important text on pedagogy. Some sections primarily address teachers, while others directly exhort parents about doing what is right for their children's salvation. According to a modern devotee, Catholic Reformation prelates pushed the book hard; it was adopted as a textbook in Catholic schools and read publicly in churches to assembled parents. Eventually it went through eleven editions.

I shall say that I found the first two parts quite boring, and I think parents who got through the whole thing must have been very devout. Even though the writing is in an easy vernacular style that shuns both classical erudition and perpetual biblical citation, I am not sure how successful the work would have been as a popular-advice manual without official backing. Let us skip over the first part, which thunders about the importance of child rearing and the sanctity of marriage, and the second, which treats each of the ten commandments and how youths should obey them, and move directly to the next seventy pages on the specifics of a Christian education for children. Antoniano wished above all to be understood by the average person, and in this he succeeds admirably, but the message has far too much hellfire and brimstone for my taste. On the other hand, Pope Pius XI made a much more positive assessment, incorporating many of Antoniano's views into his 1926 encyclical, *Christian Education of Youth*. He termed the work a "golden treatise" written by a "holy and learned Cardinal to whom the cause of Christian education is greatly indebted." Anyway, let us read the message, greatly abbreviated.[59]

The seeds of each and every sin in the huge array of human transgressions are within us at birth, ready to germinate at different times in our
lives. In adolescents, sins of the flesh burst forth (about which more in
the next chapter) and in older people, avarice flourishes. Among children, the inclination to cover their shortcomings by telling lies crops up
first. They prefer to play and will make any excuse to avoid school and
serious study. They want to do whatever they see someone else doing;
whatever a playmate has, they want it too. They are disobedient, unwilling to do anything that displeases them; they lie to avoid being punished.
All this continues until about the age of fourteen. Children are thieves,
usually of little things at the beginning. But allowing petty stealing to go
unpunished is like letting worms crawl and survive until they become
giant serpents. Human nature has a poison within all of us, the infection
of original sin. Concupiscence of the flesh rebels against our spirit and
leads us toward evil. Beyond dispute, this is true of children as well, who
seek only sweet things that delight their senses.

All is not hopeless, however, and there are remedies at hand if only
we will apply them. Children must be taught to fear the just wrath of
God. They must be raised in paternal reverence and obedience by parents who themselves set good examples of proper behavior and speech,
and who discipline with a mix of love and fear. Governing a family is
like governing a city, with the father as magistrate. He must use the rod
and the whip to correct his children, to keep them from evil and incline
them toward good, just as the biblical Solomon wrote. Many fathers are
overindulgent, especially the rich or those whose only child is a son.
Some of these excessively protective fathers run in to protest if the teacher
so much as gives their son a mild slap.

On the other hand, and this "other hand" takes up five pages against
only two for advice to use the rod, too much beating is also bad and
usually counterproductive. The prelate unequivocally condemns those
fathers and teachers who strike in anger, who let the impulse of their
passions rule their judgment, who beat for every little thing. Their rage
is such that their entire bodies shake, they scream, their faces turn red,
the pupils of their eyes glisten with fire; truth be said, their corrections
are a bigger sin than the original offenses. Leaving aside the issue of
whose sin is greater, many times such beatings render the child so bewildered and dazed that he does not get the fruit that should come from
correction. Instead, he quickly learns to become irascible and furious,
thereby doubling the harm.

Corporal punishment cures sin best when used like a medicine, administered moderately, with pauses to judge the effects of different dosages.

Fear of God and the love of doing good are always more effective than a beating. Use of the rod should be rare, although on those occasions when it is used, sufficient to carry real pain. In sum, Father Antoniano slowly concludes, the good father who intends to beat his son should be guided not by blind rage but by reasoned discretion. Fathers and teachers who mindlessly strike children in any part of their bodies within reach, especially in the head, are to be censured. The head is the seat of all the sentiments, where nature has placed those instruments meant to serve the mind's most noble gestures. Those who yank a poor boy by the hair and dangle him in the air or bang his head against the wall, or down against the bench, are unequivocally condemned. Also shameful are those who ferociously whip the child's face and eyes, leaving him permanently scarred or deformed. There is yet another danger in such behavior. When the father's anger finally abates, he feels love again and repents what he has done—or in the case of the teacher, the child's parents and relatives sharply importune him—the result being that the excessive beater now goes to the opposite extreme and refuses ever to hit or let anyone else hit children, the harm of which each person can imagine for himself.[60]

Much better would be for fathers and teachers to try St. Basil's rules for disciplining young monks. Let the punishment be related directly to the sin committed. If someone eats too much at one meal, he gets substantially less at his next sitting. If he eats too soon, there will be a long delay before tomorrow's dinner is served. On diet in general, however, Antoniano takes a remarkably relaxed approach. Children, especially girls, should drink little or no wine, and their meals should emphasize simple foods with a good balance of dry and wet items. There is no point in making children wait until fixed hours for meals, as they have different needs than adults. If they are hungry before lunch, then provide them with a healthful snack—no meat or cheese but perhaps a piece of bread, an apple, and dried figs or raisins. The church in its wisdom does not require people under age twenty-one to observe rigorous fasting; while parents may wish to impose some seasonal restrictions, these should be moderate.

Sleep and dress are the prelate's next concerns. Getting up early is good for bodily health, and morning is the best time for studying philosophy. As the biblical Solomon says, do not sleep too much or you will fall into poverty, so it is wise to get children accustomed to rising early. When the children do get up, see that they do not waste a lot of time, particularly the girls, on combing their hair, washing themselves with perfumed soaps, and excessive brushing of teeth. These vices are all the greater in rich families.

Modest dress applies to boys and even more to girls, but the real problem is with their parents who set such bad examples. Although this is a book about rearing children, Father Antoniano cannot resist noting the terrible indecency of all those supposedly honest matrons who go around in dresses with such plunging necklines that their entire breasts show, including their nipples. Just as indecent are those women who attire themselves so you would think they were men. Then there are those disrespectful women who do not wear a head veil in church, and are accompanied by husbands who keep their hats on. "I want you to know that Christ is the head of man and the head of woman is man."

Following this diatribe, clearly addressed to laypersons, the prelate returns to his main theme, again advising parents directly but in a more reasoned fashion. All boys, rich and poor, should be sent to school to learn reading, writing, and arithmetic. Girls need less, just enough reading to get through a simple prayer book and a bit of writing. Rich girls may be introduced to elementary arithmetic, but the dangers of female vanity being great, it is better that all females attend primarily to sewing and domestic chores. Certainly there is no reason to teach them rhetoric. Children should go to school voluntarily; it will not take force to get them there if you use the right encouragement. The most important thing about a school is that it have good teachers who are well trained, well ordered in their own lives, and deserving of admiration. Public schools are bad because even if the teacher is morally upright, there are likely to be wicked boys in the classroom. While rich people might continue to follow the old practice of having a private tutor come to their homes, other parents might do better to band their children together and bring in an instructor for a class with a maximum of eight pupils. However, hiring a good private teacher was not possible for some making up the wide public Antoniano hoped his book would reach, and for them he recommends an established Jesuit school. All teachers must be respected and afforded great authority over the children's education.[61]

In addition to its new catechism and to doctrinally correct advice manuals such as Cardinal Antoniano's, the Catholic Church also sponsored renewed efforts to assure that its priesthood used the confessional box properly to guide the moral lives of the faithful. These efforts, at least the ones I am concentrating on, dispensed with complex theological issues and with the universality of Latin in order to tell simple parish clergy in the vernacular exactly how to do their job better. Friar Bartolomeo de Medina's little book, for example, has all the characteristics associated with popular-advice manuals such as Mercurio's for midwives—practical, plain language moving quickly from start to finish of the business at hand—except of course for the subject matter itself. We saw in an earlier chapter how the Spanish Jesuit advised confessors to instruct married couples on sex without sin, and now we read about how to hear the confessions of boys and girls between the ages of seven and fourteen.

Above all, confessors must watch out not to inadvertently teach boys and girls to sin by asking them too many questions. Try to get the truth out of them, but do not suggest behavior they may not have gotten to yet. Ask them if they have used bad words, but don't spout forth a string yourself and question whether they have said each one. Ask about sins of the flesh, which are especially pernicious in little girls, but avoid mentioning specific body parts and actions. Start with questions about telling lies and failing to keep promises and vows. Continue your interrogation by asking about the frequency of going to mass and the time since the last confession. Ask whether they have behaved irreverently while in church and whether they have disobeyed their parents, teachers, and other elders. Move along to petty thefts, bad words, jokes, saying nasty things against other children, and gluttony. Close out with sins against chastity. There we have it; nothing here that cannot be found in dozens of medieval penitentials; it is just restated in a concise, simple way for handy reference before going to hear confessions.[62]

Other vernacular works not written explicitly by or for churchmen nonetheless carry its message. A plain, frankly rather dull, 1571 manual by Eufrosino Lapino summarizes the eight characteristics of every good student: fearful of God, reverent toward his teacher, well mannered with everyone, loving of his honor, obedient to his elders, diligent on his own, tireless in learning, and persevering in acquiring knowledge. Everything must be done in moderation except for study, which should be a daily activity. Food, dress, and fun are to be rare treats, not the stuff of everyday routine. The effort by this writer to reach out to less affluent groups is clear in the admonition to good teachers, that they must instruct not only rich children who pay well but also the poor ones who can afford only a fraction of normal fees, because these boys nonetheless have internal treasures.[63]

Another example, this time a more imposing quarto book including lots of advice on agriculture but also with major sections on choosing a wife and raising a family, is the Tuscan physician and philosopher Francesco Tommasi's *Reggimento del padre di famiglia*. The advice is often quite abstract, always on a high moral plane, unabashedly derivative, and arranged according to no logic I can fathom, yet just the sort of thing a country gentleman might have wanted among his possessions. Whether his wife and children would have welcomed the advice is open to question. A man's nature is to be loving and solicitous toward his children, Tommasi begins, and a father's neglect inevitably brings ruin to his offspring. The three obligations of parental love are to teach the child to have faith in God, to instill good behavior, and to provide an education in the liberal arts.

The necessary liberal arts, as defined by Tommasi and in his order of importance, are grammar, logic, rhetoric, music, arithmetic, geometry, and astrology. Later, according to age and ability, boys should also be taught the sciences of philosophy, metaphysics, and theology; finally, they may be introduced to specialized areas such as ethics, politics, economics, and medicine. The good teacher for every subject and at each level must be able to guide children away from their innate sensuality, toward the use of reason. He must be not merely knowledgeable but intrinsically erudite, and he must have the ability to correct errors. He must be prudent in all matters, speak well, and never use bad words or brutish mannerisms.

The text then drifts back to behavioral failures for which parents rather than teachers are responsible. The first, eating defects, is not only harmful in itself but leads directly to sexual sins in adolescence: "Lust is born from gluttony, just like a daughter from her mother" is the saying Tommasi approvingly quotes. Specifically, children must be disciplined if they eat with too much avidity, if they eat excessively at one sitting, if they eat in slovenly fashion, if they eat at the wrong times of day or indulge in snacks, if they refuse to eat the full variety of food on their plates, or if they seek food that is too refined and delicate. With equal thoroughness parents must watch over and correct improper playing habits, bad gestures, inappropriate clothing, and poor choice of companions. Children should be taught not to hate and not to be taciturn. The children of gentlefolk should never be allowed to run around in the piazza like plebeian ragamuffins.

The time for good fathers to start instructing their children is at birth, with the selection of a moral, calm wet nurse if mother herself cannot breast-feed. Do not allow the infant to cry too much, as this is a vice, but do not feed the baby on demand. Just how Tommasi thought mothers or wet nurses were supposed to accomplish these contradictory injunctions he does not say, but the assumption here clearly is that the baby and its nurturer are under the same roof with the caring father. Anyway, when children are a little older, have them do calisthenics in the cold so they become tough, not overly wanting of heat. Exercise in cold weather also stimulates the liver, which in youngsters should never be heated up with wine. Read them good Christian children's stories and saints' lives.[64]

On the matter of physical exercise, good Christians might have found further support for Tommasi's recommendations in a book with an extravagant title surely intended to boost sales:

> Governance of the Family, by Messer Nicolò di Gozze, Gentleman of Ragusa [present-day Dubrovnik], Occult Academician, in which Briefly are Treated the Truths of Economics and One Learns, No Less with Ease than with Erudition about Governance, Not Only of the City Household but also One in the Countryside; and also the True Way to Acquire and Maintain Riches

Readers of this 1589 book may or may not have found useful information on how to get rich, but they definitely had before them in no uncertain terms some advice about their children's weight. Obesity is a plague and fat people should be banned from entering the city. Overweight children should be exiled at the age of fourteen, just as they did in ancient Sparta (according to Gozze). Boys should play vigorously to grow sturdy and supple, but their games should never involve touching playmates' clothing or in any way exciting lasciviousness, concupiscence, avarice, or envy. While Gozze admired the Spartans for banishing fat adolescents, he could not bring himself to approve of their idea about letting children run around barefooted. He thought this probably was fine for peasants but absolutely was not okay for young patricians in the city. As to exercise in the nude, that must have been as unthinkable to him as it is today among American Olympic enthusiasts.[65]

Plumpness is also bad for girls and leads directly to lasciviousness and dishonesty. Virgins should not be running from house to house, nor should they be seen lingering and chatting in the piazza. Once you have your daughter properly enclosed at home, see that she does not expose herself at the windows or hang out at the balcony. Make sure she learns to sew, crochet, knit, and embroider. Silence is a grand ornament in the female sex, so instruct daughters to be taciturn, not that they should be entirely mute but they should speak prudently, no more than the time and place require. The precepts of proper Christian behavior should be instilled at an early age. Christianity is based on faith, not reason, and among the very young the tendency to believe is more developed than the rational faculties.[66]

Other parts of Gozze's book strike me as less extreme. They may serve to round out our survey of popular lay writers working within the confines of Catholic Reformation teaching on child rearing while retaining much from Greco-Roman wisdom. The gentle, caring advice we read earlier about encouraging babies to good habits comes through clearly here. If your child has trouble falling asleep, do not keep him in silence; instead rock his cradle and sing him a song. Never let his nurse, nor should you yourself, fill the baby with fear or with any sadness that might disturb his tranquility. Listen carefully to his wailing or whimpering so you can tell what's bothering him; learn what he likes and what he hates. This is important for at least his first three years, which is no small part of his life. Wet nurses who hit, shake, or frighten the baby and forbid him to cry should be severely condemned.

Beginning in his third year, gradually introduce him to exertion in cold air, because this tightens his body and increases its natural heat, making him more robust and better able to withstand fatigue. Get him accustomed to some discomforts, to doing things that are displeasing; otherwise, he will become spoiled and unwilling to accept the moral discipline of God's holy laws. Before he is seven, teach him the alphabet and introduce him to syllables, but do not fret too much over his slowness to catch on because he will learn more by play than by violent discipline.

From seven until about thirteen, children enjoy learning and usually they can be encouraged with pleasing rewards rather than strictness. They should not just be memorizing words but beginning to understand the meaning of what they read. For a change of mental pace, it would be good to follow Plato's advice and teach them to play the lyre. Take care that they do not hear or see obscenities; inclinations lead to actions, and once they are on the wrong path, it is very difficult to return them to the straight and narrow. After age seven, children develop a moral sense as they begin to understand the difference between what is good and evil, honest and dishonest, praiseworthy and vile. Diet should be regulated more toward the solid and dry than in younger children, because this will help the mind to discipline the body in choosing what is good. Rich people who indulge their children with delicate foods make a big mistake, because not only are their bodies thereby weakened but also their morals. Exercise is essential—jumping, dancing, competing in games—but not to the point of exhaustion or in ways that give rise to concupiscence or anger.[67] When Gozze moves on to advice for dealing with adolescents, he abandons these relatively benign, moderate recommendations for raising younger children, but that shift is something to be explored in the next chapter. For now, I suggest only that advice manuals written late in the sixteenth century and clearly attuned to Catholic Reformation ideas nevertheless retained a fundamental belief in the natural goodness of children, an idea that St. Augustine had rejected centuries earlier, that Calvinist thinkers already thoroughly denied, and that our post-Freudian contemporary world relegates to an arena of sentimentality unworthy of serious discourse.

Children's Books

Books used to teach boys and girls to read Italian simultaneously aimed to shape their minds and morals. While these books are not what we generally take to be advice manuals or how-to books, their didactic purposes are very explicit. They certainly did tell Renaissance people how to behave. According to modern scholar Paul F. Grendler, the most important of these readers, the one assigned to boys and girls immediately after the primer, was *Fior di virtu* (Flower of Virtue). Written sometime before 1325, it has been the subject of considerable analysis concerning authorship, use of classical references, indebtedness to Thomas Aquinas's scholastic organization, and absence of New Testament references in favor of Old Testament proverbial wisdom. Its place in the vernacular curriculum, along with other works used to teach reading, may be followed in Grendler's thorough analysis.[68] It circulated widely even in manuscript and was printed on many occasions in the sixteenth century, often with woodcuts for added visual appeal. Without further ado, let us enter the classroom and start reading.[69]

In chapter 7, we get a defense of women based on Solomon's sayings—such as the one that compares finding a good woman to finding virtue and joy—but the words of praise are quickly tempered by the same king's reminders on the wickedness of Eve, to which are added dire warnings from Hippocrates, Homer, Sallust, Plato, Avicenna, and an unnamed wise philosopher. Our unknown author then ignores the secular experts and dismisses the misogynous parts of Solomon, saying that "anger and indignation made him speak and write in that manner," probably after he had been reduced to behaving like a small child by the pagan temptress who got the best of him in his old age. The chapter concludes by asserting that women's evils are small in comparison with those done by men, and that in sins of the flesh it is women who are more often reticent and who suffer the deceits and violence of men. Exactly what schoolgirls and schoolboys were supposed to make of this disrespectful treatment of a biblical patriarch is unclear. It also occurs to me that teachers who themselves had doubts about their own authority in the classroom might have been a bit uncomfortable in dealing with this chapter.

And there is more. Thirty-four chapters follow, each usually with a story from the animal kingdom, a few maxims as often as not misattributed to one or another biblical or classical author, and a tale involving humans to illustrate the virtue or vice under consideration. The chapter headings are instructive. In order, after the six opening chapters on love and a seventh on women, they are envy, joy, sadness, peace, anger, mercy, cruelty, liberality, avarice, correction, flattery, prudence, folly, justice, injustice, loyalty, falsity, truthfulness, falsehood, fortitude, fearfulness, magnanimity, vainglory, constancy, inconstancy, temperance, intemperance, humility, pride, abstinence, greed, chastity, lust, and moderation.

"Chastity" is a matter we shall consider in the pages ahead, so let it be our lesson for today. We learn first that doves are chaste; if a partner dies, the survivor never mates again, and he or she neither drinks clear water nor roosts among green trees. After the instructive animal behavior comes a warning from St. Jerome to watch the heart, the tongue, and the eyes, followed by a list of six prescriptions to observe with special care. First, do not eat and drink to excess, for the holy fathers say you cannot quench the fires of lust on a full stomach. Second, follow the advice of Ovid (of all people) and avoid idleness. Third, shun conversation between male and female. As St. Bernard says, "For a man and a woman to converse together without sinning is a greater task than to resurrect the dead." Fourth, listen to St. Gregory and mistrust prostitutes and all those who deal in carnality. Fifth, pay heed to St. Sylvester and do not speak or linger when lust is being discussed. Sixth and last, learn from Pythagoras to avoid singing, playing music, and dancing. The chapter closes with the story of a nun who preserved her chastity by cutting out her eyes, clearly a variant on St. Lucy's martyrdom.

Although *Fior di virtu* held a preeminent place in the vernacular curriculum, it was by no means the only printed work directed to children. Schools used a variety of pamphlets that served the curriculum for teaching elementary reading skills to young girls as well as being items for their mothers and father to read at home. *El costume delle donne* (Ways of Women), which gives advice on child rearing in the form of a poem in eight-line stanzas, is typical of this genre. It begins by telling mothers to get help in guiding their children by asking divine assistance from the greatest mother of all, Blessed Virgin Mary. Then the stanzas turn more practical.

E la fanciulla si attenda a filare	Have your daughter attend to weaving
a far cusina e a servir sia presta	And at cooking and serving be diligent.
a ogni cosa che per casa e affare	When household chores need doing,
secondo el tempo cosi sia richiesta	Finish the tasks in time well spent.
con maschi non lassarla conversare	With boys don't leave them to joking,
ne sia lasciva quando fusse a festa	Nor to lascivious misbehavior before Lent.
andar nanzi atenda con discretione	Attend gala dances with discretion,
ad honesto diletto e oratione	In honest delights and pious oration.

The verses go on to warn against idleness, gazing at passersby from the window, going out of the house alone, talking too much or gossiping, drinking undiluted wine, extravagance in dress, and dousing yourself in perfume—all done in a cheerful style meant to be read aloud, possibly memorized, absorbed rather than learned or imposed. Perhaps to make the booklet more attractive to potential readers, the lengthy title promises a concluding chapter containing thirty-three things to make a woman more beautiful.[70]

A sterner warning comes in another pamphlet, wherein a prostitute laments her downfall and advises her younger sister to follow a more Godly path to marriage.[71]

La sorella tua maggiore	Your sister who is older
molto meglio se diporta	Amuses herself much better,
si stà in pate con amore	If about love she stays leery
e spezzando si conforta	And a broken heart comforts her.
tu sei pazza, e poco accorta	You are crazy, not very wise;
fa che più mai non ti senti	Make it so I hear you no more,
A gran torto ti lamenti.	Or you will lament your downfall.
Come farò io poverella	What will poor me do
con la mente si affannata;	With my mind in turmoil;
che l non vuol pur ch'io favella	Unwilling to enter a convent,
trista me disgratiata,	Wretched in my hopeless state.
voglio esser pur maridata	I too would like to be married.
faccia il Cielo, & ogni stella	God and all the stars willing,
Io son quella Villanella.	I am that Evil One.

Writings in a similar style also addressed men. Consider for example the following excerpt from a humorous poem against gambling.

O vui padre de famiglia	Oh you father of the family,
avertite el mio consiglio,	Listen closely to my advice.
fa che questo t'assotiglia	Make this your cutting edge,
guarda ben che lo tuo figlio	Look well that your son
a giocar non dia de piglio	Does not fall into gaming
te fara poi sospirare.	And bring you to grief.
Maladetto sia il giocare.	Accursed be gambling.

The stanzas go on with the "accursed be gambling" refrain to the various evils of throwing dice and playing cards.[72] Other little collections strike me as so patently goody-goody that they must have been for very young children or else possibly they were meant as a spoof. The word *frottola* in the title from which the following lines are taken certainly allows the possibility that it is a put-on. The story is about a father who has two sons, a good boy called Benedetto and a bad one named Antonio.[73] The good son speaks.

Padre il mio pensiero,	Father, my thoughts
volto e solo al studiare	Are only of studying.
Et a me basta andare	It is enough for me
vestito honestamente	To be dressed honestly
Et non si riccamente	And not in such a rich fashion
chio veggio e virtudiosi	As to turn my head.
O palesi: o nascosi	In public and in secret,
sempre esser piu stimati,	Always seeking more esteem,
Amati: & honorati	Love, and honor
che un ricco ignorante,	Than an ignorant rich boy,
Che sol, dal vulgo errante	Loved only by the plebes
e amato: & non da Dio,	And not by God.

The battle for the hearts and minds of Christian souls did not end with childhood. In the next chapter we turn to what advice manuals had to say about adolescence, and if you are not interested in historiographical asides, you might wish to turn the page now.

More than a decade ago, historian Robert Darnton published a very influential book titled *The Great Cat Massacre,* in which he analyzed the reading habits of one Jean Ranson, a wealthy Calvinist merchant from La Rochelle, France. Darnton expressed surprise at the large proportion of children's literature and works of pedagogy among Ranson's book orders, nearly a third of the fifty-nine titles he purchased between 1774 and 1785, from the Société typographique de Neuchâtel publishing house. According to Darnton, it was Ranson's modern approach to fatherhood, his new attitude toward children, his heightened sense of responsibility for their moral upbringing—all derived from reading and accepting Rousseau's premise that children were naturally good—that accounted for his taste in books.

> The remarkable thing, however, is not that he [Ranson] read this or that treatise on children but that he read any treatises at all. He entered into parenthood through reading and relied on books in order to make his offspring into so many Emiles and Emilies.
>   This behavior expressed a new attitude toward the printed word. Ranson did not read in order to enjoy literature but to cope with life and especially family life, exactly as Rousseau intended.[74]

I accept that Rousseau may have written something new to Jean Ranson, and done so in an admirably persuasive style, but there was absolutely nothing innovative in Rousseau's evocation of the good child. Perhaps Enlightenment French Calvinists had forgotten that Italians wrote, repeated, plagiarized, and read about the innocence of babes in popular-advice manuals throughout the Renaissance. Literature for children to enjoy by themselves, storybooks for parents to read aloud, guides on how to read, moral plays and poetry, heroic tales for all ages, and treatises both philosophical and practical prescribing norms for child rearing—hundreds, maybe thousands of these works sold briskly in the cities of northern Italy more than two centuries before Ranson discovered books telling him how to be a good father.

CHAPTER

· *5* ·

Adolescence

Who Was an Adolescent?

We tend to think of "adolescence" as an invention of late-nineteenth-century European bourgeois society. The classic scholarly formulation of this view may be found in the work of my colleague John Gillis, whose book *Youth and History* still repays careful rereading more than twenty years after its original publication. He details the "discovery of adolescence," between 1870 and 1900, the "era of adolescence," from 1900 until 1950, and the "end of adolescence," since midcentury. He cites an impressive array of scholars and documents concerning this modern invention and the heyday of adolescence, a life stage especially nurtured in middle-class, two-parent, two-child, loving families that kept their offspring at home until marriage, or at most sent them off to a controlled school environment during the year and to an equally well-supervised camp in the summer. Gillis separates the adolescent teenager from the young adult in his or her twenties, linking the rise of the adolescent to specific demographic and economic trends, namely, smaller and wealthier families. Working-class boys who left school for a factory at age eleven, or girls sent out of the home as servants by the age of fourteen, had no adolescence. For the more fortunate ones, the years of adolescence were supposed to be a carefree time of self-indulgence and self-discovery. Even the powerful forces of sexuality, a taboo subject among earlier Victorians, might be explored, at least in a tentative, controlled way. The twentieth century saw the idea of adolescence democratized throughout the Western world, although still foreshortened for the poorer classes and extended for the well-to-do. Boys wallowed more fully in adolescent freedom than girls, clearly because the consequences of sexual experimentation were less for them and also because they stayed in school longer and married later. In the euphoric celebration of adolescence, there was initially little concern with the darker consequences of peer pressure, sexual precocity, and standardized testing (and failure) that today engage several scholarly disciplines.[1]

The picture of adolescence Gillis drew initially achieved wide acceptance and still retains substantial validity. It accurately portrays the experience of Western teenagers over the past two centuries. Nevertheless, when our gaze shifts back five hundred years, to examine advice manuals telling Italian Renaissance and Catholic Reformation parents and teachers how to cope with adolescent behavior, we may be struck instantly by similarities with modern concerns. Maybe the nineteenth-century "invention" analyzed by Gillis and others is actually a "reinvention." "Boys will be boys" is both the title of Gillis's chapter on the discovery of adolescence and the signature theme of Renaissance historian Richard Trexler's work on Florentine youths in the fourteenth and fifteenth centuries. Similarly, the Victorian taboo on discussing sexuality that late-nineteenth-century manuals on adolescence cast aside did not result in the first ever mentions of teenage sex. Much earlier there had been a very lively, public dialogue, with explicit reference to all sorts of sexual behavior. I want to avoid the mistake of reading modern ideas into old books, but I also want to convey fully what the old books have to say, even when their injunctions and prescriptions happen to have a contemporary ring.

In this chapter, I use the word "adolescence," because I believe it to be the most accurate translation for modern readers of what the original texts describe. In using this term I do not imply that it carries all the cultural baggage associated with modern, Western "adolescence," but I also do not accept that present-day usages and experiences necessarily deny or corrupt the meaning of terms understood in a somewhat different but nonetheless entirely coherent fashion by other people in an earlier society. I could sidestep some of the semantic implications here simply by using the more neutral word "teenager," but that would belie my sense that sixteenth-century advice manuals do indeed deal with a stage in the life cycle they consciously treat as adolescence. The stage was defined not only by age boundaries but also by familial dependency, self-exploration, sexual experimentation, and societal toleration of misbehavior.[2]

The joys of adolescence are captured nicely in the verses of a Renaissance carnival song, attributed to Antonio Alamanni, that extols the progression of life's ages:[3]

Vien l'etá d'amore ardendo,	Next comes the age of love burning,
c'ogni còr gentile invita:	With every gentle heart invited,
gioventú, lieta, ridendo,	Youthful, gay, laughing
vien cantando e molto ardita.	They come singing and high spirited.
O che dolze e bella vita!	Oh what a sweet and beautiful life!
chi va a caccia e chi fa versi,	This one goes hunting and that one writes verse,
chi d'amor non può tenersi,	While another's love bursts all bounds,
tanto è vago il suo bel fiore.	So charming is its beautiful flower.

At the outset of this book, I noted Matteo Palmieri's division of the life cycle into six stages, the third being adolescence *(adolescenzia)*. He writes that adolescence begins with the termination of childhood *(puerizia/fanciullezza)*, at the age of discretion *(anni della discrezione)*, and ends at age twenty-eight. This lack of chronological precision about when adolescence begins is no less interesting than the exactness of the closing demarcation, and both merit further exploration. Palmieri's division of the life cycle eventually settles on multiples of seven, with the age of virility starting at twenty-eight, old age at fifty-six, and decrepitude at seventy. Counting backwards, the reasonable age for discretion in this scheme would be fourteen, which would also produce symmetrical spans of fourteen, twenty-eight, and fourteen between the age breaks from adolescence to virility, virility to old age, and old age to decrepitude. Collapsing infancy and childhood into a single span from birth to adolescence, which the humanist explicitly does according to an alternate division he labels as the age of ignorance, would then produce a string of fourteen, fourteen, twenty-eight, and fourteen, for a total of seventy. Palmieri discusses at some length Dante's reference to the age of thirty-five as the halfway point in the life span, again a multiple of seven, so it is reasonable to suppose he was aware of all these numerical niceties, as were late-medieval and Renaissance intellectuals generally. The original text does not exclude categorically that seven may be the age of discretion, which would produce a less regular but still orderly pattern of multiples of seven, with the string of seven, twenty-one, twenty-eight, and fourteen still adding up to the requisite seventy. But other didactic advice in Palmieri makes it unlikely that he meant to suggest so early an end to boyhood.[4]

We are left with the phrase "age of discretion." What does Palmieri mean by age of discretion? Certainly he does not mean age of puberty, a physical change understood to be beyond the individual's volition. Sexual awareness and capacity are subjects openly and fully discussed in the manuals we are reading, so there is no proto-Victorian or other kind of taboo here. Rather, Palmieri aims to define adolescence on more subtle grounds than the purely physical process of maturation. To explore when and how an individual begins to know the difference between vice and virtue and to make choices, he introduces the Y symbol, telling readers that from a single road, ultimately there is an absolute break between the two paths to follow. The symbol confirms what we have seen already about humanist views on childhood behavior. Little boys and girls are at the stem or base of the Y, and no sins they may commit can lead them fatally away from reaching the path of eventual goodness and salvation. The irreparable fork in the road comes at the vertical halfway point in the Y, which is to say at age thirty-five when, Palmieri reminds us, Dante began his literary descent into hell. Behavioral choices after the age of seven move one increasingly along the path of good or evil, but the point of no return comes only at midlife. The "age of discretion" is not a precise moment but a process of moral and spiritual formation that takes place over many years, is accompanied by intellectual and physical growth, starts at different ages for different individuals, and proceeds at varying rates but always reaches a finishing point or summation at the age of virility. Palmieri foregoes the symmetry of exact numbers to emphasize instead the fluidity of adolescence, quite a remarkable intellectual break-through when contrasted with his more rigid, less-interesting exactitude in declaring that virility ends at age fifty-six and decrepitude starts at seventy.

During adolescence, beginning at the age of discretion, the individual proceeds along the path of vice or virtue by personal choices. Because we are inclined from birth to enjoy evil (whether the consequence of original sin or simply the delights of nature is not entirely clear), the self-restraint needed to obtain eternal salvation must be developed carefully. Fathers must be especially diligent in teaching children to know and then freely choose good. In the early years, children behave well out of fear or because teachers and parents forbid their doing bad things, but then they outgrow such restraints. Youths taste the delights of the world and follow whatever satisfies their appetites. The younger ones are particularly malleable; they should be kept separately, out of conversation with the older ones already hardened in evil doings. More than at any other age, now is when the young ones should learn patience when being re-buked, something most of them accept badly just when they need it most. Although Palmieri knows his Dante well and has a thoroughly Christian belief in hell, much of his thinking on adolescence draws directly, although without acknowledgment, from Quintilian, as do his views on child rearing.

Advice on forms of punishment also follows Quintilian, continuing and even expanding upon admonitions not to break the child's will. If you want to raise a servant or a mechanic, Palmieri moralizes, then maybe you should beat the boy on occasion, but physical punishment is contrary to nature and not good. Furthermore, it is likely to turn natural filial love into hatred. Rebuke should be enough, and even this according to age; cite good examples of other youths he knows, vilify the bad ones, have him converse with the good ones, reward proper behavior with things he likes, and give the treats to others if he misbehaves. When he is bad, punish him with a long examination of his behavior rather than with deep passion. Put him in isolation, deny him delicate foods, prohibit his wearing a favorite outfit—whatever will cause a fuller reflection on the error committed. Whippings give only brief suffering; quickly forgotten, they wrongly give the impression that the bad behavior is now fully paid for and, therefore, the sin is easily repeated. Choosing good comes not from fear of a painful beating but from the desire to flee from sin.[5]

The Sins of Adolescence

Palmieri's text, written in the fifteenth century and appearing in several printed editions in the first half of the sixteenth century, drew heavily from the liberal, tolerant educational philosophy of Quintilian and Plutarch. A rather different view of adolescence is to be found in the thundering Catholic Reformation writings of Cardinal Silvio Antoniano. He it is who brought us the metaphor of the tree of sin planted at our birth, from which the first branches were childish lying and tattling. Now the same metaphor serves to define adolescence as the time when the tree of sin goes into full foliage, usually beginning around age fourteen and continuing until twenty-one or so. The prelate explains as follows:

> Adolescents are self-indulgent, greedy, and ever ready to grab for more, even though this constant grasping is often volatile and contradictory, changing from one moment to the next, quickly tiring of the old and ready for anything new. Their desires are like the thirst that comes from a high fever—insatiable. Young men enjoy only hunting and horseback riding; they waste money, are totally impractical, and will not listen to advice. They are easily deceived, malleable as wax, sociable only with their own kind, quick to make friends if it leads to pleasure seeking, merrymaking, and gaming.
>
> Much more could be said about the sins of youth but their worst enemy, as philosophers through the ages have pointed out, is their sexual desire, which dominates their lives. Incontinence of the flesh, which infests most of them and against which they offer little resistance, is what sinks them, especially if they lack fatherly supervision,

whether because their father is dead or simply because he and other family members cannot be bothered.[6]

Against such evil one might imagine Cardinal Antoniano invoking all sorts of hard punishments, but in fact his prescriptions turn out to be extraordinarily moderate, pretty much the things good parents think they should do today, recommendations that undergird commonplace divisions such as those between junior and senior high schools. He tells the father that his best chance to instill virtue in his child is at a very young age, so he should participate actively in the early formative years and not wait until his teenager has gone bad. Be especially vigilant about watching your child's companions, for nothing leads a child astray so surely as an older youth who entices the younger ones into corruption. Encourage good behavior with rewards and promote friendships with peers of good moral character. Many times a child will refuse to take even the best advice from his father, so all these and other suggestions might better come from one of the father's respected colleagues.

Proper upbringing for adolescent girls requires a mother's special attention. Do not send your daughter out on errands such as shopping or delivering a note or whatever; just go yourself. Do not let her go out and about in the company of old maids *(zitelle)*. Do not let her hang out the window or balcony to show herself off and flirt with passersby. Keep your eyes open and look for bad signs such as undue, sudden, extra attention to personal grooming and dress. Take her with you to confession, often. Above all, the vigilant mother should keep her daughter busy, so occupied with in-house chores that she has no time for idle thoughts and sinfulness. While it is true that women should not engage in violent exercise of a manly nature that might be indecent to their modesty, still they should not be too languid and lazy. Housework—I suppose some mopping, scrubbing, polishing, shining, sweeping, and hauling, although Antoniano does not say precisely—promotes bodily vigor and therefore the ability to procreate when the time comes after marriage. The female sex by nature is lewd and frivolous and at this age of little consequence. But there is always hope that good early upbringing, along with fear of God and a saintly example from her mother, will bring a good result anyway.[7]

Secular writers could be just as harsh in their judgments about young women, often without the redeeming hope expressed by clerics such as Cardinal Antoniano. Nicolò Gozze, who may be recalled for his tirade against obesity in boys, had something to say about beauty in girls. The four necessary virtues in young women are modesty, piety, chastity, and beauty. Beauty and chastity go together because beauty without chastity is like adorning a pig with precious jewels. Nor is chastity without beauty in the least praiseworthy, more a sorry reality than a virtue. Women generally are too loquacious and would be better off staying mute than babbling on as they do. They should stay home. Putting beautiful ornaments on an ugly woman just accentuates how hideous she really is. She will end up like the biblical Jezebel, who painted her eyes and adorned her head before looking out her window to entice the warrior Jehu. The outraged conqueror instead had Jezebel pushed to the ground, where her blood splattered and dogs ate her flesh so there was nothing to bury save her skull, her feet, and the palms of her hands (2 Kings 9:30–37). The lesson is clear enough![8]

There existed in the sixteenth century a substantial literature about women, some of it by women, who granted sexual favors and received some form of financial compensation. Later scholars read these texts with great pleasure and drew a portrait of the "honest courtesan," perhaps best exemplified by Imperia, Veronica Franco, Caterina di S. Celso, and Tullia of Aragon. By day they played music and wrote poetry, while at night they entertained high prelates and courtiers. Hundreds of years later, they found a place of scintillating esteem in Jacob Burkhardt's version of the Renaissance.[9] Erudite antiquarians such as Guido Biagi, who headed the Laurentian and Riccardiana libraries in turn-of-the-century Florence, brought very clear preconceptions to their archival and bibliographic work. After evoking rhetorically the joys of an evening with Tullia, Biagi writes, "This intelligent sympathy, indeed, was rarely looked for in the family, for the housewife of this time was either a fear-inspiring virago with a masculine mind, capable of protecting her virtue by sheer force of arms, or else she was a creature wholly absorbed in domestic matters, with no understanding for anything beyond her prayers and her pantry."[10]

My own survey of sixteenth-century literature focuses on the world portrayed in popular-advice manuals, where one finds few "courtesans" but plenty of prostitutes and whores, the women required by law to stand naked to the waist on the Bridge of Tits (*Ponte delle Tette*) in Venice, to entice young men away from their penchant for sodomy. One also finds in these books some recommendations for wives who clearly were neither viragos nor house nuns, something I shall explore in the next chapter. A good example of popular condemnation of prostitution is Giovanni Antonio Massinoni's thirty-page book containing both *Il flagello delle meretrici* (On the Scourge of Prostitutes) and a second tract titled, *La nobiltà donnesca ne' figliuoli* (Womanly Nobility in Your Children), reprinted in 1599, by his homonym Giacomo. There are three reasons young men should stay away from prostitutes, advises the author. First, they create confusion in your life; second, their insatiable lust will exhaust you; third, their diseases will kill you. The worst is that you are being loved not by a woman but by a whore. And this whore outdoes a pig for filth, a heap of dung for vileness, a wind for instability, a scorpion for wickedness, a lion for pride, a dragon for cruelty, and a snare for tenacity. She will put you in your grave.[11] On the other hand, a little book of bad verse appeared in 1553, promoting itself as a guide to selecting among the forty best prostitutes in Florence, so the advice manual's range should not be underestimated, especially when spoofs are included.[12]

The most important advice about prostitution printed in sixteenth-century Italy undoubtedly is the "honest courtesan" Veronica Franco's letter 22, analyzed so brilliantly in a recent book on Franco and her world by literary critic Margaret Rosenthal. Franco, whose clients included Henry of Valois, king of Poland and the future King Henry III of France, wrote and published (probably at her own expense, in 1580) a stinging indictment of the social circumstances that forced young women such as herself into female subjugation, often as in her own case with the encouragement of her mother who had earned her living in the same occupation. According to Rosenthal, and her analysis is highly suggestive, Franco's message is not one of repentance but of indignation at the cruel and violent life of the prostitute, a life of inequality and suffering. She and her sisters have been excluded from the vaunted freedom of Venetian citizens, and they do not share in the empire's prosperity. Her letter then turns more practical and specific. It is addressed to a friend who already has rejected Franco's offer to pay for her daughter's entry into a home for young girls "at risk." The precipice is near, warns Franco, and now you must strip your daughter of the embellishments meant only to deceive a prospective suitor. Do whatever is necessary to preserve her chastity and with it her right to marry honestly and avoid the certainty of damnation for both mother and fallen daughter. Franco backs her words with money, repeating her desire to help in any possible way. Although we do not know how this advice was taken, archival documents record that Franco was active in supporting the work of refuge houses for impoverished fallen women in her native city. As Rosenthal demonstrates convincingly, Veronica Franco saw clearly and condemned unequivocally the economic and social realities that pushed a young woman onto the path of becoming a courtesan.[13]

A rather different challenge to the dominant Catholic Reformation attitude that adolescents are fundamentally corrupt—and personally responsible for their sinfulness—comes from the pen of another woman, the Venetian feminist Moderata Fonte. She grants that young women sometimes seem shallow or fickle, but argues that this sorry outcome is entirely due to their being raised without proper discipline, and is not a result of any deficiency in female nature. In Fonte's dialogue, the female interlocutors quickly go beyond a defense of women's equality to assert their manifest superiority over men. Fonte was one of a circle of literary Venetian women who wrote poetry and pioneered in setting out a consciously female voice in the burgeoning field of *querelle des femmes* literature. Although published in the same year (1600) as Lucrezia Marinella's more successful work, Fonte actually wrote her tract eight years earlier. After centuries of obscurity, she has been rediscovered in the past decade and is now receiving the full scholarly appraisal she so richly deserves. Critics especially laud Fonte's insistence on the pleasure that women may take from their own learned conversation and her rejection of the minor roles assigned to them in classics such as Castiglione's *Courtier*. *Il merito delle donne* (The Worth of Women) is clearly an erudite dialogue meant for an elite audience, so it falls outside even my loose definition of the advice-manual genre. Nevertheless, its message is of great importance, and I shall return to it briefly in my analysis of advice for widows. A fine English translation, with an excellent introduction, became available in 1997, so you can read this pioneering writer for yourself.[14]

Turning now to Giovanni Michele Bruto's recommendations on the proper education of a young gentlewoman, we have what is clearly an advice manual in the sense that it advises a noble father on raising his daughter. Significantly, however, it lacks the problem-oriented, indexed, quick-fix character of how-to books aimed at middling folk. Since Bruto was a Protestant exile forced to publish abroad, I assume that very few Italians could have read his precepts. Still, the highly unusual publication in 1555, of a French translation with the Italian on facing pages, and in 1598, of an English translation in large print, with both the French version and the Italian original in small-print columns on facing pages, calls for a closer look at the contents. The title page of the 1598 edition states explicitly that this format is "for the better instruction of such as are desirous to studie those Tongues," and the translations in fact are very literal, quite easy to follow. My sense is that the book would not have been used to instruct little English boys on how to read French or Italian, because the subject matter would have bored them to tears, but as a teaching tool for girls, the book could simultaneously have served the purposes of language education and moral edification. It seems plausible that elite mothers also might have used it to teach themselves French and Italian. Such evidence of female literacy in England by the end of the sixteenth century is not at all surprising, but the 1555 and 1558 editions in French and Italian indicate an earlier and wider market than one might expect, at least based on the authoritative and denigrating recommendations of prelates such as Cardinal Antoniano, which barely allowed that women should read one language much less two.

As to specific advice, most of what Bruto wrote apparently did not outrage genteel women teaching themselves to read a foreign language, however much it may offend modern sensibilities. Mothers fit to raise a daughter properly are rare, he begins, because the great affection they bear toward the child compromises their wisdom and virtue. Fathers are even worse, being more indulgent and delicate in satisfying their own pleasures than wise and diligent in seeing to their children's welfare. As soon as their daughters can read a little and distinguish one word from another, they give them amorous, impudent songs to memorize. Embers from vices learned in infancy later get stirred up by the evil conversations of various persons and lead the young woman astray. Therefore, it is better for fathers to find a wise matron to read to the child stories of virtuous and renowned women, holy scriptures, histories, things that give reading pleasure while inspiring her to choose virtue over filthy abomination. A girl's mind is very delicate and must not be made yet more feeble and effeminate by being exposed to things likely to make her forget her good reputation. Watch out for the mischief done by dames bringing gifts of dresses and jewels, by prattling maids and servants passing idle time at the fire, by fellow children no matter how innocent they appear, and by men who disguise their wicked intentions in religious garb or noble title. Just keep the girl away from all these dangers and under a ceaselessly watchful eye.

The wise matron (today we would use the word governess, but "wise matron" is what the 1598 English edition used for the Italian *savia donna* and the French *bonne dame*) must sugarcoat any behavioral corrections that become necessary; her own countenance should always be pleasant and merry, full of amiable and delightful gestures. Do not discipline so heavily that the girl is paralyzed by fright or bitter reprehension. "Above all things" the wise matron holds "her hands from beating or striking her, as a beastly and inconvenient kind of correction, to a frank and honest mind." The girl must be raised to choose good voluntarily and happily, not out of fear.

While Bruto obviously recommends that a gentlewoman learn to read, he has grave reservations about introducing her to philosophy and science, especially at a tender age. Better to follow the infallible truth of Jesus Christ, who despised the wisdom of the world as an enemy to an honest religious life. The loss in not reading the Christian poets will be outweighed by the good that comes from complete ignorance of the foolish loves of the Greek gods, Ovid's amorous books, and Homer's adulteries and fornications. There is good in Plato's discourses, but inevitably the girl would come upon the impudent actions, loves, and dalliances of Alcibiades. Then there is the danger that comes from the insatiable lust of men, for surely if she were to study philosophy and science, the girl's teacher would be a male. Even St. Jerome in the desert among wild animals sometimes imagined himself to be in the company of beautiful Roman women, so what chance can there be of finding an honest teacher? No sensible father would prefer a learned daughter of suspect reputation over one who is ignorant but pure. She may read Boccaccio's lives of famous women but definitely not the *Decameron,* which decent men read only for the magnificent style, not the actual content.[15] Now that the Holy Scriptures have been translated, these also should be read, along with accounts of the sacred Christian virgin saints and martyrs. Among pagan works, Plutarch's moral treatises are fine, as well as those of his *Lives* that touch upon women. The noble young girl must abstain wholly from music, for under the guise of honestly soothing the mind's passions, it opens the gates to all sorts of vices, as happened to Agamemnon, Ulysses, and King Saul. Stick with needlework and tasks done with the distaff, spindle, and loom—all this in a book to assist elite female readers in learning French and Italian.[16]

Another and far more curious variation on the popular-advice manual is a little work by Orazio Lombardelli, published in Florence in 1579, *De gli ufizii e costumi de' giovani* (On the Duties and Habits of Youth). On the title page he identifies himself as *Accademico Humoroso* (Humorous Academic), while in other writings he lists himself as *Tranquillo Umoroso,* thus highlighting his membership in Cortona's *Accademia degli Umidi.* These "academies" were literary societies where men of intellectual pretension gathered to present their witty efforts, sometimes in the form of misogynous tracts that cleverly mimicked more serious work.[17] In a solidly scholarly vein, Lombardelli wrote in defense of pure Tuscan pronunciation, including use of *Z* instead of *T* in certain words, and achieved a brief moment of fame for his commentary on Torquato Tasso's *Gierusalemme Liberata.* Nevertheless, when he ultimately obtained a post at the University of Siena after many years of languishing as a private tutor, it was not the one in Tuscan language he coveted most. Even the twentieth-century literary scholar who goes to great lengths to rescue him from obscurity admits that he was a second-rate opportunist who jumped at any chance for the limelight.

Among his other publications, *Il giovane studente* (The Young Student), done in the form of a letter to his brother Leonardo, provides rules for students to follow in improving their abilities to memorize. Other sections of this rather prissy epistle treat diet and sleep, recommending that everything be done in moderation: don't retain urine and excrement; don't walk outside in rainy or windy weather; don't leave your room at night except for an emergency; don't get too close to a hot fire. Be like the plebeians: eat good bread, well leavened and thoroughly baked, and drink fresh, clean water.[18] Completely ignored by modern literary scholars is his tract *De gli ufizii e costumi de' giovani,* but what possibly may have been inappropriate for inclusion in a bio-bibliographical essay on a relatively minor Tuscan critic is precisely the publication I want to explore a bit further.[19]

In many respects the work, dedicated to no less a personage than Francesco de' Medici, grand duke of Tuscany, and divided into four books, reads like a rigid tirade against all that is wrong with the sinful world of late-sixteenth-century Italy. The second page laments over printing presses that spew forth works that blaspheme the name of God and the merits of the saints in silly love songs, lascivious elegies, and wicked comedies. Even members of the clergy usurp the church's wealth while producing joke books; in addition, so many of these ignoramuses are around with their thousand ways of tricking people that you no longer can distinguish a thief from a cavalier of true religion.

The next page provides a list of the characteristics of young men not at all unlike the entirely serious tirade of Cardinal Antoniano, except that Lombardelli struts out his estimable command of Tuscan epithets rather than engage in moral analysis. Young men are proud, ambitious, vainglorious, swaggering, arrogant, boasting, impatient, peevish, hard to please, dandies, featherbrained, restless, contumacious, superficial, intriguing, litigious, precipitous, furious, always ready for a fight, without a thought for the future, with no regard for justice or injustice, unwilling to listen to wise counsel or exhortation, and without any respect for place, time, or person. When it comes to acquiring something of the fine arts and sciences or seeking honor and a good name, they suddenly become infirm, disabled, crippled, shuffling, somnolent, lazy, and disobedient to their elders. They abandon themselves so much to debauchery and drunkenness that they become crazed, frenzied, rabid, stoned, deaf, mute, and blind.

As with any parody, there is an ample bite of truth, and it comes when Lombardelli satirizes the advice manual with a list of ten reasons why young men behave as they do. What I like best about the list is how

cleverly each reason is utterly beyond the control of the youths themselves.

1. Young men have hot blood, a natural consequence of the mix of hot/cold
and wet/dry bodily humors appropriate for their age and needed for their further
growth.

2. Young men have been treated badly as infants, with either too much or too
little affection, discipline, nurture, or whatever.

3. Young men are inexperienced, something only time and experimentation
can resolve.

4. The fathers of young men are more concerned with making their children
wealthy than with making them good, just as the church teaches all the time.

5. Young men are only following the bad examples they see and hear in their
fathers' daily behavior.

6. Young men hear the conversations of adults and are lured into sin.

7. Adults indulge and encourage young people to debauchery and drunkenness and allow them to sleep off resulting hangovers until two in the afternoon.
Merchants provide food and drink on credit, shopkeepers sell dirty books and
lascivious pictures, dances and fairs abound, massage parlors and beauty spas
encourage undressing. And in the rare cases when a father tries to impose some
order on his wayward son, for sure the mother butts in and starts yelling at her
husband. Then the home itself becomes a war zone as she goes out and about
telling her darling's teachers and advisors unending fables about the cruelty of
her husband toward the misunderstood little wretch.

8. Young men are corrupted by the public and private spectacles of dishonest
women. These flatterers and enchantresses lure mere boys into gaming and to
the wicked life, where the participants are naked, either with obscene gestures
and words or in actual deeds. In readings of verse and poetry, in satiric comedies
of love triumphant and other theatrical displays, authors shamelessly say anything
that might get a laugh.

9. The whole world has lost respect for the precepts of true religion.

10. The future is so uncertain that there is no use in following the good and
true path anyway.

Lombardelli continues his mockery of advice manuals in book 2 by
offering fourteen specific remedies to overcome the vices of youth. Book
3 then provides detailed ways of looking for signs of probable virtue or
possible vice in a young man, and of distinguishing one from the other.
Mostly these are variations on the "everything in moderation" theme
found so commonly in prescriptive literature, but several recommendations are quite vicious, as in the advice that a young man should converse
with old-timers because even if they are illiterate idiots, they still have
lots of experience and can remember how the things of the world have
changed. Other rich sources of sick humor are the fervent and frequent
warnings to avoid all conversation with women. Apparently his book had

some popularity, because Lombardelli added a table of contents, giving it even more fully the masquerade of being an advice manual, for reprintings in 1584 and 1585, by the same publisher who presumably had sold out of the 1579 edition. All this was before his moment of glory resulting from his discourse on Tasso. *De gli ufizii e costumi de' giovani* may have been read more for its humor than as serious advice, at least I think that was the case for many readers, and so I shall not stay with it further except to note that among the array of popular books in the sixteenth century, we find not only the advice manual but also literary spoofs of this genre.[20]

An even more ambiguous work is Simeon Zuccolo's *La pazzia del ballo* (The Insanity of Dancing), published in 1549. In my view this pseudo-erudite tract was consciously meant to be humorous even as it carried moral advice against the evils of dancing. Perhaps the author was a monk who delighted in recalling the joys of dancing in his youth and could not resist the worldly temptation to publish his little masterpiece of just thirty-one octodecimo leaves. Pride of authorship comes through in his preface, as does his clever way with words. But one could also read the book as an entirely serious, very misogynous tirade by an embittered old man who detested youthful sensuality as expressed in the liveliness of dancing. Yet again, one could read it as an instructional manual teaching readers how to do the tarantella, the dance of the hair, and other Italian dances of the time—at least that is how someone at the Library of Congress classified the book.[21] A 1969 reprint makes it reasonably available, so you could obtain a copy and judge for yourself. For the moment, allow me to provide some feel for the text.

Zuccolo tells his readers that dancing began with the gods who listened to celestial music; it is used as a part of religious expressions throughout the world. Initially this sounds more like anthropological analysis than reasoning by a dogmatic cleric, but let us continue. The first cause of the desire to step lively and dance is mankind's natural cheerfulness, merely analogous to a dog wagging its tail and jumping up and down when you feed it. Upon further reflection, therefore, Zuccolo concludes that the tradition of dancing on feast days, even holy days, is pagan and rude, not truly religious at all.

The second cause that incites men and women to dance is the debauchery that ensues from drinking wine to excess. Bread and meat, even if eaten in abundance, do not have this effect, only wine. What happens is that the wine flows, good cheer follows, and it is festival time. You see this especially at *Carnevale* (Mardi Gras), when everyone starts dancing and quickly all sorts of dishonest, swinish sexual behavior follow. Crazy mothers and fathers actually lead their sons and daughters off to the festival, carrying around not only a fife but also a trombone and maybe some gaming dice. They are all ready to sing and dance through the night, gradually shedding that honest shame without which you cannot really say a girl is a virgin, a wife is chaste, or a widow is honest.

Dancing is akin to a full-scale riot. The women begin by offering men a gloved hand, but soon enough the dancers are not content with clutching dead animal skin so off comes the glove. Initially the woman proffers only one little bare finger but then two, three, and four join them, and finally her whole hand. Today women go even further, offering not only a naked hand but also their arms, shoulders, breasts, and other voluptuous parts. They behave just like the public prostitutes who entice clients with bittersweet tastes and touches here and there. All the while their husbands look on and allow this to continue, their horn of jealousy drowned in wine (*Bacco/becco* is the play on words that enlivens the original). With great pomp and vainglory, these husbands lead their wives and daughters to the ball—plucked, painted, and well greased as if to an arena to joust with adulterers and lover—where they get to see just how far libidinous desires can go.

The third cause of the urge to dance is the music itself. Musicians, fife players, and singers are by nature a bizarre lot, likely to be fanatical and highly volatile. A dance is akin to a fair at which horses are being sold. The buyer first examines the merchandise visually from head to toe, and when he finds a promising animal, he separates it out to see how it moves, at first trying a walking gait, then a trot, and finally a gallop. Dancers resemble a tarantula in their movements, and that is not the only similarity. The hat dance is a representation of adultery in which husbands and wives leave their normal places and of necessity take other partners.[22]

One might make a great deal of Zuccolo's little book or not much at all. The only real advice it clearly contains is a warning to husbands and fathers to keep their wives and daughters away from dance halls. There are no traces of other writings by him, nor do we know anything about him; the work was not reprinted until the twentieth century—as a curiosity piece. The original clearly was a cheap edition, possibly one that sold well, but of course we cannot say exactly how well. Although many advice manuals include warnings about the evils of dancing, I know of only one other Italian text devoted exclusively to examining the morality of dancing. Rinaldo Corso's *Dialogo del ballo* (Dialogue on Dancing) appeared in 1555, six years after Zuccolo's tirade, and at least one literary scholar surmises that it may have been a direct response to Zuccolo. Corso's interlocutors eventually agree that dancing is not evil, but their

verbal road to that conclusion is rather sterile when compared with Zuccolo's lively wit.[23] In any event, no pamphlet war about dancing ensued.
Shifting the comparative focus does not help much. Only the vagaries of
the Library of Congress's catalog scheme put La pazzia del ballo in the
same subject category as serious sixteenth-century books on how to
dance, such as Fabritio Caroso's Il ballarino (1581) and his Nobiltà di
dame (1600), and to compare it with these elegant tomes for aristocrats
and their dance instructors would be ludicrous.[24] Approaches taken from
literary criticism also do not get us very far. Funny or at least clever as
Zuccolo may be, he does not rank anywhere near a Boccaccio or an Aretino. Alas, even Zuccolo's erudition is but a thin veneer and cannot withstand more than passing scrutiny. All this said, his little book did find a
publisher and an unknowable number of readers. Perhaps in Rinaldo
Corso it also found a respondent. Be that as it may, Zuccolo's sentiments
made it to the world of print, and they strike me as reflective of a variety
of sixteenth-century attitudes: moral prejudice against popular musicians
and artists; dancing as sexually charged, flirtatious, and licentious; husbands and fathers as accomplices in their women's degeneracy; delight
in sensuality as entirely natural.

Dancing and carnival gave special license to sins of the flesh but advice
givers cared equally about the demands of modesty in daily habits and
dress. Matteo Palmieri is less concerned with modesty itself than with
curbing the adolescent desire to show off, to be seen, noticed, and admired. Young men and women should dress in accord with the common
fashion in their community, that is, in the appropriate attire the occasion
demands. Men's garments should not be delicate, neither polished nor
appliquéd, and should not be a kaleidoscope of colors. Always flee from
every feminine ornamentation and from exaggerated coiffeurs: no frizz-
ing straight hair or artificially removing natural curls.[25] Another moralist
warns that even a prince, for whom there should be no rules against
fine and delicate clothing, must avoid the appearance of being girlish or
effeminate, and he ought not to become more concerned with appearance than with substance.[26] Monsignor Sabba da Castiglione adds a reminder to avoid like the plague any use of musk or similar odors and
powders more appropriate for vain women than for true young gentlemen. Recall the proverb: it is not always good if someone is always perfumed.[27] The humanist Enea Silvio Piccolomini, perhaps better known
as the crusader Pope Pius II who died in 1464, while preparing for a
holy war against the Turks, casts the bigger issue with a magnificent
economy of words: "Dressing and undressing beyond necessity stem either from poverty, as certified by Diogenes, or from vulgarity."[28]

More than a century later comes Nicolò Gozze's reminder that our senses are like portals through which experiences pass to our inner selves. Moderation of the senses during adolescence, therefore, will result in a lifetime of equilibrium. Good guides, both parents and teachers, will not let young people see ugly, obscene things, because these will stay tenaciously in their minds and become objects of desire further along. The ears must be protected from hearing dirty and dishonest stories because, as Aristotle says in book 7 of his *Politics,* hearing is next to doing. Sense of smell can also be a problem if teenagers learn to sniff things that excite their lust, especially perfumes worn by lascivious women. Then there are speech, taste, and touch. Saying dishonest words and telling lies not only arouse concupiscence immediately but also so accustom the mind to false reasoning that the thinking process itself becomes corrupted and the youth incapable of recognizing and holding to the truth. It is better for adolescents to be more taciturn than loquacious, in proper accord with their lack of expertise on worldly matters, and to learn by listening, thereby growing in prudence, training, and judgment.[29]

Gozze drifts off to his next topic, excessive eating and drinking, without realizing that he has failed to cover the sins of touching and tasting, but no one ever said popular-advice manuals were uniformly logical and consistent. In any event, in the array of manuals that an avid collector might acquire, these sins do not go unnoticed. Panfilo Fenario, in a rather large and pompous religious tract, presents at great length and with some repetition the general argument that, because mankind is endowed with free will, once a human being chooses sin, he or she becomes worse than a beast. Fenario divides sin at least partially according to which of the five senses performs the evil act. The worst of the tactile sins is touching the genitals, because this distorts God's purpose of procreation; touching, therefore, is more sinful than seeing, smelling, tasting, or hearing the genitals. While logically this hierarchy may seem to treat sodomy lightly, the author's intent surely was otherwise. The theology here is a mishmash anyway; the argument confuses intent with consequences and intermingles the sense that commits the sin with the object upon which it is committed.[30] Let us return to the more practical advice of Gozze.

Regulation of eating and drinking has many facets. Meals should not be gulped down quickly and avidly because that hurts the stomach, like throwing wood helter-skelter on a fire. Eating more than can be digested harms the body's overall complexion. Tell youngsters also not to eat with dirty, sweaty hands or spill all over their clothes. Meals should be served in a timely fashion, neither too soon nor too late. Even more important than control in eating is a tight rein on drinking. Immoderate consumption of wine arouses sexual desire, offends the brain, and makes people behave scandalously. And when all the senses are brought firmly under the mind's regulation, then it is appropriate to release some of the tensions of a spirit enclosed in such a somber body with rigorous exercise like a game of handball or soccer or scrimmaging. Best of all is playing music, long known as just the right medicine to cure sadness.[31] Lessons from nature and from the Bible all teach us the virtues of moderation, writes another moralist. Just think about why God gave no other creature of man's stature so small a mouth and stomach. And remember that Adam and Eve got into trouble over a mere apple, not a calf.[32]

Wine and sex also caught the attention of Annibale Guasco, as shown in a letter to his daughter Lavinia, published in Turin in 1586, advising her on proper behavior as she left home to become a court damsel. Wine should be heavily diluted with water, for pure wine is the great enemy of chastity. Even the poorest, most ugly young woman becomes rich and beautiful if she remains chaste. Chastity is just like a dress, and any little mark stains it. No one would want to wear a soiled dress for all to see, no matter how elegant the fabric and design. The stain cannot be removed with water or with any solvents; it remains even after the dress has been reduced to ashes and dust. A dishonored woman remains exactly that forever, on this earth and after she dies.[33]

The problem of chastity evoked a substantial popular literature, finding its way even into parlor games of the *Jeopardy* sort,[34] and as we might expect, occupied a central place in Catholic teaching on morality. We now return to advice manuals for confessors, a genre that must have had a high multiplier effect as the priest used the confessional to interrogate and instruct his parishioners. How-to books for confessors served as conveyors of how-not-to-sin information for laypersons. A cleric in 1572, who turned to page 217 of Lodovico Gabrielli da Ogobbio's *Methodo di confessione* (Method of Confession), would have found there simple vernacular explanations of seven major kinds of sexual sin, both for his own edification and to guide him in using proper words when questioning laypersons—all in a handy octodecimo format:

1. Fornication is defined as sexual intercourse between a man and a woman, neither of whom is married.
2. Rape is sexual intercourse outside of marriage with a virgin.
3. Adultery is sexual intercourse between a man and a woman if either is married.
4. Incest is sexual intercourse between persons related by blood or as in-laws, unless there is a matrimonial dispensation.
5. Sacrilege is any sort of sexual activity with a person who has taken religious

vows. It is also sacrilege if a priest or monk sins with a woman who has not taken vows herself.

6. Sodomy is the gravest of all sexual sins because it violates nature and denies procreation.[35]

7. Conjugal excess is when husband and wife behave inappropriately with each other or in regard to the time, place, or technique of sexual intercourse.

All sexual sins are mortal sins, not just the seven specifically designated above; some examples of sins not to be treated lightly are looking at lewd pictures, talking dishonestly with women, fondling and kissing women, singing dirty songs, and reading lascivious books.

Moving on from definitions to practical advice on how to combat lust—whether in the confessor or the parishioner is not always clear—the manual suggests following precepts proclaimed centuries ago by renowned theologians such as Gregory the Great (540–604) and Isidore of Seville (d. 636). If you desire a woman, try to conjure up a clear image of how her body will be when she is dead. Or if that is too difficult and you can only think of her in a living condition, concentrate on the fluids in her nostrils and the phlegm in her throat; focus on the contents of her bowels. She may look nice and be attractive on the outside, but internally she is full of ugliness and dirt. If you saw a filthy mark or some spittle on her dress, surely you would be put off, disgusted to touch her even with the tip of your finger, but that is what all of her is like on the inside. Unlike thirst or hunger, lust is insatiable. The more you think dirty thoughts, the greater your urge to keep thinking them; the more you commit sexual sins, the greater your desire to do it again, while your satisfaction actually decreases. Consider carefully how brief is the bodily joy against how enormous is the eternal punishment in hell. You who have committed carnal sin, know that you've been shipwrecked and should fear the sea and flee from danger. You did not choose to conserve in their entirely the gifts God bestowed upon you at birth, but at least start holding onto whatever is left.[36]

While this pocket-sized guide is ambiguous about whether priest or parishioner might be doing the sinning and getting shipwrecked, no uncertainties mark Gaspar Loarte's *Avisi di sacerdoti et confessori* (Advice to Priests and Confessors). His book means to advise confessors on what to say when penitents tell of having committed sexual sins. Begin by reminding the sinner of his or her guardian angel. Ask the name of the angel. Do they know that the angel is watching over them physically, literally there in the room at the bedside when the sin is being carried out, thoroughly disgusted by all the hideous sights and horrid sounds? The best penances for sexual sins are the hard ones—no chance here to get off with a few Hail Marys. Demand that the penitent whip the offending flesh, undertake extended fasting, abstain from favorite foods, discipline the body, and wear a hair shirt. Tell him or her to sleep fully clothed on a board or on the floor, keep vigil all night, or get up very early in the morning. Suggest a long, arduous pilgrimage, hospital service, or a tour of duty cleaning public latrines. These are the penances that work best to macerate and mortify the flesh, rendering it subservient to the spirit. However, rich people and other parishioners of delicate complexion may not be able to cope with such physical self-punishment even if they are young, so have them gather offerings if they are poor or pay directly for rearing an orphan if they can afford it.[37]

Somewhat less extreme advice comes in Bartolomeo de Medina's book on the same subject, translated from the 1579 Spanish original into Italian as early as 1584, and reprinted at least three times by 1600. It offers an excellent example of what we have been seeing throughout on the power of the vernacular. A manual for confessors surely could have been written in Latin and used throughout Catholic Europe in a single edition. So why the vernacular and the expense of translation and publication in other vernaculars? Perhaps parish priests just weren't very good at Latin anymore, if they ever were, but I believe there is more to it. The clergy needed advice on how to deal with delicate questions of sexual sin using vocabulary parishioners could understand, neither technical to the point of obfuscation nor so crass as to provoke derision or shame. The printed vernacular book gave them exactly the approved word or phrase for penis (virile member), vagina (dishonest part), sexual intercourse (act of Venus), and whatever else they needed to say or hear in the confessional box. It is also possible that publishers thought some laypersons would want to read these books, which talk about sin so openly, explicitly, even arousingly.

The Council of Trent recognized the problem of language explicitly. Its intent that the faithful know precisely what was sinful meant that everyone had to be able to say the names of the sins. Surely this need to understand the words spurred the outpouring of popular-advice manuals for confessors (and parishioners) that occurred in the latter half of the sixteenth century. These little books may be sorely lacking in theological sophistication, but they are rich with help for carrying out daily pastoral duties. Confessors must approach the subject of proper sex with appropriate discretion, the council advised; they must use words that will not offend the sensibilities of pious laypersons or excite laughter in church. On the subject of adultery, pastors must use extreme caution and prudence. They should treat "with great delicacy of language" a subject that requires moderation rather than copious speech. The gathered high prelates had come to believe that by fully and diffusely detailing the variety of ways in which men and women might depart from the church's injunctions against illicit sex, the priest might be lighting upon those very topics that serve to inflame rather than extinguish the fires of sin. Remind parishioners of Christ's teaching that, whosoever looks on a woman in lust already has committed adultery with her in his heart (Matt. 5:27). Teach them these words in your homily, but omit details about the many and varied other species of immodesty and licentiousness, of which each individual may be admonished privately and only as the necessities of time and person require.[38]

Studying all this new language might arouse lust in the confessor himself, thought Friar Bartolomeo de Medina, so he assures the priest reading his book that there is no sin if the man of God accidentally ejaculates while hearing a particularly libidinous confession or pouring over relevant materials for noble purposes. To get humid and feel certain titillations when obliged by duty to talk with a woman is excused. The battle against lust is hard, unending, and dangerous, so confessors should concentrate on these five remedies. First, resist wicked thoughts, even fleetingly and jokingly. Second, watch and control the senses, especially the eyes, which are the first point of attack by the forces of carnal desire. Third, work constantly, never allowing yourself an idle moment. Fourth, remember always that God is actively watching you. Fifth, flee all occasions of contact with women of suspect age, even holy ones who have taken vows.[39]

Another late-sixteenth-century, pocket-sized manual on how to make a good confession, this one apparently intended by its author, Brother Cherubino da Firenze, both for the clergy and the faithful, addresses the difficult question of intent, one that had plagued theologians for centuries. He reduces the problem to an easily understood set of guidelines. First, the friar provides a list of what is sinful: forcing your partner to have sex; touching or looking at dishonest body parts, yours or anyone else's; talking, singing, or reading dishonest things;[40] kissing with lustful intent; naming or listening to others name sinful organs or acts; sending or carrying letters or other missives containing provocative materials; receiving gifts for engaging in dishonest acts; inducing others to behave sinfully; wooing and courting in church or other inappropriate places.

Then he turns to sinful carnal desires. If you consent mentally, you are obligated in confession to name the desire and the category of person you had in mind doing it with—a virgin, a married person, a relative, or whomever. Good confession requires telling the circumstances and specific objects of sinful acts, so the priest may determine the exact transgressions. Each occasion of desire must be recounted separately; the penitent must recall whether and with what means she or he tried to ward off the evil thoughts. In the case of someone in love, there may be innumerable sins of lustful thought; each one must be examined diligently, individually. Inducing sexual craving on the part of others toward yourself—what we might call flirting—is also a grave sin. In confessing their sins of desire, the faithful must omit nothing out of shame; nevertheless, their vocabulary always must remain decent and modest, yet not so obscure or genteel that the priest falls to understand exactly what the penitent actually had in mind.

Genuinely uncontrollable flashes of carnal desire are not wrong in themselves, but lingering over them for enjoyment definitely is sinful. Even wet dreams may not be sinful if you are immediately and truly sorry, hoping with all your heart never again to suffer such loss of bodily control. You should pray before going to bed not to be plagued in this way; as a practical matter absolutely avoid heavy eating and drinking before going to sleep, since these activities increase the likelihood of nocturnal pollution.[41]

The stakes involved in sins of the flesh were high indeed. In 1568, the Camaldolesian monk and prolific author of saints' lives Girolamo (Brother Silvano) Razzi published a treatise on domestic economy, meant I believe for clerics as background material for their preaching, or perhaps for very devout Catholics wishing advice on how to live according to Christian ideals. A chapter on sins explains that the seven mortal sins, in ascending order of their seriousness, are pride, envy, anger, sloth, avarice, gluttony, and lust. This hierarchy is very different from what is found in Dante's *Inferno*, a matter Brother Silvano mentions specifically. He prefers to follow traditional teachings that measure the severity of a deadly sin by how much damage it does to others and then to one's own soul. This somewhat arcane emphasis on consequences rather than intent is seen as well in Brother Silvano's warnings about what happens to lustful people. They become foolish, inconsiderate, precipitous, self-absorbed, unloving toward God, fixated about life on earth, phobic about death, and desperate as they contemplate their final judgment and loss of eternal happiness.[42]

I close our survey of recommendations about combating lust by returning to *The Catechism of the Council of Trent*, obviously not meant directly for public consumption but clearly of great importance in determining what the faithful read and heard. We have already learned that confessors should not go into great detail about the varieties of lust, and that they should use delicate language to name sexual acts and body parts. Still, plenty of good material remained for rhetorical flourish. Pastors should remind parishioners of the destruction of Sodom (Gen. 19), of the punishment of the Israelites who fornicated with the daughters of Moab (Num. 25), and of the slaughter of the Benjamites (Judg. 20). Tell them that even those who escape death will suffer intolerable pangs and tortures for all eternity. Teach them that while they are still on this earth, blind infatuation will cause sinners to lose regard for God, for personal reputation and honor, for family, indeed for life itself. They will lose confidence and good judgment, becoming incapable of discharging any sort of normal duties, as happened even to King David (2 Sam. 11) and to the wise Solomon (1 Kings 11).

Provide the congregation with clear guidelines on how to combat lust—avoid idleness, stay away from intemperance in food and drink, and watch out especially for the EYE, which is the most insidious inlet for lust. Pastors should admonish and reprove female parishioners against excess concern with ornamentation. Especially warn young minds against obscene conversation, because dirty language is like a torch that lights up passions in an immature mind. Effeminate and lascivious songs and dances also lead to lust, and are to be carefully avoided. All amatory and obscene books go in the same category, as well as any printed images that appear indecent. The best way to repress the violence of lust is frequent recourse to confession followed by communion. Add to this a regimen of unceasing, devout prayers accompanied by fasting and alms, vigils, pious pilgrimages, and other austerities.

Making Fun

Some advice on questions of conception and child rearing may have struck you as funny, at least I hope so. But the intentions of the original authors—with obvious exceptions such as Ortensio Lando's satire on why a sterile wife is a good thing and possible spoofs like Lombardelli's on adolescence—were entirely solemn, and I believe sixteenth-century readers took the pages in front of them seriously. Even male impotence and husbands who failed to satisfy their wives' sexual desires—subjects so merrily explored by Boccaccio and other fiction writers—did not elicit humor in the specific form of an advice manual. As we move on to advice on whether to marry and how to choose a spouse, however, it becomes clear that the how-to-do-it format served as a vehicle for all sorts of humor, often misogynous and occasionally pornographic. Readers of these books surely were looking more for good laughs than for sound prescriptions. Still, this form of making fun reveals something about social mores and about the power of inexpensive print to speed the circulation of new, outrageous, even vicious ideas. By taking a glance at how men lampooned women (only rarely does satire directed against men take the form of an advice manual, although such humor is common enough in short stories of the *Decameron* genre), we gain perspective on how both sexes understood their relations and interactions.[43]

The literary efforts of Count Giovanni Maria Bonardo, better known as a scientist than a humorist, illustrate nicely how the printed word allowed opportunities for an idle nobleman to dabble in different fields. His works display little intensive study and no original research, but they all have a pleasing, folksy way of conveying information in the vernacular to an audience beyond the university, undoubtedly due to the considerable efforts of his editor, Luigi Groto ad Adria. Among his publications, we find a 1586 book on how to manage the farm and increase crop yields, perhaps intended for the gentleman farmer without too much leisure time, at least to judge by its brevity. Several years earlier, he had published an equally sweeping and superficial survey of secret and rare, animate and inanimate elements found throughout the world. Earlier, there had been an astronomy book providing the size and distance in Italian miles of all the spheres in the universe, beginning with hell and moving along through the planets and stars up to where the saints reside in heaven. In a lighter vein, there was a book on madrigals.[44]

In the midst of all this publication activity, Bonardo also found time to write his reflections on life's pleasures and pains, among which of course was marriage. These jottings had been mislaid at his editor's shop for sixteen years before being published in 1586; Groto must have located them only shortly before his own death in 1585, and reportedly he remarked that "it almost would have been better not to have found them." A modern critic comments wryly that Bonardo's agriculture book was "more sober and lucid." Anyway, in good pseudoscientific fashion, Bonardo weighs the pluses and minuses of taking a wife. The good thing is that you will not require an alarm clock to get up early in the morning nor will you need to read fables to fall asleep. Unfortunately, the downside looms larger. The count admits, speaking from his heart, that you will get no rest anyway, because of the infinite miseries marriage brings. If your wife is richer than you, she will be insufferable; if she is of higher rank, she will not respect you; if she has more relatives, you are threatened with visitors everyday. If she is too pretty, she will want to be adored constantly, and because everyone desires her, she will give you good reason for great concern; but, if she is ugly, your life will be a living death. If she is poor, she will spend all her time scheming to get rich, and if she is already rich, she will think only about getting wealthier without risking the loss of what she already has.

If she gives birth often, you will have to do the work of both husband and wife, because she will be too busy to run the household and supervise the servants. She will become jealous and won't let you go out, even to see your own relatives. Once the house gets fuller than a schoolroom, she will start acquiring clothes for herself, thereby impoverishing you, while she lets your children run outside naked. To cut a good figure in her new wardrobe, she will send the youngest first to one wet nurse and then to another when the first runs out of milk. Your children will give you so much trouble, you will wish you never had them. If she cannot conceive, she will never be happy, she will have no desire to build up the family riches, and the births of children among your relatives will be days of darkness, not celebration. In the end, everyone will think that her sterility is a punishment from God upon you, so you must be an evil person.[45]

Whereas Bonardo's humor was embedded in a publication record that included works in popular science and always prominently featured his title of count, embellished with the pompous addition of "illustrious," other misogynous tracts circulated anonymously. The *Compagnia della lesina* (Company of Lesina) series of little chapbooks appeared as early as 1591, in Mantua (at least that is the earliest edition I have found with Lesina in the title), and continued to be enlarged and reprinted throughout the next century. Advice from the *Compagnia della lesina* purports to deal with savings and thrift, and it uses this motif to satirize a vast range of targets, including the choice of a wife. If you are forced to marry, the author recommends, make sure the girl has a big dowry and a small body, this in obedience to the rule of the wise philosopher who said to take as much as you can of what is good and the least possible of what is bad. A little wife will take up less space in bed, so you can either economize by purchasing a smaller bed or else keep more room for yourself. There will be savings on the yards of fabric needed for her clothing, and these coins do add up over the years. She will be too short to expose herself at the window, so she won't need as many garments anyway. Then there is always a chance that if she climbs on a stool to do her household chores, she will fall off and kill herself, so you will be rid of her and your bank account can really soar.[46]

Somewhat more ambiguous is the recommendation to choose a woman that others do not want. It comes from Angelo di Forte, a mercurial figure who published a critique of Avicenna's supposed errors, along with books on alchemy, astrology, and the plague. His suggestion, contained in a cheap-looking octavo pamphlet of about forty unnumbered pages, could be read with some refashioning as a churchly prescription to look past superficial beauty toward inner character and virtue, some examples of which we will examine shortly, but I am inclined to take it as a satire on such sanctimonious advice. Nobody wants women who are old, lame, hunchbacked, ugly, crippled, or deformed, says Forte, because such creatures do not spark the flames of lust in a young man. This is really too bad, because so long as these unfortunate women are still made of flesh and bone, they too have natural longings. They know they are not wanted, that no one could possibly be jealous over them, and that they must be very timid in making sexual advances. Therefore, anyone of them will make an excellent wife, as the sweet love that burns in her breasts is fueled by union with a husband so good that he saw past her defects and chose her above all others. The pretty ones, on the other hand, are desired by all who see them, and they soon start to linger with one or another admirer in playful flatteries. You get started thinking too many heavy thoughts, your spirits get tired and you feel only anguish. Her love of being loved vanquishes any sense of virtue she may once have possessed, and you are left with the sorry consequences.[47]

Sixteenth-century readers might find very similar sentiments in verse form in works such as *Stanze in lode della donna brutta* (Stanzas in Praise of the Ugly Woman). The rhymes playfully remind young men that beauty fades quickly. Moreover, since only male semen determines the appearance of your offspring, it would be better to leave the pretty girls to some dwarf or Ethiopian and choose for yourself a reliably ugly wife, so you can be certain the children she conceives are actually yours.[48]

I found a different humorous take on desirable physical qualities in a strange little book that includes lots of black magic and secrets for tricksters, including how to make dogs chase after your enemy by secretly smearing secretions from a bitch in heat on his shoes, powders to make a fire inextinguishable, potions to cause sleeplessness or inability to swallow, and recipes to get rid of foot odor, kill fleas, and prevent insects from eating your grain supply. Amidst all this mishmash is a repeat of the yardstick found in several literary traditions that to be truly beautiful, the ideal woman should have things in threes, as follows:

Three white—flesh, teeth, and face
Three black—eyes, lashes, and pubic hair
Three red—lips, cheeks, and nails
Three long—body, hair, and hands

Three short—teeth, ears, and feet
Three wide—chest, hips, and forehead
Three narrow—mouth, vagina, and waist
Three large—thighs, buttocks, and nature
Three soft—hair, lips, and fingers
Three small—mouth, nose, and breasts[49]

Then there is advice apparently given with superficial sobriety that nonetheless may have struck male readers as humorous and that unquestionably has a misogynous tone. The dialogue by Ciro Spontone titled *Hercole difensore d'Homero* (Hercules, the Defender of Homer) is a good example. The interlocutors take up the subject of beauty in a woman, but instead of focusing on Platonic philosophical questions, they drift into specifics. Her alluring eyelashes should be dark, her eyes not too protruded or recessed, her nose not too long or short but in proportion with the round visage it adorns, and her cheeks not so white as to appear pallid and with a natural blush. She should have a courteous and smiling mouth, small and surrounded by coral lips that sublimely imprison clean teeth, a round neck and large breasts, a small body, high hips, straight legs, small feet no longer than her hands, and fingernails not too curved. Altogether she should exude purity on the outside and a touch of enchantment on the inside. But if a woman does not have all these features and is something less than a Venus, she should just make do with what the mirror tells her.[50]

Among many satires of the serious-advice manual, one of my favorites is Ortensio Lando's *Paradossi* (Paradoxes), which contains a variation on the cuckold theme that so delighted sixteenth-century readers. In my chapter on conception, I could not resist including his recommendations in favor of marrying a sterile woman, and now I am equally unwilling to pass over in silence his advocacy of keeping an adulterous wife. A wife who is faithful soon gets to be bold and imperious, Lando warns, insolent, proud, and completely unafraid of her husband. But once she finally finds a lover, she instantly becomes more attentive and affectionate toward her husband. Even better, she may become financially useful if her new man has a high title and is known in the right places. Staying with an adulteress gives you personal freedom and a life of tranquility. It allows you to repudiate her without resort to poisons or knives. This modern tendency to combat adultery with weapons is absolutely deplorable. The ancient practice among pagan husbands who found themselves cuckolded was much better: shut up and ignore it.[51]

Were there a prize for the most viciously misogynous advice-manual spoof I have come across, a top contender would be in the writings of

Giuseppe Passi. He held memberships in several literary academies, including one at his birthplace of Ravenna, and wrote a string of humorous tracts on human deficiencies, magic, and speaking so as not to offend, each of which went through multiple printings. Then in 1609, he withdrew from the world to join a Camaldolesian congregation of hermits. Well before this early retirement, however, he published *I donneschi difetti* (The Defects of Women), opening the treatise with a warning against women who color their hair and wear costume jewelry. At great length he advises men to follow the wisdom of Aristotle and pay no heed to women's counsel, giving numerous examples of men who listened to their wives and ended up dead. Other chapter titles explain that women are proud, avaricious, intemperate, lascivious, carnal, libidinous, luxurious, angry, choleric, furious, dissolute, gluttonous, drunken, wine bibbers, invidious, indolent, lazy, vainglorious, ambitious, ungrateful, cruel, adulterous, prostitutes, whores, ruffians, sharp tongued, chattering, gossiping, grumbling, lying, false, caustic, curious, pertinacious, obstinate, litigious, contentious, ribald, discordant, disputatious, witches, sirens, venomous, pernicious, superstitious, conjuring, cheating, hypocritical, fraudulent, deceiving, jealous, tyrannical, thieving, fickle, inconstant, unstable, lightheaded, credulous, silly, brainless, cowardly, vile, timid, fearful, and vain.[52]

Not everyone thought Passi's book was so funny. Among his outraged detractors was one woman ready to match him in the business of hurling invectives. Lucrezia Marinella, the Venetian poet and daughter of advice-manual writer Giovanni Marinello, published her book *La nobiltà et l'eccellenze delle donne* (On the Nobility and Excellence of Women) as an explicit response to Passi. According to her chapter titles, women are temperate, continent, courageous, intrepid, prudent, just, faithful, courteous, tolerant, patient, strong, and loving toward family and country. Men, by contrast, are avaricious, incontinent, drunk, gluttonous, undisciplined, irascible, bestial, overbearing, arrogant, lazy, negligent, sleepy, tyrannical, usurping, ambitious, vainglorious, unjust, angry, murderous, fraudulent, perfidious, deceitful, perjuring, obstinate, pertinacious, ungrateful, discourteous, unfaithful, volatile, hateful, evil, thieving, assassins, rapacious, plundering, vile, fearful, petty, blasphemous, ungodly, divining, witches, conjurers, lying, mendacious, jealous, preening, bleached, painted, polished, heretical, schismatic, crybabies, and gamblers.[53] Both these battle-of-the-sexes works might be excluded as falling outside the advice-manual or even the "advice-manual-spoof" category, but such an exclusion could not be applied to Giuseppe Passi's subsequent tract *Dello stato maritale* (The Married State).

The opening epistle to readers declares that this new book is the first installment of what he promised in his earlier *I donneschi difetti*, to wit, specific instruction for men on how to govern virgins, matrons, widows, and nuns. Even though virgins logically should come first, Passi writes that he is skipping to the matron category because of the pressing need to take the blinkers off all those simpletons who either didn't read *I donneschi difetti* very carefully or who misunderstood it. Anyway, Passi protests, he never said not to take a wife but only told the truth about what living with one would be like, much as the oracle sees the future but does not alter it. Nor will the promised sequels on governing virgins, widows, and nuns be forthcoming, he teases, since he has decided to let them live happily ever after.

As to matrons, *Dello stato maritale* begins with an eight-page table of contents precisely in the style of an advice manual, the better for readers to find exactly what they need at any given moment. Just name the problem and locate a quick solution. On getting your wife to obey your commands, turn to page 160; if she climbs on top for sex, see page 132, for how to get her off; for help in not being jealous, try page 150; and so forth. The book itself is filled with pseudoerudite citations of ancient Greek philosophers (printed in Greek) and biblical texts (provided in Latin) to show that most women are evil by nature. Garbled reformulations of saintly theologians such as Bonaventure, Aquinas, and Ambrose also abound. Alongside these are numerous examples of good women who were brave warriors, who stood with Mary at the cross, or who suffered martyrdom to preserve their virginity. Still, says Passi, there is no need to say that one woman is better than another because they say it for themselves, all the time. As to marriage, the first rule is never to marry a widow, because she will always put the merits of her first husband under your nose, an observation Passi proves with numerous erudite citations beginning with Moses and concluding with Jerome. The other cardinal rule is that an old man should not marry a young woman. Women are generally insufferable anyway, and a young one will be impossible to satisfy. Keep impure women away from your house, because they will turn your wife into one of them. Never let your wife mount you or read lascivious books, because she will become permanently unrestrained. Do not hit her, especially in front of others; it does no good and will just make her misbehave even more.[54]

The tradition in which Passi wrote went back at least to the twelfth century, and poems such as *Le malitie delle donne* (The Cunning of Women) were printed widely as soon as there were printing presses. Although not nearly so vitriolic as the prose verbiage in *Dello stato maritale* and *I donneschi difetti,* these stanzas brought amusement, at least to some readers, by mercilessly bashing women. They advise variously against choosing a rich wife, one who is poor, pretty, amorous, or a foreigner, or, as in the following lines, a young one.

Se la pigli giovenetta	If you choose one who is young,
Ti convien amaestrare	You will have to train her
Quella lingua maledetta	To curb her accursed tongue.
Mai farà, che barbotare	She will do nothing but mutter
E con suo mormorano	And with her constant complaining,
Darà voce fino al Cielo	Her voice to the sky ringing,
E non stimarà un pelo	She won't give a hoot
De lo tuo minacciare.	If you threaten to give her the boot.[55]

The next manual we shall consider may read like a spoof to us moderns, as I believe it did to some contemporary readers, but other sixteenth-century people no doubt took it seriously. I refer to Cosmo Agnelli's *Amorevole aviso circa gli abusi delle donne vane* (Loving Advice On the Abuses of Vain Women). He had been issuing printed warnings for Christian women on how to behave for at least sixteen years before this work appeared in 1592. For Agnelli, three abuses stood out among all the rest: hair coloring and styling, powdering and exposing the breasts, and wearing high-heeled shoes. Notably absent from this tirade, as well as from popular-advice manuals generally, whether loving or not, is a parallel condemnation of exaggerated fashion statements by young men. Moreover, the exclusive focus on women by clerical authors like Agnelli carried over as well to sumptuary legislation approved by secular politicians.[56]

Dyeing or bleaching your hair blond is a reprehensible practice that does violence to nature and offends the Supreme Author who gave you the color you have. If God wanted you to be blond like a German or a French woman, he could have easily made you so. Your eyes will not be more alluring just because your hair is bleached. Lightening your hair wastes the world's most precious commodity—time. It is amazing to see women seeking this imaginary beauty by spending hours in the sun, sustaining all kinds of pain, using poisonous dyes, and inhaling noxious sulfur fumes with their heads over the fire. Their poor husbands come home early from work expecting to find them at prayer, or if their wives are out, assuming that maybe they've gone to mass, and instead these women are off sunning themselves or sitting at home in stony silence attending to their coiffeurs. The dangers have been known for centuries, ever since the great physician Galen wrote about how hair coloring ruins the head and makes a woman unfit for bearing children. Blond hair is good for whores, dark for proper matrons. And what are we to say about those women whose hair has turned white, so now they dye it blond or black as if no one will notice how hoary they've become? Agnelli then misquotes both St. Paul (1 Tim. 2:9–10) and St. Peter (1 Pet. 3:3–4), ascribing to these authoritative letter writers injunctions against bleaching the hair when in fact the biblical texts fulminate only against curls or braids. Still, the spirit of Christian teaching is fully and fairly captured in his diatribe, and the scriptural references allow him a segue to his attack on exaggerated hairstyling.

Fashionable women braid their hair and pile it up in the shape of a plume, a tower, a crest, or a horn—at least that is what Agnelli saw. Then they strut around with their proud chins in the air, thinking they are beautiful and alluring but in fact looking ridiculous, more like satyrs and horned demons than women. Imagine, some of them actually skip going to mass because their hair is not styled to suit them. Who can calculate how much money they waste each year at the hairdresser? Not only could the money have gone in charity to support the poor, but these hairdressers—a lascivious lot—fill their clients' ears with salacious gossip and turn them into equally dishonest women.

The second great abuse of women is that they powder their faces and breasts to show off. Grandiose hairstyling and facial makeup are bad enough, but the worst of all is arousing men's lust by exposing your paps. The naked breast could be allowed as perfectly natural, but if a woman first adorns her bosom and then displays herself, something else must be going on. She is advertising merchandise for sale; she has turned God's rule of natural harmony into total chaos. Agnelli then cites approvingly canto 23 of Dante's journey through purgatory in *The Divine Comedy*, wherein the great poet condemns the ways of Florentine women who parade around displaying their breasts and paps. Next comes a tirade against women who do not wear a veil to cover their heads in church, followed by a return directly to the evils of powdering and a warning that applying plasters to lighten the skin inflicts great physical as well as moral damage. The skin gets old and wrinkled before its time, becoming pale and flaccid. Your teeth fall out, your breath smells foul, and you get into the bind that you are so decrepit and ugly that you really cannot go out in public without putting on a mask of makeup. Ovid's poetic warnings against facial treatments still rang true fifteen hundred years later:

> Your first concern, girls, should be for proper behavior:
> With a fine personality, features are sure to please.
> Love of character's lasting, but age will ravage beauty,
> The pretty face wrinkle and line,

Till a time will come when you'll hate to look in the mirror,
And misery etches those furrows deeper still.
But probity lasts well, will endure for ages, can carry
Love with its weight for years.[57]

The third abuse Agnelli warns against is wearing inordinately high-heeled shoes. Women think that strutting around from this magnificent perspective makes them alluring, but true beauty always consists in proper proportions. Elongating your legs with heels that are a quarter or even half an arm's length leaves you looking like a monster, with the head and torso of a child perched on the legs of a giant. What beauty can there be in having your knees nearly where your chin should be, in being unable to take four steps without danger of imminent collapse, in tumbling over should you try to kneel, and in being unable to arise without assistance? How does it look in church when, at the moment the priest raises the holy sacrament, there you are standing in pompous arrogance while you should be prostate on the floor? God sees everything. Back at home, high heels prevent you from attending to the household chores any good wife and mother should be doing.

All this is what in Latin is known as *fucus*, falsity about stature, falsity about hair, falsity about coloring. Because of the weakness of their sex, women do not have the right to introduce legitimately these usages, nay, corruptions of proper usages. Agnelli continues his loving advice with a protest; he is not saying all ornamentation is evil, only that which goes to excess. Too much gold, too many jewels, a collection of precious dresses—all these bring ruin to the house and disorder to the world. A married woman, and only a married woman, not a daughter or a widow, may wear a modest amount of real gold: to please her husband, to display to everyone his financial success, and to keep his thoughts from straying to lascivious behavior with other women. Indeed, if these are truly your motives, with no personal vanity involved, then wearing precious jewelry and looking good is a meritorious act. But let's face it, such instances are rare indeed, vastly outnumbered by the vain falsifiers you see every-where.[58]

With Cosmo Agnelli's loving advice about bleached hair, plunging necklines, and high-heeled shoes, which I hope readers have found at least moderately funny but which he definitely wrote to inspire female sinners to give up their ungodly fashions, or at least to give comfort to those pious women who shunned such finery in favor of modest attire, we have returned from the muck of theologically dubious misogyny such as *I donneschi difetti* and the *Compagnia della Lesina*. We are back onto the main road of Catholic prescriptions concerning women's behavior. Men hewed just about all of that road, in Italy as everywhere in Europe, a point strongly emphasized, for example, in Suzanne Hull's book *Women according to Men*. Nevertheless, we should not assume that female writers, whether published or not, necessarily offered a sharply different direction. Since we are now looking at fashion, this seems like a good place to set forth a quotation from a letter written on February 12, 1487, by the eighteen-year-old widow Laura Cereta. She meant the letter to be public, and she specifically sought eternal fame through her writings. Her husband had died only months before, so obviously this was a difficult time in her life, a period in which apparently she depended more on the consolation of religion than she would in later years, but there is no evidence that she subsequently changed her views on women's vanities. Apart from internal pronouns that identify the author as a woman, what distinguishes this text from Agnelli's diatribe may be more a matter of style than substance, something worth pondering.

> Wives are bewitched by rich display; more witless still are those [husbands] who, to satisfy the appetite of their wives, destroy their patrimonies. . . . Let those who do not believe me attend the services of the church. Let them observe weddings packed with seated matrons. Let them gaze at these women who, with majestic pride, promenade amidst crowds through the piazzas. Among them, here and there, is one who ties a towering knot—made of someone else's hair—at the very peak of her head; another's forehead is submerged in waves of crimped curls; and another, in order to bare her neck, binds with a golden ribbon her golden hair. One suspends a necklace from her shoulder, another from her arm, another from neck to breast. Others choke themselves with pearl necklaces; born free, they boast to be held captive. And many display fingers glistening with jewels. One, lusting to walk more mincingly, loosens her girdle, while another tightens hers to make her breasts bulge. Some drag from their shoulders silken tunics. Others, sweet-scented with perfumes, cover themselves with an Arabian hood. Some boost themselves with high-heeled shoes. And all think it particularly modish to swathe their legs with fine soft cotton. Many press softened bread on their faces, many artificially smooth their skin, stretched with wrinkles; there are few whose ruddy faces are not painted with the luster of white lead. In one way or another they strive by means of exquisite artistry to seem more beautiful than the Author of their beauty decreed. The impudence of some women is shameful. They paint their white cheeks with purple and, with furtive winks and smiling mouths, pierce the poisoned hearts of those who gaze on them. O the bold wantonness

of lost modesty! O the weakness of our sex, stooping to voluptuous-
ness! We have only to hang from our ears little ornaments trembling
with precious stones and emeralds, and we shall not differ from pa-
gans. Was it for this, by chance, that we were begotten, that we might
worship in shameless devotion the idols of our mirrored faces? Did
we renounce display in baptism so that, as Christian women, we
might imitate Jews and barbarians?[59]

Choosing a Spouse

For a fitting vantage point as our gaze shifts from frills and cosmetics to
serious advice on the lifetime commitment of choosing a spouse, let us
return to *The Catechism of the Council of Trent*. First, there is an innate
tendency in both sexes toward marriage, wrote the assembled high prelates; such a union provides for mutual aid and support during the discomforts of life and in the feebleness of old age. Second, marriage offers
the only proper, stable way to realize the desire for a family. Third, marriage is a remedy against concupiscence and is the prudent choice for all
those who are aware of their own frailty and who are unwilling to bear
the assaults of the flesh. These are the basics, and as long as the primary
good intentions remain in the foreground, it is not to be condemned if
in choosing a wife a man gives weight to his desire to leave an heir, to
his prospective bride's dowry, and to her beauty, illustrious descent, and
congeniality.[60]

Even narrower ground had been sufficient for St. Paul, who held that
the reason for marriage is quenching the physical passions, and who does
not directly mention economic gain, procreation, defense of family interest, or maintenance of social order. Paul's authoritative letter to early
Christians (1 Cor. 7:1–7) begins in thoroughly one-sided fashion, arguing that men would be better off not touching women while offering
no parallel praise for the benefits of female continence. Although the rest
of the passage explicitly gives husbands and wives equal rights to claims
on the conjugal debt, the sexist coloration remains. Not surprisingly,
most advice manuals written by men follow Paul's archetype, giving little
consideration to female sexual urges as a reason for marriage. In other
contexts, to be sure, the manuals treat women as lascivious daughters of
Eve. The catalyst is the sexual act itself. To put the matter in the same
crude way as the manuals do, as long as a virgin does not know what
she is missing, then her sex drive remains low; only after introduction to
the carnal act does she become insatiable. Since male advice-manual
writers assume a world of virginal brides who have little choice about

being passed from father to husband, their recommendations generally address lustful grooms.

The secular physician/charlatan Leonardo Fioravanti accepts Pauline wisdom without question, reformulating the matter in his usually direct manner. There is nothing a man likes better than sex, he asserts, and those who are not married get exhausted in every sense of the word in their quest for carnal satisfaction; moreover, they are constantly at risk of serious disease. "I advise everyone who intends to use this vice to take a legitimate wife, as holy and divine law commands."[61]

A more discursive, equally pious statement may be found in the layman Francesco Tommasi's 1590 guide for the father of the household. He repeats disapprovingly the old adage that you should pick a wife with your fingers, using them to count how much money she has, and with your eyes, to see how beautiful she is. Tommasi freely concedes that women are very wicked, generally behaving badly and displaying excessive pride. But these defects are just part of their nature; they do not constitute a sufficient reason not to marry. Propagation of the race is man's duty, and so he must marry. But it takes eleven repetitive pages to get through this advice.[62] Equally tedious and unconvincing in my judgment is the dialogue by Annibale Romei claiming in good Platonic fashion that no one is so beautiful that they do not have some ugly aspect, nor anyone so ugly that there is not something beautiful in them—a hand, a breast, an eye, character, something. So, yes, love grows from beauty, but everyone (Romei is referring exclusively to a female "everyone" here) has some beauty and therefore some reason to be loved.[63]

Monsignor Sabba da Castiglione's collection of 133 ricordi (actually, highly prescriptive memoirs) is unusual for so openly combining rigid Catholic tenets with crude humor directed against women. Although largely and perhaps understandably ignored by modern literary critics, the book was very popular in its day, going through three editions (the last one posthumous) and growing from 72 to 133 memoirs between 1546 and 1554; there followed nineteen printings between 1559 and 1597, in Mantua (1), Milan (2), and Venice (16). While I recognize its important place in antiheretical writing by midcentury churchmen, my interest in the Ricordi focuses on its practical recommendations for laypersons. Depending on which of its six hundred pages the reader flips to, or locates by using the handy table of contents at the back, anyone seeking information about how to be a true gentleman could find everything here from injunctions on visiting holy places to advice on how to dress.

In a lengthy examination of the joys and pitfalls of marriage, Sabba da Castiglione begins with Socrates, ascribing to the Greek philosopher the insight that you will repent either way. If you do not marry, you will miss the sweet delights of having children, along with the loving companionship and support of a wife. If you do marry, you are headed for a life of constant warfare, without peace or truce, that will leave you no moment of repose and will turn even your nights into harsh, cruel battlefields. Instead of finding a quiet bed, you will lie in an armed camp with an unceasing din of complaints and laments all about. If your bride is beautiful, she will be sought after by everyone; if she is rich, she will try to rule you. If you have children and they are obedient and wonderful, you will be in constant fear that you may lose them or that they will be led astray by evil companions. Remember that offspring who start as good little goslings still turn into bad geese. Total misery awaits you if your children turn out to be contumacious, rebellious, disobedient, lazy, and ribald.

When a very wise man was asked if he meant to take a wife, he answered, "of course, by the hair." And did he intend to lead her? "Straight down to the river." And would he touch her? "With a stick." And would he place a ring on her? "Yes, in her nose, like an ox." A widow should marry only a widower, because then when she starts saying her first husband was better at "this," he can respond that his first wife was better at "that." "I think there is no greater penance in the world, not even the harshest flagellation, than to have to patiently tolerate for love of God a wife who is crazy, contradictory, impudent, and bestial as some of them are. Such a fate is much worse than that of the Christian martyrs in heaven who only suffered a few moments of bodily pain, eased by the consolation of Jesus Christ. These poor husbands really should be canonized for martyrdom and put in the book of martyrology and the catalog of saints, so during the litany we can say an Our Father for them."

Embedded in all this levity, however, is a sterner and more traditional message. Monsignor Sabba explains to his readers that a good woman should have six characteristics, like the lily that has a sweet odor protected by six thorns hidden by six pedals. Failure to adhere to the good leads to very specific sins, as the following chart shows:

GOOD BEHAVIOR	FAILURE
Sobriety in food and drink	Gluttony and drunkenness
Honesty and decorum in dress	Lasciviousness and vanity
Custodianship of the eyes and ears	Licentiousness and excess curiosity
Moderation and temperance in speaking	Gossiping and telling dirty jokes
Abhorrence of dishonest persons	Falls into worldly sin and scandal
Devotion to honest chores	Laziness leads to lasciviousness

Little wonder, then, that Sabba da Castiglione closes this chapter on choosing a wife with a thankful reminder that he decided instead to become a cleric in the order of the Knights of Jerusalem.[64]

From a less ponderous, misogynous perspective, but one that also found great favor among sixteenth-century readers, we have Leonardo Fioravanti, who follows his advice about quenching male sex drive with a declaration that marriage is the best of all friendships. Whereas all other human relations are based either on will or on biological necessity, this one rests equally upon both. In a section addressed primarily to male needs, he proceeds to outline the seven benefits of marriage. The first is that a father's memory rests in his children, allowing him to be reborn through his sons. The second is that the sin of adultery and consequent eternal damnation may be avoided. The third is the good companionship that comes to a happy couple. Fourth, married men and women stand to obtain numerous legal benefits. Fifth, in some instances peace and happiness are restored among families that had been hostile to each other, and these new alliances produce prosperity. Although Fioravanti promises to give seven reasons why a man should marry, he apparently ran out of things to say on this topic after five. He drifts off instead into recounting various oddities in wedding ceremonies from exotic civilizations, such as exchanging toenail clippings and pieces of each other's ears, which I suppose fascinated the reading public.[65]

Some men wanted to marry a virgin. If they turned to Lorenzo Gioberti's book *Errori popolari,* they could find advice on how to verify virginity, or at least on what signs they needn't bother about. This was the section of his book that had gotten him into much trouble back in France and had necessitated an apologetic defense in the revised edition. He advises readers to forget about the popular adage that after a girl has sex, her nipples turn dark. You'd be better off making judgments based on the sweetness of her facial expression and on her general demeanor. Also, don't count on claims that by measuring the proportions of her neck, chin, and head you can tell anything, because it is not true that sexual intercourse makes a girl's neck larger—that just happens normally during puberty. Nor is there any factual basis to the lengthened-tip-of-the-nose theory. Some folks claim that if you grind up a piece of aloe and have your prospective bride swallow it, she will urinate incontinently if she is a virgin. Others look for the same result after putting leaves of dock on the fire and having her inhale the smoke. But neither test is reliable, since the outcomes can be faked anyway. The only way to tell for sure is to do a vaginal examination, and even this can be very tricky. Ways for a bride to deceive her husband on their wedding night have circulated for centuries.[66]

The general consensus among advice-manual writers is that girls rush too quickly into marriage. This opinion, conveyed in lighthearted poetry such as the *Lamento de una gioveneta la quale fu volunterosa de esser presto maridata* (Lament of a Young Woman Who Wants to Hurry Up and Marry), also emerges in the stern warnings we considered earlier from Michele Savonarola on how people no longer live very long because they are born to parents too young to have strong seed.[67] Another manual we reviewed extensively, Giovanni Marinello's *Delle medicine partenenti all' infermità delle donne,* copies directly from Savonarola: women should marry between the ages of eighteen and twenty-five, while their husbands should be the same age or older, up to thirty. Women at this age are best able to sustain the rigors of pregnancy and childbirth. If either partner is too young, then the risk increases that the fetus will form imperfectly. However, too old, especially for the woman, is also not good. First, a girl who stays at home too long gets set in her ways and is no longer really obedient to anyone. Second, she becomes too old to attend vigorously to raising her own children.[68]

Nicolò Gozze, whose advice we perused concerning obesity, getting rich, wearing makeup like a Jezebel, and table manners, also weighs in with vigor on the proper age to marry. He praises Marsilio Ficino's dialogue on Plato's *Republic* but realizes that many of his readers may not have it at their fingertips; anyway, while it recommends twenty-five as the age when a man should marry, Gozze thinks thirty may be more perfect. Upon further reflection, he approves of Aristotle's suggestion that eighteen for women and thirty-seven for men is best, because this gives them each about the same number (thirty-two or thirty-three) of reproductive years in that women are fertile until fifty and men virile until seventy. So taken is Gozze with his display of classical erudition here that he ignores all the issues concerning husband/wife relations, raised in a wide range of sixteenth-century tracts, that advocate lesser age differences between spouses.

Instead, Gozze moves to consideration of very youthful marriage. He seems to hold to some sort of theory that each man has a total number of reproductive years, so he suggests that if you wait until you are old, say fifty, then you could keep sexually active into your eighties. If a male starts too soon, anytime before seventeen, sex interferes with his growth and at fifty he will be tapped out. For girls anytime younger than sixteen is too young and will lead to difficult pregnancies and birth deformities. Although the church allows girls to marry at age twelve and boys at fourteen, this is only a concession to what is biologically possible, not an indicator of what is best. While you don't want a wife who is very young for physiological reasons, you also don't want an old one; she can't be taught anything and will be impossible to live with. Like the saying goes, writes Gozze, you can't get an old ox to plow; in the same way an old bride is hardened and ungovernable. A young wife is tender, easy to discipline, whereas with the old one, neither domestic tranquility nor conjugal love lasts long. There will be continuous fighting, discord, and shouting and great disorder in the family.[69]

Lest we dismiss Gozze, along with so many other writers of advice manuals featured in my book, as obscure misogynists writing in crass ways that catered to the tastes of country boors and uncultured men of commerce, I want to introduce briefly—just to get them on the record here—a few words from Torquato Tasso. He ranks high among the literary giants of sixteenth-century Italy. Readers already may be wondering why I have made little mention thus far of the obvious leaders in the field of Italian prescriptive literature generally and courtesy books in particular: Castiglione's *Courtier*, Giovanni Della Casa's *Galateo*, and Tasso's "Father of the Family" (*Il padre di famiglia*). I take these works, all of fundamental importance, to be "dialogues," rather than advice manuals, clearly aimed at an intellectually and economically elite group of people, and in my concluding remarks I shall explore further the usefulness of distinguishing between a dialogue and an advice manual. But it is worth emphasizing here that the two genres do not differ so greatly in their views about what is proper behavior, at least in life situations relevant across class lines. Age at marriage is one such universal concern. In some cultures what is considered a proper age to marry may vary greatly according to class, based on property considerations, the ability to sustain a home, or practices of living in extended families. In sixteenth-century Italian literature, on the other hand, the uniformity of suggested behavior for all classes is striking. Thus, to listen to Tasso's dialogue with a Neapolitan gentleman is to hear differences from what we have been reading all along consisting more in tone than in essence:

> Now, if we turn to the matter of age, I say that a husband should try to find a young wife rather than an old one. Not only are young women more fit for bearing children, but they are also, according to Hesiod, better at receiving and adopting the habits that a husband wants to impart to them. Moreover, since the life of a woman is ordinarily shorter than that of a man, and since women, whose natural heat is not proportionate to their excessive humidity, grow old faster than men, a husband's age ought to exceed that of his wife by

enough years so that the beginning of the old age of one of them is not out of step with the old age of the other, and so that one does not become incapable of procreation before the other.

If a man takes his wife under the conditions that I have just described, it will be much easier for him to exercise the superiority that nature has granted men, and if he cannot make his natural superiority felt he will sometimes find his wife so recalcitrant and disobedient that, in place of the companion whom he expected to help lighten the burden that our humanity brings with it, he will confront a perpetual enemy who is as contrary to him as unbridled desire to reason. Indeed, women are related to men as desire is to the intellect, and just as desire, which is in itself irrational, is informed by many beautiful and comely virtues when it subjects itself to the intellect, so a woman who obeys her husband adorns herself with virtues that she would not possess if she were rebellious.[70]

These sweet, even sugarcoated, words are part of a philosophical dialogue rather than a book of rules, but the message for Tasso's readers (or those of Castiglione or Della Casa) is of a piece with the less-elegant phrasing of Gozze, Marinello, and Fioravanti.

One of the more unusual variants on male/female age differences I have come across is in Domenico Bruni da Pistoia's little book *Difese delle donne*... (In Defense of Women), published in 1552, and reprinted seven years later. From the tone of the opening protests against the calumnies of misogynous writers I had expected another woman-bashing spoof, but this one remains a straight defense of gender equality right to the end. According to Bruni, the fact that by law a woman may marry without parental consent at sixteen, whereas a man must be eighteen, means that women are superior to men. They are wiser and they mature sooner. From this it follows that they are more perfect than men at an earlier age and can testify in legal actions, run a household, and make contracts. Nor is this all. Women have more beautiful bodies than men, they are better at predicting the future, and they are more charitable.[71]

In addition to their general consensus on the proper age for marriage, advice manuals also agree that prospective spouses should be of similar social standing and economic means. According to the physician Marinello, if a husband is more noble than his wife, he will tend to treat her like a child; he may even hold her in disdain and grow to hate her. If he is of lower rank, she will treat him as a loathsome idiot, and as so often happens with children who are taught no paternal respect, she will become degenerate.[72]

Fioravanti, usually unrestrained in making exaggerated claims for his recommendations, shifts to a remarkably judicious tenor in offering his first rule: bride and groom should be of equal blood. This rule may not bring you total happiness, he concedes, but at least it will result in your avoiding the worst disasters and scandals that arise from an unhappy marriage. If the partners are unequal, for example, if an aspiring merchant marries his daughter to a rich peasant, then at their first dispute one will suspect the other of marrying only for the money. The one of higher rank will refuse to address his or her mother-in-law as "mother." The woman who marries a man of higher status or wealth would be better off burying him right away; that way she only has to cry for a day, whereas otherwise she will shed tears for a lifetime.[73]

The second part of Fioravanti's first rule, at least according to his way of arranging things, applies equally to the rich merchant, the poor gentleman, the shrewd peasant, and the modest courtier: no father should accept as a daughter-in-law a girl who knows more about how to beautify herself than about cooking and sewing. The third part of the first rule reverses the gender, saying that fathers should not give their blessing to a future son-in-law who struts around with false nobility but does not know how to ride a horse well. Beware of the prospective groom who is too good at cards, dice, or checkers.

Fioravanti's second big rule is addressed to the man seeking a wife: choose one whose personality is similar to yours, someone you can truly love. Marriage to a woman you do not love will be a prison; better that the hearts embrace before the hands touch. Forced marriages against a son's will (a daughter's wishes get no mention) will bring fights among the in-laws, scandals, threats, and litigation. However, warns the physician/charlatan, one cannot condone marrying impulsively, secretly, or by running away, because a marriage made for love alone, without a careful assessment of familial interests, quickly turns to pain and anguish. Love that begins as a thunderbolt ends just as quickly, exiting the same way it entered.

Use the following list of characteristics to make a judicious evaluation of a proposed spouse. The prospective good wife walks gravely, knows house duties, treats her husband-to-be patiently, promises to be loving and nurturing about raising children, behaves affably with neighbors, conserves possessions with diligence, displays good breeding and personal honor, befriends only good companions, and loathes all immature behavior. The prospective good husband speaks in measured fashion, makes corrections in a reasonable manner, keeps in good faith anything told to him in confidence, gives counsel prudently, displays care and diligence in governing his possessions, responds with patience if his spouse-to-be importunes him, guards jealously the prospect of rearing his children properly, conserves and enhances his personal honor vigilantly, and treats everyone honestly.[74] There you have it—rather like *The Rules*, 1564 style.

For one of the more thorough guides on choosing a spouse, we turn to Lodovico Dolce. The *Enciclopedia Italiana*'s entry refers to him as very prolific but the possessor of only second-rate literary talents; moreover, he was a plagiarist. Thus, he personifies nicely the sort of author we are interested in examining more closely.[75] Recent scholarship moves beyond literary snobbery and assesses him far more positively—as a pioneer among those who wrote directly for the market rather than for a patron, a distinction introduced some thirty years ago by historian Paul F. Grendler and one I shall return to in my conclusion, because it points so clearly to a key difference between an advice manual and a dialogue such as *The Courtier*.[76] Among some 184 works Dolce wrote, edited, translated, plagiarized, or somehow had a hand in for the prominent Venetian publishing firm Gabriele Giolito de' Ferrari between 1542 and 1568, the book of immediate concern to us is his 1545 *Dialogo di M. Lodovico Dolce della institution delle donne* (Dialogue on the Instruction of Women). Later editions saw the title grow to *De gli ammaestramenti pregiatissimi, che appartengono alla educatione, & honorevole, e virtuosa vita virginale, maritale, e vedovile* (On the Most Valuable Governance Related to the Education, Honor, and Virtuous Life of Virgins, Matrons, and Widows), and added promises that the reading would be light and sweet, with the inclusion of aphorisms, unusual documents, prudent advice, wise counsel, useful rules, and pious maxims, along with both the usual table of contents and an index to let the reader find the most notable matters at a glance. The preface tells us that there are many books available for men on how to lead a proper life but nothing of equal quality offering rules for women. Signor Dolce has been laboring just like a busy bee gathering flowers from all the world's documents touching upon the female lifestyle, and now he intends to fill the gap with this book drawing on the wisdom of many philosophers.[77]

In fact, the book copies mercilessly from the erudite work of Juan Luis Vives, *De institutione feminae christianae*, completed in 1523, at the commission of his fellow Spaniard, Queen Catherine of Aragon, the wife Henry VIII of England would soon divorce. Vives's effort so impressed the queen that she asked Thomas More to translate it, but more pressing matters of state arose and he simply approved an English version by Richard Hyrde prior to its appearance in 1529. Translations into other languages, including Italian, followed in due course, often in versions in which this work was coupled with translations of Vives's 1523 *De ratione studii puerilis* and his 1529 *De officio mariti*. Dolce may or may not have been aware of the imminent Italian version (1546) of these three Vives works combined in one volume, but he certainly knew of the originals. He must have decided there would be sufficient demand among readers, so that his variant of instructions for women, which actually appeared in the preceding year (1545), could compete successfully with the original in a rival translation. Queen Catherine may have thought highly of Vives's style, but the work certainly was not "light reading" of the sort Dolce proposed. Dolce's editorial judgment must have been good, for his version went through additional printings in 1547, 1553, 1559, and 1560, as against just one reprinting in 1561, in Milan, for Vives. Dolce's name made it to the market again in 1622, with a freshly updated posthumous edition included in a single binding with classic works by Agnolo Firenzuola and Alessandro Piccolomeni.[78]

A modern scholar hails Vives's work as the "leading theoretical manual on woman's education of the sixteenth century," a pioneer in making the transition from medieval convent education to the effective application of humanist principles. Especially significant are his emphasis on instruction in the vernacular and his suggestion that students of vernacular grammar keep individual notebooks like those recommended by humanists for boys learning Latin. His stress on obedience looms large, however, as does his disdain for women who read frivolous romances. The call for pious modesty and the emphasis on learning practical skills such as embroidery, cooking, and home economics all have a familiar ring. What was good for the famous educator who taught Mary Tudor apparently was good for Dolce as well, so he unstintingly and uncritically copied virtually every idea; in reading him we are also reading much of Vives.[79]

Dolce promises that his book will teach virgins how to remain pure, married women to be faithful, and widows to be tolerant and chaste. The purpose is didactic, not eulogistic or humorous, and in this it differs markedly from contemporary works such as Lodovico Domenichi's *La nobiltà delle donne*. Although retaining the formal structure of a dialogue, the treatise becomes a totally one-sided instructional discourse by Flaminio to Dorothea; later editions added a problem-oriented table of notable matters, typical of advice manuals. As a further aid to thumbing through the work as an advice manual rather than reading it as a dialogue, marginal entries are provided, looking like biblical postils but giving quick summaries of the content matter of each page or paragraph. The book claims to be complete, the only guide male and female readers will need, beginning with infancy and ending with widowhood. The opening chapter urges mothers to breast-feed their own children for all the reasons we have already considered, and the pages that follow exhort parents to raise their daughters in piety and modesty, by being good example themselves and displaying sober affection. The girl's books should be serious and inspirational, her food moderate and plain, her dress designed not to call attention to herself; she should not play cards, dice, or checkers. She should go around only with her mother, whose own demeanor will set the example of proper womanly propriety in the manner of walking, talking, and laughing. Teach your daughter never to engage in secret conversations with men. Neither give her too much praise nor denigrate her skills at dancing, singing, or playing a musical instrument.[80]

We come next to a chapter advising a father about choosing a virtuous husband for his daughter. A girl raised in a truly virginal state neither knows nor wishes to know of carnal union with a man, so she has absolutely no worldly experience on which to base the choice of a husband. She will accept happily whomever her father elects for her.[81] The exemplary father must put himself in his daughter's place and think about her happiness, setting aside any considerations about how the son-in-law might prove useful to his own interests. Some fathers look only at wealth and noble lineage, failing to give enough attention to what it will be like for the daughter to live under the same roof with this man and share his bed. Making good family alliances or ending a feud is not sufficient reason to punish your daughter. Do not be a merchant of your daughter when you should be her father.

Two issues need to be considered about marriage: a lifetime of companionship and a partnership in raising children. Good companionship is most likely among equals, so do not try to marry your daughter to someone either superior or inferior to yourself in rank. A household where there is no love quickly falls into ruin. The second rule is that the prospective couple should be of similar personality and habits. You can't expect a wolf to live together happily ever after with a lamb, and the same goes for people. Take care not to seek a groom-to-be who has more talents than are appropriate to his station in life. It's enough if he is sufficiently industrious to assure fulfilling the family needs; he need not be so ambitious that the children constantly have to tighten their belts. Speaking plainly, while riches are not to be despised, and while they may be used to give charitable sustenance to the poor, too much wealth is not good. Reread Boccaccio's story of the Florentine who chose love and became destitute, obtaining in poverty what he could not as a rich man. Fair enough, there cannot be matrimony without patrimony, but it is enough if the wife is fruitful and knows how to run the household and her husband is a good provider. Some consideration should be given to good looks, but these are fragile matters, of little moment. The groom-to-be should be healthy and of clean lifestyle, for the immediate benefit of his wife and so that he will have strong seed to produce robust children. He should not be too young but also not so old that he is likely to die or be unable to support the family until the children are grown.[82]

In the chapter summarized above, Dolce attempts to give specific recommendations to a father about choosing a husband for his daughter in a narrowly how-to style. This much set forth, the author then introduces a new chapter, complete with numerous examples and aphorisms, describing the ideal prospective son-in-law in a discursive, literary "who/ what" style. Character and habits outweigh all other considerations; assuming these are present, the good husband also should be intelligent, prudent, and highly educated. And don't be shocked when I say both husband and wife should be literate, so that both may participate fully in religious offices as well as in civic life and all other human endeavors. The marriage of such a couple will be filled with contentment, like the tree that bears abundant fruit, whereas a marriage based only on the weak threads of worldly riches or sexual desire will flounder in disarray and fighting. Recall all the trouble between Paris and Helen; that's what happens when lust drives a woman to take up with an infamous man or when a scholar on pilgrimage is smitten by some whore. Follow instead the path laid out by Penelope and Ulysses. Life is a lengthy voyage toward death. Since that is where we all end up eventually, your daughter would be better off marrying a poisonous snake and reaching her destiny quickly than having to suffer for years with a rich villain. The woman who prefers crying in silks to laughing in a coarse skirt is a fool, as is the bride who would choose hatred in the opulent room of a rich palace over the adoring hugs and kisses of her loving husband in an unassuming hotel.

Nothing is worse than the living hell of a husband and wife who hate one another, and nothing is so suave as a couple who love each other, who depend on each other for life itself, in whom the desire of one is the desire of the other. With love, family governance goes smoothly in all matters. When the mother wishes to instruct her child in something, the teacher is at hand. When the wife needs counsel in the face of adversity, a wise adviser is ready with exhortation and comfort, whatever it takes to sail the turbulent seas of life. The good husband treats his wife sweetly, not only with words but by example, so that she truly thinks she has found not a man but an angel delivered from heaven for her sustenance and companionship through all her days. "Believe me, such happiness has no match on earth, only among the saints in paradise. . . . What else can I say? It's time to move on to the rules for married women."[83]

CHAPTER

· *6* ·

Marital Relations

Lodovico Dolce—how appropriate that *dolce* means "sweet" in Italian—
certainly paints an idyllic picture of marital bliss for the young man and
woman who wed for love. Assuming they, or their parents, have given
due attention to the equality of their social conditions and the compati-
bility of their personalities, everything will be fine. How accurately this
amorous picture reflected daily experience, at least for some marriages
some of the time, is hard to judge. Dolce absolutely believed that the
man should wear the pants. He governs the family while his wife assists
him, most often by being deferential. While a lifetime of caring and companionship is the very definition of marriage for Dolce, he does not intend a companionate marriage as we moderns understand the term. So
also, the partnership he specifies for raising children means an alliance
between two unequal persons—a father who rules and a mother who
obeys. Divided rule, familial democracy, mutual veto, and equality were
all unimaginable to him. Advice-manual writers, including Dolce, considered the analogy between husband and wife jointly governing a household and multiple magistrates presiding over a city, such as existed in
Venice; but clearly they rejected any form of shared authority, opting
instead for absolute, singular kingship under the familial roof.[1] Inversion—the woman on top—indeed was plausible, occasionally as reality
and regularly as entertainment, but parity was too much out-of-the-
question to serve even as humorous text.[2]

Renaissance people accepted that fathers should rule. Even treatises
written by women that most persuasively argue for equality of the sexes
or occasionally for female superiority do not go on to challenge societal

norms about family governance. And yet we know that economic realities—for example, husbands away for extended periods on business or military ventures—meant that many wives had to run their own households, making major economic decisions when necessary. Moreover, demographic factors such as high mortality from disease and normal aging for late-marrying men necessarily left widows in charge, to rule themselves as it were. What historian Barbara Diefendorf found for sixteenth-century Parisian widows, I believe was true of Italians as well. Law and custom tried to limit the power of widows because women were deemed competent, not incompetent.[3] Popular-advice manuals are quite explicit in telling women how to cope with the realities of life, including absent or dead husbands. Men should rule, even though women could rule; indeed, according to at least one writer who feared that female empowerment might lead to mass maritucide, precisely because women could rule.[4]

A more disturbing reality was physical abuse. We shall see in a variety of ways that society did not tolerate husbands who governed their wives by beating them. While doing research in Rome, I came across a book published in 1601, describing the aims and privileges of all the charitable institutions in the Eternal City. The listing runs to 421 pages and includes several entries on shelters for battered wives. Among these was the monastery of Santa Marta, which opened in 1542, with Augustinian nuns in one section of the building and former prostitutes in the other, the separation being more for convenience than for moral redemption, I suppose, since no contact was allowed between the two groups. As time went by, however, not enough former prostitutes came to live there, so half the building remained empty. The nuns then changed their charitable objective to offering shelter for wives in bad marriages, who no longer wished to stay with their husbands or whose husbands had thrown them out. Women who could pay their own support had to do so, but others were taken in anyway as charity cases. Apparently the problem of under-utilization disappeared.[5]

These are the extremes, the heavenly joys of wedded love in a patriarchal household as proposed by Dolce versus the convent in Rome for abused, despised wives. Men who wrote advice manuals told couples who read their works how to get closer to the bliss and avoid the hatred. Writers and readers shared the belief that pleasure was attainable in a relationship among unequals. It seems not to have occurred to anyone that greater equality might have led to greater happiness. The burden of command was no lighter than the burden of obedience. The injunction that a husband provide for his family was neither more nor less essential than the obligation of a wife to conserve what the family possessed. The rewards of behaving with civility, decorum, and even kindness accrued to both spouses. Someone had to rule the family, just as someone had to steer the ship, a metaphor used over and over again in advice literature.[6] That someone normally was the husband and father, although in his absence or if he died, then the wife and mother could be that someone—sometimes without much ado, other times only with difficulty. But having two people at the helm was a formula for shipwreck, certainly no way for a family to prosper. Fathers did rule, and mothers could rule on occasion, but there could not be two rulers. However much this patriarchal view may offend modern sensibilities, it had a logic.

Contemporary feminist scholarship beginning with the late Joan Kelly and more recently reflected in work by Kathleen Casey, Constance Jordan, Margaret King, and Margaret Rosenthal, among others, demonstrates persuasively that the sixteenth century was not a good time for women. However much Renaissance rhetoric reasserted the meaning of liberty, wives may have found themselves more deeply under the authority of husbands than they had been in earlier centuries, in both Protestant and Catholic cultures. Opportunities for unmarried women also may have narrowed. With regard to advice manuals and their writers, three recent findings, or rereadings, seem especially relevant. The first concerns bedrock humanist texts like those of Francesco Barbaro and Juan Luis Vives, which the new scholarship sees in a far more unfavorable light, one with a misogynist hue, than did earlier readings (sometimes by the same scholar, as in the case of King on Barbaro). The second is the discovery of protofeminist nuggets in what were once treated as relatively less important, clearly woman-bashing texts. The third, and in my judgment the most important endeavor, is the recovery and critical evaluation of works by women, especially the rich writings of Veronica Franco and Moderata Fonte, published centuries ago but long ignored.

Indeed, Franco and Fonte explicitly foreshadow the presentist assertion by King that the companionship and subordination simultaneously required of Renaissance wives were necessarily contradictory injunctions. In my judgment, however, this argument has been well articulated but not yet proved. There is plenty of evidence, most of it conceded by King, that wives whose voices have come down to us referred to their husbands in terms of deference and endearment, all in the same figurative breath. We can properly call these women victims of male oppression if we so choose, but that is not how they saw themselves, at least not according to their words and deeds. In the pages that follow, we shall be examining advice to married couples, written by men, read by men and women. I do not see this literature as part of a grand, conscious effort to increase the subordination of wives but rather as an effort by writers of varying talents, who shared society's largely unquestioned acceptance of patriarchal ideals, to instruct married couples on how to live in harmony. The authors thought they were doing some good, probably with an eye to making a little money publishing and occasionally to entertaining their audience. The Renaissance did not invent misogyny and male dominance.[7]

From the Humanists

Sometime around 1300, an Italian mother supposedly sent her daughter off to be married—with a loving kiss, wishes for happiness, and a set of rules on dealing with her new groom:

> Avoid anything that might annoy him. Do not be joyful if he is sad, or sad if he is joyful.
> Find out what he likes to eat and if your tastes do not agree with his, do not show it.
> If he is asleep, sick, or tired, do not disturb him; if you must do so, be gentle.
> Do not rob him, lend his goods, or give them away.
> Do not be too curious about his business but if he confides in you, keep his secrets.
> Be good to his family and friends.
> Do not do anything important without seeking his advice.
> Do not ask him to do things that are impossible or might damage his honor or position.
> Be attractive, fresh, clean, modest in appearance, and chaste in behavior.
> Do not be too familiar with the servants.
> Do not go out too often; the man's domain is outside whereas the woman's is in the home.
> Do not speak too much, for silence is a sign of modesty and chastity.
> Do not make your husband jealous.[8]

As we have seen in looking at advice manuals on conception, pregnancy, child rearing, and adolescence, sixteenth-century writers borrowed freely from the past. Every precept from this late-medieval manuscript appears somewhere in Renaissance popular-print culture, and much else as well.[9]

The classical tradition also looms large. What Aristotle was to advice on conception and Quintilian to recommendations on child rearing, Plutarch was to marriage guides. Indeed, his *Coniugalia praecepta*, which takes the form of an epistle to a newly married young couple, was translated into Italian and printed in its entirety several times during the sixteenth century. Thus did a philosopher/historian become transformed into the author of an advice manual, one sufficiently lowbrow that modern scholars dispute its true provenance. No matter—for us pseudo-Plutarch is Plutarch, just as he was to readers who consulted him in the sixteenth century.

Married people should achieve their mutual desires by persuasion, not by fighting. The husband leads and sets the preferences, but both parties must agree. Governing a wife should be like the soul ruling the body— intertwined in good will for mutual benefit—not like controlling a piece of property. Of course, married couples should not be seen kissing, yet how much more disgraceful it is for them to squabble in public. Especially at the outset, when physical attraction fuels the fires of love, a marital relationship is fragile, not yet centered on character and rationality. A husband must not humble his wife, and he should respect her above all others. Unlike the moon, which shines when the sun is away, a wife should radiate only in the company of her husband, staying at home and out of sight when he is not around: "Most women, if you take from them gold-embroidered shoes, bracelets, anklets, purple, and pearls, stay indoors."

A wife ought to have no feelings of her own; instead, she should join with her husband in seriousness as in sport, in sobriety as in laughter. The bride must not be so afraid of appearing wanton that she is too reserved to laugh and joke with her husband. A man who is not cheerful with his wife, who does not join her in being lighthearted and in play, is just teaching her to seek her own separate pleasures. Husband and wife should not indulge in unholy and unlawful sexual intercourse with others. Their own lovemaking should welcome the possibility of offspring. Elsewhere in Plutarch's discourse, however, this semblance of mutuality becomes strained, as he advises the wife to accept her husband's extramarital debaucheries as a sign of his respect for her due modesty. Further along, the scholar/moralist reconsiders and advises husbands that since these little flings cause their wives great pain and suffering, it would be better to give up such trivial pleasures. In lovemaking between husband and wife, she should not behave like a whore and take the initiative, nor should she feel annoyance when he comes on strong.

Shifting from sex to money, Plutarch advises married people to pool their resources in a common fund, so there is no thought of what is mine and what is not. If it happens that the wife has contributed the larger share to this joint estate, still the estate should be said to belong to him. Just as wine has more water in it than anything else and yet we still call it wine, so it should be with joint property. Even if the husband brings less, their wealth bears his name. A wife's hold on her husband should

arise not from her beauty, dowry, or high birth but from her sweet conversation, good character, and unfailing comradeship. Her companions
should be her husband's acquaintances, not her personal friends. She
should talk to her husband or through him, not directly to strangers, lest
her words betray her feelings—exactly as disrobing would expose her
body. The wife should do what she can to assuage her mother-in-law's
natural jealousy, being nicer to her husband's parents than to her own.
She should keep silent when her husband is angry but console him with
words of comfort if he is sullen. Fighting in the bedchamber is especially
destructive of the intimate union that marriage should be. A wise wife
closes her ears to the backbiters who warn of her husband's evil ways.

If his words have not done so already, Plutarch's closing passages may
strike an especially offensive chord to modern ears. Women cannot conceive children without help from a man, yet they certainly do develop
uterine "moles" (what we would diagnose as fibroid tumors) all by themselves. So also, unwanted tumors can grow in women's heads if they
fail to receive the seeds of good doctrine from their husbands. Left to
themselves, wives may conceive all manner of bad ideas and low designs.[10]

I have put Plutarch freshly before us as a reminder that Italian humanist and Catholic Reformation advice manuals were by no means breaking
new ground in their highly restrictive prescriptions for wifely behavior.
Without any doubt, Francesco Barbaro had Plutarch on his desk when
in late 1415, he sat down to write what became his famous essay "On
Wifely Duties," a work described by Margaret King as being "of fundamental importance for the understanding of Venetian humanism, of
Venetian culture, and perhaps of aristocratic consciousness in Europe
for centuries to come."[11] Addressed to Florence's Lorenzo de' Medici
(1395–1440, brother of Cosimo il Vecchio) on the occasion of his forthcoming marriage to Ginevra Cavalcanti, its popularity more than a century later in print culture among a considerably wider audience owes
much to its youthful, self-confident, quick-paced, plainly didactic style.
The language is unequivocal, even folksy, and the references to classical
wisdom and nature's mysteries are done with admirable nonchalance.
"On Wifely Duties" is not a dialogue or a symposium that leaves room
for philosophical doubt or disputation but a handy little guide, one that
became available in vernacular translation to inform anyone who could
read. Its unabashed defense of aristocratic privilege no doubt grated the
sensibilities of some literate plebeians, but what Barbaro wrote about
marital relations may well have seemed every bit as desirable in a burgher
household as in an aristocratic villa. The goal of *unanimitas*—the forging

of multiple desires and potentially conflicting needs into a single will in a harmonious and loving marriage in which fathers ruled and mothers obeyed—appealed to the physician no less than the prince, the clerk no less than the courtier, a pope's mother no less than a professor's.[12]

King places emphasis more on class than gender in highlighting the theme of preserving noble privilege in Barbaro's work.[13] Recent scholarship, on the other hand, stresses the darker side of familial *unanimitas* when the participants hold such unequal power. Constance Jordan, for example, features Barbaro in her treatment of humanists who applied Christian ethics to the subject of relations between husbands and wives. The place of religion is more complex than Jordan allows, however, since Plutarch's *Coniugalia praecepta*, which undoubtedly was Barbaro's primary source of inspiration, is hardly a Christian treatise. The humanist's emphasis on procreation may have come from St. Augustine, but it also is found clearly and forcefully in Plutarch. Whatever their origins, the precepts Barbaro lifted from earlier thinkers and wove into a fresh text, translated and printed for all to read a century later, certainly put severe limits on a wife's autonomy. Consider the following:

> I therefore would like wives to evidence modesty at all times and in all places. They can do this if they will preserve an evenness and restraint in the movements of their eyes, in their walking, and in the movement of their bodies; for the wandering of the eyes, a hasty gait, and excessive movement of the hands and other parts of the body cannot be done without loss of dignity, and such actions are always joined to vanity and are signs of frivolity. Therefore, wives should take care that their faces, countenances, and gestures (by which we can penetrate by careful observation into the most guarded thoughts) be applied to the observance of decency. . . .
>   . . . I would have wives be seen in public with their husbands, but when their husbands are away wives should stay at home.[14]

According to Jordan and other scholars such as Kathleen Casey, Italian male rulers consciously led the way among all European men in successfully blocking the expansion of female economic power into political decision making. Historian Stanley Chojnacki demonstrated how elite women used their control of dowries to favor daughters over sons and in a variety of ways to threaten the patriarchal establishment. The men responded vigorously. Now we understand why Barbaro studied Plutarch, saw the advice about mixing all the marital property together and calling it the husband's, and passed this wisdom (including the wine metaphor) along to Lorenzo de' Medici, the Venetian aristocracy, and eventually to many sixteenth-century married couples. Jordan's conclusion is compelling on the wife's fate: "What must be noticed is that her transformation into an object and symbol has depended on a kind of violence. Men agree to cease hostilities among themselves because they can agree to exchange women among themselves. In the process women lose their capacity to speak and be heard; they have value or are virtuous only as the means by which the continuity of society is guaranteed."[15]

Renaissance husbands consciously placed narrow restrictions on women's behavior, treating wives and daughters at best as mindless extensions of male selves, incapable of independent judgment, and at worst as property to be exchanged in accordance with the needs of a stable, self-satisfied patriarchy. How else are we to take the following advice from Barbaro?

> Yet I think we ought to follow the custom—for good mores have so decayed,—that our wives adorn themselves with gold, jewels, and pearls, if we can afford it. For such adornments are the sign of a wealthy, not a lascivious, woman and are taken as evidence of the wealth of the husband more than as a desire to impress wanton eyes. . . . Moreover, jewels and gold may often easily be of great use in business and public affairs.[16]

The indictment by Jordan and other feminists may sound a bit harsh, yet it rings true. Sixteenth-century advice manuals told married couples that the way to get along was for the husband to command and the wife to obey, an injunction repeated hundreds of times over. No reading of these texts could reasonably come to any other conclusion. So, why did historians for decades portray a Renaissance for women as well as for men? The answer has several parts. In the first place, there had been a major dissenter to the old consensus. Twenty years before Joan Kelly's fundamental essay answered her question, "Did Women Have a Renaissance?" with a resounding NO, Ruth Kelso had published a book of great erudition, based on close reading of hundreds of Renaissance texts from throughout Europe, titled *Doctrine for the Lady of the Renaissance*. She concluded in no uncertain terms, based on overwhelming evidence drawn from Barbaro and over eight hundred other treatises, that Renaissance doctrine limited women's roles—to being helpmates and reproductive vessels for their husbands. She found that, between 1400 and 1600, even relatively progressive writers held to a theory of not one but two human races: naturally superior men and naturally inferior women. Kelso alludes only briefly, however, to "the challenge of comparison between these thoughts of men of another age and our own which I constantly felt but with restraint praiseworthy or not have not taken up." In my view Kelso's restraint adds enormously to the richness of her work, which allows us to see Renaissance thought on its own terms while leaving no doubt about where she stands. Her restraint was due less to self-effacement than to rigorous analysis of her own situation. Writing in 1956, she was skeptical about how much progress men had made since the sixteenth century in accepting women as equals.[17]

What of everyone else before Joan Kelly? Sad to say, historians and literary critics were asking different questions, or they found Renaissance ideas about female inferiority to be merely quaint, harmless, or possibly congenial. Readers may recall Guido Biagi's voyeuristic imagery from the Florentine archives, quoted earlier. He was typical. A related question is whether the Renaissance invented, or at least greatly reinvigorated, what Kelso terms the theory of "two human races." She makes no such assertion, and I am inclined to support her assessment even against the weight of recent feminist scholarship claiming that humanist thought, along with both the Protestant and the Catholic Reformations, actually made things worse for European women than they had been before 1400. It seems to me that a firm judgment either way is not presently possible; moreover, we come no closer to a conclusion by decrying the vicious treatment of women in Renaissance tracts without examining earlier views. What the Christian, Venetian patrician Barbaro wrote in the fifteenth century about wives keeping silent and being subservient came directly from the first-century, pantheist, Greek scholar Plutarch. Similar sentiments may be found in the aphorisms of Florentine lawyer Francesco da Barberino around 1300, or placed in the mouth of a mother to her daughter at about the same time somewhere in Italy and probably much earlier in England, or in civilizations adhering to the teachings of Confucius, Buddha, or Mohammed. An argument about the specific material conditions that enhance patriarchal misogyny, however powerful as a descriptive analysis, takes on explanatory validity only in a comparative context, and this context we have not developed sufficiently.

Finally, there is the intriguing question of what happened to women who did not fit the new, or the not-so-new, model of a wife as an obedient, speechless, reproductive extension of her husband. Obviously in Catholic Europe there was the institutional alternative of the convent, but I am more interested in women who stayed in society, and in particular in the status of widows. Further along in this chapter I shall take up what advice manuals say widows should be doing. That exploration should shed light not only on widows themselves but also on their sisters whose husbands were still alive. After all, how does one go from being a helpless, mindless, silent appendage to being the head of a household, often with children to raise and a patrimony to defend, whether it consisted of an estate or a few meager household goods? But first I want to return to relations among living husbands and wives in sixteenth-century Italy.

Since Francesco Barbaro's "On Wifely Duties" is so heavily a rehash of Plutarch, there is no need to stay with it further. The main point I would make is that, while his treatise did have an audience in early print culture, it never became the sort of canonical text that twentieth-century scholarship would suggest. Barbaro's recommendations had to compete for readers against a wide range of advice manuals, many with somewhat different approaches to marital relations, even if they all presupposed male supremacy. We begin with Matteo Palmieri, another fifteenth-century humanist whose work reached print in the sixteenth century. He observes that every sensible man wants a wife who is honest, a woman of good habits. However, we don't always get what we want in life. What should a husband do if he finds himself with a vexatious, haughty, vain wife, one constantly ready to cross him and answer back? Palmieri advises that you try to get her to mend her ways; if she won't, then practice bearing your burden in silence. This light-hearted treatment continues with a reminder of what Socrates said when someone asked him how he managed to get along with his intractable wife, Xanthippe: "I learn at home how to put up with the abuses I receive when I step outside."[18]

Socrates' wife turns up again in Desiderius Erasmus's 1523 colloquy on marriage, translated by midcentury into German, Spanish, French, Italian, and English printed editions.[19] Once again, as with Plutarch, we have here a major intellectual whose work—at least this colloquy—circulated widely in the sixteenth century as popular pulp. Using Eulalia ("sweetly speaking") as counselor to the shrewish Xanthippe, Erasmus stays closely with Plutarch's words but reshapes the *Coniugalia praecepta* into a lively exchange between two women who calculate for themselves how best to cope with brutish husbands. Xanthippe's Nicholas is rapidly dissipating her dowry on wine, whores, and dice. When he eventually comes home, he snores all night and even pukes in bed. They shout at each other constantly, she giving as good as she gets. On one occasion, he raised a club at her and she had to defend herself with a footstool, like an Amazon. Eulalia warns her pugnacious friend that there can be no dissolution of marriage, putting a stop to Xanthippe's curses upon whoever robbed women of the right to divorce only by reminding her that Christ himself so willed it. Sweetly Eulalia describes how she tries always to be agreeable with her husband, just as do tamers of elephants and lions, and how trainers of horses use calls and caresses to soothe these mettlesome animals. How much more fitting for us wives to employ such arts upon those with whom we must share bed and board for life, happily or not. Cook what he likes and make up the bed to suit him. If he seems depressed, put on a worried look. Of course it is right for a wife to reprove her husband if something important is at stake, but just wink at the trivial matters. If you must reprove, let it be in private, with wit and pleasantry, after which quickly introduce a more cheerful topic. If you must take your complaint out the door, let it be to your in-laws, with great restraint, so they will see not your hatred but his fault. Hold back something in what you tell them, so your husband will know tacitly that you handled the problem with courtesy.

Eulalia continues with examples extolling how accommodating some women are, like the wife who discovered her husband in adultery and provided the lovers with luxurious bedding or another who cooked them fine meals. This is just too much for Xanthippe, who vows to dump the contents of her chamber pot on her husband if she catches him going off to some sweetheart. Returning from the comic to the practical, Eulalia claims that no creature is so fierce that it cannot be tamed, although the effort may take several months of cheerfulness and turning the other cheek. Above all, let there be no quarreling in the bedroom because complaining during sexual intercourse spoils the very medicine that rids men's minds of vexation and cures their ills.[20] Look not at his faults, which only disgust you and provide a handle that cannot hold him anyway. Instead, mark his good points and thereby "take him where he *can* be held." Eulalia learns that Nicholas and Xanthippe already have a fine son (conceived well before marriage, when he tickled her so amorously that one thing led to another) and now she is pregnant again, so obviously he is a good plowman working a fertile field. All his friends think he's a great fellow, so there must be something likable about him. He is only twenty-four and probably still needs to learn the joys of being head of a family. To clinch her case, Eulalia asks Xanthippe about her stepmother and her mother-in-law, learning that both these old hags wish her dead. Don't give them the supreme satisfaction of seeing you separate from your husband and maybe lose your son. Finally Eulalia promises to speak directly with Nicholas, and "when I get a chance, I'll tell him a fib about you—how lovingly you spoke of him."[21]

Humorous, fast-moving talk among women is also the didactic strategy employed in Antonio Brucioli's *Dello ufficio della moglie* (On the Duties of a Wife), published in Venice in 1526, with new editions in 1537 and 1544. The structure is that of a philosophical dialogue, pretty much like those written by humanist scholars mainly for their own edification. It is the third in a big collection of thirty dialogues on subjects typically of interest to humanists, such as the virtues, educational theory, and republicanism. Most of Brucioli's works, including his dialogues on natural philosophy and metaphysics, are just too highbrow for inclusion in my survey of popular-advice manuals, but I make room for his treatment of wifely duties because its playful, practical recommendations strike me as just the sort of thing every literate sixteenth-century Italian would have enjoyed. Scholars remember Brucioli primarily for his troubles with the Inquisition. Together with his brothers, he ran a formidable publishing business in Venice; on his own he translated the Bible and wrote numerous biblical commentaries. These had a Lutheran tinge that led, in 1555, to formal charges, an eventual abjuration of his heresies, and an order to burn all his writings. His retraction displeased the Inquisition, however, because it lacked sufficient clarity, so he was jailed again in 1558, a sentence transmuted to house arrest after the interrogating judges found him "mentally tired" and accepted some sort of bail/bribe paid by a friend.[22]

Brucioli was sufficiently prolific and Protestant to get himself listed as a condemned author in the indexes of Rome for 1557, 1559, and 1564, making illicit even the chitchat we shall now examine between Lucia and her young companion, the newly married Lisabetta, but that little detail only adds to the dialogue's charm.[23] The "sisters" agree that husband and wife should be equal, but Lucia wisely stresses the advantages of being conciliatory and proceeds to tell Lisabetta how to encourage her husband toward good habits and away from undesirable and contentious behavior. Always be cheerful in word and deed, watching for the times when he tends to be angry and keeping silent if need be. Use words of submission, at least occasionally, and feel truly sad when he seems perturbed. If he appears burdened with worldly cares, don't chatter and make merry in his presence. Be vigilant in attending to household chores, learn to cook foods that particularly delight him, and decorate the bedroom in a pleasing fashion. You'll find his love for you growing by leaps and bounds.

Lisabetta interrupts to express some doubts about the one-sidedness of all this advice, but she is ready to listen again as Lucia discusses when and how a wife should reproach her husband. When his mind is thoroughly at peace and no one else is around, pleasingly and with sweet words pray him to consider, for the good of his family, his reputation, and his health, mending his ways a bit and desisting from whatever little this or that offends you. Then cut the discourse short and shift immediately to happier subjects. The biggest problem with women is that once they start talking, they just don't know when to stop. Don't let things get out the door because it is much easier to patch up a dispute when only the two of you are involved. Lisabetta objects that it would take a philosopher to keep track of all these subtleties in observing her husband's moods and responding just so, but Lucia assures her that it's all quite elementary for a clever woman. Absolutely avoid discord in the bedroom. Certain women are so contentious that they continue to fight and remonstrate during sex, thus turning a pleasurable occasion for lifting cares from a man's mind into yet another vexation.

Honor your in-laws, trying always to be at peace with them and holding them as dear as you do your own family. Show respect for their age and don't barge in as if you are now the boss of the whole house. Be careful that no word or deed casts doubt upon your fidelity. This is easy enough if your husband is always first in your heart, so that no one can confuse or mislead you. Speak as little as possible, avoiding discussion unless forced by the occasion and answering questions rather than asking them. Flee from women of questionable reputation even if they be ladies of great renown. Ignore the gossip of servants, who always want to raise a big fuss about this or that person's behavior; keep things calm, protecting your husband from such concerns. Use all your arts to persuade your husband that everything you do is out of love for him, displaying toward him a certain reverence, even fear, that you might be displeasing him in some way.

I see that you are very pretty, Lucia tells Lisabetta, so I must warn you that just as straw burns brightly but dies out unless good wood is added to the fire, so also newly married love inflamed by a shapely body fades quickly unless enriched with good habits, prudence, and mental love. A woman who would rather command a blockhead of a husband than obey a wise one is like those who prefer to gather around a blind man than to follow one illuminated with intelligence and reason. Finally, Lucia reminds Lisabetta to be the opposite of the way the moon is with the sun—to shine only in her husband's presence and never when he is away. This, of course, brings us directly back to Plutarch's *Coniugalia praecepta*, from which we have never really strayed very far in reading Barbaro, Palmieri, Erasmus, and now Brucioli.[24]

Dialogues among female interlocutors at least give the appearance of allowing for the validity of a woman's counsel, even though the author is male. A more condescending, outright misogynous form of printed advice takes the form of a letter from father to daughter. In my previous chapter I presented Annibale Guasto's admonitions to his daughter about preserving her chastity as she left home to become a court damsel. Its tone is very similar to the published letter we now peek at, written by Pietro Belmonte to his daughter Madonna Laudomia on the occasion of her (re?)marriage to Antonio Diotallevi, a nobleman from their native Rimini. He begins by reminding her that she has four brothers whose reputations would be harmed by any misbehavior on her part and also that as an infant she was raised on her mother's own milk in addition to what her wet nurse supplemented, so she owes much to that saintly progenitor as well. A display of rather unfocused fatherly erudition follows, beginning with the Greeks and Romans, carrying on through St. Augustine and Dante, and concluding with contemporaries such as Giovanni Della Casa and Annibale Caro. The crumbs of practical advice are very restrictive indeed, thoroughly encased in citations from the classics. Now that she is married, Laudomia should not go out without her husband to weddings or festivals, nor even to a funeral. She must not so much as imagine setting foot out of the house without his knowledge, nor should she let anyone whom he does not approve into their home. For the adulteress Belmonte recommends live entombment, without clarifying whether he is thinking about his own dearest Laudomia or simply musing more generally. Elsewhere we get aphorisms ascribed to various ancients, such as the advice that it is better to live homeless on the street without a roof over your head than in the house of a loquacious woman. Then there are compulsively exact recommendations about how every item among the household belongings must be kept in its precise place, in accordance with where proper decorum says things should be, so her husband can easily find whatever he needs at a given instant.

The thinness of this book's erudition and intelligence lead me to believe it may have expressed male notions about the limits of female intellect and education—how much Belmonte thought a woman could absorb, to state the matter bluntly—and that it was meant as a wedding gift for moderately literate daughters of aristocrats about to marry, rather than as a treatise for humanists or as something husbands should read to their wives. It is clearly and exclusively an advice manual with absolute prescriptions, not a dialogue with room for doubt or for alternative views. Although lacking the usual table of notable matters, there are summary notations in the margins describing the content of each paragraph or page, presumably to facilitate the thumbing and rereading appropriate for a how-to book.[25]

We continue to peer into private correspondence that its author surely meant us to see by perusing Orazio Lombardelli's instructions to his wife Delia, written shortly after he married this sixteen-year-old of good family in 1574. Lombardelli, who may be remembered for his rhetorical invectives, perhaps humorous in intent, against adolescents, and for his list of ten reasons for their horrible behavior, all no fault of theirs, is dead serious in explaining to Delia what he expects of her. He has left her in the countryside to attend to matters there (possibly supervising the vintage, since it is autumn) while he is busy in the city (no doubt Siena), which may explain the formality of a written document. He must have thought Delia would have some leisure time at her disposal, as he opines that reading and rereading his instructions will give her more opportunity to ponder their wisdom than oral communication would allow. Ruth Kelso, to my knowledge the only modern commentator besides myself who has read this text, suggests that one may see between its lines a rather uptight man of letters who is not quite sure how to cope with his spirited young wife, a reading I certainly share. Be that as it may, there can be little doubt about how Lombardelli structured his advice. It comes in exactly 180 short paragraphs, *"capi"* he calls them, although they are clearly not "chapters" in the normal sense of that term. In the printed version, each is numbered (in Arabic, not Roman numerals—quite unusual) like a bullet in a word-processor-produced presentation, highlighted by indentation, and cross-referenced by number as necessary. Whereas his work on adolescents wanders about aimlessly at great length, the style in this epistle is quick and pointed. In stark contrast with the advice manual about adolescents, his words for Delia are stripped of grandiloquence and are defensively buttressed by a simplistic mixture of proverbial wisdom laced with allusions to Greek, Egyptian, Lybian, and biblical authorities. My sense from all these characteristics is that Lombardelli meant his paragraphs to be read by Delia and other new brides like herself, rather than by the male literati addressed in his other works. He wrote *Dell' uffizio della donna maritata* (On the Duties of a Married Woman) in a condescending style, reflecting his perception of females as less intelligent beings as well as his fears about womanly independence. In this respect, the work is very similar to Belmonte's epistle to his daughter.

The message itself is rather less innovative than the packaging—lots of unacknowledged Plutarch and nothing so extreme as live entombment for the adulteress. Paragraph 3 warns than God will punish a wife who is unhappy with her lot in life by making her permanently depressed. Number 13 admonishes her not to do or say anything without her husband's permission, unless it is clearly for the good of the family, and 18 adds that she must obey willingly even before his command arrives. Paragraph 19 tells her that tending to a sick husband comes before going to mass, and number 166 adds that she should know her herbs and medicinals. Other regulations dictate that she must be cheerful and lively in her husband's presence, respectful in giving only the briefest counsel, and a calming influence in every circumstance, changing her mood to suit his. With strangers do just the opposite: no laughing, flirting, dressing immodestly, or parading about. Avoid lascivious perfumes and ostentatious jewelry. The best women are the ones you hear little or nothing about; being known by everyone is not a healthy sign, nor is having nicknames or being praised in songs.

Other prescriptions provide fascinating glimpses into the writing and reading habits of a burgher wife. Do not read letters addressed to you or to other women without your husband's permission (par. 106), and do not write letters unless absolutely necessary (107). "What is built in a year of reading good books crumbles in a week of reading bad ones" (144), so stay away from love stories and battle epics. Instead, he recommended reading Juan Luis Vives, *On the Duties of a Christian Woman;* blessed Lorenzo Giustianiano (patriarch of Venice), *Doctrine of No Little Use to Those Newly Entering Religion and Desiring to Lead a Religious Life;* Jean Gerson, *Imitation of Christ;* Diego de Estella, *The Contempt of the World;* Luis de Granada, *The Sinners Guide* and *A Memorial of a Christian Life;* and Pope Gregory I, *Dialogue.* "These few should do for a while" (145), he added, because "books should be few but read carefully and fully understood" (146). "After a few years with the above texts [N.B. all were available in printed Italian translations from their Latin originals and all required a high level of literacy.], you may read more liberally from saints lives and devotional tracts" (147, referencing par. 142). We are advised in paragraph 148 that the time for wives to read is after dinner and when shops are closed on holidays, because household duties come before everything else (149).

An afterword to Lombardelli's sixty-five-page book contains a letter to his uncle Ricciardo telling us that Delia died at the age of nineteen from complications following the birth of her son, who also did not survive. The death brought tears to all who knew her, for her charity, prudence, faith, modesty, and sense of duty were exemplary. On this lugubrious note, his comportment manual for Delia ends, to be shared with other newly married women in a 1583 printed edition.[26]

More palatable, at least to my taste, is the explicitly humorous advice of the *Compagnia della lesina,* which may be recalled for its recommendation to save money by marrying a little woman with a big dowry. Do not let her out of the house unless it be for some honest purpose; whatever you allow, do not let her stop off at your child's godfather so she can cuckold you in the Boccaccio style. Keep her at home, like a fixed star, and away from the company of vagabond women, who are like shooting stars. Either way, women naturally have tails like a comet and they get easily lost, like chickens. We men may be the fire, but women are the fuel and the devil blows on the flames. All married members of the *Compagnia della lesina* are ordered to return home at a decent hour, to provide amply for the family's needs, not to play cards and hang around at the local tavern, and especially not to chase after other women. You are not to speak about your wife to others except to praise her honesty and make sure you wear the pants, not she![27]

From the Church

Renaissance Italian humanists closely followed Plutarch in giving advice primarily directed toward wives. To learn what efforts or sacrifices husbands should make to keep their marriages harmonious, we turn instead to the church. *The Catechism of the Council of Trent* took as its central text Paul's letter to the Ephesians (5:25–28) telling husbands to love their wives just as Christ loved the church: "Husbands should love their wives as they do their own bodies. He who loves his wife loves himself." A husband should treat his wife with courtesy on every occasion and honor her always. He should recall that Eve was Adam's companion, not his servant, that God formed her from Adam's side, not from his feet. Still, wives should be reminded that Eve was not drawn from Adam's head, so she should understand why her role is to obey, not command. A husband is obligated to exercise some honest pursuit that yields sufficient income to provide for his family's sustenance. He must avoid the languor of idleness, from which every vice flows. Finally, he must govern his family, correcting moral errors when necessary and keeping all the members steadfast in their respective tasks.

The assembled high clerics had no hesitation about extending their message in the clearest of terms as it related to sex: "It must therefore be taught, that, united in the bonds of mutual love, husband and wife are enabled by the grace of this sacrament, to repose in each other's affections, to seek no alien and illicit attachments, no criminal intercourse; and to preserve marriage honorable in all, and the bed undefiled" (Heb. 13:4). The indissolubility of marriage that Erasmus jested about in his dialogue between Eulalia and Xanthippe was no joke; moreover, according to the church, it had the benefit of making couples slower to anger and dissension. Even if a couple does separate, friends should find it easier to reconcile a husband and wife who are stuck with each other for life. Two interrelated lessons are critical in making husbands understand their duties. The first is that sexual intercourse is not to be used from motives of sensuality or pure pleasure; lovemaking must be restrained within the limits of self-control. The second lesson cites the authority of St. Jerome (against Jovinian 1:49) and warns that "a wise man ought to love his wife with judgment, not with the impulse of passion; he will govern the impetuosity of desire and will not be hurried into indulgence. There is no greater turpitude than that a husband should love his wife as he would an adulteress."[28]

The Council of Trent, of course, also approved numerous prescriptions for wives. The catechism begins with some definitions to help parish priests explain fundamental tenets to the faithful. The word "matrimony" tells us that the object of marriage is to conceive, bring forth, and raise children. The word "wedlock" highlights the fact that a lawful wife is locked to her husband. The word "nuptials" comes from Latin *(nuptiae, nubendo)* and reminds us that brides veil themselves out of modesty, as a sign that they will be obedient subjects to their husbands. The lesson continues with a citation from one of St. Peter's letters (1 Pet. 3:1–2), which enjoins wives to accept the authority of their husbands, even those who are not Christian, to win them over to faith without speaking a word but solely by good conduct, purity, and reverence.

The dilemma that had confronted St. Peter continued to confound Catholic Reformation prelates. They accepted the leading role of women in the initial spread of Christianity; these devout forebears frequently had struggled against stubbornly pagan husbands, and their behavior had been anything but obedient or feminine. The years before the Protestant Reformation also had witnessed intense female spiritual innovation—in Italy, as in Europe more generally—with an explosion of new saints cults, a far greater number of trials for heresy, and a series of female challenges to the magisterium. Confronted by a choice between innovative spirituality and defense of male dominance, sixteenth-century Catholic leaders made the same decision as Peter had 1500 years earlier: even holy women must be silent.

And yet the crucial role of mothers could not be ignored or curtailed too greatly. The catechism states explicitly that a principal duty of wives, alongside their primary responsibility for taking care of domestic concerns, should be to train their children in the practice of religion. Their Christian obedience had to come of free will, not force. A wife compelled by necessity might leave the house unaccompanied, but her preference should be to remain at home; she should willingly seek her husband's permission to go out. Except for God, she should love no one more than her husband and esteem no one more highly. This will come naturally if she has followed the church's advice to seek virtue and congeniality in a prospective groom rather than wealth or good looks. The wife must yield to her man in all things not inconsistent with Christian piety, and this she must do voluntarily and cheerfully.[29]

Bartolomeo de Medina, in his manual to assist confessors in giving spiritual guidance to parishioners of all social strata, begins with the mundane observation that a husband must provide for his wife's material needs. He must not mistreat her by hitting her or with verbal abuse. He must control his temper and refrain from excessive jealousy. Yes, wives tend to be a bit disobedient, fastidious, and negligent of household duties, but harshly criticizing every little flaw is not the way to get along. Wives must do their part too. They must not go out of the house against their husbands' wishes. Stop! I want to suggest that this is a much less restrictive prescription than what we saw in Plutarch, Barbaro, Belmonte, and other humanists. According to this churchman, wives may go out, even shine when the sun is away—like the moon—so long as they are discreet and their husbands do not object, of course. Surely he will allow her to go to mass during the week while he is at work. The good wife must be truly loving, and not merely put up with her husband. Her primary concerns should be the children, not vanity and pomp in her own attire. She must not hang out the window or otherwise let herself be viewed by outsiders as if she were for sale.[30]

Further hints that wives had some leeway may be found in the breezy stanzas of churchly poetic advice such as El costume delle donne. Do not ask your husband for too much money is what one line admonishes, without specifying how much is too much. Your churchgoing should be out of contrition, not pomposity, says another, nor should your eyes be wandering about taking in the scene while you mouth your prayers. When mass is over, do not hang around chatting; instead, go straight home and prepare something good for your husband to eat.[31] What have we here? Women who go to mass, perhaps with children in tow, while husbands spend Sunday morning having a drink in the piazza? Matrons who catch up with each other and begin informal marriage negotiations for their daughters? Wives who let their cooking chores take second place to socializing on the church steps? Ladies who assemble before God to check out the latest hairstyles and fashions?

Francesco Tommasi, whose advice for the country gentleman consciously furthered the efforts of post-Tridentine Catholicism to regulate the daily lives of the faithful, expands ever so slightly the wifely freedoms hinted at in Bartolomeo de Medina's confessional and in popular verse.

A husband should treat his wife not as a servant but as a confidante. Even the great Aristotle was wrong in warning men not to take counsel from a woman. A husband should accept advice from his wife, so long as it is given after careful consideration, in a reasoned manner. Nor should he keep secrets from his wife, mistrust her in any way, or be jealous.[32]

Monsignor Sabba da Castiglione offers a more authoritative viewpoint as he begins his prescriptive memoir on wifely behavior by reminding readers that Mary deferred to Joseph at the temple. The biblical incident referred to concerns the twelve-year-old Jesus who had been missing for three days when his parents came upon him back in Jerusalem, intently interrogating his elders. Jesus says to his parents, "Why were you searching for me? Did you not know that I must be in my Father's house?" Mary understands in her heart the meaning of her son's rebuke but still respectfully joins her husband in expecting and accepting filial obedience from the boy (Luke 2:45–51). What was good for the Mother of God must be proper for all other mothers, so no further historical examples are needed; indeed, they would be sacrilegious says the cleric as he moves on to more complex matters.

A wife must accept the reasonable, just, honest commands of her husband, but she must not obey requests that are against God's laws. The monsignor is so conservative that initially one might doubt how much solace he provided women who hoped to get support from the church for assistance in confrontations with their husbands. Still, further reflection suggests that modern scholars who view the Protestant abolition of confession as a loss for wifely independence, or at least as the removal of one restraint on patriarchal dominance, have a point. Churchmen, we noted earlier, had a lot to say about what should go on during lovemaking, always couching their advice in the language of obedience to God's laws. Certainly a woman could refuse sodomy or anal intercourse; on many days of the year she could lawfully refuse sex altogether. Monsignor Sabba allows for yet more interference, telling the wife to do everything reasonable to delight her husband but adding that if he wants to take you along to balls, comedies, tournaments, games, and other light entertainments you find offensive or lascivious, then just say no. Do not go. In this meddling logic we see a high churchman—writing in a big, authoritative book that went through nearly two dozen printings—assuming that women are capable of judging whether something is morally offensive, and then allowing them to act on their own judgment in direct denial of their husbands wishes. I believe it was the author's intent to place church authority above patriarchal rights. Moreover, this intent was understood and accepted by sixteenth-century readers, thereby providing some meaningful freedoms to pious wives.

These good women may have been more receptive to the remainder of Monsignor Sabba's advice than we would be. Your clothing should not be too airy, light, or vain. It should always be without frills, clean, and without stains, sweat marks, or dirt, because otherwise you look uncaring, more like a scullery maid than the proprietress of your home. Your speech should be grave, pleasing, moral, mature, weighty, and sparing. If you must correct something in your husband, do so out of charity—with affection, love, tenderness, and modesty. Do not become too possessive about things in the house, even as you carry out your duties of guardianship. Attend to your husband when he is ill. Teach your daughters to read, at least enough so they can follow the prayer book in an intelligent way; say the rosary with them everyday. Take them to church, dressed in accord with your station in life, not to see and be seen. Keep busy yourself and occupy your daughters with sewing and other useful skills. Do not let your husband bathe with your sons, because children should not see their parents naked.[33]

Another influential prelate, listed as Monsignor Agostino Valerio, bishop of Verona, on the title page of the octodecimo pocket manual we now open, used the vehicle of a letter to his married sister, Laura Gradenigo, to instruct wives on proper behavior. He claims to have published his little book with pretty borders, to meet repeated requests from members of the Company of the Madonna in Verona for a few words of spiritual guidance meant expressly for matrons. His Latin treatises on ecclesiastical rhetoric and his adoring biography of St. Charles Borromeo, which correctly spell the author's name as Cardinal Agostino Valiero (rather than Valerio, as it is found in his advice manual for married women), are much better known and were reprinted widely, whereas there were only two quick printings of his *Instruttione delle donne maritate*, so perhaps it was something of a vanity edition. Be that as it may, the work is humorless to a fault, unlike, for example, Monsignor Sabba da Castiglione's attempt at being funny in suggesting a husband put a ring in his wife's nose; it shuns as well the rhetorical flourishes that make a modern reader smile at Cardinal Antoniano's advice, even when that was not the prelate's intention.

Valerio's chapters are short and quick, easy to digest or to recommence for the woman with only a few minutes free between one household chore and another, which strikes me as exactly the way he intended the book to be read. Being at peace, doing everything in moderation, is the key, for a willful woman is like a serpent, a dragon. Love your husband above everyone except God, yet not so arduously that you are overcome with jealousy. Always be a bridge, a peacemaker between your husband and his brothers and sisters, between your children and their father, between your parents-in-law and their son. Never give counsel to your husband unless you are asked; even then, avoid any hint of audacity. If you must correct some fault in your husband, use the third person: "they say that such-and-such leads to loss of honor" or "it would be displeasing to God." Keep your eyes cast downward and your mouth shut except for absolute necessities; dress to cover up, not to attract attention to yourself; close your ears to useless talk; flee from public spectacles and comedies where the devil lurks to find new recruits and bring pious souls to ruin. Have faith and prepare for a long life—like the biblical Sarah—but if you are called to an early grave, think of your fate as God's way of protecting you from further occasions to sin. Keep your face and your hair as God made them for you, lest on the day of judgment he should stand before you and demand to know what you did with the gifts he gave you. How would you respond? Finally, no one has ever gone to the theater, a ball, or a worldly festival without coming home spiritually weakened, so skip all such vain entertainments. Instead, spend more time reading this little book of mine![34]

Now that we are back to cosmetics, let us return briefly to the loving advice of Cosmo Agnelli, with his tirades against women who curl and dye their hair, wear facial and body makeup, and go around in high-heeled shoes. What was merely scandalous for virgins threatens society itself when practiced by matrons. Whether such behavior is a mortal sin or only a venial transgression depends on the intention. All women who paint, powder, stuff, curl, bleach, and alter themselves, because they are consciously displeased with what God has given them, are mortal sinners in that their intent is to countermand the will of God. Just as any decent painter would be furious if someone came along and recolored his canvas, so God will judge harshly anyone who alters his handiwork: "Can you imagine if a limb of Jesus Christ should be transposed onto some whore? Beware, God is watching." Also guilty of mortal sin are those who put their vanity ahead of their immortal soul by refusing to go to mass if they are having a bad-hair day, as are those who use cosmetics to lure men into lascivious thoughts or actions. Married women have an additional occasion for mortal sin if they wear makeup or high heels against the express command or even the unspoken intent of their husbands, no matter what the reason. Matrons who set a bad example for their daughters bear the children's sins.

For all women—virgins, matrons, and widows—when the apocalypse comes, sweet perfumes shall be replaced by fetid stenches, curly blond hair by baldness, precious belts by harsh ropes, and breast corsets by hair shirts. That is how God will punish women for their arrogance and lasciviousness. Remedies against sin are at hand and are not all that difficult to implement. In the public sphere, bishops and priests should speak up to encourage republics to pass statutes and ordinances governing the honesty of women. The great majority of women would support legislation outlawing exposed breasts, jeweled dresses, makeup, and bleached hair, knowing the tranquility it would bring to society. Priests and confessors should unite now to devote serious words from the pulpit on these matters. In their private lives, pious women should reform of their own accord, setting aside fears that their husbands will no longer find them attractive, relying instead on the true beauty of their honesty, generosity, judiciousness, and nobility of spirit.[35]

On a more cheerful note, let us return to the folksy rules of Brother Cherubino da Siena. He it was who despaired of getting married couples to desist from kissing each other's dishonest parts, who scolded husbands for demanding the conjugal debt when their wives were preparing for holy communion, and who urged wives worried that their husbands might stray to liven up the sexual activities at home. Although the bulk of his marriage manual is devoted to sex, a few opening pages touch on other matters. Initially the friar offers balanced sets of rules: three things husbands owe their wives; three that wives owe their husbands; and three mutual obligations. The first duty of a husband is to instruct his wife in whatever she may need to improve her spiritual health, everything from the Lord's Prayer to the Ten Commandments to Brother Cherubino's own little *Regola della vita spirituale.* Alas, husbands are just as ignorant as wives these days, so the blind lead the blind and they both fall into ruin. Men first must get proper instruction at church themselves and then impart what they have learned to their spouses.

The second duty—husbands must correct their wives if they fall into female fragilities and occasions of sin—comes with an interesting twist. Just as no one but a husband may have carnal knowledge of his wife, so also no one but a husband may chastise his wife. Moreover, the correction must always begin with the most benign approach first, just as the good physician treats a sore initially with innocuous egg whites, then with a stronger plaster, and only with the razor and lance as a last resort. Correction should be loving and sweet, with the husband using himself as a good example (the presumption being that he is one) and appealing to her wish not to offend God and ruin the family's reputation. Don't shout "you're crazy," but instead say something like, "you spoke almost like one of those foolish, mad women do." Harsh words make her worse, not better. But if sweetness does not work, and your wife seems to possess a vile, rustic spirit, then use astringent words and threats to terrorize her into better ways. If this fails, take a stick and give her a good beating. Save beatings for the really big defects, like blasphemy, calling on the devil for help, hanging out the window, or flirting with dishonest young men. In short, do not hit her out of anger but only in a controlled way, out of charitable concern for her soul. Even then, always try kindness first.

The husband's third obligation is to provide for his wife's material needs: food and drink, clothing, shoes, a roof over her head, furnishings, and a suitable lifestyle. These must be provided in sickness as in health. She has brought to the marriage her dowry, in accordance with local customs, so her share in bearing the weight of marriage is accounted for. Considering that the husband has taken possession of his wife's dowry (communal property arrangements), it would be a cruel injustice for him to leave her wanting and not to provide for her needs. Her body should be nourished with the same concern he shows his own flesh.

Brother Cherubino moves along quickly to the three obligations of a wife. First, be in constant fear that you do nothing that might displease your husband in word, deed, or gesture. Behave with reverence toward him, responding with words of humility and calling him "Mister" or "Sir." However, "most delightful daughter of mine," if your husband orders you to do anything against God's commandments, do not obey him, for God's law is higher than man's. But if you are not sure whether your husband's orders are bad or good, just go ahead and do whatever he asks; should your obedience lead to evil, the sin will be his.

Second, take care of domestic duties to the best of your ability: cooking, cleaning, and keeping the house in order. Just think about how hard your husband is sweating, worrying, overworking, and stretching himself to provide for you and for your house. Like they say, "one hand washes the other and both wash the face," so this obligation is entirely fair.

Third, admonish your husband when he sins, gently and sweetly comforting him so he won't do it again and choosing carefully the right moment to reproach him so he will be in a receptive mood. Preface your correction by addressing him as "my Mister, my Sir," and tell him to reform out of love for you, that nothing could give you greater consolation than to see him freed from mortal sin. Pious wives are uniquely able to bring their husbands to salvation, yet how many there are who instigate their consorts to carry on vendettas and behave hatefully or who exceed their mates in vanity when they should be curbing excess pride. God created woman in the Garden of Eden to help man, not to bring him to eternal ruin.

Finally there are the three mutual obligations, the first of which is living together in cordial love. Be ready to sacrifice even your life for one another, as Christ did for his church. You must be able to truly forgive any transgression so long as your spouse is remorseful. Your love must be total, never one-sided or reserved. Brother Cherubino then abandons this mutual approach, turning for inspiration to the apocryphal Book of Tobit. There he finds five worthy injunctions given to Sarah by her parents as they sent her to her new groom, without locating any corresponding advice for husbands. For me the most poignant aspect of Sarah's story is that she had been betrothed seven times, only to find her fiancé, on each occasion, dead by morning, before the marriage could be consummated (Tob. 3:7–8)! But the friar makes no mention of Sarah's horrifying personal experiences and instead embellishes on the admonition by her parents to honor her new mother- and father-in-law (Tob. 10: 12). Although I doubt that Brother Cherubino meant some form of sly humor, I must confess to finding ironic comedy in his advice that, like Sarah, a wife must love no man but her husband, "so long as he lives on this earth." Another curious inversion of Sarah's circumstances comes with the friar's urgent appeal that stepmothers be kind to the children their husbands may bring from a prior marriage, especially the little helpless ones.

The fourth admonition—to preserve the family's assets—seems routine enough but shows once again the great confidence with which popular-religious-advice manuals assign to wives responsibility for administering the household wealth, including wine and grain stores, linens and clothing, and even the family's most prized possessions. This obligation extends from a housewife of modest means to one who must govern a staff of servants and slaves. Such responsibility, of course, was not compatible with portrayals of woman's innate inferiority, absolute incompetence, and constant need for supervision. My judgment is that practical self-help books meant for a wide readership, such as Brother Cherubino's, were less misogynous than some of the more esoteric, philosophical humanist tracts we have seen, precisely because the popular manual succeeded only when it sold and was read, which happened only if, in fact, it delivered useful information on how to run a household or how to avoid discord in marriage. The reality was that wives and mothers exerted considerable power even when fathers ruled, that the necessities of daily life ameliorated the ideals of patriarchy. The friar had it right when he advised wives not to add to their husbands' worries while they were away on land or sea by burdening them with the possibility of returning to a house in disarray, the children gone astray.

The fifth bit of wisdom Brother Cherubino found in the Book of Tobit is that wives should be circumspect—so restrained in word, act, and gesture that their husbands love them spontaneously, without reservation or gnawing jealousy. His little manual then returns to mutuality, taking on a tone that might be appropriate during a modern-day marriage-counseling session. It is equally reprehensible when either spouse embraces a lover. No allowances (such as those Plutarch granted) can be made for male flings, nor can any exception be justified as providing a safety valve for excess male lust while preventing a pious woman from being introduced to lascivious ways. Carnal knowledge outside the marriage undermines your own capacity to love your spouse and destroys her or his ability to love you. Mutuality also applies to the honor he must bestow upon her and she upon him, with each partner giving without looking first to receive and then enjoying the true love that follows. Finally, reciprocity must govern how spouses support each other, especially against the malicious, insidious gossip of outsiders. Of course little disagreements arise between husband and wife, just as crockery and utensils clank against each other in a cupboard; if two people are to talk with each other night and day, sharing everything under one roof, first one and then the other must be ready to forgive and show a little extra patience. When one pulls the string, the other should let go. Husbands do not need to win at every point, although wives have even more reason to let the man triumph and graciously put up with him. Whatever goes wrong, don't let twenty-four hours pass without reconciling and asking forgiveness—this goes for both of you but especially the wife.

The second obligation, after the multifaceted one to love with cordiality, is to live together under one roof. The basic reason is control over sexual urges. So important is this obligation that it holds even if one partner is blind, deaf, dumb, ugly, or sterile. Theologians agree that you need not live with a spouse who has leprosy but even then you should move to a nearby residence and continue to serve your partner's needs. If one or the other goes away on pilgrimage or business and no word comes from her or him, whether for a hundred or a thousand years, still you may not remarry unless absolute confirmation of your spouse's death arrives. The holy church decreed this rule to put a stop to those ignoramuses who said you could remarry after waiting without news for seven years, then seven months, seven weeks, seven days, seven hours, and finally a mere seven minutes. The third and final mutual obligation, the one that takes more words to explain than all the others combined, is the conjugal debt. Brother Cherubino's advice on this subject I have already considered in my earlier chapter on conception, so it need not detain us further.[36]

By way of closure on this brief look at churchly advice for married couples, I want to take a glance at the monk Tommaso Garzoni's views. He was a very popular and prolific author who wrote some rather strange books, but since none of them could be considered an advice manual, he is largely outside my landscape. An acerbic critic of the decadent world around him, Garzoni was a quintessential Catholic Reformation cleric, one with an exceptionally clever pen, perhaps a little insane or else way ahead of his time in using craniognomy to explain the scurrilous sonnets of poets like Pietro Aretino. In another work, a collective biography of biblical women in the *querelle des femmes* genre, he asserts that women by nature are more pious than men and therefore more similar to God, regardless of physical appearances. No one governs a home more sagaciously than a woman. Man was created from dust lying outside paradise, whereas woman was created from a rib, surely more noble than a clump of earth, from within the Garden of Eden, making her more perfect in God's eyes, according to our monk.[37]

In reading Garzoni, I am sometimes uncertain about whether his weird sense of satire has duped me, but in this instance I do believe he intends to stake out a progressive, provocative stance in defense of woman. If so, then he is only a little in advance of the position taken by his fellow churchmen, who without exception defend the equality of a woman's soul and her right to a place in heaven. Sixteenth-century neo-Aristotelians saw women as a separate, inferior species. Neoplatonists, on the other hand, envisioned a unified, single human essence, cloaked though it clearly was in a superficially different exterior. Judged in terms of the fundamental divide between two or one species, church teachings put Catholic writers—no matter what their misogynous tendencies, laments about female silliness, and jeremiads on worldly sin—squarely with the Neoplatonists. A soul—potentially pure, fully worthy of salvation—resided in every person, male or female. This tenet, whether believed or not, put rigid limits on how churchmen might advise husbands and wives to treat each other. Humanist tracts may be charged with reducing women to chattel—the possessions of fathers who traded them off to husbands—a logical, plausible reading today even if it was not the intent of their authors or the understanding of their original audience. For Catholic writers, by contrast, no amount of male denigration and ridicule in this world could deny a woman's essential humanity, her place of honor in God's order. Small consolation to be sure, the sort of religious pablum fed to black slaves in the antebellum American South, but to understand in any serious way the dynamics of either culture, we need to explore how subordinated people coped, even while we assert the injustice of their circumstances. The paradox extends to all of Catholic Europe, perhaps beyond, as exemplified so well in a quotation from the Oxbridge cleric Francis Meres in his *Gods Arithmeticke*. Equality of the sexes was out of the question on this earth:

> Therefore love your husbands here, and if they reward it not, it shall be rewarded in Heaven. Be obedient to them here, and ye shall be made equal with them in Heaven. Be humble and lowly here, and ye shall be exalted in Heaven. Be clothed with modesty here, and ye shall be clothed with honor in Heaven.[38]

From the Gentlemen

Writers who had not taken formal religious vows also contributed to the steady stream of moral-advice manuals published in Catholic Reformation Italy. Giacomo Lanteri, an engineer who served at the papal court and also under King Philip II, was known primarily as a mathematician, with special expertise in the construction of military fortifications. Toward the end of his life, however, he wrote a more reflective treatise on household economy, divided into two parts. The first contains four dialogues by men—on construction of the villa, supervision of servants, income and economic gain, and management of household expenditures. The gist throughout is moderation, on why it is more important to conserve wealth than to strive endlessly after more income, and on the virtues of charity. The second part brings in female interlocutors, who get only two dialogues. The one on solicitude I shall spare my readers entirely, but I do want to pause briefly over the discourse on female chastity (*honestà feminile*). Neither as clever nor as funny as many I've read—in fact, rather longwinded sermonizing at its worst—the premise is that a married woman is in constant danger of losing her good reputation. Sometimes even a single improper gesture, perhaps seen by an unexpected and unnoticed observer, can bring infamy on a woman who in reality is chaste. Keeping friends with someone who subsequently turns out to be of ill repute similarly besmirches a good woman. Avoid reasoning that could somehow be construed as lascivious, the best way being to avoid reasoning altogether. Do not gossip with servants, nor let their bickering and petty stupidities disturb your husband's tranquility of mind. Do not

spend the whole day bending your husband's ear about all the possessions you lack that your friends and neighbors already own. Painting your
face is patently dishonest and brings the household to ruin. Instead, imitate the German and Belgian women who dress properly with high collars
and closed bodices. Follow their honest example, and do not seek to
pursue the latest fashions that change at every whim. Venetians in the
old days had it right when they kept their women veiled. That was outstanding, truly holy legislation, because it instantly solved the social problems created by male lust. Gradually over the centuries, veils have come
up and collars have gone down, so that now women go around with their
entire breasts exposed. What indecencies are left?[39]

From Nicolò Gozze, the occult academician of Dubrovnik, come similar recommendations: if your wife is haughty or domineering, refuse to
show her a happy face under any circumstances because otherwise she
will ride you forever, just like plopping onto an easy chair. If she behaves
with humility, on the other hand, always be radiant and on your best
behavior. Wives who are generally prudent and judicious may be corrected with gentle admonitions, but if your woman is intemperate and
fearless, then reproach her with tough, harsh words. In governing his
wife, the good husband keeps experimenting with various mixes of love
and fear until he comes up with proper dosages. By setting the rules, you
will avoid excessive jealously, which kills you more easily than a knife
and nourishes great anxieties in your heart. Listen to your wife's counsel
if her words are spontaneous and unexpected, because often a woman's
intelligence is more intuitive and crafty than a man's, as with the biblical
Rebecca, Rachel, Deborah, Judith, and Ester. However, unless she is
extraordinarily discreet, do not reveal your secrets to her or you may
repent until your dying day. Gozze closes this part of his treatise by instructing women in the seven obligations of a good wife:

1. Guard over all the family possessions inside the house.
2. Let no one into your home without informing your husband.
3. Do not dress or adorn yourself beyond your means or beyond the customs
of your locale.
4. Do not put your nose into your husband's affairs, especially political doings.
5. Imitate the honest ways of your husband.
6. Revere your husband not with servile fear but with filial respect.
7. Be happy and evenhanded with your husband, in good times and bad.

On a loftier closing note, Gozze offers a rule that applies equally to husband and wife: share fully in each other's sentiments so that, like knots
tied tightly against one another, they are stronger than either alone would
be in providing a proper foundation for the family.[40]

Leonardo Fioravanti, the purveyor of quack elixirs and professor of secrets we consulted in chapter 2 for his guaranteed cures of sexual dysfunctions, also offers sixteenth-century readers his wisdom on what every woman must know to run her household properly. His book on the so-called mirror of universal science, like all his other works, went through numerous editions, clearly selling briskly to a wide audience that included both lesser nobility and business and craftspeople. All wives, he declares, should know how to bake bread, sew, wash, iron, and cook. A noble woman must not disdain domestic knowledge, both to be a better supervisor if she has a servant and to lend a hand as needed. Next, in a put-down typical of the popular-advice-manual genre, Fioravanti warns that nobility does not come with eating too much, sleeping excessively, and talking constantly. Women who get their exercise doing chores at home do not have the time and energy to stroll around the piazza, an activity that is the mortal enemy of chastity: "Rich, young, healthy, strong, pretty, attractive, and carefree woman who has liberty—I ask you—what are you thinking when you sit on a thick cushion, other than setting your mind on how to keep enjoying what you have." Beware that such blessings are ephemeral, seemingly an alluring way to cruise through life but all a cruel deception.

The doctor/charlatan/philosopher then climbs to an even higher rhetorical plateau as he invokes the husband observing his ideal, steadfast helpmate:

> What a great pleasure to hear his wife arising in the morning at an early hour to start on the housework, without combing her hair and putting on stockings, with her shirtsleeves rolled up and her arms bare, getting the servants to work and giving the children their clothes to put on. What a joy to see her do the laundry, wash the sheets, sift flour, make bread, sweep the house, fill the lamps, get lunch going, and then pick up her sewing needle. I don't think those women are any good who do nothing but go to sleep at midnight and arise at noon, telling dirty stories all evening. These women do little else than sleep, eat, and gossip. If you look at their little corner of the house, everything radiates in splendor, but elsewhere the house is a shameful mess, dirty and dusty, more like a barn than a home.[41]

Dr. Fioravanti's directed his prescriptions primarily at city housewives, whose domestic space was fairly limited, perhaps to an area that could be properly dusted and swept by midmorning. Rural women had yet more responsibilities, enough to keep them on the go from sunrise to sunset and beyond into the night. Virtually all sixteenth-century

agricultural-advice manuals for country gentleman that I have seen—
dozens of them—contain at least some reference to the duties of *La
Signora*, the wife who was central to successful management of the family
property, however great or humble. Xenophon's *Oeconomicus* provided
the classical model, serving for this subgenre in ways similar to Plutarch's
Coniugalia praecepta for treatises on marital relations: a source to plagia-
rize, translate, cite, modify ever so slightly, even improve upon, but rarely
to ignore. A recent translation by Sarah Pomeroy, with an outstanding
scholarly introduction, makes Xenophon's work readily accessible, so
here I only wish to highlight a few points. The illustrious Alessandro
Piccolomini translated the text into Italian in 1540, and Lodovico Dolce,
among others, translated and frequently reprinted favorites by Xenophon
such as *Anabasis* and *Cyropaedia*, ensuring that Italian writers of farmer's
almanacs who could not themselves read the original Greek still had easy
access to its content, as well as to other writings by this revered authority.
Pomeroy suggests that for the Italian scene, Aristotle's *Oeconomica* may
have been more influential than Xenophon's *Oeconomicus*, a conclusion
that in my judgment holds only for fifteenth-century humanists writing
in Latin. Once we get to printed vernacular texts in the sixteenth century,
whether in England (as Pomeroy recognizes) or in Italy, Xenophon
clearly held his own against any and all Greco-Roman authors.[42]

Pomeroy's careful reading of Xenophon establishes him as a "separate-
spheres-of-influence" theorist, but one who absolutely did not denigrate
the domestic realm as inferior. Like Plato, Xenophon treated the soul as
having no sex, with men and women equally capable of moral perfection. This separate-spheres view sat more comfortably with nineteenth-
century feminists than with the post–Second World War generation,
writes Pomeroy, although exceptions must be made for Carol Gilligan
and other recent authors who deny that "gender difference undervalues
women and look for a way for women to fulfill traditional female roles
without handicaps." Changing tastes notwithstanding, writers of farmer's almanacs in sixteenth-century Italy, I believe, saw no contradiction
in accepting both the overarching framework of patriarchy and, within
that paradigm, the separate- (and valued) spheres model they found both
in Xenophon's ideas and in the realities all around them in the countryside. The reader of Xenophon joins Socrates in learning from Ischomachus that his wife manages within the home, on her own. She attained
this capacity by achieving self-control as a child, through prayer, and
most recently from her husband's good instruction on how she must go
beyond maidenly restraint to realize the full measure of her God-given
abilities. Thus, she became ready to fulfill her role as queen bee for the

hive, as quartermaster for the army, as boatswain for the trireme, as pilot's mate for the merchant ship, as chorus master for the dance. Once Ischomachus explained to her how offensive he found her facial powder, rouge, and platform shoes, she readily gave up these false adornments, gaining a natural flush to her complexion by following his advice to walk a lot, sift flour, and knead dough. And so she became a truly ideal wife.[43]

Treatises like Piccolomini's translation of Xenophon may have been too pretentious for most farmers, while large and elegant agricultural-advice manuals like Estienne's surely carried prices meant for sale only to the wealthy. But the marketplace also made room for modest, practical works such as Giuseppe Falcone's book of 366 octavo pages. In all these tracts—highbrow and low, expensive and cheap—we see that ideas about proper women's roles more consistently cross class divides than do norms for men, confirming once again the observation Kelso made some forty years ago. Women of all classes, except perhaps for royalty, ran country households in hands-on fashion, whereas elite countrymen who wished to devote themselves to contemplation, politics, and recreation employed factors. Falcone's advice captures nicely the world of the respected rural family: one with some property to manage, conserve, and pass on to children; one able to hire a few hands for the busiest days of harvesting but otherwise laboring on its own; one local people might aspire to imitate without appearing ludicrously ignorant of social barriers.

A Carmelite friar who also published a hagiography detailing the merits of several early saints from his order, Falcone displayed admirable breadth of interest with his eminently practical, no-frills farmer's guide. Reprinted many times throughout the century following its initial appearance in 1597, the book opens with a table of notable matters, so as to help readers intending to reconsult its pages whenever particular needs arose. The prose eschews proverbs and biblical precepts, devoting itself instead to detailed recommendations about matters promised by the lengthy title, which may be translated as "A Work of Agriculture, More than Necessary for Everyone Wishing to Increase Crop Yields and All Those who Practice Agriculture, [telling] How to Plant, Grow, and Prune Trees, Cultivate the Garden, and Sow Acreage in accordance with the Quality of Fields and Meadows; How to Put Up Buildings, Houses and Edifices Pertinent to the Villa; and with Remedies for the Various Infirmities of Oxen, Horses, and other Animals." The title goes on to boast that this treasure chest of advice is drawn from every Greek, Latin, and Italian author who has written on the subject, thereby presumably reassuring the farmer with only limited money to spend on books that he now possesses all that is worth knowing, that he need not add to his library or envy what is on the shelf of his richer neighbor. The section on his wife's duties is addressed directly to her, in a plain but not condescending style. Falcone leavens his text with an occasional joke, as when he explains that in the countryside, husbands take care of outdoor tasks and wives of the house itself, because otherwise women would do the men's work and then kill off their unnecessary appendages.

Above all take care of your own self as a devout, God-fearing woman, govern your children and other family members diligently, and obey your husband. Be patient and kind to everyone, discreet, and not jealous. Love your home, leaving it only on necessary business, and in general stay within the courtyard. Be severe with hired laborers who slough off on work; do not be litigious; flee from dances, music, and festivals, and keep your daughters away as well. Attend to cleaning the house, the linens, the tablecloths, and the entryway. See that everything is neatly put away in its proper place, not strewn all over helter-skelter.

Do not trust anyone with your keys to the pantry and granary. Watch carefully over your teenagers, especially the girls. Be the first to get up and start work in the morning, the last to retire at night. Before going to bed, prepare what is needed for tomorrow. Do your chores without muttering because service rendered with hostility is not well received. Do not encourage your women friends to come over and chat; if they show up uninvited, just send them away. Follow your husband's orders in everything and willingly serve the needs of your neighbors. Encourage your children to be industrious, telling them, "Do you see me? Do you see your father? Do you see what we do?" Don't curse or use foul language and dirty words. Gather wood spread around the courtyard and stack it by the fireplace. Save the grape stalks for kindling or for feeding the oxen in winter. Carefully dry the residues from the grape harvest for making oil for the lamp in the stable. Keep an honest count of the eggs, chickens, capons, butter, and cheese you have sold.

Do not pay too much attention to beautifying yourself, but take care to be personally clean. On Saturday you should wash your hair and your *venere* (genitalia), using a shampoo made by pouring a ladle of good, cold ashes into a pail of water and boiling it until it is reduced by a quarter, not more. This is the perfect washing solution.

For Sunday, have a white shirt or blouse ready for each member of the family. In doing the wash, neither waste soap and wood nor ask women in to help; use the young women of your own household instead. As to the courtyard, see that the chickens and other animals do not ruin the seedlings. If you lend something to a neighbor, be sure to get it back as soon as possible. Immediately after you finish eating, clean up, so your house doesn't look like a tavern. Attend to mending clothes and linens.

Put the chickens in their coop in timely fashion. Know how to castrate the young roosters. Do your spinning in the evening. Bake bread only with your own household members, without gossiping too much while you're at it. Bread should not be eaten fresh out of the oven; instead, wait for it to become dry and firm.

Do not touch that bottle of good wine. Just drink the table wine, watered down, saving what little there is of unadulterated wine for the hot season ahead. At the table, first offer a blessing, then eat lightly, silently, and in peace. Wait until all family members have arrived home before sitting at table. Do not set out a big spread; give each person an appropriately sized bowl of *minestra,* and do the best you can to see that everyone is content with what is before them.

Put the little ones to bed first, before your working-age children even come home. The good wife who attends to the house is like money in the bank *(guadagna cinque soldi),* even if no one recognizes her contribution. Take especially good care with the milk—know how to make butter, ricotta, and cheese, properly salted. Make sure all the courtyard animals and fowl are fed at the right times.

You are not a good housewife unless your garden is neatly planted, seeded, hoed, and weeded. Never let the chickens, ducks, and other animals enter the vegetable patch. Watch that the lard, sausages, and salamis do not go rancid. See that the furnace and the stove are in good order so that your bread is properly cooked. Each year make new underclothing for everyone in the household brigade. Keep the chicken coop locked with a key, and go everyday before noon to collect the eggs. Each evening count the chickens to make sure they are all in the coop; check that no animal has disturbed the beehive.

For large purchases and sales, wait for the boss, but attend to the little things yourself, because the head of the household should not be bothered with details.[44]

Indeed, this manual is filled with details—it is in the details that I see useful clues about the identity of the wife who read such a book or whose husband read it to her and held her to its standards. She was the married copossessor of a modest farm somewhere along the Po Valley or the Veneto, a geography captured nicely by printings of the book itself in Pavia (1597), Brescia (1599), Treviso (1602), Venice (1603, 1612, 1628), place unknown (1619), and Piacenza (1691). She was a good Catholic, although too busy to go to mass except on Sunday. Her heavy responsibilities were universally understood to be absolutely essential to the survival of her household. If her work was not precisely equal to her husband's, nevertheless she was considered equally necessary in their mutual endeavor. If she neglected her duties, turned to drink, or became chronically ill, then another woman—perhaps her eldest daughter or possibly her husband's unmarried sister—had to come and take her place. If she died, then her husband remarried quickly, for she could survive without him much more successfully than he without her. She offset the drudgery of her days by stealing moments to exchange ideas and information with women of her age and status who did exactly what the advice books told them not to do: pop over to a neighbor's kitchen unannounced at midmorning to look in on what was baking, make an informal arrangement to do the wash jointly in the afternoon to save on firewood, bring over a secret salve for that persistent wart or aching knee, stop by with freshly picked wild berries when she had gathered more than her own family could eat but not enough to bother selling at the market, go over to the village intermediary (usually a woman) with a few eggs or a cheese to be brought to market for sale the next morning. The lifestyle prescribed by Falcone in the sixteenth-century is remarkably similar to what I have observed personally during extended stays in rural Italy and Croatia. To be sure, young women today reject such a seemingly mundane existence and move to the city, along with the men who cannot survive without them. But their grandmothers lived that way, as did their forebears for centuries.[45]

Farmers who held extensive pasture lands, who perhaps resided a little higher up in the Apennines or in the foothills of the Alps, might have turned instead to Count Giovanni Maria Bonardo's *Le ricchezze dell' agricoltura* (The Riches of Agriculture). I introduced him in chapter 5 as the dilettante who balanced in satiric, pseudoscientific fashion the pros and cons of taking a wife, jauntily concluding that the scales tipped heavily against marriage. But that was a different treatise, intended for an audience of literati, whereas the readership for his little agriculture book seems to have been moderately well-to-do landowners, neither day laborers nor nobles on great estates with servants and sharecroppers to do the work. The title page reveals something about marketing strategies. Whereas Falcone assures readers that his work includes the wisdom of every known Greek, Roman, and Italian expert on the subject, Count Bonardo trumpets the claim that almost nothing in his book has been taught before by any writer, either among the ancients or the moderns. However false that claim may be, the opening pages are arranged conventionally according to the yearly calendar, with summaries of what needs to be done each month, beginning with January. Following the December listing are chapters detailing how to do each task previously specified in monthly order, but this chronological presentation applies primarily to the husband's obligations. The full treatment of the wife's rather formidable list of jobs, by contrast, knows no season and offers little repose.

During the day the farmwife should tend to the cows and milk them; make butter and cheese; care for the pigs and feed them; keep the fire going; and preserve the lards, fats, hams, salamis, bacon, sausages, and similar items. During the evening she should prepare flax for weaving into linen (a sticky mess of a job, not for anyone with delicate hands). On an annual or semiannual basis, I suppose, although the frequency of this work is not specified, she should shear the sheep (a task requiring strength and dexterity), then wash and comb the wool in preparation for making clothes for the family. Closer to home, her responsibilities further include keeping the vegetable garden filled with herbs for *minestra;* watching over the chickens and pigeons; preserving herbs, fruits, turnips, and other tubers; drying seeds for all the plantings; tending the bees; and making honey and wax. Moving on to indoor tasks, she should oversee all the household furnishings and linens, with a constant eye on what may be needed in the days or weeks ahead. The final recommendation could have been left unsaid: be the last to go to bed at night and the first to arise in the morning, keeping watch over everything. Perhaps on his own estate, Count Bonardo's wife had maidservants to assist her, so maybe she did not have to do all her prescribed work herself, but my sense of this manual is that its tone, style, likely price, and content meant that it was directed primarily to men and women who worked the fields and tended the animals with their own hands—all day, all year.[46]

One of the authors Bonardo surely borrowed from heavily—despite his claim to complete originality—was the popular almanac by Agostino Gallo. Structured as a dialogue, and expanded over several reprintings from ten to thirteen and then to twenty days in duration, it largely abandons philosophical discourse and instead provides practical how-to aids such as a calendar of what needs doing on the property each month, an index of notable matters, a glossary of technical terms, and marginal summary notes to enable the busy farmer to quickly locate exactly what he must know to complete the task at hand. Some editions are further enhanced with nearly two dozen woodcuts showing details of farm implements used in the Brescia region, from which I surmise that a talented craftsman/farmer could have fashioned his own tools. I shall spare you the book's wisdom on how to prune, plant, hunt, and fish.

Instead, let us zoom in on advice from chapter 18, about how to deal with a wife who does not share your appreciation of the countryside, given in the same matter-of-fact style as the admonitions in chapter 17, to keep busy when it's raining, and the recommendations in chapter 19, on snaring birds. If your wife is a good woman, as so many of them are, there is no problem. But some women do not appreciate the joys of country living, about which Gallo waxes ecstatic for many pages, because they have so much smoke in their chimney they won't put up with staying outside the city. They want to come and go as they please, showing off their charms to this one and that. They think about nothing more than running here and there, wherever caprice takes them, invariably turning up where there is dancing, a comedy, a play, games, debauchery, or a tournament. They want to hang out at the doorstep all day or at the window like a crazy woman with no sense of shame, scandalizing the whole city. Such antics had not been customary among the ancients; they were introduced later by the barbarians and now have spread throughout Italy. It's like a cancer, one that feeds upon the blind husbands and stupid fathers who are the real culprits for permitting such vituperative comportment. The best remedy against this pestilent seed would be to execute a proper sentence against every evil woman: "Just as the bad daughter should be given death as her dowry, worms as her wedding gown, and a coffin as her home, likewise the infamous wife should have her eyes gouged, her tongue cut out, and her hands chopped off. Or, better yet to rid the world of her, burn her alive."

The interlocutors soon realize that their recommendations for cleansing the world of wicked women have no chance of being implemented, so they turn to other evils of the city, like the dishonest merchants who cheat an honorable matron, a licentious widow, a comely virgin, or a cloistered nun with equal unscrupulousness. Alas, this part of their conversation again becomes depressing even to themselves, dwelling as it does on city streets where muggers lurk, tricksters and racketeers abound, killers roam free, and thieves prey everywhere. All these criminals deserve gruesome summary executions alongside the world's evil women, but that won't happen either. The discussants eventually realize they can achieve peace only by returning to the countryside, presumably with writer and reader both better able to see the demands of housework, gardening, and animal husbandry not as drudgery but as fruitful endeavors—God's work.[47]

A sixteenth-century *mariazo* listing the virtues of a good peasant wife also extols the joys of rural life, but in a more upbeat style. The verse was probably meant for recitation from a theater stage as much as for reading at home.[48]

La sa stizar el fuogo	She knows how to stoke the fire,
la sa lavar squele	She knows how to wash the pots and pans,
la fa ben papardele	She makes great noodles,
la stria ben fen in prò	She mills grain well at the stream,
la sa ingrassar un bo	She knows how to fatten an ox,
la mena a pascolo i puorci	She guides the pigs to pasture,
la sa ben vendere e comprare.	She's shrewd at buying and selling.

I opened this chapter by exploring humanist prescriptions for a happily married life, beginning with the sugarcoated misogyny of Plutarch's letter to the bride and groom, touching upon the treatises of Francesco Barbaro and Matteo Palmieri, and then sampling the lively dialogues of Desiderius Erasmus and Antonio Brucioli before swallowing a dose or two from the harsh familial epistles of Piertro Belmonte and Orazio Lombardelli. The model that emerged from all these writings featured absolute patriarchal authority for the husband and narrowly circumscribed behavior for his subservient wife.

Against this philosophical ideal, I then surveyed briefly advice set forth by the church, including the Council of Trent's authoritative pronouncements, several vernacular confessors manuals, and a few diatribes by literary-minded monks. For all the ranting and raving about women's evil ways, embedded in abundant evidence that men's obsessive fear of female sexuality pervaded Catholic Reformation writings, a few significant limits to male domination appeared. Above all, there is God, whose will no husband may command his wife to disobey. And how is a wife to know God's will? There is much advice telling her to seek the opinion of her confessor, yet between the lines—occasionally in them, if I have read without excess liberty—is the progressive notion that the wife herself defines whether a command is unchaste. The injunction from Monsignor Sabba is worth repeating: do everything reasonable to delight your husband, but if he wants to take you along to balls, comedies, tournaments, games, and other light entertainments that you find offensive or lascivious, then just say no. Do not go.

The third grouping of authors, dominated by gentlemen agriculturalists, took us away from the ideal worlds of both the humanist's study and the monk's cell. We entered the homes of wives who had to put supper on the table—raise it, cook it, and clean up after it. I let the lunatics among this group, who recommend mutilating and burning evil women alive, speak for themselves. Moreover, I fully concede that humanists may have harbored such thoughts even if their civility kept them *in pectore*, with the notable exception of Pietro Belmonte. Churchmen, too, perhaps took satisfaction in believing that such a fate awaited Eve's sinful daughters in the next world. Still, amidst all the burdens of guarding chickens, shearing sheep, keeping the fire going, cooking, cleaning, nursing sick children, and catering to her husband, I think the rural housewife had some freedom.[49] Not just the freedom to say "no," granted by the church against a husband who wanted to take his wife to a lewd show or engage in sodomy, but also the freedom to say "yes," to make decisions about whether to sell an egg or eat it, buy a personal treat or put an extra penny in the charity box, mend a sheet one more time or use it for rags. Trifles, you may say, but the stuff of real life for many women.

From lamentations by male writers of all persuasions, we know that headstrong city women went about as they pleased, strolling in the piazza, gossiping, flirting, and reading dirty books. Their female cousins in the village may have led a more drab existence by our standards, yet in their world survival meant they had to acquire knowledge, develop skills, exchange ideas, respond to adversities, and make decisions. As a practical reality, they could not have been brainless automatons living in childlike subservience to their almighty husbands and still have run their households successfully. Little wonder, then, that almanacs for farmers consciously set out huge "spheres of influence" for the good wife. She was expected to get done whatever needed to be done, to use her own discretion in accomplishing her part in a mutual endeavor.

Widows

When the old man died, the idealized portrait of Renaissance household patriarchy had to undergo subtle variations, even outright negations. Let the opening revisionist be a female voice. Moderata Fonte's delightful *querelle des femmes* dialogue, *Il merito delle donne,* is a work I have already mentioned, and here I wish only to note the setting for its discourse. Seven women gather in the widowed Leonora's garden: a second widow; two matrons; two maidens, one of whom already has determined never to marry; and a newlywed freshly returned from her honeymoon. Leonora recently became the proud inheritor of the magnificent villa that her six guests have come to see. Word is out that, although she is rich and beautiful, Leonora has no intention of remarrying, a choice her friends eagerly desire to hear more about. Her spinster aunt bequeathed her the property, after having spent lavishly throughout her lifetime in adorning the place with fountains and statuary expressing her misandry. In such conducive surroundings the women proceed to dissect the opposition, quickly overcoming their inhibitions that some male intruder might report their conversation to the smug Venetian authorities. They may employ their intellects at leisure since their invitation rests on no man; there is no one to tell them when to go home.

Day one starts slowly until Leonora breaks the ideological logjam with an unequivocal declaration of her intention to remain a widow, about which more shortly. The air now cleared, the maiden Corinna provides the lightening rod for a storm of invective that sees the destruction of every rationale for male domination, expressed brilliantly in sonnets and citations of the classics. Eventually the guests return home for a well-deserved repose, determined to reassemble early the next morning. Dawn breaks and their gondolas arrive just as Leonora finishes her toilette, the prompt start allowing not for chores but for a wide-ranging discussion in which discourses on astronomy and biology yield to joyful analysis of cosmetics and fashion. The ladies display easy familiarity with Greco-Roman theories of the four bodily humors as they construct a self-indulgent, gluttonous parody of male-authored advice manuals on health and diet such as those by Michele Savonarola and Giovanni Marinello—hardly surprising for a woman like Fonte who was well-established in the milieu of Venetian publishing and who may have been an acquaintance of Lucrezia Marinella, the erudite daughter of Giovanni. Amidst conundrums such as whether there are more fish in the sea, birds in the air, or animals on land, and amazing tales about exotic places like the Sea of England, where the water freezes so you can walk on the ice gathering immobilized fish, the interlocutors sprinkle liberal doses of phylogeny. Using the inexperienced maiden Virginia as a foil, the wiser ones excoriate men at every turn of the page.

Before all this flowing discourse, however, the orientation of the dialogue had to be established early on day one. The two widows engage in the following exchange after newlywed Elena remarks in passing on how charming her hostess is and her hope that they will get together more often:

> *Adriana (the elder widow)*. She sure is gracious, pleasing, and beautiful; there's nothing else to say. What a shame you don't want to remarry, being so young and pretty.
> *Leonora (the young widow)*. What, me remarry? I'd rather drown than submit again to any man. I escaped from slavery and imprisonment. Are you now suggesting I voluntarily become enchained again? God watch over me.

Cornelia, a matron, gives Leonora a kiss and exclaims that her hostess is much more intelligent than she had previously thought. Leonora seems

embarrassed at the compliment and suggests that all partake in a refreshing glass of chilled wine. They do, enjoying as well their hidden
companionship, laughter, games, and fruits. As the widow Leonora will
remain safe from male predators, the dialogue among women may begin
in earnest.[50]

Precisely how many women were in Leonora's circumstances and how
many made her choice we simply do not know. I am not referring here to
her property holdings—the enchanting garden adorned with sculptured
misandry and the Venetian villa reached by gondola—since my concern
is not with the richest one tenth of 1 percent but with the middle-class
and upper-middle-class people who I believe bought and read advice
manuals. Even when the property was modest—a farmhouse with tools
and a few acres of land or a struggling shop with a sparse inventory, some
debts, and the bare necessities in crowded familial quarters on the floor
above—the challenge to patriarchy was similar. How could the wife confined only yesterday to silence, mindless drudgery, and house arrest—
all to mollify her husband's paranoia about her chastity—today go about
town on business of the most urgent sort, making decisions about herself
and her children? If relatives helped out during the initial period of shock
and grief (or secret rejoicing as the case may be), who looked after things,
however few the possessions, in the months and years that followed?

As one of my colleagues observed, "Rudy, these are very complicated
questions you're asking; no one can resolve them fully for any society."[51]
Answers to even the simple queries continue to elude us. How many
widows were there? How old were they when their husbands died? How
frequently did they take another spouse? If they remarried, what interval
elapsed between one marriage and another? How many children or other
persons, and of what age and sex, depended on them at the moment they
became widows? What were their assets and liabilities, and what legal
control did they have over the disposition or payment of each? Then there
are more complex questions. How capable were widows of handling the
business and personal affairs newly thrust upon them? What were their
emotional, intellectual, and experiential strengths and weaknesses? How
could they get assistance from relatives, friends, businesses, or charities?
What were the up-front and hidden costs of such aid? Finally, there are
the historian's traditional concerns. How did the circumstances of widowhood change over time, place, class, and culture?

Although we do not know enough to answer fully any of these questions, we know a little here and there, enough to reassure me that I am
justified in asserting that widows were a challenging anomaly to patriarchal norms everywhere in early modern Europe, although in varying de-

grees. Legal approaches to property in marriage oscillated between the extremes of total conjugality, the mixture recommended by Plutarch, and strong linearity, husband and wife each retaining control over natal family property, passing her and his holdings individually onto offspring. Either way, indeed at every point along the conjugal/linear spectrum, surviving women at some point exercised meaningful control over assets and liabilities, either as wives over their personal, natal wealth or as widows over the conjugal mix. Men—be they fathers, husbands, or sons—could and did write laws to circumscribe the freedom of their daughters, wives, and mothers to control property, but nowhere were such controls absolute, if for no other reason than that such extremism would have threatened to extinguish entirely the interests of competing male relatives. Legal records abound telling of conflicts over women's property occurring between father and son, husband and father-in-law, brother and brother-in-law, not to mention stepchildren, bastards, lovers, friends, and institutional vultures. Moreover, a wife had to deal with restrictions from the grave as expressed by written testament. Still, we may recall that the Magna Carta itself placed a widow's rights before those of her dead husband's creditors. By no means do women emerge from the vast array of legal documents as witless, helpless victims. If the Florentine widow and epistler Alessandra Strozzi was not exactly typical, undeniably she was possible.[52]

Patriarchy had its limits. A careful study by Samuel Cohn Jr. found that Siena's women responded enthusiastically to Catholic Reformation spiritual calls, at least upon their deathbeds. More women made wills, increasingly bequeathing pious gifts, so that their recorded charity increased sixteenfold between 1550 and 1650. In their living years these women joined sex-segregated confraternities and in their graves they remained with their sisters—not their husbands—thus reclaiming their bodies by choosing religious sorority over family ties. Cohn reports that half the women who made a free designation, in the period 1550 to 1599, elected burial apart from their husbands or fathers (or other male lineage), reversing the 1450 to 1550 pattern, when patriarchy had extended even to the burial ditch. The proportion of loners rose to nearly two thirds between 1600 and 1649, and reached almost three quarters by 1650 to 1699. Post-Tridentine Sienese widows also exercised increased control over property. Already by the late sixteenth century, husbands' wills less often threatened wives with loss of inheritance if they remarried or were unchaste, or in some cases limited the good-behavior sentence to one year, after which the widow became truly free. Companionate wills by healthy married couples also became more numerous, containing

mutual provisions for saying masses, expressing full faith in each other's
decision-making capacity, and leaving the estate with no strings attached
to whoever survived. The words agreed upon by Cristofano and Maria
tell it all: "They wish not to impose any weight or aggravation on one
another, because each of them confides in the good conscience of the
other, that the one who survives will have performed as many suffrages
as possible for the health of their souls."[53]

Just as I am confident in asserting that widows exercised some control
over assets and liabilities, even though I remain necessarily vague about
the exact details, so also I state categorically that there were many widows
around, more than there were widowers, even though I cannot say exactly
how many lived in most places in Europe in any given year. A good
anchor point on numbers comes from David Herlihy and Christiane
Klapisch-Zuber's study of the Tuscan census of 1427 (Table 1), a little early for my purposes but so thorough as to justify a quick presentation:

Table 1. Marital Status in Tuscany, 1427

	Florence	Cities	Towns	Countryside
Men over age 12				
Married	48%	59%	63%	65%
Widowers	4%	4%	3%	4%
Unmarried or indeterminate	48%	37%	34%	31%
Total number of men	13,514	8,897	8,481	59,145
Women age 12 and over				
Married	53%	58%	62%	65%
Widows	25%	24%	21%	17%
Unmarried or indeterminate	22%	18%	18%	18%
Total number of women	12,101	9,165	8,698	59,301

More people married in the countryside than in the city, especially the
big city of Florence. Men whose wives died usually remarried, whether
they were urban or rural residents. Women whose husbands died usually did not remarry, especially in the city. According to Herlihy and
Klapisch-Zuber, whose work may also be consulted for details about how
the indeterminate category might be apportioned, approximately 10 percent of Tuscan women were already widows at age forty and fully 25
percent by age fifty. Their numbers were partially balanced in the male
population by the prolonged or permanent bachelorhood of men who
reached the age of fifty without ever marrying, some 12 percent in Florence and over 5 percent in the countryside. In short, a supply of mar-

riageable men existed, but the demand by widows was weak. According to Herlihy and Klapisch-Zuber:

> These figures would prove, if proof were needed, that widows remarried only reluctantly or with difficulty. The great majority, after the death of their first husband, viewed the prospects of a second marriage with about as much enthusiasm as men viewed their first. This hesitation was nonetheless subdued in the countryside; there, the proper management of a farm required male help. But it was very pronounced in the city, where widows could live independently, on salary, rent, or public charity.

Actually, women were considerably more reluctant to remarry than men had been to marry in the first place, if one goes by the numbers instead of by the misogynous humor of advice manuals. However, leaving that problem aside, the emphasis by Herlihy and Klapisch-Zuber on widows who chose independence, even when it meant relying on welfare, rings true.[54]

Legal restrictions nominally aimed at protecting the rights of children whose fathers died also worked to discourage widows from remarrying. In Florence, the *Magistrato dei Pupilli* (magistrate for wards), which was founded in the late fourteenth century and lasted into the nineteenth century, undergoing a major reform in 1565, had specific authority to intervene if a widow who controlled a patrimony on behalf of her children remarried. Taking a second husband instantly rendered her legally dead with regard to her prior marriage, so that the court acted exactly as if her children were total orphans with both parents deceased. Further penalties came in the requirement of chastity many dead husbands legally imposed on their children's mothers, although this may have been enforced only for flagrant violations or when families battled over other issues. Still, guardianship of their children gave widows power and many chose to retain their authority by not remarrying.[55]

I am especially interested in these widows, because they are the women most likely to have been too mature to return to their natal household yet too young to turn power willingly and completely over to an eldest son. They best fit the male stereotype of the merry widow with an insatiable, and now liberated, sexual appetite. They were more likely than older widows to have made a choice about remarriage, possibly influenced in their decision by what they read in an advice manual. There is some reality behind the ridicule found in Vincenzo Maggi's 1545 *Un brieve trattato dell' eccellentia delle donne* (A Brief Treatise on the Excellence of Women), which reports that Brescia's finest widow at long last has decided to remarry. It seems the city's bachelors have been crucified so thoroughly by their widow/lovers that they have become spineless, willing to let women govern them, so now she can choose one among the lot and ride him mercilessly. Maggi adds that as the widow announces her decision, her head is high in the air, filled with tyranny.[56]

Evidence gathered throughout preindustrial Europe, scattered and incomplete though it may be, further confirms the presence of significant numbers of mature, capable women who lived successfully in freedom from the immediate yoke of household patriarchy. For seventeenth- and eighteenth-century France, scholars have found that widowers remarried more than twice as frequently as widows, 50 percent compared with 20 percent. Moreover, widowers who remarried tended to wed celibate women rather than widows. Another study of France in the sixteenth and seventeenth centuries also found higher remarriage rates for widowers, adding that they remarried much sooner than did widows. This study found the typical age at widowhood for women to be thirty-five to forty. Widows were reluctant to remarry even when their material circumstances forced them to change residences. One study found that for preindustrial Sweden, class was more important than gender, as peasant widows remarried but pastors' wives did not, although another survey came to the opposite conclusion; in both studies men remarried more frequently than women. For seventeenth- and early-eighteenth-century England, analysis of parish registers shows that men on average remarried sooner after widowhood than did women, with the interesting variation that more women than men remarried very quickly, say within three months of their spouses' death, after which a reverse trend set in and held over the long run, with women who got past the first ninety days waiting longer to remarry if they did so at all. My judgment is that precipitous remarriage reflected the extreme vulnerability of some widows, but that those in a position financially to remain independent were more likely to do so than widowers. A thorough study of the village of Abingdon, from 1540 to 1720, confirmed the desire of widows to protect their independence by refusing remarriage, as well as the pressures against this choice. For seventeenth-century Germany, demographers again found widowers remarrying sooner and more frequently than widows, in both Protestant and Roman Catholic regions. Overall, then, from the Mediterranean to the Baltic, from the thirteenth to the eighteenth centuries, in the cities and in the countryside, among Catholics and Protestants, we know that many widows chose to struggle for survival and independence. We also know they did so with remarkable success.[57]

Advice manuals could not have helped much. A widow might consult household economy books meant for patriarchal settings and simply wear the pants herself, but guidance addressing her specific needs was sparse indeed. In all times and places, including our own by my eyeball survey of bookstores at the local shopping malls, advice manuals for maidens and married women outnumber those for widows by a huge margin.[58] Looking backward a couple of millennia, we may recall that Cicero's famous essay on old age portrays an idealized world comprised solely of men! Male sexual urges disappear and no women are around in any capacity whatsoever, as the retired warriors and statesmen take to the fields for a life of leisurely farming.[59] On elderly women there is nothing. Alas, the most famous Greco-Roman passage concerning widows probably is the vicious put-down from Pericles' funeral oration, in which he comforts the parents of fallen soldiers, spurs on their surviving brothers and sons, and then turns to the widows before him: "If I am to speak also of womanly virtues, referring to those of you who will henceforth be in widowhood, I will sum up all in a brief admonition: great is your glory if you fall not below the standard which nature has set for your sex, and great also is hers of whom there is least talk among men whether in praise or in blame."[60]

Shifting the focus back to sixteenth-century Italy, I found no books addressed specifically to widowers and many fewer tracts for widows than for virgins and wives, even including works of the dialogue genre so popular among humanists. Moreover, much of the verbiage specifically addressed to widows is merely a rehash of recommendations for virgins. In the case of Cosmo Agnelli's so-called loving advice against extravagant hairstyles, cosmetics, plunging necklines, and high heels, for example, the title promises a book useful for virgins, widows, and matrons, but anyone seeking explicit recommendations for each category would have been sorely disappointed. Widows are especially disgraceful if they make themselves alluring when they have no intention of remarrying, but that is about Agnelli's only special notice of this category of woman.[61] Among better-known writers, the advice manuals of Juan Luis Vives, in translation, and of Lodovico Dolce, which is heavily taken from Vives, also apply their restrictive prescriptions for virgins and wives even more fully to widows, but without breaking significant new ground.[62]

The most striking area of differential treatment is advice to widows against remarriage. These recommendations often convey a bitterness about the married state not found in manuals on whether to marry in the first place, which frequently are more satirical than didactic. In ancient and medieval times, prescriptive writers invariably assumed that widows would remarry, especially if they were young, and moral authorities made no condemnation of the choice.[63] With the Catholic Reformation, however, a virulent hostility to remarriage (re)surfaced, finding its inspiration in the writings of St. Jerome. His preference for the virginal state was well known, as was his spiritual counsel for the wealthy widows of Rome who bankrupted themselves in following his advice. Ever the master of plain speaking, Jerome told his disciple Marcella that a widow had only one duty: to remain a widow. About Marcella's resolve there can have been no doubt, but others in his spiritual circle, like Furia, needed more support:

> The trials of marriage you have learned in the married state: you have been surfeited to nausea as though with the flesh of quails. Your mouth has tasted the bitterest of gall, you have voided the sour unwholesome food, you have relieved a heaving stomach. Why would you put into it again something which has already proved harmful to you? "The dog is turned to his own vomit again and the sow that was washed to her wallowing in the mire." Even brute beasts and roving birds do not fall into the same snares or nets twice.[64]

Both the quotation and the "flesh of quails" reference are biblical (2 Pet. 2:22, Num. 11:31–35), although the context in both cases has nothing to do with widows.

Still, Jerome's metaphors found their way into works such as Bernardo Trotto's *Dialoghi del matrimonio, e vita vedovile* (Dialogue on Matrimony and Widowhood), first published in 1578, and reprinted twice in the next five years. Like Leonora in Moderata Fonte's dialogue, Hippolyta, also a widow, is determined to keep her personal freedom. The question of remarriage is purely rhetorical. You who have experienced how much anguish matrimony brings, you who have tasted such a fill of carnal food that it made you fastidious and caused you to vomit, why would you now want to return to the same poison, like a dog licking its own vomit, like a pig washed of so much filth returning to the miserable mud?

Literary critic Constance Jordan sees Trotto's tract as a feminist piece that places him in the front rank among authors who show how women can use power. On the other hand, Ruth Kelso provides a more conventional reading, one that situates Trotto squarely among deeply religious authors writing in tune with Catholic Reformation efforts to control female sexuality and power in any form. The historical situation favors the latter interpretation, as do the Turin-based publication circumstances of Trotto's book; the straightforward reading also makes it unnecessary to turn St. Jerome's meaning upside down. Hostility to remarriage sometimes expressed feminist liberation (for example, Fonte's widow Leonora), in which case the talk was mostly about power and money. At other times it expressed patriarchal repression of women (for example, Jerome and Trotto), in which case the talk was mostly about sexuality and filth. Either way, those who opposed remarriage logically had to accept the ability of women to rule themselves, even if many among them feared where self-rule might lead. In this limited sense only, strict Catholic reformers were protofeminists.[65]

Control over public disorder permeated advice for widows, even as obsessive concern with chastity ran afoul of biology. When applied to married women, the universally accepted four-humors theory suggested that a dutiful husband, apart from looking after his personal desires, should have intercourse with his wife as often as necessary to heat up and moisten her body against its melancholic tendencies or else, if she was choleric by nature, as infrequently as possible so as to keep her system properly cool and dry. Now with her husband dead, the same line of reasoning suggested that a widow needed at least some doses of sex to keep her hot/cold, wet/dry bodily mixture in good order, especially as her internal balances had become accustomed to knowing the flesh and receiving injections of hot, wet sperm. Less-scientific thought eschewed these puzzles, holding simply and resolutely that once a woman experienced sex, she became too weak to resist carnal stirrings. Clearly, the immediate way to preserve public morality was remarriage. And yet Renaissance advice manuals did not urge widows to take a second husband, relying instead on injunctions against lewd behavior and lascivious public appearances.[66]

Giovan Giorgio Trissino, best known for La Sofonisba, a play hailed as the originator of modern Italian tragedy, as well as for various works of poetry, comedy, and linguistic analysis, was a wandering courtier and erudite humanist who found favor wherever he went, serving as an ambassador for Popes Leo X and Clement VII before accepting the title of count palatine from Emperor Charles V. Trissino's personal life was less successful. He and his first wife married in 1494, when both were sixteen, because his wealthy family, anxious over his frail health, wanted heirs as soon as possible. Their precautionary actions bore fruit, as the couple had two children, including son Giulio. Then Madonna Trissino died young, sometime shortly after 1500. The widower Trissino arranged to raise their children himself, even while he launched his career as a roving courtier. At some point in his travels, he became intimately acquainted with Margarita Pia Sanseverina; his Epistola del Trissino de la vita, che dee tenere una donna vedova (Letter on the Proper Lifestyle for a Widow), which we are about to consult, may have been written on the occasion of her entry into a convent, perhaps as some sort of literary vengeance after she dumped him. She had been widowed for over a decade, and whether she followed his rules of conduct while they were lovers cannot be known, nor is there any reason to suggest that he had even formulated the rules before she opted for a nunnery rather than his wealthy estate.

The jilted suitor returned home, and in 1523/24, obtained a papal dispensation to marry his kinswoman Bianca Trissino, very beautiful and very recently widowed from another Trissino, who had named Giovan Trissino as his executor. The remarriage took place just before the birth of their son Ciro, and a daughter followed in 1526. Bianca Trissino already had eight children by her first marriage to a Trissino, which may help explain why she apparently was such a tiger about defending the interests of her new son Ciro against her grown stepson Giulio. The stakes were high, as Giovan Trissino had inherited a great fortune from his noble, illustrious family. Perhaps due to all the fights over money, Bianca had formally separated from her husband some years before her death in 1540. However, her demise did nothing to ease the familial conflict, which saw Giovan Trissino evicted from his own house by a court order handed down by the magistracy in Vicenza and confirmed by an appellate court in Venice. The embittered old man penned literary maledictions on both cities, went off to Germany where he found no peace, and returned to Rome where he died in 1550, driven insane by melancholy.[67]

The dedication of Trissino's *Epistola* to Margarita Pia Sanseverina starts in pure acid, with an acknowledgment that we all prefer to hear ourselves praised, not lectured at, and that we rightly disdain those who presume to tell others what to do, especially when their advice is unsolicited. Then he smugly reminds her that he has long known her to be an exceptional person, one who does not follow the crowd, one who will accept his counsel. She must consider herself as having been born with a man's spirit and body, he continues, poisoning this injunction to be what she is not with an immediate recommendation to forego thinking about astronomical mysteries and focus instead on the virtues of prudence, temperance, justice, and toleration. Further along, platonic drivel about true virtue is rudely interrupted by a tirade against women who try to appear taller by wearing platform shoes, failing to see that these make them look ridiculously disproportionate while they stand and serve only to give people a good laugh when, after a fall, everyone realizes how short these pompous women really are.

The rules then become specific. Get to know the reputations of the women and men in your city; give only a passing notice to the wicked ones, but converse more openly with those of honor. Avoid hearty laughter and audacious speech: one is a sign of being featherbrained, the other of a violent soul. It is not beautiful to speak of things that are ugly. Don't talk too much; silence is the great ornament of a woman. Don't stand completely mute but talk only from necessity, always observing gravity, honesty, and liveliness in your words. Don't start analyzing the doings of the Turks in Constantinople or the soldiers in Egypt, the deliberations at the Diet of Augsburg or the armed conflict in Geradadda (perhaps Djérada in Morocco). Nothing is more unbecoming than to hear women reasoning about war and disputing about statecraft. Don't contradict or quibble, nor be longwinded, contentious, and obstinate. When you are going about town, don't be too elegant to greet everyone but keep your salutations brief—better a nod than words.

Trissino next interrupts himself with an admonition that he has been going on so long about proper speech for a widow that he has let more important matters slip by. Above all, you must adore God, honor and revere the saints, seek always to please God, obey his commandments, willingly attend mass, and give generously to the monks. However, don't try to out-saint your neighbors and become such a house nun that people whisper behind your back. If you want to pray, do so behind closed doors in your room. The call to moderation goes on and on. Don't be too anxious to receive invitations to wedding receptions and festivals, but don't be overly reticent about going when you are invited. Don't accumulate superfluities in your home, but don't be caught in short supply of necessities. Don't insist on delicate foods, but don't be Spartan either. Govern your family and servants diligently, so that you are neither cruel nor lax. Dress them so as to bring honor on yourself, not in accord with how little they deserve. Never be two-faced, saying one thing with your tongue while holding another thought in your heart.

Trissino's conclusion is rather condescending, perhaps to be expected from a jilted suitor. If you read all that I have written, and examine it diligently, you will find the seeds of everything pertinent to the lifestyle of a proper widow. And if some particular at first seems strange, just don't do it; however, you will see what peace of mind comes from acceptance. Nor do I say you should be content with reading only what I have written; indeed, I urge you to read lots of books and to take from each one its counsel on how to live properly. Just as the man who wants to build a beautiful palace consults diverse artisans and experts, so have I constructed the epistle I now send you by drawing on a wide range of ancient philosophers. Trissino was very proud of his ability to read Greek, a talent Margarita surely lacked.[68]

A more conventional advice manual is Giulio Cesare Cabei's *Ornamenti della gentil donna vedova* (Ornaments of the Gentle Widow), published in 1574. To the best of my knowledge it was never reprinted, perhaps because readers did not much favor its holier-than-thou pontificating, especially from someone with no formal clerical status. The writing is rather dry, containing neither the promises of heaven nor the warnings of hell that give zest to other Catholic Reformation didactic works. The message is oppressive without any comic relief, intentional or otherwise, or even enough misogyny to stoke an angry reaction. Nonetheless, Ruth Kelso rightly selects this text as emblematic of Christian emphasis on humility for women, stated far more explicitly for widows than for virgins and matrons. Her analysis focuses on twelve commandments for the truly modest, humble widow to follow. Among these, the four that most struck me in reading the original treatise were those dealing with external appearances, that is, with matters others could see and gossip about.

Although Cabei, like other writers, expresses concern with interior goodness, he is also typical in giving primacy to preserving public decency. The unsaid reality is that a widow, especially a young widow, will be observed constantly—by envious in-laws, tattling friends, resentful children, lascivious confessors, lustful laymen, spiteful testators, greedy lawyers, and dishonest shopkeepers—all instantly ready to find fault and spread the word about any real or imagined indiscretion. Therefore, the widow must carry her body with grave modesty and honest shame, avoiding not only display but any bold, forceful, sudden, or carefree motion. Her eyes certainly need a huge *(grandissimo)* brake and her head must be absolutely free of any libidinous thought, lest her eyes betray the immodesty. It is all right not to cry constantly or take deep sighs with every breath, but the chaste widow also does not laugh or even break into a broad smile. Finally, her words need to be few, only necessary responses; she should never speak unless spoken to and never be the conveyor of gossip. Thus neutralized as a possible provocateur of male desire, she may go about town doing charitable works, perfecting her piety, and presumably conducting life's daily business.[69]

An extremely rare book published in Rome in 1570, *La vedova del Fusco* (The Widow of Fusco), presents a startlingly more positive view of widows. About the presumed author, Horatio Fusco Monfloreo D'Arimini, we know absolutely nothing, and my strong suspicion is that the author in fact was a woman, probably a widow, who wished to mask her identity. She was clearly a person educated in classical history and mythology, although not in Greek and Latin languages; although she had no interest in specific biblical injunctions, she possessed a profoundly Christian sensibility. The book had only one printing, and is more cultured that the usual how-to manual, but I think you will want to know about it anyway.

La vedova del Fusco begins as follows: "The tight knot of marriage broken by her husband's death, the woman becomes a free being—like a bird flying in the air that goes wherever it pleases. And because prudence always has been her principal ornament, she now truly is able to make judgments, dress discreetly, be chaste and of pure beautiful spirit when, having the liberty to sin, she does not sin." Until the lion is unchained, the horse unbridled, the bird uncaged, you cannot know their true natures, and so it is with a wife; only when the nuptial ties are dissolved, so that she is master of her thoughts and deeds, can her soul reach perfection and integrity. Some will go astray, those shoved off by their mothers to a wet nurse, those taught the importance of virginity but not of honesty, those treated by their fathers as so much merchandise. They will become the widows who eat constantly, imbibe before supper, seek precious wines, in summer refuse drinks without ice cubes or snow, loll in bed all day, get aroused in the pleasures of Venus at the least provocation, and pass the nights in debauchery.

The good widow, by contrast—nurtured in prudence from birth, now outside of paternal and marital controls, free to give herself to another man but demurring—achieves the highest state of self-realization. Theologians may laud virginity, yet it is more perfect to have known the flesh and then to renounce it. Her husband's death sawed her body in half, taking away the part filled with charity and love where she buried her worldly cares, leaving her bereft of the captain, consort, and master of her will. Heart inflamed with tears of grief and doing her best to console her children, now she buries the cold cadaver honorably, displaying soulful love and reverence. She sets aside any thought of remarriage, brings in a mature woman of good character to assist her at home, shuts the door to suitors, puts away her jewels and ornate dresses, finds a good teacher for her children, follows a sober diet, attends mass regularly, and shuns festivals. She does not gossip, judge others, tell jokes, or shout in the piazza.

An extended roll call of great widows follows, drawn heavily from Greek and Roman heroines but continuing into the present, that is meant both to inspire the reader and to display the author's erudition. The last ten pages return to an examination of why some widows are good and others bad, interspersed with advice on choosing a husband for his good character rather than his physical appeal, virility, or wealth. This section is less innovative than the earlier pages, with their forceful argument that a girl's upbringing determines her behavior as a widow; their biting comment that the virtue of chastity belongs not to the girl but to her father, not to the wife but to her husband; and their triumphantly ironic assertion that only the widow is potentially meritorious—free to choose good over evil.[70]

In our perusal of advice on conception back in chapter 2, the writings of physician Michele Savonarola loomed large. Now, as our look at widowhood closes out the life cycle, allow me to conclude with advice from another Savonarola: Michele's famous grandson Girolamo, the fiery Dominican preacher executed for heresy on May 23, 1498, on a scaffold in Florence's Piazza Signoria. Some seven years earlier, at the onset of his triumphal years, the moral reformer had written a brief tract on widowhood, clearly meant for women to read, one that would provide guidance and inspiration. Four editions appeared in rapid succession before his death, and his work continued to be popular through the first half of the sixteenth century, with an additional eight printings, six in Venice and two in Milan, of collected tracts including the exhortation for widows. Savonarola's writing is fiercely logical, quick paced, fanatic, and dogmatic, a fascinating read even today.

He begins with an appeal to women to remain in widowhood. True enough, you can remarry without fear of sin, but how much better your spiritual life will be if you have only one master to serve, not two. First of all, you may have found it hard to meet God's demand for your whole heart when you were tied to a husband who was tedious or, worse yet, perverse, irreligious, libidinous, jealous, or otherwise unjust. Not only do such men make it difficult to serve God, they are a constant impediment with their backbiting and yelling, as well as their sinful carnal desires, eventually inviting in the devil himself. More often than not, unfortunately, widows who remarry tend to choose just such husbands, God's punishment for their failure to realize the grace of their liberation. Second, it is better to remain a widow because that way you are freed from carnality. If you stay by the fire, you get hot, and the same goes for concupiscence; the more you do, the more you desire, alienating yourself further from God. Third, if children are born of your remarriage, caring for them is a great burden and hinders your spiritual growth, as daily experience shows. Fourth, a widow is less distracted by familial governance than a married woman. Fifth, a widow is more liberated, not only from lust but also from avarice and pride, the three sinful roots of every evil. While the matron has to think about attiring herself and her children in accordance with her station in life, a simple black dress suits the widow, who thus is given no occasion for vainglory. Sixth, a widow may decline invitations to weddings and festivals, thereby avoiding these occasions for sin, which are especially pernicious these days. Last, society is more suspicious of widows than of married women and therefore denies them unhealthful practices such as conversing with men, strolling around the streets, and sitting at the window. The brakes applied out of regard for shame are converted into virtue, since ostentatious public activity even in married women offers numerous occasions for sin. For all these reasons, the widow is much freer to do good than is a married woman.

There are several distinct categories of widows, Savonarola continues, and there is no point in trying to be what you are not. Some think only of remarriage. A widow's choice to remarry is good if she is in the flower of her youth and lacks any religious vocation, lest the devil tempt her. Also without sin is the widow pressed by temporal conditions to remarry, or who realizes that God did not give her the gift of being able to live chastely. These are the standard Pauline injunctions, which Savonarola accepts. However, when a widow seeks remarriage out of lust or avarice, looks for riches, or demands a man of high rank, then her choice is sinful. All widows determined to remarry, be they good or bad, have nothing to do with the current discussion, so the preacher moves on, literally leaving them behind.

Among true widows who have no desire to remarry, there are also the good and the bad. Those who remain widows only because they lack a dowry or are afraid of marrying a loser or cannot find a husband, or for whatever occult reason, are bad. They do not serve their inner chastity and are a public danger to the dissolute youths who chase after them. They go around in bright, modish dresses with their veils or kerchiefs pulled up and folded so not much is covered. They lift their eyes shamelessly, voluntarily keeping company with young men, laughing with them and bantering about things that are not religious. Less evil, but still excluded from the monk's intended audience, are those widows who refuse remarriage not out of love for God but for earthly concerns: love for their children or their riches or fear of marrying someone worse than their first husband. These women are not in the mold of St. Anne (Savonarola's model of the ideal widow, as portrayed in Luke 2:36–38, who, upon her husband's death after seven years of marriage, spent the next six decades or so in constant prayer and fasting). They rarely go to confession, pray, fast, or turn out to hear a sermon; for them Savonarola can only offer a prayer that they do not use up God's grace here on earth and lose their heavenly reward. Another sort of widow truly wishes to serve chastity and God but is held back by family ties, whether the care of children or other relatives. For her God will wait patiently. Others, however, if they really wished to serve God could separate from family obligations, yet out of pusillanimity or compassion they do not. In these cases there is a need for careful counsel and full consideration of the circumstances. Finally, there are those ready to abandon all worldly attachments, to live out their earthly lives in pleasing God. Savonarola addresses the remainder of his treatise to these true widows.

The demands are great, as are the eternal rewards. You must prefer death over dishonoring your Creator. Having lost all hope of consolation in this world, you must strive only not to lose grace in the next. The essential starting point is a pure heart, from which you reach ever greater perfection by subtle mental examination and daily scrutiny of your appetites and desires. Whatever part of your soul loves things created by God does not love God himself. You must love God so totally with all your heart and mind that you have no memory of worldly concerns. Do not exalt at the first signs of grace because only perseverance will be crowned; indeed, live always in great fear that you will lose God's favor and return to the worldly muck from which he lifted you.

This exhortation, a clear invitation to follow the well-defined path of the female mystic, yields to distinctly more practical themes in book 2 of Savonarola's text, revealing with wonderful candor the pitfalls that await even a conventionally pious widow. Having lost your carnal husband, at least see that you do not lose your spiritual groom; then, maybe, you will ultimately reuinite with your earthly companion, assuming he is in a healthy place. Wear black and go heavily veiled for the rest of your life. Draw within yourself. Shun all conversation with strange men, especially young ones. Avoid as much as possible familiarity with your relatives, especially your male in-laws, because nothing inflames lust like a prohibited affair. And if you are too old for such dangers, reject intimacy anyway, because it sets a bad example for the young and deflects your mind from prayer. Disdain conversation with strange women, particularly the vain young ones, because as Solomon said, "the friend of crazy people becomes similar to them" (Prov. 13:20).[71] Don't be too close even with your own blood relatives and members of your household, who are a distraction that could lead you into interactions with worldly people.

Flee from holy men who are really seculars, because the spirit is easily converted into flesh. Truly holy men fly from women and truly holy women fly from men. Don't be intimate with holy women unless they are well proved, because these days you find many who don a mantel of piety but have the devil in their hearts, wickedness on their tongues, and gall in their minds. Don't be too familiar with priests, even if they are your relatives. Be on your guard if they come frequently to visit because a good monk or priest shuns women whenever possible and seeks solitude to contemplate the divine mysteries. Above all watch out for the ones who lead a busy life and ask only for a little companionship. Even the others who seem straight enough in their cassocks may solicit you with gifts of little religious images and holy objects that frequently turn spiritual affection into carnal love: "I am suspicious of conversations with priests and monks, no matter what their condition." No woman should feel safe because she is old or because the monk or priest in question is old. The fire of concupiscence burns as long as the flesh survives and the devil, always ready to ignite it, never dies. Hold the clergy in as much reverence as you like, just don't converse with them.

Choose your confessor with utmost care. Too many of them linger over confessing a widow, seeking out some useful tidbit or weakness to realize their own lascivious desires. A woman who loses her husband, it being illicit for her to converse with secular men, often seeks consolation from priests, many of whom, being very wicked, trap them with a thousand snares. So, devout widow, find a saintly old confessor. Talk to him only for confession and about things directly related, such as your spiritual conscience, and this only briefly and infrequently. Even though regular confession is good, reasoning too much in church with the clergy is not. Such behavior engenders scandal in the minds of all participants and is a waste of time that may lead to yet other sins. Finally, once you've found a good confessor, stick with him and don't be like those airheads who wander from church to church, wanting to speak with every religious in town. Don't hurry to confess before each visiting preacher, saying you do so out of devotion, because that sort of devotion just dissipates your mental purity.

Practicality continues in Savonarola's next chapter on fasting, which rapidly extends to a more general appeal for moderation of the five senses. In common with virtually all male spiritual counselors, Friar Girolamo warns against excessive food deprivation. The usual regimen of church-approved fasts should be sufficient. So long as there is no damage to your health, abstinence on Fridays is fine in warm weather, and you might add special fasts at other times, perhaps on the vigils of Holy Days. Equally important is what people of every condition should do: eat in accord with natural necessity, not to excess. Finding the middle way between the sinful extremes of self-starvation and gluttony is not easy, but widows should err on the side of too little rather than too much, because nature is content with sparse, simple food and drink.

Fasting should extend to all superfluous delights and bodily sensations. Your eyes should not wander about observing worldly vanities, especially in church and other public places. The eyes reveal much about a woman's modesty and sobriety, so the widow, especially when men are around, should humbly lower her gaze to the ground. Let the ears abstain from hearing pernicious, useless words. Remember that at the last judgment, we shall have to explain each idle word. Especially shun gossip and listening to bad things about your neighbor, which often happen in the midst of a nominally pious discussion. Men have such loose tongues these days that it is difficult to converse without hearing some bad words, so just don't talk to them. Speaking, like hearing, leads easily from the superfluous to the idle and then to evil, so be parsimonious with words. Don't let your nose linger to enjoy libidinous odors like those perfumes and oils meant not as medicine but for sensual delectation. Spiritual people should smell of good reputation and exude an odor of sanctity wherever they go, not stink of lascivious scents that offend the angels in paradise. Deny your palate the sweet salads and luscious fruits, but do so privately lest you fall into vainglory. Do not so much as let a man touch your hand. A woman's flesh is like wax, and every touch leaves an impression. Earth is good and water is good, but when you mix them, you get mud. Having once known a man, the widow is especially vulnerable to the rekindling of carnal desire.

Your prayer should be mostly in silent solitude, with your mind elevated to God. Frequent, short, fervid supplications are better than long infrequent litanies. Fortified by isolation from the world of men, denial of the bodily senses, and devout prayer, the widow who has achieved interior spirituality now is ready to read book 3, wherein Savonarola examines her obligations to humankind. The first is to teach by good example. Her piety should be seen by all in her plain dress, reserved speech, calm disposition, humble heart, and accommodating ways. She should not be too austere or judgmental, because that yields no fruit in bringing others to salvation. Sinners quickly deride the holy widow for vaingloriously thinking she has become a saint; be ready to talk of God's love with sweet, sugared words. That's the way to call men to divine love.

The second obligation is to spread the word of God. Granted the apostles prohibited women from public preaching, still nothing prevents you from privately exhorting people to goodness. You should teach your inferiors, for example, your sons and daughters, grandchildren, and servants.

With other persons you may not initiate doctrinal instruction, but if you are truly asked, you really know what you are talking about, and you are not giving the appearance of being too holy, then go ahead. You should prepare for these private lessons by having memorized the Articles of Faith, the Ten Commandments, and the wise counsel of the church fathers. These things you will have learned from the preachers, from reading vernacular books or those in Latin, if you know grammar, or from experience, which is more reliable than words. The best teacher of all is the illumination that comes from holy prayer and divine love. Do not put great faith in visions, however, until you first reveal them fully to your confessor and are sure they are not the devil's work.

The widow is also responsible for governing her household and instructing all its members in proper behavior in accord with their stations in life. Some widows may be too young for this responsibility, not so much in years as in sentiment, and temporarily they must accept the role of student instead of teacher until they become sufficiently mature to govern. Savonarola's assumption, notwithstanding this disclaimer, is that widows are capable of exercising full dominion over their household— this is what should happen, later if not sooner.

In closing, the friar explores the dimensions of a pious widow's ministry. Toward her superiors, such as her parents, she should instruct only by prayer and by example. If they err and follow the path of sin, however, they are no longer her superiors, so she may do whatever it takes to get them straightened out and back on the right road. With her equals, the widow may minister with prayer, good example, and humble correction. She may even resort to exhortation and chastisement but only in charity, not by exerting claims to superiority. Moreover, she should not seek out each sinner in town to engage in her or his salvation. There is enough to do concerning one's own soul without going around poking into other people's lives. With her inferiors, the widow may demonstrate superiority, retaining always in her heart a saintly humility and using asperity only if sweetness fails. Great discretion is needed in adjusting instructional methods to the age of the learner and focusing on the particular fault that needs correction. The cardinal rule is to instruct and correct with charity, with a desire to save a fellow soul. For superiors and equals who stubbornly refuse to reform, simply say a prayer and let them be. In the case of inferiors, on the other hand, restrain them from bringing harm to others, with threats and blows if necessary. Finally, remember that even St. Anne did not announce the coming of Christ to everyone, only to those who truly awaited redemption.[72]

I did not give extended space to Girolamo Savonarola's tract because I think it was a major factor in determining how sixteenth-century widows behaved. Rather, I hope it makes clear for you, as it does for me, the contradictions inherent in Renaissance patriarchy. Accepting widow-hood as a valid, even admirable choice meant rejecting the ideological underpinnings of male control: Aristotle's logic of two sexes, one superior and one inferior. Practice further confirmed that the Greek philosopher was wrong. The Italian widow was not an Amazon-like classical demi-goddess, providing grist for Boccaccio's tales of great warriors, or a heroic virgin defending her Christian faith. She was the norm, at least for a time, in most women's life cycles, going about the streets conducting business and attending to her needs and answering for her decisions to no man.

Friar Girolamo's invitation to a place in paradise may have appealed to only a few of his readers. Yet, even those with other plans and those who accepted his promptings initially but then fell by the wayside surely understood its earthly assumptions. A widow controlled her destiny. Life's circumstances might not have prepared her initially to meet her full responsibilities, but her innate capacity was there. By her will and by her actions, always with God's grace, of course, she could achieve salvation. Along the way, she would take care of her own affairs here on earth. Yes, she would wear black and keep her eyes lowered so as not to arouse libidinous male thoughts or give rise to public scandal. But her selfhood was never in question. She was able to recognize good and to choose it over evil—just as the obscure Fusco would assert many decades later. She needed little if any help from men, most of whom Savonarola warned her were morally depraved. Set against the challenge of being responsible for her own salvation, the burdens of governing what had been her husband's domain seemed light enough. Now sure of her own worth, she was ready to govern others, beginning with her own household and eventually extending to the men and women of her community.

CHAPTER

· 7 ·

Then and Now

Printing was invented in Germany and made its way to Rome, then to the diverse regions of Italy, so that now there is no province without a printer: truly an art of the utmost genius—and very profitable, an empire that caused a world sleeping in ignorance to reawaken, as everyone already knows. Before the coming of this glorious art of printing, one found very few literate people, due to nothing more than the prohibitive cost of books, so that only those rich enough to buy them could become learned. It necessarily followed that the poor remained ignorant and scorned; without books they could not study. Those who mastered Latin and Greek, with their eloquence and their new language, dazzled the illiterate masses with these marvels. The Doctors in those days were truly happy; they were revered and adored like divine beings; despite all their falsehoods and lies, they were deemed good. And when the talk turned to Philosophy, the poor people, who didn't know much, were humbled by listening to citations of Plato, Aristotle, Seneca, Carneades, and other ancient philosophers, thinking that what they heard must be referring to another world. In this way the Doctors could lead on the donkeys with as many carrots as they pleased, there being no one to contradict them. But then this blessed printing press emerged, so the majority of people, both men and women, know how to read; what's more important, Philosophy, Medicine, and all the other sciences have been translated and printed in our maternal language, so that everyone can know his or her part; maybe the day will come when we shall all be Doctors of some sort because already in our times the majority, even the women, speak of Philosophy, Medicine, Astrology, Mathematics, and as many sciences as there are in the world, without being Doctors; this way no one gets fooled anymore, because all who are willing to tax their brains a little can be among the learned. And the cause of all this is the printing press.

That is how Dr. Leonardo Fioravanti, the prolific writer and purveyor of medicinal wonders, whose books hawked elixirs to keep your penis erect or even to raise you from the dead, understood the impact of the printing press.[1] He reached his conclusions way back in 1564; I cannot add much to what he figured out long ago.

Our journey through the world of sixteenth-century-Italian, popular-advice manuals is at a close, so my task as your guide comes to an end. I have done the writing, you the reading; had we been face-to-face, you could have interjected questions here and there. This absence of spontaneity is especially limiting right now, when my preference would be to set aside academic expertise and join you instead for an informal chat, maybe over drinks or lunch. I sorely miss not knowing what interested you during our trip, what was boring or confusing, what I said that seemed doubtful or wrong. I miss knowing what you have made of my book, which for better and for worse surely was not always what I intended. Yes, there will be professional book reviews in the weeks or months ahead; at www.amazon.com, self-appointed reviewers can use the Internet to say what they think, and I can even respond; maybe over the next decade there will be a few scholarly citations or even disputations. But all of this is not really interaction, at least not in an intellectually invigorating way. There is little alternative to continuing in serial, monologue mode.

I think I've shown you pretty much the range of what sixteenth-century-Italian people of the middling sort could have read telling them how men and women should behave toward each other. I say this knowing that more than a few advice manuals surely have disappeared entirely, neither rescued for posterity by some confiscating authority actually seeking to curtail circulation nor cared for by a curiosity-seeking bibliophile nor auctioned off from the dusty shelves of a once-noble family's estate. Hardly a visit goes by to a rare-book room when I do not come across some interesting item that's new to me, so experience even more than humility tells me I must have overlooked some relevant works despite my privileged stays in research libraries in Italy and elsewhere. Nevertheless, notwithstanding vagaries that caused an unknowable number of volumes to go missing centuries ago, compounded by my own present-day scholarly lapses, I am confident that seeing more books would not significantly alter the landscape. Among the missing treatises, I do not believe there is some work extolling the virtues of companionate marriage or explaining why God commands parents to break their children's wills by beating them. If nothing else, sixteenth-century publishers were merciless plagiarists, ready to print anything that would make a profit. If an idea circulated, I'm sure I saw it somewhere.

More problematic than the unseen is how I've shown you what I did see. My seemingly innocent disclaimers about letting the texts speak for themselves are not to be swallowed whole. True, I do not glory in unpacking a text so thoroughly that no one can put it back together; nor could I ever outgrow my historical training enough to declare authorial intent to be irrelevant. Still, my preferences necessarily shaped choices about what you should see. I like prose that gets to the point, makes sense on first reading, and allows for a chuckle—at least in how-to books. I told you forthrightly which advice manuals struck me as boring, and undoubtedly I short-changed them, devoting instead a disproportionately large number of words to conveying the jokes and the exotica, with relatively fewer given over to the dross. Although I tried to provide accurate renditions of the texts—alerting you to which ones went through frequent reprintings, exercising care not to take words out of context, advising you of alternative interpretations—in the end this advice manual is my creation. No one in the sixteenth-century could have read anything exactly like it. Moreover, probably no single sixteenth-century person actually consulted as many how-to books as I imposed on our imaginary Tuscan couple. It may well be that a translation, a photograph, or an exhumed corpse would have captured past realities more faithfully and fully. On the other hand, actually translating the hundreds of sixteenth-century books I have read would be a waste of time, at least in my judgment. Some of the best—Isabella Cortese's *I secreti,* Moderata Fonte's *Il merito delle donne,* Simeon Zuccolo's *La pazzia del ballo,* and sections of Friar Mercurio's *La commare*—are available in modern translations or reprints, but these are the gems, published primarily as curiosity items to display on your coffee table or to give as gifts to those who already possess everything.

Instead, I've winnowed carefully—saving you from sifting through all the repetitive, plagiarized, verbose, imitative, badly written words that abound—composing a coherent portrait from the kaleidoscope my eyes saw there: just the highlights, skipping the redundancies while lingering over the new and offbeat. That's what a guide is for, right?

Another self-imposed limitation in my guide work is that I omitted several sites completely. Our journey began as I pointed to scholarly findings suggesting a broader-reading audience among sixteenth-century Italians than some of you may have imagined. Still, everyone concedes that a majority of the population could not read (on that point Fioravanti was exaggerating, as usual); the illiterate included virtually all poor, marginal, and enslaved peoples. Printed advice read aloud or retold in summary form could have reached them, something I believe happened in the countryside with chapters of expensive, elitist agricultural treatises devoted to home remedies for farm laborers; perhaps literate midwives passed the wisdom of Friar Mercurio's book along to their ignorant assistants; confessors' manuals explaining sins of the flesh surely had a ripple effect; we know that Cardinal Antoniano's book on child rearing was pushed from the pulpit. Still, I make no claim that our literary journey has penetrated deeply into the daily lives of an illiterate majority. Taking control of your own destiny, becoming your own Doctor and Philosopher—the breakthroughs hailed by Fioravanti—do not come with listening to the wisdom of others, whether that wisdom is from a printed book or a scribe's page.

At the other end of the socioeconomic spectrum, where resided that 1 percent of the population about whom 99 percent of history books seemingly are written, I've made scant reference to courtesy manuals, the most famous of all sixteenth-century-Italian books after Machiavelli's *Prince*. Count Baldassare Castiglione's *Book of the Courtier* (1528) established the genre among print works, instantly making Italy the place in Europe to observe and perfect the art of courtly manners. At a time when English royalty ate with greasy hands as they spilled jugs of ale over themselves, when French nobles boorishly goosed one another as they danced, and when German princes outdid each other in farting at the table, Italians taught by printed words the exquisite virtues of nonchalant elegance in every gesture. Although no one ever quite matched the *Courtier*'s literary polish, imitative challengers rolled off the presses throughout the sixteenth century: Giovambattista Nenna of Bari's *Il Nennio* (1542), Sperone Speroni's *I dialogi* (1542), Archbishop Giovanni Della Casa's *Galateo* (1558), Girolamo Muzio's *Il gentilhuomo* (1571), Stefano Guazzo's *Civil Conversation* (1574), Torquato Tasso's *Il forno* (1580), and Annibale Romei's *Discorsi* (1585), to name only a few of the most famous. Eagerly consumed by Italy's urban nobility, translations brought the new civility to France, England, Spain, and eventually even to the uncouth Germans.

The *Courtier*'s publishing history is the subject of an entire book, quite informative, by modern historian Peter Burke. A few particulars are especially relevant at this moment. The pace of translations and the frequency of reprintings make it clear that Castiglione's book outsold every advice manual I've discussed in the preceding chapters. Many, many people must have bought it who had no chance ever of being invited to a dinner dance at a count's villa. Perhaps it was for these dreamers that later editors (including our own Lodovico Dolce) tried to transform the *Courtier* from the open-ended dialogue Castiglione wrote into a closed-instruction manual, a "recipe-book" to use Burke's phrase. The "dialogue was flattened and decontextualized by its editors," who added a detailed index, an appended laundry list of the qualities expected in the perfect courtier and lady, and marginal paragraph notations—precisely the trappings of a popular-advice manual: "The buyer of one of the later sixteenth-century editions scarcely needed to read the book to be instructed," concludes Burke.[2]

The *Courtier*'s metamorphosis nicely illustrates what you have missed because of my decision to concentrate on advice manuals to the exclusion of several well-known philosophical dialogues, even though they offer recommendations of a sort on how men and women should comport themselves. The dialogues I did include tended to be closed in their prescriptions, with one speaker clearly doing the talking while everyone else listened, with no serious doubts allowed about the instructor's conclusions, with little sophistication used in justifying the positions taken, and with emphasis placed on rules and on how to achieve results, not on the tortuous, uncertain, occasionally blocked path to truth. It is no surprise that open, less rule-oriented, more theoretical treatises generally dealt with concerns quite distant from the daily lives of literate merchants, professionals, and well-to-do farmers. Even though philosophical dialogues enjoyed considerable popularity, and must have been bought by commoners as well as aristocrats, they did not promise specific outcomes or offer practical advice to anyone. They were read for enjoyment, not profit; for edification, not know-how. As literary critic Virginia Cox demonstrates persuasively in her recent book entitled, *The Renaissance Dialogue,* the fixing effect of the printing press, combined with the Catholic Reformation's taste for ask-no-questions rules, favored the crass style of an advice manual over the leisurely pace of a dialogue.[3] Centuries later, of course, dialogues came to be reprinted, analyzed, and deconstructed, while advice manuals languished in obscurity. So be it. Our journey has been through the tenements, not the palaces; you can return to visit the monumental stuff easily enough. I also skipped Pietro Aretino's *Sei giornate* (Six Days), which needs a fresh monograph or two all to itself.

Female Authorship

Addressing the dearth of female Renaissance poets, Ann Rosalind Jones notes that, "to be a professional writer and a woman in the sixteenth century was a very rare thing." Class decorum inhibited aristocrats of either sex from turning to the printing press, and an "even stricter modesty surrounded women's writing, which was often published only after their deaths."[4] These insights apply to the advice manual as well. Men did nearly all the writing; about that there can be no doubt. Women did much of the reading; about that I hope you are persuaded. In order to reach some assessment of how sixteenth-century men and women may have experienced this imbalance, let us recall briefly in their chronological order three tantalizing bits of information about publication opportunities. First, Lodovico Dolce in 1545, prefaced his advice manual for maidens, matrons, and widows with the statement that, while there were many books telling men how to behave, none instructed women, so he would fill the void. Second, in 1561, *I secreti della signora Isabella Cortese* went on sale; it must have done well, as it subsequently went through six reprintings. Third, Moderata Fonte never published her wonderful *Il merito delle donne*, completed in 1592; it appeared posthumously only in 1600, the same year as Lucrezia Marinella's angry response to Giuseppe Passi's vicious misogyny. What might these three little facts about Dolce, Cortese, and Fonte suggest?

Dolce may not have been among the most talented of literary men, but he did have a good sense of the book market, doing prolific work for the Giolito firm in Venice as a translator, editor, and writer. Indeed, Peter Burke names him among the very first professional writers. Unlike painters, sculptors, and even court jesters, who for centuries had been doing their work full time, very few writers earned their livelihood from the pen alone until the printing press came along, and then not until the middle of the sixteenth century. Dolce, and a half dozen pioneers like him, wrote not for a patron but for the market. He exaggerated when he said there were no advice manuals for women, for surely he knew of Vives's treatise, but he was correct about the general balance of things.[5]

Male writers prescribed behavior for men just as freely as they did for women, and with equal certitude, pomposity, and intrusiveness. Indeed, books nominally addressed solely to women's needs, such as Marinello's advice in *Delle medicine partenenti all' infermità delle donne*, contain lengthy sections on problems such as male impotence. Apart from advice on obviously gendered topics—hunting for him, childbirth for her—my survey of sixteenth-century-advice manuals found a roughly equal profusion of words addressed to men and to women, with the single exception of widowers, for the simple reason that the only useful recommendation for them was to find another wife quickly. Husband and wife were told jointly how to engage in proper sex; mother and father were both in-

structed on child rearing, bride and groom each received advice on getting along with one another after the physical passions cooled. To be
sure, in some manuals the mode of address varies by gender, as in
Brother Cherubino's attempts to reason with husbands while he more
often cajoles their wives. These variations are important, and I have tried
to portray them accurately for you. Yet I would reject the implication
that male writers were especially willing to tell women how to behave,
something they did not do as freely with men. Printers had to survive in
a competitive market, and apparently advice for men sold equally well.

Our second little fact is Mrs. Isabella Cortese's book of secrets. It
stands alone in the how-to genre of sixteenth-century Italy for its bold
proclamation of female authorship, as if this might enhance sales, which
perhaps it did. Maybe other books listing a male author were written by
women; maybe this book was written by a man. What intrigues me most
is not actual authorship but why no Italian publishing entrepreneur
picked up on Mrs. Cortese's commercial success by trying a sequel. My
sense is that most printers would have typeset anything they thought
would earn a few soldi, so the likelihood is that similar works of female
authorship did not present themselves. The man with the printing press
simply did not encounter the woman with literary talent. By way of a
global comparison, according to historian Dorothy Ko, already at this
time in China the woman reader-writer was becoming not an isolated
individual but a type: "The debut of women as author and audience was
in itself one of the most conspicuous elements in the urban culture that
had been taking shape in the Jiangnan market towns since the mid-
sixteenth century." In Italy, at about the same time, likely barricades
between publishers and potential women authors, especially after midcentury, were Catholic Reformation requirements for licenses to print,
pay arrangements for authors, the vagaries of patronage as it shifted from
the court to the literary agent, and the exclusion of women from the
burgeoning printing trade itself. But these barricades certainly were not
insurmountable, nor do they explain why women's writings apparently
found publishers more readily as posthumous works.[6]

Our third tidbit is Moderata Fonte's reticence to publish. She was not
unique. Elissa Weaver's study of sixteenth-century Tuscan convent theater finds many talented nuns sharing their plays with other sisters, but
in manuscript form only. These women also wrote—and also did not
publish—saints lives, poetry, letters, chronicles, and spiritual works.[7] No
Italian translation of Christine de Pisan's poetry or prose appeared in
the sixteenth century (although English and Portuguese versions reached
print). Only in 1640 were selections of Laura Cereta's letters published,

and then in their original Latin, making them far less accessible. Against these nonpublishers are some women who did: Tullia d'Aragona, Celia, Vittoria Colonna, Veronica Franco, Lucrezia Marinella, Gaspara Stampa, and Laura Terracina probably are the best-known secular female authors whose vernacular works were printed under their own names in the sixteenth century. They are among a total of twenty-six names listed in a recent thorough survey by Luciana Borsetto.[8] About a third of the group wrote clearly religious tracts, although not all of them were nuns; another third were "honest courtesans" who wrote poetry and letters; the remaining third carried noble titles (except of course for Mrs. Cortese) and wrote both prose and poetry. A 1559 collection devoted entirely to women's writings, edited by Lodovico Domenichi, collected verses by more than forty female poets. Some of these published authors, along with a few new names, also found a place in the mixed-gender compilations of Girolamo Ruscelli, Lodovico Dolce, and half a dozen "in memoriam" or "in-praise-of" anthologies.[9]

The list of female authors is long if one begins with low expectations but short when compared with the relative significance of women writers before the printing press. Certainly there is nothing in sixteenth-century books to match the influence of religious writers like Angela of Foligno, Catherine of Siena, and Catherine Vigri.[10] While a precise tabulation would be impossible, my sense is that the already small ratio of female to male writers in the scribal culture may have diminished even further during the first century and a half of the printing press. Why? If there was no conspiracy among publishing firms to exclude women, which I believe there was not, except possibly for religious tracts that appeared once the Catholic Reformation magisterium determined to curb individualistic expressions of female piety; if there was no lack of a market for what authors identified as women might have put into print, which I believe there was not; if there was no dearth of talented female writers in the sixteenth century, which certainly there was not to judge by the quality and quantity of works they continued to write by hand, then perhaps women themselves were reluctant to present their writings in the public, unguarded domain of print. Writing is always an exposition of the self. In the medium of handwritten words, women writers controlled to some degree who would see them, who would read and respond, whether a sister in another convent, an absent lover, or a patron. The printed book led a life of its own—displayed on a street merchant's stand, bought as a commodity, passed from one hand to another, shunned or praised anonymously.

I believe that when Moderata Fonte, using the venue of ladies gathered in the widow Leonora's garden, expressed fears that the Venetian patriarchy might be spying on their conversation, she truly spoke for herself. Her thoughts were private, hers to be divulged to whomever she wished and kept from those she chose to exclude. As a child she had conserved all her writings in a box, and when her treasure got washed away in a local river, she rewrote every word from memory, so she was not shy about her talents. Still, her work was private. For as long as *Il merito delle donne* remained in manuscript, she could share its misandry with her circle of literary-minded, female, patrician friends alone. As a young woman, Fonte had published *Tredici canti del Floridoro,* dedicating her chivalric epic to Bianca Cappello, the Venetian noble who ran off with a lover and bore his illegitimate child before making her way to the bed of Francesco de' Medici, eventually becoming the grand duchess of Tuscany. Very little followed in print.[11] After being pushed into marriage with Filippo de' Zorzi, a man chosen for her, Fonte may have had less time for writing, since her biographer tells us she always put household chores first. She was a devoted mother who played the harpsichord and the lute, sang to her children, breast-fed them herself, and taught them to play the viola with such skill that the world listened in amazement. Her own abilities remained extraordinary, although her subject matter shifted from feminist concerns to topics more appropriate for a matron, such as funeral eulogies and reflections on Christ's Passion. These verses her husband, the local bishop, or even the entire Venetian patriciate were free to buy, sell, read, and criticize as they pleased, although she preferred to publish anonymously. Indeed, her husband wrote a prefatory sonnet for the *La Resurrettione* (The Resurrection) poem.

Il merito delle donne was another matter entirely. Might Fonte's role as wife and mother have been compromised if her husband had read Leonora's diatribe against marriage? ("What, me remarry? I'd rather drown than submit again to any man. I escaped from slavery and imprisonment. Are you now suggesting I voluntarily become enchained again? God watch over me.") Was Leonora's more benign view of marriage at the very end of the dialogue just a bit too perfunctory, coming only after all the lacerating words had been written? We do not know how much of her book-in-progress she showed Messer Filippo de' Zorzi, but we do know that she took her copy to the grave—literally—as she completed the dialogue one day before she died in 1592, at age thirty-seven, giving birth to her fourth surviving child. Apparently the widower did not do a very good job of caring for his family—too busy at work, according to Fonte's biographer—and the children, aged ten, eight, six, and newborn, sorely missed their mother's tutelage.

For eight years Zorzi, a member of the elite citizen class and a government lawyer who dabbled in poetry, apparently did nothing to get his
late wife's work into print, at least not this work. I strongly suspect her
La Resurrettione poem prefaced by his sonnet (1592) did not actually
reach the press until after she died, perhaps as some sort of eulogy. Be
that as it may, her feminist dialogue received no such assistance. Nor
did sufficient support come from her dearest friend's husband, Giovanni
Niccolò Doglioni, himself a widely published author who, in 1593, wrote
the biographical sketch containing all we know about Fonte, wherein he
unstintingly touted his role as her marriage broker and literary patron.
One phrase in this biographical sketch suggests that publication, in 1593,
was imminent: ". . . *Il merito delle donne:* the very work that is being
published alongside this account of her life."[12] But nothing happened.
Whether Moderata Fonte's final wish had been to keep her thoughts
about men in manuscript only, or whether her husband would have been
too embarrassed by the book, I cannot say. What we can be sure of is
that a work of incontestable literary merit by a well-connected female
author, clearly in a *querelle des femmes* genre that sold well, remained private. My guess is that the widower, Filippo de' Zorzi, blocked publication
of *Il merito delle donne* until his dying day in the summer of 1598. Once
he was out of the way, however, events combined to rescue the work
from permanent obscurity. In 1600, Lucrezia Marinella accepted a commission from the Venetian publisher Ciotti to write a response to Giuseppe Passi's vitriolic misogyny; she accepted a deadline of only two
months to do the work, clearly placing considerations of market timeli-
ness ahead of quality. (In a second edition Marinella apologized for the
imperfections in the earlier version caused by these time constraints.)
The first edition appeared in August 1600, and its polemic verve no
doubt caught the attention of Venice's book producers and consumers.
Whether Marinella then touted the *Il merito delle donne* manuscript, or
Doglioni once again intervened as the late Fonte's literary agent, we cannot be sure. Several experts lean toward the latter view, but I think Doglioni had foregone his chance back in 1593; my guess is that Lucrezia
Marinella—a confident, new, young author—was the critical patron.
One way or another, the book appeared on November 10, 1600, with a
prefatory poem by Moderata Fonte's eighteen-year-old son Pietro and
a presentation from her sixteen-year-old daughter Cicilia. Her recently
deceased husband went entirely unmentioned. Thus ended the deep reticence by respectable Italian women to send their prose to the printer,
for all the world to examine and purchase. Henceforth, nuns, charlatans,

and high-class prostitutes with literary talents had to compete for book-shop space with honest matrons.[13]

The messages carried by popular household-advice manuals would change more slowly. Female authorship of how-to books remained relatively infrequent in the decades, even the centuries, ahead. Nor did a distinct, different voice emerge until very recently, such that one could contrast "women according to men" against "women according to women" as clearly in guidebooks as one finds the distinction made, for example, in *querelle des femmes* literature or for that matter in poetry and fictional prose more generally. Brother Cherubino gave way to Alex Comfort, Dr. Michele Savonarola to Dr. Benjamin Spock, Antonio Tagliente to Theodore Seuss Geisel, Matteo Palmieri to Richard Ferber, and Cardinal Silvio Antoniano to Bishop Fulton J. Sheen—to name just five modern male experts whose once-prized books are gathering dust in my attic. Even as we speak, while female authors have taken over the market for advice manuals about catching a husband and about pregnancy, good-sex recommendations generally come from male-female joint authors, while men going it alone still do very well in the child-rearing sector.

The Internet

Before saying *arrivederci*, I want to make one final, brief stop at Bill Gates's *The Road Ahead*.[14] We've heard the distant charlatan Leonardo Fioravanti tout the power of information in the sixteenth century, and now we jump ahead more than four hundred years, across an ocean and a continent, so that a visionary entrepreneur in Seattle can forecast our destiny. I use the term "visionary" to capture Gates's own words: "When I was nineteen, I caught sight of the future and based my career on what I saw" (4).

Actually, I have the CD-ROM version of *The Road Ahead* on my computer as I write this paragraph, replete with thousands of hypertext links. The screen is split for simultaneous tasking, and I have followed Bill's advice to install a sound card, so now I can both see and hear what he has to say. However, since at this moment there is some glitch about setting up the right icons to make all this happen, my eyes are focused temporarily on the paperback edition; "completely revised and up-to-date" is the hype on the title page (the sort of thing I'm accustomed to reading on many sixteenth-century title pages). The cover shows a photo of Bill Gates, hands in his pockets, standing casually, beckoning me to join him along a road that stretches prominently behind him. Yes, behind him; at least if he turned his back, however rude that might be, the road would lie ahead. I know Gates thought carefully about this pose, since he explicitly mentions the photo as one of the few parts of his book "which we finished well ahead of schedule" (xv). It merits closer inspection.

Unlike the most famous road I know, the yellow-brick one that Dorothy took to rescue her dog Toto from the Wicked Witch of the West, this road is a dingy asphalt color. The orange-divider stripes demarcate just two lanes, nothing like I'd imagined the information superhighway would look. I can't even tell whether this is a two-way street, since there are neither signs nor traffic, vehicular or human, in either direction. Whereas Dorothy met friends along the way who turned out to be crucial in allowing her to reach the Wizard of Oz, no one seems to be around to assist Bill Gates. This is peculiar since the book itself is wonderfully generous in giving profuse credit to the many friends our author affectionately acknowledges in his life (in addition to the two co-authors who apparently accompanied Bill on his journey as a writer). Nor do I see, even with a magnifying glass (Microsoft's symbol for getting to the Internet but a tool I use the old-fashioned way), a workstation or something of that sort looming in the distance, like the Wizard's castle, to encourage the walkers on their journey. Alongside the road, there is not much— no flora or fauna whatsoever unless maybe the out-of-focus brownish stuff is wheat, and we're looking at a prairie rather than a barren desert. The sun is shining above some wispy Microsoft-logo-type clouds, possibly another torture since there are no trees. Perhaps they were cut down during the age of print.

A switch to the "Companion Interactive CD-ROM" version, which now has popped up on my screen, confirms my worst nightmares. The photo of the road behind holds firm for only two seconds, too little for me to think much about it, before I'm hurtled forward, without Bill or anyone else to guide me, and lifted in the air. Good thing, because suddenly the road bursts into apocalyptic flames, spreading fire over interconnected paths looking every bit like supposed landing strips for UFOs flown by denizens of lost civilizations on the Gazca plain—hardly what I mean by a companion. Before it got firebombed, the two-lane road ahead had led me to hope it would be a two-way street, so that I could ask Bill questions and hear him reply. "Join Bill Gates for a discussion of how technology will shape our future" is what the screen said momentarily. Then another explosion occurred, this one looking like a nuclear fireball. After a bit more flashing and shaking, the screen finally settled down, but as it turns out, my mouse can click only on his preset questions to get his prerecorded answers, hardly what I mean by interactive. Now that I've heard the eighteen canned Q & As a few times, while getting visually glazed over watching Bill's talking head on my screen, I think I'll click back to the book itself.

To my great relief, Bill Gates writes that he does not find highway imagery any more useful than I did; a market is the metaphor he prefers to describe the future of information exchange. Perhaps revealing the range of his experience, the markets he mentions are shopping malls, farmers' markets, bookstores, and the New York Stock Exchange (6). Alas, American shopping emporia are nothing more than enclosed-highway strip malls, stores to be bypassed in fixed sequence; farmers' markets carry only agricultural produce; bookstores are highly organized; and the New York Stock Exchange functions under tight regulations—altogether nothing approaching Internet anarchy. Nevertheless, the market metaphor suits me if we can switch the locus to downtown Istanbul. In its vast *souk,* Asia meets Europe, Muslim sells to Christian, ragamuffins jostle matrons, and the buyer's desire determines the price. The market changes much too rapidly for anyone to invest in a proper directory of the shops—although with some practice you could draw a mental map of what is probably where—but it's equally exhilarating to sip tea with a goldsmith, then exit left for goat entrails or right for kid gloves, as the mood strikes you. Filled with chatter and intriguing smells, the market is exposed to the weather, unpredictable, and truly interactive—exactly what Bill Gates's CD-ROM and the world it describes are not.

Yet the *souk* and the Internet do have a fundamental commonality, one shared with the world of sixteenth-century Italian books. By no means do shoppers in any of the three locales have equal access to the dazzling array of merchandise before them. Gates can be disarmingly humble: "[*The Road Ahead*] is meant to be a serious book, although ten years from now it may not appear that way. What I've said that turned out to be right will be considered obvious and what was wrong will be humorous" (xv). He also can be ecstatic about the democratizing possibilities of what began as his toys. You can stay in your humble cabin in the Ozarks and visit the Louvre, examine a rare da Vinci *Codex,* get lifesaving medical consultations, see any film you wish at anytime of day or night, chat with your friends around the world—all for free. His optimism reminds me of Leonardo Fioravanti's prediction: "the day will come when we shall all be Doctors . . . even the women."

As we know, things did not work out quite that way. Intellectual elites gained considerable power over the press; the poor remained despised and exploited, denied anything remotely like equal access to education; men took greater control from women over healing, using books as one of their principal weapons; universities developed new disciplinary guidelines to make "Philosophy, Medicine, Astrology, Mathematics, and as many sciences as there are in the world" less accessible than ever before, hiding not behind Latin, which at least could be translated, but behind impenetrable vernacular jargon, itself cloaking little if anything.

Historians and capitalist entrepreneurs don't always see eye-to-eye on things. Henry Ford's dumb remark that "history is bunk" still rankles. Bill Gates, by contrast, is music to my ears:

> Success is a lousy teacher. It seduces smart people into thinking they can't lose. And it's an unpredictable guide to the future. What seems to be the perfect business plan or the latest technology today may soon be as out-of-date as the eight-track tape player, the vacuum-tube television, or the mainframe computer. I've watched it happen. History is a good teacher, though, and observing many companies over a long period of time can teach us principles that will help us with strategies for the years ahead. (38)

I agree; history is a good teacher. I hope you have found rummaging around with me in old advice manuals informative and entertaining. I have—ciao!

NOTES

For sixteenth-century books I consulted, the publisher is included for better identification. Names of printer/publishers have been standardized using listings from Rhodes, *Silent Printers,* and Ascarelli and Menato, *La tipografia del '500 in Italia* (see note 17 to chapter 1). For works lacking publication information, I give the name of the library (Biblioteca Nazionale Centrale di Firenze [BNF]) and the shelf mark for readers who may wish to locate the originals.

Internet site http://intranet.rutgers.edu/bell/ provides a machine-readable copy of the notations, available for usual scholarly use and accessible with the user name "bell01" and the password "doithow."

Chapter One

1. Dale Carnegie, *How to Win Friends and Influence People* (New York, 1936), 233.

2. See Luigi Balsamo, *Bibliography: History of a Tradition,* trans. William A. Pettas (Berkeley, 1990), 46–51, on the publishing context of Possevino's work. On pedagogical matters, see Susanna Peyronel Rambaldi, "Educazione evangelica e catechistica: da Erasmo al gesuita Antonio Possevino," in *Ragione e "civilitas,"* ed. Davide Bigalli (Milan, 1986), 73–92. On the Index of Prohibited Books, see J. M. De Bujanda, *Index des livres interdits,* esp. vol. 8, *Index de Rome 1557, 1559, 1564* (Sherbrooke, 1990).

3. See Gabriella Zarri, ed., *Donna, disciplina, creanza cristiana dal XV al XVII secolo: Studi e testi a stampa* (Rome, 1996), 397–732, for the listing of 2,626 vernacular works addressed to women and an explanation of how it was compiled. This is a wonderful source for what it contains, but how I wish the team had kept better track of items they saw and excluded as insufficiently religious or not clearly enough directed at women. Many of the advice manuals we shall consider in the chapters that follow are missing entirely from the Zarri list. While some,

like Orazio Lombardelli's *Dell' uffizio della donna maritata,* indeed may no longer be available in any Italian library, others, for example, Mrs. Isabella Cortese's *I secreti* are ubiquitous. Admittedly not a very Christian text, nonetheless *I secreti* was enormously popular and must have been read by a goodly number of Italian housewives; so while its exclusion by the Zarri team is entirely understandable, in this instance good logic does not aid cumulative scholarship. Even a computer-readable version of the rejects would be most helpful.

4. On the scribal culture, see Armando Petrucci, *Writers and Readers in Medieval Italy: Studies in the History of Written Culture,* ed. and trans. Charles M. Radding (New Haven, 1995), 169–235. The earlier classic study and starting point for all scholars engaged in this field is Elizabeth Eisenstein, *The Printing Press as an Agent of Change,* 2 vols. (Cambridge, 1979).

5. J. Rawson Lumby, *Bernardus de cura rei famuliaris, with some Early Scottish Prophecies* (London, 1870), provides a wonderful example of how a Latin text might become the source for vernacular literary efforts. St. Bernard's original text also may be found here.

6. For the "art of love" work, see Leon Battista Alberti, *Hecatomphila de misser Leon Battista Alberto. Hecatomphila che ne insegna l'ingeniosa arte d'amore; Deiphira che ne mostra fuggir il mal principiato amore, pur hora venuta ne le mani de gli huomini* (Venice: Francesco Bindoni & Maffeo Pasini, 1534). Other editions of this work, or of the Deiphira section alone, were published in 1524, 1528, 1534, and 1545, and there were translations into French in 1534, and into English in 1598. The latest edition I know of is 1863, rather unfortunate since this is an important work in the genre of courtly love and its popularity in the sixteenth century is of significance. For the text on household economy, see Xenophon, *La economica di Xenofonte, tradotta di lingua greca in lingua toscana, dal S. Alessandro Piccolomini, altrimenti lo Stordito Intronato* (Venice: Comin da Trino, 1540).

For works that did not find a publisher, see Paolo da Certaldo, *Libro di buoni costumi,* ed. Alfredo Schiaffini (Florence, 1945). An earlier edition by Salomone Morpurgo (1921), iii–xxxix, provides what little is known about this manuscript and includes the ironic circumstance that in the same hand that transcribed Certaldo's writings at the Riccardiana library in Florence, there is a copy of St. Bernard's epistle "De cura rei famuliaris."

The publishing history of Alberti's book on family governance is summarized in Renée Neu Watkins, ed. and trans., *The Family in Renaissance Florence: A translation . . . of I libri della famiglia by Leon Battista Alberti* (Columbia, S.C., 1969). In some ways Alberti's *I Libri* suffered an even more unkind fate than Paolo da Certaldo's work. When the third part (the one adapted from Xenophon) reached print for the first time in 1734, it appeared under another name, that of the fifteenth-century Florentine Agnolo Pandolfini, a mistake that went uncorrected until a second edition appeared in Naples in 1843, still incomplete. There was another incomplete edition in 1845, and not until 1908, when a new version became an instant classic used in Italian schools, did the book achieve a wide audience. For intellectual reasons why Alberti's work may not have had much popularity in the sixteenth-century, see Giovanni Ponte, "Etica ed economia nel terzo libro 'Della famiglia' di Leon Battista Alberti," in Anthony Molho and John

A. Tedeschi, eds., *Renaissance Studies in Honor of Hans Baron* (Florence, 1971), 283–309; however, Ponte's argument cannot account for the success of Piccolomini's translation of Xenophon.

The list of works completely neglected in the sixteenth century could be extended quite a bit, but none can have been as obscure as Francesco da Barberino, *Reggimento e costumi di donna,* ed. Giuseppe Sansone (Rome, 1995), which was thought to be lost entirely until it was rediscovered in 1667. It is a wonderfully humorous collection of advice for women from all stations in life, and demonstrates clearly that the themes I shall explore in my book are by no means unique to the sixteenth century—but the fact remains that absolutely no one in the sixteenth century could have read it!

7. Horatio F. Brown, *The Venetian Printing Press 1469–1800* (Amsterdam, 1969, rpt. of 1891 ed.), 73–92; 77 and 79, respectively, for the quotations. Claudia di Filippo Bareggi, *Il mestiere di scrivere: Lavoro intellettuale e mercato librario a Venezia nel Cinquecento* (Rome, 1988), is essential on relations between intellectual endeavor and the market realities of sixteenth-century publishing. On the economic conditions, privileges, and censorship attending incunabula production in Venice, see Leonardas Vytautas Gerulaitis, *Printing and Publishing in Fifteenth-Century Venice* (Chicago, 1976), 1–56. On privileges and prohibition, see William A. Pettas, *The Giunti of Florence: Merchant Publishers of the Sixteenth Century* (San Francisco, 1980), 153–84.

8. Steven Ozment, *When Fathers Ruled: Family Life in Reformation Europe* (Cambridge, 1983), follows a life-cycle structure similar to the way I organize my chapters, going from marriage to childbearing to child rearing; in turn, this is how the original books themselves understood things. Suzanne W. Hull, *Women according to Men: The World of Tudor-Stuart Women* (Walnut Creek, 1996), does the same, with chapters on rules for wives, conception, care of babies, and raising daughters. This book rests on Hull's meticulous scholarship over many years, reflected also in her earlier *Chaste Silent and Obedient: English Books for Women, 1475–1640* (Huntington Library, 1982).

9. William Eamon, *Science and the Secrets of Nature: Books of Secrets in Medieval and Early Modern Culture* (Princeton, 1994), 4, for the how-to qualities of these books, 94–96, on the impact of print culture on books of secrets, and 234–35, on print and how-to tracts.

10. Ruth Kelso, *Doctrine for the Lady of the Renaissance* (Urbana, 1978, rpt. of 1956 ed., includes a foreword by Katharine Rogers).

11. Nowhere is such a life-cycle approach more explicit than in the writings of the influential humanist Matteo Palmieri. He composed *Della vita civile* (On Civic Life) in 1439. Among the half dozen treatises he wrote, it was the only one to appear in print in the sixteenth century. This quite erudite text, with its primary concern being civic government, probably did not appeal to many householders as a book to consult about their everyday needs. Still, he wrote in Italian precisely so that his friends who did not read Latin or Greek might benefit from his knowledge of classical pedagogy and of philosophers who had treated politics and ethics. In book 1 of *Della vita civile,* Palmieri begins at the beginning, so to speak, with the conception, breast-feeding, and parental care appropriate for a

future good citizen. He tells us that human life is divided roughly by age into six parts. The first is called infancy and goes from birth until the baby begins to speak. The second is childhood, which continues until the boy or girl reaches the age of discretion. The third is adolescence, which lasts until twenty-eight years of age and is marked by corporal growth and strengthening. There follows until age fifty-six the stage known as virility, during which time the natural forces are sustained and even prosper. Then comes the fifth part of the life cycle, known as old age, that lasts until age seventy. Finally, there is decrepitude, from seventy until death. Palmieri notes that other philosophers have divided human life into only two stages—the period of ignorance and the period of cognition—but he himself follows the more complex, multistage model as he gives advice on how parents should handle infancy, childhood, and adolescence.

For an excellent introduction to Palmieri's writings and career, see George Carpetto, *The Humanism of Matteo Palmieri* (Rome, 1984). For the first printed edition, see Matteo Palmieri, *Libro della vita civile* (Florence: Li heredi di Filippo Giunta, 1529, which was followed by a 1534 ed. in Venice). I used one of several more readily available modern editions, Felice Battaglia, *Della vita civile di Matteo Palmieri e De optimo cive di Bartolomeo Sacchi detto Il Platina* (Bologna, 1944), 25–26, for the life-cycle material.

12. Roger Chartier, *The Order of Books: Readers, Authors, and Libraries in Europe between the Fourteenth and Eighteenth Centuries,* trans. Lydia G. Cochrane (Stanford, 1994), 5, for the quotation, and 1–23, for relevant theoretical propositions on premodern reading. Also see David D. Hall, *Cultures of Print: Essays in the History of the Book* (Amherst, 1996), 1–14.

13. Natalie Zemon Davis, *Fiction in the Archives: Pardon Tales and Their Tellers in Sixteenth-Century France* (Stanford, 1987), 4, explains her handling of pardon tales in a way that closely parallels what I intend to do with advice manuals:

> My historian's eye will not focus on morphologies of the tale, on production from a universal grammar, or on arrangements of functions, 'indices,' and propositions that might be found in any time or place. Rather I am after evidence of how sixteenth-century people told stories (albeit in the special case of the pardon tale), what they thought a good story was, how they accounted for motive, and how through narrative they made sense of the unexpected and built coherence into immediate experience. . . . My method here will in part resemble that recommended by Barbara Hernstein-Smith, attending closely to the means and settings for producing the stories and to the interests held by both narrator and audience in the storytelling event. But I will also be conceiving of 'structures' existing prior to that event in the minds and lives of the sixteenth-century participants: possible story lines determined by the constraints of the law and approaches to narrative learned in past listening to and telling of stories or derived from other cultural constructions.

Analogously, I shall try to summarize what authors wrote and people read, attempting to portray the advice given primarily from the perspective of a sixteenth-century householder. I shall try to discern and give due weight to authorial intent, and I shall attempt to reach conclusions about probable audience based on mundane factors such as the book's size and likely cost, as well as its content. I shall note Greco-Roman precedents, biblical teachings, and works by church fathers, seeing these less as inexorable determinants of the advice given than as constraints and inspirations in a broad and varied historical legacy. When I insert myself and my twentieth-century experience into the telling, it will be more to question or maybe to poke fun at modern-day received wisdom and political correctness than to castigate sixteenth-century people for not being "with it," whatever that "it" might have been.

Even more problematic than my presumption to read texts on behalf of people long dead is whether reading advice meant following it in some fashion. A good starting point for considering the impact of reading in premodern societies is the chapter titled "Do Books Cause Revolutions?" in Robert Darnton's *Forbidden Best-Sellers of Pre-Revolutionary France* (New York, 1995), 169–246. Darnton's answer is a very cautious "not no," at least to judge by the proposed third volume of his trilogy on reading. That planned study of how contemporaries saw events in the months immediately preceding Bastille Day, based upon minute investigation of what they wrote down and printed for others to read, would make no sense unless the answer, somehow, is "yes—books do cause revolutions." Hardly less exasperating than Darnton in its ambiguity is Roger Chartier's iffy answer to his earlier and very similar question—"Do Books Make Revolutions?"—in his *Cultural Origins of the French Revolution,* trans. Lydia G. Cochrane (Durham, 1991), 67–91. Indeed, Chartier suggests that it might be better to reverse the causal arrow and consider how the Revolution "made" books (89). (In the original, "En un sens, c'est donc bien la Révolution qui a 'fait' les livres, et non l'inverse" [112–13])

One must be chastened by such scholarly hesitation in addressing well-established historical questions. When it comes to interrogating sixteenth-century-advice manuals, I feel most confident about conveying to you what people read, rather more speculative in asserting on how they read, and least sure in suggesting the impact of reading on daily comportment. I do not believe that popular-advice manuals were "made" by people's behavior, but who knows for sure? And exactly what people "made" of what they read in advice manuals is probably unknowable, although on occasion I shall ruminate.

This rather old-fashioned way of looking at things past has contemporary practitioners. See, for example, Margaret R. Sommerville, *Sex and Subjection: Attitudes to Women in Early-Modern Society* (London, 1995), 5–6, for the method, and the rest of her fine book concentrating on the English scene for its application.

14. Paul F. Grendler, *Books and Schools in the Italian Renaissance* (Aldershot, 1995), conveniently collects several of Grendler's essays on these issues. See especially, "Form and Function in Italian Renaissance Popular Books," *Renaissance Quarterly* 46, no. 3 (1993): 451–85. Grendler in turn cites Lucien Febvre and Henri-Jean Martin, *The Coming of the Book: The Impact of Printing 1450–1800,* trans. David Gerard (London, 1976), 87–90, and Rudolf Hirsch, *Printing, Selling, and Reading, 1450–1550* (Wiesbaden, 1974), on how to recognize a popular book.

15. See the essay titled "Aldus Manutius: Humanist, Teacher, and Printer," in Grendler, *Books and Schools,* 5, for an evocative description of the book-selling scene in Venice: "By 1501, Venice had published almost twice as many books as Paris, her nearest rival, and nearly one-seventh of all the books printed in Europe. Sixteenth-century tourists did not come to Venice to visit a glass factory and to buy glass trinkets; they came to buy books." For a detailed exploration of why Venice dominated book production on the Italian peninsula, see Luigi Balsamo, "The Origins of Printing in Italy and England," *Journal of the Printing Historical Society* 11 (1976–77): 48–63. For the actual process, see Martin Lowry, *Nicholas Jenson and the Rise of Venetian Publishing in Renaissance Europe* (Oxford, 1991), 173–206. The chapter titled "The Printer, the Reader, and the Market" includes an analysis of sales by category of books (196), but even the author cautions against making too much of such quantitative exercises, a warning that would be even more applicable to later periods when sales were much higher. On the decline of printing in Venice after 1600, see Ivo Mattozzi, "'Mondo del libro' e decadenza a Venezia (1570–1730)," *Quaderni Storici* 72 (1989): 743–86. For a more general discussion of books as commodities, see Lisa Jardine, *Worldly Goods: A New History of the Renaissance* (New York, 1996), 135–80.

16. See Balsamo, *Bibliography: History of a Tradition,* 31, for the particular lament, and 1–60, more generally, for the bibliographic scene from the Middle Ages through the sixteenth century.

17. Fernanda Ascarelli and Marco Menato, *La tipografia del '500 in Italia* (Florence, 1989), 10, provides the overall number and in a text of over four hundred pages summarizes what is known about individual printers and editors. For the Venetian scene in particular, see Dennis E. Rhodes, *Silent Printers: Anonymous Printing at Venice in the Sixteenth Century* (London, 1995), and Bareggi, *Il mestiere di scrivere.* On Florence, see Pettas, *The Giunti of Florence.* Also see Eamon, *Science and the Secrets of Nature,* 147. For information on average print runs for Europe generally, see Rab Houston, *Literacy in Early Modern Europe: Culture and Education 1500–1800* (London, 1988), 156–62. Also see the estimates, generally quite conservative because they do not attempt to measure the circulation of books among multiple readers, by Paul Slack, "Mirrors of Health and Treasures of Poor Men: The Uses of the Vernacular Medical Literature of Tudor England," in Charles Webster, ed., *Health, Medicine, and Mortality in the Sixteenth Century* (Cambridge, 1979), 237–73. Slack's analysis of the probable readership for medical works of different sizes, formats, and subjects influenced my thinking about the Italian publishing scene as well.

18. Brian Richardson, *Print Culture in Renaissance Italy: The Editor and the Vernacular Text, 1470–1600* (Cambridge, 1994), 91, on competition, and generally, for printing in Venice and Florence.

19. Grendler, "Aldus Manutius," 5–23. On Aldus Manutius, also see Martin Lowry, *The World of Aldus Manutius: Business and Scholarship in Renaissance Venice* (Oxford, 1979), 257–99, for an estimate that this single publisher, admittedly an important one with contacts throughout Europe, may have reached a total output of between 100,000 and 120,000 books. For a valuable, although fleeting,

ray of light on the question of sales of individual items, see Rudolf Hirsch, "The Art of Selling Books: Notes on Three Aldus Catalogues, 1586–1592," in his *Printed Word: Its Impact and Diffusion (Primarily in the 15th–16th Centuries)* (London, 1978), part 30. Also see the discussion of octavo sizes and prices in Harry George Fletcher, *New Aldine Studies: Documentary Essays on the Life and Work of Aldus Manutius* (San Francisco, 1988), 88–91. Eamon, *Science and the Secrets of Nature,* 239, reports that charlatans sold books of secrets, often little more than pamphlets, for "a few soldi apiece," necessarily a bit vague and yet overall in keeping with the point I am making about accessibility.

20. A high level of literacy among nuns is suggested in Elissa Weaver, "Spiritual Fun: A Study of Sixteenth-Century Tuscan Convent Theater," in Mary Beth Rose, ed., *Women in the Middle Ages and the Renaissance: Literary and Historical Perspectives* (Syracuse, 1986), 173–205. For further discussion of literacy rates in Europe generally, see Carlo Cipolla, *Literacy and Development in the West* (Baltimore, 1969), 45–61, and Houston, *Literacy in Early Modern Europe.* Houston estimates that as many as two hundred million books and chapbooks were published in Europe in the sixteenth century (166). On readership in city and country in France, and by class, see Natalie Zemon Davis, *Society and Culture in Early Modern France* (Stanford, 1975), 189–226. Eamon, *Science and the Secrets of Nature,* 94–105, is excellent on the German scene, and see 126–33, on pre-1550 best-sellers. For an estimate that 45 to 60 percent of Florentine boys may have attended school and therefore presumably grew to be literate adults, see Peter Burke, "The Uses of Literacy in Early Modern Italy," in Peter Burke and Roy Porter, eds., *The Social History of Language* (Cambridge, 1987), 22. Also see Peter Burke, *The Historical Anthropology of Early Modern Italy: Essays on Perception and Communication* (Cambridge, 1987), 110–31, and in particular 112, for the conclusion that literacy rates in northern Italy were the highest in Europe from about the year 1000, until the seventeenth century, when efforts were made in the Dutch Republic and Sweden to achieve virtually universal literacy. Somewhat lower estimates for literacy and for the vibrancy of the Italian publishing scene may be found in Harvey Graff, *The Legacies of Literacy: Continuities and Contradictions in Western Culture and Society* (Bloomington, 1987), 121–23. Still, Graff concludes that a "veritable avalanche of treatises aimed at a variety of forms of self-help and improvement, from praying to singing and accounting, rolled from sixteenth-century presses." On religious books and a wide readership, see the introduction to Anne Jacobson Schutte, *Printed Italian Vernacular Religious Books, 1465–1550: A Finding List* (Geneva, 1983), 1–3. On elementary schooling, see Paul F. Grendler, ed., "Education in the Renaissance and Reformation," *Renaissance Quarterly* 43, no. 4 (1990): 774–823.

21. Pettas, *The Giunti of Florence,* 11–12, includes the disdain for printing among Florentine humanists and the Medici family as a major factor in Venetian dominance of this new industry.

22. Grendler, "Form and Function in Popular Books," 453. Also see his "Chivalric Romances in the Italian Renaissance," *Studies in Medieval and Renaissance History* 10 (1988): 59–60, 83–89.

23. The reverse also is true in that writing in Latin often was a socially or

politically charged choice. See the insightful essay by Peter Burke, *"Heu domine, adsunt Turcae:* A Sketch for a Social History of Post-medieval Latin," in Peter Burke and Roy Porter, eds., *Language, Self, and Society: A Social History of Language* (Cambridge, 1991), 23–50. Cecil Grayson, *A Renaissance Controversy: Latin or Italian?* (Oxford, 1960), 14, persuasively points to the printing press's dependence on a wide audience as the most important factor in determining the triumph of vernaculars over Latin in scholarly as well as in popular writing. On the specific reluctance of physicians to publish in the vernacular, see Richard J. Durling, "A Chronological Census of Renaissance Editions and Translations of Galen," *Journal of the Warburg and Courtauld Institutes* 24, no. 3–4 (1961): 240–41, and note 55.

24. Maria Luisa Altieri Biagi, Clemente Mazzotta, Angela Chiantera, and Paola Altieri, eds. *Medicina per le donne nel Cinquecento: Testi di Giovanni Marinello e di Girolamo Mercurio* (Turin, 1992), 12. Biagi et al. ascribe to Mercurio other medical works, including a commentary in Latin on Hippocrates and another on syphilis. However, there may be some confusion here between Girolamo Mercurio who died in 1615, and certainly wrote the *La commare* book, and the more famous Girolamo Mercuriale who died in 1606, and is best known for Latin works on children's diseases and on gymnastic exercises. Friar Girolamo Mercurio wrote another big treatise in the vernacular that we shall return to, *De gli errori popolari d'Italia. Libri sette* (Venice: Giovanni Battista Ciotti, 1603), and in this work he frequently refers back to his *La commare*. But there are no specific references by title in either of these two vernacular books to any of the other writings ascribed by Biagi to Mercurio. The *National Union Catalog* clearly identifies Mercuriale, not Mercurio, as the author of the Hippocrates commentary and the syphilis treatise but misascribes *La commare* to Mercuriale (vol. 377, p. 23). Of the two books I am certain Mercurio wrote, *La commare* was the resounding success.

In subsequent citations of Mercurio, I shall give the book and chapter of the original *La commare*. If the material cited is included in the selections of Biagi et al., then in parentheses I shall give the page numbers for the readily available Biagi edition. For material not in Biagi, I shall give the page numbers from the 1601 edition of *La commare* (Venice: Giovanni Battista Ciotti), which I used. This edition contains a book 3 on the care of young children that Mercurio completed in 1600, and integrated into the updated version of *La commare*. According to Felice La Torre, Mercurio's book went through at least eighteen editions during the next century or so; see La Torre, *L'utero attraverso i secoli: Da Erofilo ai giorni nostri* (Città di Castello, 1917), 102–3.

25. Margaret Spufford, *Small Books and Pleasant Histories: Popular Fiction and Its Readership in Seventeenth-Century England* (Athens, 1981), 50–75, provides a wonderful example of common sense brought to bear on important historical issues concerning literacy and readership. See also the fundamental essay by Roger Chartier, "Culture as Appropriation: Popular Cultural Uses in Early Modern France," in Steven L. Kaplan, ed., *Understanding Popular Culture: Europe from the Middle Ages to the Nineteenth Century* (Berlin, 1984), 229–53. On female book ownership, well before the use of printing in Europe, see Susan Groag Bell,

"Medieval Women Book Owners: Arbiters of Lay Piety and Ambassadors of Culture," in Mary Erler and Maryanne Kowaleski, eds., *Women and Power in the Middle Ages* (Athens, 1988), 149–87.

26. Anne Jacobson Schutte, "Teaching Adults to Read in Sixteenth Century Venice: Giovanni Antonio Tagliente's *Libro Maistrevole*," *Sixteenth Century Journal* 17, no. 1 (1986): 3–16. For a thorough assessment of early books on how to read, one that suggests learning to read may not have been as simple as Tagliente suggests, see Piero Lucchi, "La santacroce, il salterio e il babuino: Libri per imparare a leggere nel primo secolo della stampa," *Quaderni Storici* 38 (1978): 593–630.

Chapter Two

1. For a thorough introduction to premodern biological understanding of reproduction see Angus McLaren, *Reproductive Rituals: The Perception of Fertility in England from the Sixteenth to the Nineteenth Century* (London, 1984), and Ian Maclean, *The Renaissance Notion of Woman: A Study in the Fortunes of Scholasticism and Medical Science in European Intellectual Life* (Cambridge, 1980), 28–46, and specifically 37, on sex determination. Also essential is Thomas Laqueur, *Making Sex: Body and Gender from the Greeks to Freud* (Cambridge, 1992), 25–62. The many parallels between what I present throughout this chapter and what McLaren finds for England suggest a European-wide understanding of biology, rather than language-specific knowledge, even at the level of popular manuals on topics as diverse as herbals, anatomy, and witchcraft.

For an uncompromising indictment of Aristotle as "antifeminist to the core," see Maryanne Cline Horowitz, "Aristotle and Woman," *Journal of the History of Biology* 9 (fall 1976): 183–213. On the political implications of Aristotelian biology, see Sommerville, *Sex and Subjection*, 16–23. Also see Constance Jordan, *Renaissance Feminism: Literary Texts and Political Models* (Ithaca, 1990), 29–34, 259, for the suspicion that the Greek philosopher did not get along very well with his wife.

2. On Aristotelian dominance in popular-advice manuals, see Daniela Frigo, *Il padre di famiglia: Governo della casa e governo civile nella tradizione dell 'economica' tra Cinque e Seicento* (Rome, 1985), 11–12. For an excellent introduction to Greco-Roman and Christian texts on the physiology of conception and motherhood, see Clarissa W. Atkinson, *The Oldest Vocation: Christian Motherhood in the Middle Ages* (Ithaca, 1991), 23–63. Also see Thomas Laqueur, "Orgasm, Generation, and the Politics of Reproductive Biology," *Representations* 14 (spring 1986): 1–41, particularly on Galen. An excellent introduction to medieval texts on female reproductive biology is Claude Thomasset, "The Nature of Woman," in Christiane Klapisch-Zuber, ed., *Silences of the Middle Ages* (Cambridge, 1992), 43–69; and see Danielle Jacquart and Claude Thomasset, *Sexuality and Medicine in the Middle Ages*, trans. Matthew Adamson (Princeton, 1988), esp. 48–138. Also of fundamental importance is Joan Cadden, *Meanings of Sex Difference in the Middle Ages: Medicine, Science, and Culture* (Cambridge, 1993), which thoroughly documents the presence in medieval texts of virtually every belief and prescrip-

tion, popular or otherwise, found in the sixteenth-century books considered throughout this chapter; and see also Monica H. Green, "Women's Medical Practice and Health Care in Medieval Europe," *Signs* 14 (1989): 434–73.

3. See Biagi et al., *Medicina per le donne*, 7–15, for a thorough discussion of the significance of the choice to write in the vernacular. Parallel findings for England may be found in Alison Sim, *The Tudor Housewife* (Montreal, 1996), 78–93.

4. Lorenzo Gioberti, *La prima parte de gli errori popolari. Nella quale si contiene l'eccellenza della medicina, & de' medici, della concettione, & generatione; della gravidezza, del parto, e delle donne di parto; & del latte, e del nutrire i bambine. Tradotta di franzese in lingua toscana dal mag. M. Alberto Luchi da Colle* (Florence: Filippo Giunta, 1592), hereafter cited as *Errori popolari*, except when Mercurio's original reference was to *Errori populari*. For the publishing history of the original, and for a superb English translation, see Laurent Joubert, *Popular Errors*, trans. and annotated by Gregory David de Rocher (Tuscaloosa, 1989). De Rocher is also the translator and annotator of two other works by Joubert: *Treatise on Laughter* (University, 1980), and *The Second Part of the Popular Errors* (Tuscaloosa, 1995).

5. Davis, *Society and Culture in Early Modern France*, 224–25, 258–67. Also see pages xiii–xxvi, of the de Rocher translation of *Popular Errors*, and Eamon, *Science and the Secrets of Nature*, 162, 259–62. Eamon views "popular errors" books as elitist, and I certainly agree that they belong at the quality end of the advice-manual spectrum, while de Rocher emphasizes Joubert's great respect for popular traditions, a reading I share. Beyond matters of tone and style, the errors Joubert denounces come overwhelmingly from Greco-Roman scientific treatises. On how readers may remake what they read, see Carlo Ginzburg, *The Cheese and the Worms: The Cosmos of a Sixteenth-Century Miller*, trans. John and Anne Tedeschi (Baltimore, 1980), esp. 28–54.

6. Gioberti, *Errori popolari*, 64–66.

7. Gioberti, *Errori popolari*, 73. The exploration of a "one sex, two genders" biology by Laqueur, *Making Sex*, 25–62, is immediately relevant here.

8. Gioberti, *Errori popolari*, 70–73.

9. Francesco Tommasi, *Reggimento del padre di famiglia* (Florence: Giorgio Marescotti, 1580), 89. This quarto tome of 561 pages joins extended treatments on family relations with advice on agricultural methods. The intended readership was probably gentlemen who owned country estates; they received a heavy dose of moralizing along with the advice about what to plant. For bio-bibliographical information and an introduction to Italian books in this "country-estate" genre, see Marino Berengo, "Un agronomo toscano del Cinquecento: Francesco Tommasi da Colle Val D'Elsa," in aa.vv. *Studi di storia medievale e moderna per Ernesto Sestan*, vol. 2 (Florence, 1980), 495–518. Also see Frigo, *Il padre di famiglia*, 40–41; 49, note 5, in which she concludes that in Tommasi the primacy of knowledge *(sapere)* is so submerged that the book in essence "becomes one of the instruments in the strategy of the post-Tridentine church to control and influence daily life and its values."

10. Roberto Ridolfi, *Vita di Girolamo Savonarola*, 6th ed. (Florence, 1981), 4–6, 492. On Avicenna, see Nancy G. Siraisi, *Avicenna in Renaissance Italy: The*

Canon and Medical Teaching in Italian Universities after 1500 (Princeton, 1987), and also her chapter, "The Changing Fortunes of a Traditional Text: Goals and Strategies in Sixteenth-Century Latin Editions of the *Canon* of Avicenna," in A. Wear, R. K. French, and I. M. Lonie, eds., *The Medical Renaissance of the Sixteenth Century* (Cambridge, 1985), 16–41. Especially strong on the connections between Greco-Roman and Arabic medicine related to conception is Marcia C. Inhorn, *Quest for Conception: Gender, Infertility, and Egyptian Medical Traditions* (Philadelphia, 1994), 55–67.

11. We are most fortunate in having the carefully edited and complete text of Luigi Belloni, *Il trattato ginecologico-pediatrico in volgare: Ad mulieres ferrarienses de regimine pregnantium et noviter natorum usque ad septennium di Michele Savonarola* (Milan, 1952), which is the edition I shall cite throughout my work. The thorough introduction (v–xxxv) provides an account of Savonarola's life and writings. Among Savonarola's printed works is *Trattato utilissimo di molte regole, per conservare la sanità, dichiarando qual cose siano utili da mangiare, & quali triste . . .* (Venice: Gli heredi di Giovanni Padovano, 1554), which I was able to consult at length in Rome. It does not include the "Degli atti venerei" section that turns up as pages 261–75 of the later and better-known revision, *Libro della natura et virtù delle cose, che nutriscono, et delle cose non naturali, con alcune osservationi per conservar la sanità, et alcuni quesiti bellissimi da notare, raccolto da diversi autori greci, et latini, et arabi, prima per M. Michel Savonarola medico padoano, poi di nuovo con miglior ordine riformato, accresciuto, et emendato, et quasi fatto un altro per Bartolomeo Boldo, medico bressano* (Venice: Domenico & Giovanni Battista Guerra, 1575). The one from 1554, a sextodecimo of 84 leaves in tiny print, grew in the later version to 299 more elegant quarto pages divided into twenty-five chapters as follows: cereals, herbs, tubers, citrus fruits, sweet fruits, birds, fresh water fish, eggs, dairy, wine, water, salt, oil, honey, spices, fragrances, air, exercise, rest, sleep, vigils, intake and evacuation, sexual intercourse, conservation of good health, and further reflections on conservation of health. Although much of what these early manuals convey about diet and good health is covered in my next chapter in the section on diet and lifestyle during pregnancy, they also contain a wealth of interesting material that space precludes me from discussing here. For a modern edition of a copy of the handwritten original, see Jane Nystedt, *Libreto de tutte le cosse che se magnano: Un' opera di dietetica del sec. XV / Michele Savonarola* (Stockholm, 1988). A photostatic reprint (Padua, 1991) of the 1515 printed edition also exists.

12. Savonarola, *Ad mulieres ferrarienses*, 55–58.

13. Giovanni Marinello, *Delle medicine partenenti all' infermità delle donne. Scritte per M. Giovanni Marinello, & divise in tre libri: Nel primo de' quali si curano alcuni difetti, che possono sciogliere il legame del matrimonio; nel secondo si rimove la sterilità; & nel terzo si scrive la vita della donna gravida, sino che sia uscita del parto, con l'ufficio della levatrice* (Venice: Francesco de' Franceschi, 1563). A small selection of its chapters can be found in *Medicina per le donne*, edited by Maria Luisa Altieri Biagi et al., which also contains excerpts from Mercurio. However, since that edition includes only five chapters from Marinello's original forty-nine, I shall cite the original throughout. Marinello's book on beauty aids, *Gli ornamenti delle*

304 NOTES TO PAGES 26–27

donne (Venice: Francesco de' Franceschi, 1562), also may be consulted in a selected modern edition by Luigi Pescasio (Verona, 1973).

Lucrezia Marinella's book, *La nobiltà et l'eccellenza delle donne co' diffetti e mancamenti de gli uomini* (Venice: Giovanni Battista Ciotti, 1600), contains a series of citations and recitations about famous women from Greco-Roman antiquity, some real and some not, with many lifted directly from Plutarch. The presentation is a mirror image reversal of the format used by misogynist texts of the era, especially the work of Giuseppe Passi to which it is a direct response. See Plutarch's essay "Concerning the Virtues of Women," in *Moralia*, bk. 3, 242E, for passages heavily borrowed by Marinella. I use the Loeb Classical Library translation by Frank Cole Babbitt (London, 1927) throughout. For a modern assessment of Marinella, see Patricia Labalme, "Venetian Women on Women: Three Early Modern Feminists," *Archivio Veneto* 5, no. 152 (1981): 93. Even her charitable view allows that Marinella's style is a bit overwhelming and that she can be "tendentious, even tiresome to a modern reader." For biographical details and a good introduction to the corpus of Marinella's work, see the entry on her by Paola Malpezzi Price in Rinaldina Russell, ed., *Italian Women Writers: A Bio-Bibliographic Sourcebook* (Westport, 1994), 234–42. As a translation of Marinella's book is promised in the University of Chicago Press's series The Other Voice in Early Modern Europe, you will soon be able to make your own judgment. On Plutarch's essay, see Philip Stadter, *Plutarch's Historical Methods: An Analysis of the* Mulierum virtutes (Cambridge, 1965).

14. Lodovico Domenichi, *La nobiltà delle donne* (Venice: Gabriel Giolito de' Ferrari, 1549), quoted in Piero Camporesi, *Juice of Life: The Symbolic and Magic Significance of Blood*, trans. Robert Barr (New York, 1995), 93. See William Barker, ed., *The Nobility of Women by William Bercher 1559* (London, 1904), 44–62, for a thorough exploration of the plagiarism from Agrippa, and 74–75, for further plagiarism from the work of Galeazzo Flavio Capra. Paul F. Grendler, *Critics of the Italian World, 1530–1560: Anton Francesco Doni, Nicolò Franco, and Ortensio Lando* (Madison, 1969), 67, specifically includes *La nobiltà delle donne* as one of Domenichi's original works, a conclusion with which I do not concur.

15. For an English translation of Agrippa, preceded by an excellent introduction, see Henricus Cornelius Agrippa, *Declamation on the Nobility and Preeminence of the Female Sex*, trans. and ed. Albert Rabil Jr. (Chicago, 1996). See Jordan, *Renaissance Feminism*, 122–26, on Agrippa and Domenichi as male feminists, but then 149, on Domenichi as a misogynist. Domenichi might better be characterized as an opportunist, which would account both for the Agrippa plagiarism and his several editions of poetry by women, on which see Margaret F. Rosenthal, *The Honest Courtesan: Veronica Franco, Citizen and Writer in Sixteenth-Century Venice* (Chicago, 1992), 302, note 90.

16. Marinello, *Delle medicine*, 243–48.

17. Marinello, *Delle medicine*, 70.

18. Marinello, *Delle medicine*, 243–48; for a repetition of many of the same points, with references to the ancient Greeks but not to sixteenth-century authors, see Mercurio, *La commare*, bk. 1, chap. 13 (Biagi et al., 95–97).

19. Savonarola, *Ad mulieres ferrarienses*, 10; Marinello, *Delle medicine*, 70. Gio-

berti, *Errori popolari*, 69, warns that God punishes husbands who are unfaithful while away on a business trip by rendering their semen too weak to produce legitimate heirs.

20. Castore Durante da Gualdo, *Il tesoro della sanità* (Milan, 1982), 34, for an edition by Elena Camillo of the 1586 original published in Rome. Camillo's excellent bibliographic introduction discusses the medieval origins of the regimens contained in this work. Also see Tiziana Pesenti's entry on Durante in the *Dizionario biografico degli Italiani*, vol. 42 (Rome, 1993), 105–7.

21. Bartolomeo Boldo, *Libro della natura*, 263. For full bibliographic information, see note 11.

22. Ugo Benzi, *Regole della sanità et natura de' cibi, di Ugo Benzo, senese. Arricchite di vaghe annotationi, & di copiosi discorsi, naturali, e morali dal sig. Lodovico Bertaldi. Et nuovamente in questa seconda impressione aggiontovi alle medeme materie i trattati di Baldasar Pisanelli, e sue historie naturali; & annotationi del medico Galina* (Turin: Li heredi di Giovanni Domenico Tarino, 1620), 714, for the specific reference to the dangers of too much sex. Benzi's commentaries on Hippocrates (Ferrara, 1493) and Galen (Venice, 1517) also were printed. For complete biographical information, see Dean P. Lockwood, *Ugo Benzi: Medieval Philosopher and Physician, 1376–1439* (Chicago, 1951), esp. 382–98, for the publication record.

23. Michele Mercati, *Instruttione sopra la peste. Nella quale si contengono i piu eletti e approvati rimedij, con molti nuovi e potenti secreti cosi da preservarsi come da curassi* (Rome: Vincenzo Accolti, 1576), 112.

24. Marinello, *Delle medicine*, 4–7.

25. *Cicalamenti del Grappa intorno al sonetto* 'Poi che mia spreme è lunga à venir troppo' *dove si ciarla allungo delle lodi delle donne et del mal francioso* (Mantua: [Venturino Ruffinelli], 1545), 14. This work is a sexually explicit lampoon of Dante's ethereal *La vita nuova*.

26. Cherubino da Siena, *Regole della vita matrimoniale* (Bologna, 1969, rpt. of 1888 ed. by Francesco Zambrini and Carlo Negroni), 97. Plutarch, *Moralia*, bk. 2, "Advice to Bride and Groom," 139A. The rotten fish analogy repeated by Francesco Barbaro is most easily found in the excerpt provided in Benjamin Kohl and Ronald Witt, with Elizabeth Welles, eds., *The Earthly Republic: Italian Humanists on Government and Society* (Philadelphia, 1978), 198. The sixteenth-century translation by Alberto Lollio that I consulted is *Prudentissimi et gravi documenti circa la elettion della moglie; dello eccellente & dottissimo M. Francesco Barbaro, gentilhuomo venitiano al molto magnifico et magnanimo M. Lorenzo de Medici, cittadin fiorentino* (Venice: Gabriel Giolito de' Ferrari, 1548). For a modern assessment of Barbaro, see Margaret L. King, *Venetian Humanism in an Age of Patrician Dominance* (Princeton, 1986), 92–98. See also my chapter 6.

27. Biblical citations are from the New Oxford Annotated Bible, which uses the text of the New Revised Standard Version.

28. Bartolomeo de Medina, *Breve instruttione de' confessori. Come si debba amministrare il sacramento della penitentia* (Venice: Bernardo Basa, 1600), 155. This is a translation of the Spanish original by Bartolomé de Medina, *Breve instrucción de como ha de administrar el sacramento de la penitencia* (Salamanca, 1580), cited

306 NOTES TO PAGES 32-34

in Romeo De Maio, *Donna e Rinascimento* (Milan, 1987), 239, note 48, which was itself preceded by a Spanish 1579 edition at Çaragoça. Other Italian editions appeared in Venice, 1584 and 1587, and in Rome, 1588. De Maio identifies Bartolomeo de Medina as a "virulent antifeminist."

29. Donald Weinstein and Rudolph Bell, *Saints and Society: The Two Worlds of Western Christendom, 1000–1700* (Chicago, 1982) , 90ff., for this and other accounts of married saints.

30. Theodore Buckley, trans., *The Catechism of the Council of Trent* (London, 1852), pt. 2, chap. 8, question 34. Subsequent citations will use the following format: 2.8.34.

31. Tommasi, *Reggimento del padre*, 95; Bartolomeo de Medina, *Breve instruttione de' confessori*, 164.

32. Cherubino da Firenze, *Confessionario* (Florence: Filippo Giunti, 1563), 48–54. On earlier vernacular confessionals for laymen and laywomen, see Anne Jacobson Schutte, "Consiglio spirituale e controllo sociale: Manuali per la confessione stampati in volgare prima della Controriforma," in Convegno Internazionale di Studi Lucca (Lucca, Italy, 1983), *Città italiane del '500 tra Riforma e Controriforma: Atti del Convegno Internazionale di Studi Lucca, 13–15 ottobre 1983* (Lucca, 1988), 45–59. Schutte highlights clearly the economic pressures of publication ("*Il loro scopo principale era far denaro*" [47]) and the attempt to control secular behavior evident in pre-Tridentine confessional manuals, characteristics that became even more pronounced after 1550.

33. Lynne Lawner, I modi: *The Sixteen Pleasures, An Erotic Album of the Italian Renaissance* (Evanston, 1988), provides a wickedly spirited English translation of the sonnets, copies of the original illustrations and some later versions of them, and a scholarly introduction.

34. Savonarola, *Ad mulieres ferrarienses*, 23.

35. Bartolomeo de Medina, *Breve instruttione de' confessori*, 78; Bernardo Trotto, *Dialoghi del matrimonio, e vita vedovile* (Turin: Francesco Dolce, 1578), 90; Boldo, *Libro della natura*, 265. Jordan, *Renaissance Feminism*, 157, classifies Trotto as a "feminist," but apparently his feminism did not extend to permitting women to initiate sexual foreplay.

36. Hull, *Women according to Men*, 96–97, takes a far darker view than I do of the consequences for women of the assertion that a woman is more likely to conceive if she experiences orgasm, a notion found in many advice manuals. She cites Jane Sharp, a female writer who, in her 1671 midwifery book, "repeated the same misconceptions about orgasmic conception that male writers were promoting." The male writer she highlights is Nicholas Culpeper, whose 1675 book made the startling assertion that "there never comes conception upon rape," from which Hull immediately reaches the following conclusion: "For the woman, pregnant from a rape, the law was no protection. Confused, bewildered, fearful of public humiliation, such a woman would fail to bring charges. Not surprisingly, few rape cases were recorded in the sixteenth and seventeenth centuries." Blaming the victim for rape clearly has a long history. However, Culpeper, like all the Italian writers I know, elsewhere held only that orgasm made conception more likely, not that it was a requirement, a distinction Hull is fully aware of. She sees

the same words I do—"The greater the woman's desire of copulation is, the more subject to conceive she is"—and concludes that "the belief in orgasmic conception became one of the most devastating and confusing misconceptions for many unfortunate women." My understanding, equally beyond proof or refutation, is that advice manuals told fathers who wished to conceive a son to become tender, caring lovers with their wives. Perhaps some female readers were emboldened enough to ask their husbands sweetly for improved performance! Cadden, *Meanings of Sex Difference*, 93–104, thoroughly explores medieval treatises on sexual pleasure and conception.

37. Savonarola, *Ad mulieres ferrarienses*, 41–43; Palmieri, *Della vita civile*, 17.

38. See my "Telling Her Sins: Male Confessors and Female Penitents in Catholic Reformation Italy," in Lynda L. Coon, Katherine J. Haldane, and Elisabeth W. Sommer, eds., *That Gentle Strength: Historical Perspectives on Women in Christianity* (Charlottesville, 1990), 118–33.

39. Cherubino da Siena, *Regole*, v–xxii, for the publication history. For biographical data, see Roberto Rusconi's entry on Cherubino da Spoleto in *Dizionario biografico degli Italiani*, vol. 24 (Rome, 1980), 446–53. Also see the appraisal by Anne Jacobson Schutte in "Printing, Piety, and the People in Italy: The First Thirty Years," *Archiv für Reformationsgeschichte* 71 (1980): 13–15, which concludes that on sexual behavior between married couples Brother Cherubino could "find extenuating circumstances to excuse almost any transgression." For a recent treatment, see Margaret L. King, *Women of the Renaissance* (Chicago, 1992), 40–41. In my judgment, King inverts the meaning and context of Cherubino's advice by seeing it as restricting a wife's sexual expression when in fact Cherubino consistently assumed, rightly or wrongly, it was husbands who sought payments of the conjugal debt and wives who wished to refuse.

On fifteenth-century editions, see Maria Doglio, ed., *Galeazzo Flavio Capra. Della eccellenza e dignità delle donne* (Rome, 1988), 115. The folksy, down-to-earth, forgiving quality of Brother Cherubino's book may well account in large part for its success in early print culture. At least that is my editorial judgment when I compare it with the turgid prose of more respected works (never published in the sixteenth century) addressed to women, such as St. Antoninus of Florence's *Opera a ben vivere*. Although written in the vernacular, this advice became available only in the nineteenth century in Francesco Palermo, ed., *Opera a ben vivere di Santo Antonino, Arcivescovo di Firenze* (Florence, 1858).

40. Cherubino da Siena, *Regole*, 7–25.

41. For a thorough analysis of the variety of Catholic teaching on "sex and the married penitent," see Thomas Tentler, *Sin and Confession on the Eve of the Reformation* (Princeton, 1977), 186–232. For more recent scholarship on the pre-Reformation confessional, see Pierre J. Payer, "Confession and the Study of Sex in the Middle Ages," in James A. Brundage and Vern L. Bullough, eds., *Handbook of Medieval Sexuality* (New York, 1996), 3–31. This essay builds upon Payer's two authoritative earlier works, *Sex and the Penitentials: The Development of a Sexual Code 550–1150* (Toronto, 1984), and *The Bridling of Desire: Views of Sex in the Later Middle Ages* (Toronto, 1993). For an insightful assessment of the increasing use of the confessional in post-Tridentine Catholicism, and especially

on the feminization of confession, see Stephen Haliczer, *Sexuality in the Confessional: A Sacrament Profaned* (New York, 1996), 7–41, esp. 34–35. Also see Jean-Louis Flandrin, *Sex in the Western World: The Development of Attitudes and Behaviour,* trans. Sue Collins (Chur, 1991), 117–28, although care must be taken when the author's anticlerical outrage exceeds his scholarly caution, for example, in the unqualified assertion on page 184 that a wife could not use menstruation as a reason to refuse payment of the conjugal debt; the issue was much more complex and in fact theologians came to differing conclusions. Tentler mentions some vernacular tracts from Germany, France, and England but omits the Italian scene, and in any event is more concerned with differences of approach among serious thinkers who wrote for each other in Latin than with how theological disputes reached actual married penitents through the medium of print. He recognizes clearly, however (184–85), that as the clerical message widened its focus to include the laity, it tended to become must less insistent about careful examination of conscience and motivations for initiating sexual intercourse. For a thorough treatment of the Italian scene, see Pino Trombetta, *La confessione della lussuria: Definizione e controllo del piacere nel cattolicesimo* (Genoa, 1991).

42. Cherubino da Siena, *Regole,* 50.

43. Cherubino da Siena, *Regole,* 60.

44. Cherubino da Siena, *Regole,* 80–88. I shall not consider Bernardino da Siena directly since his sermons did not find a publisher in sixteenth-century Italy, although he did have an influence through popular writers like Cherubino da Siena. See Roberto Rusconi, "St. Bernardino of Siena, the Wife, and Possessions," in Daniel Bornstein and Roberto Rusconi, eds., *Women and Religion in Medieval and Renaissance Italy,* trans. Margery Schneider (Chicago, 1996), 182–96.

45. On St. Bonaventure, see Emma Thérèsa Healy, *Women according to Saint Bonaventure* (New York, 1955). On St. Thomas Aquinas, see Kari Elisabeth Børrensen, *Natura e ruolo della donna in Agostino e Tommaso d'Aquino,* trans. Liliana Lanzarini (Città di Castello, 1979).

46. Cherubino da Siena, *Regole,* 92–97. For a lively survey of "situational" sin, see G. R. Quaife, *Wanton Wenches and Wayward Wives: Peasants and Illicit Sex in Early Seventeenth Century England* (New Brunswick, 1979), 165–85. The standard authority on all this is Albert the Great, to whose views Cherubino adds nothing, but the way in which he expresses the accepted admonitions so that laypersons can understand and obey is just wonderful. On Albert the Great, see Tentler, *Sin and Confession,* 189–90.

47. Cherubino da Siena, *Regole,* 98ff.

48. Actually, the citation by Mercurio is wrong. Where Augustine does write about Jacob's sheep raising, it is only to say that he caused sheep of different colors to be born, not how he did it. Still, the actual account in Genesis 30:37–39 says that Jacob was able to produce striped, speckled, and spotted flocks by setting peeled rods of poplar, almond, and plane in front of the drinking water where the animals bred, thereby presumably altering their states of mind.

49. Mercurio, *La commare,* bk. 1, chap. 12 (Biagi et al., 92–95).

50. Gioberti, *Errori popolari*, 82; Anonymous, *Thesoro di secreti naturali. Raccolti per fedel honostij* (Genoa and Florence, n.d., ca. 1600), no pagination, BNF shelf mark Palat. (14) X.4.1.67; Marinello, *Delle medicine*, 57–60. See Eamon, *Science and the Secrets of Nature*, 239–59, for a general discussion of these anonymous books of secrets. On Galenic tests for fertility and a variety of elaborations, see Thomas Rogers Forbes, *The Midwife and the Witch* (New Haven, 1966), 37–38.

51. Charles Estienne, *L'agricoltura et casa di villa Carlo Stefano, gentil'huomo francese, nuovamente tradotta dal Cavaliere Hercole Cato* (Venice: Aldo Manuzio, 1581), 378, for the chickpeas. Among his major works are an important anatomical study, *De dissectione partium corporis humani* (Paris, 1545), and a thousand-page classical dictionary/encyclopedia, *Dictionarium historicum, geographicum, poeticum,* that went through twenty revisions and editions (all in Latin) from its original publication in 1553, to the last revised edition in 1693. The most readily available version of the *Dictionarium* is a New York, 1976 reprint of the Paris, 1596 edition.

52. Estienne, *L'agricoltura*, 137, 299.

53. Eamon, *Science and the Secrets of Nature*, 168–93, brings this great "professor of secrets" to English language readers. Also see pages 249–50, for Fioravanti's full awareness of the power of print in undermining classic medical authority. In Italian, see Domenico Furfaro, *La vita e l'opera di Leonardo Fioravanti* (Bologna, 1963). Ample selections and summaries from Fioravanti's texts are provided, and herein I cite Furfaro's page numbers for easy reference, as well as the original chapter locations for readers who have access to them. The cure is taken from *La cirugia* (Venice: Gli heredi di Melchiorre Sessa, 1570), bk. 3, chap. 57 (Furfaro, 75–76). The case against anatomy is from the preface to book 2 of the same work (Furfaro, 57). The praise of chickens' lifestyle is from *Il tesoro della vita humana* (Venice: Gli heredi di Melchiorre Sessa, 1570), bk. 4, chap. 78 (Furfaro, 131). See *Capricci medicinali* (Venice: Lodovico Avanzi, 1568), bk. 1, chap. 51 (Furfaro, 152), for the resuscitation claims. An earlier and harsher assessment of Fioravanti may be found in Andrea Corsini, *Medici ciarlatani e ciarlatani medici* (Bologna, 1922), 77–81.

54. Isabella Cortese, *I secreti della signora Isabella Cortese ne' quali si contengono cose minerali, medecinali, arteficiose, e alchimiche. Et molte de l'arte profumatoria, appartenenti a ogni gran signora. Con altri bellissimi secreti aggiunti* (Venice: Giacomo Cornetti, 1584), 89, for the erection remedy, 124–25, for the toothpaste, and 197, for the skin cream. The biographical information and the commandments come from the opening of book 2. A 1995 Milan reprint makes this rare work readily available. Also see Eamon, *Science and the Secrets of Nature*, 137, 194.

55. A thorough modern assessment of Dioscorides is in John M. Riddle, *Dioscorides on Pharmacy and Medicine* (Austin, 1985). Briefly, Dioscorides gathered his remedies while spending some forty years observing plant life, and it is likely that he had access to Egyptian medical literature which, drawing as it did from millennia of funerary science, was far more advanced than anything known in Europe. His influence on Galen and on generations of Arab scientists was enormous, and his reputation increased over time. In fact, one of the early books

published by Aldus Manutius, who may be remembered as the Venetian printer I used partially as a yardstick for estimating book prices, was a 1499 Greek edition of Dioscorides.

The Mattioli edition I used is *De i discorsi di M. Pietro Andrea Matthioli sanese, medico cesareo et del Serenissimo Principe Ferdinando Arciduca D'Austria etc. Nelli sei libri di Pedacio Dioscoride anazarbeo, della materia medicinale parte prima. La quale contiene il primo & secondo libro. Dal proprio autore innanzi la sua morte ricorretta, ampliata, & all' ultima perfettione ridotta. Con le figure grandi, tirate dalle naturali & vive piante, & animali, & in numero molto maggiore, che le altre per avanti stampate. Con due tavole copiosissime spettanti l'una à ciò, che in tutta l'opera si contiene: e l'altra alla cura di tutte le infirmità del corpo humano* (Venice: Felice Valgrisi, 1585). It runs to 1,527 numbered pages plus over 100 pages of introductory materials and indexes, as well as an appendix. Vernacular editions appeared as early as 1544.

56. On books of herbs and the extraordinary popularity they enjoyed, see the introduction by Erminio Caprotti to Apuleius Barbarus, *Herbarium Apulei 1481; Herbolario volgare 1522* (Milan, 1979), xlix–liv. For a modern introductory dictionary on herbals, see George Hocking, *A Dictionary of Terms in Pharmacognosy and Other Divisions of Economic Botany* (Springfield, 1955). Especially useful on toxicity questions is James A. Duke, *CRC Handbook of Medicinal Herbs* (Boca Raton, 1985). Also see Margaret B. Freeman, *Herbs for the Mediaeval Household for Cooking, Healing, and Divers Uses* (New York, 1943), 17–32; William R. Thomson, *Herbs That Heal* (New York, 1976); and Rosetta E. Clarkson, *Herbs: Their Culture and Uses* (New York, 1942), 123–99.

On the printing history of Mattioli's edition of Dioscorides, see John Riddle, *Contraception and Abortion from the Ancient World to the Renaissance* (Cambridge, 1992), 149. More generally on the printing of books of herbals, see Karen Reeds, *Botany in Medieval and Renaissance Universities* (New York, 1991), especially the annexed essay titled "Publishing Scholarly Books in the Sixteenth Century." On Mattioli and pharmacology, see Richard Palmer, "Pharmacy in the Republic of Venice in the Sixteenth Century," in A. Wear et al., eds., *The Medical Renaissance of the Sixteenth Century,* 100–17; also see Palmer's "Medical Botany in Northern Italy in the Renaissance," *Journal of the Royal Society of Medicine* 78 (February 1985): 149–57; also see Frank J. Anderson, *An Illustrated History of the Herbals* (New York, 1977), 163–72. Still of general interest is the classic work by Agnes Arber, *Herbals, Their Origin and Evolution: A Chapter in the History of Botany 1470–1679* (Cambridge, 1953, rpt. of 1938 rev. of 1912 ed.), 92–103, for the Italian scene.

57. Mattioli, *Discorsi,* section on *Membra virili;* Estienne, *L'agricoltura,* 193, 244–45, 251, on reducing sexual desire; Marinello, *Delle medicine,* 17–20, on combating nocturnal emissions by taking icy baths or sitting on a cold rock.

58. Castore Durante, *Herbario nuovo di Castore Durante, medico e cittadino rómano* (Rome: Bartolomeo Bonfadini & Tito Diani, 1585). For biographical and bibliographic information, see Durante, *Il tesoro della sanità,* which also provides a modern edition of this work (Venice: Andrea Muschio, 1586). Anderson, *An Illustrated History of the Herbals,* 187–92, notes Durante's adherence to the rather

dated alphabetical format of Mattioli but fails to credit Durante with an efficient indexing system. In my judgment, it was the functional indexing, identifying which diseases are cured by what herbs, that kept the *Herbario nuovo* in print with many editions over the next 130 years.

59. Durante, *Herbario,* 68, on betel, and 450, for the negative opinion on truffles. However, the same author in *Il tesoro,* 97–98, says that truffles do excite the appetites of Venus and multiply sperm production, so one should not expect consistency in these recommendations. Just as an aside, readers willing to pay ten times as much for a white truffle may be amused to know that according to Durante, black truffles, which he considers "male," are better than the "female" white truffles.

60. Durante, *Herbario,* 32, 51, 62, 100, 154, 155, 179, 196, 198, 202, 212, 252, 261, 285, 338, 361, 400, 415, for things that produce sperm and aid coition; 68, 86, 245, for herbs that inhibit sperm production; and 289, for retarding ejaculation.

61. Christoforo Acosta, *Trattato di Christoforo Acosta africano medico, & chirurgo della historia, natura, et virtu delle droghe medicinali, e altri semplici rarissimi, che vengono portati dalle Indie Orientali in Europa. Nuovamente recato dalla spagnuola nella nostra lingua* (Venice: Francesco Ziletti, 1585), 316–18. The original was published at Burgos in 1578, as *Tractado de las drogas y medicinas de la Indias Orientales.*

62. Marinello, *Delle medicine,* 20–21.

63. Savonarola, *Ad mulieres ferrarienses,* 9, 11, agrees, adding the wisdom from Aristotle that snakes curl up before coition in order to keep their sperm warm on its long journey.

64. Marinello, *Delle medicine,* 51–54, 62–70; he draws heavily from Savonarola.

65. Marinello, *Delle medicine,* 22.

66. Marinello, *Delle medicine,* 23.

67. Marinello, *Delle medicine,* 23, on bathing; 25, on ogling young women; and 35, on the grub rub. On the use of love potions sufficiently illicit or scandalous to attract the attention of church authorities in Marinello's city of Venice, see Guido Ruggiero, *Binding Passions: Tales of Magic, Marriage, and Power at the End of the Renaissance* (New York, 1993), 88–129.

68. Girolamo Menghi da Viadana, Minore Osservante, *Compendio dell'arte essorcistica et possibilita delle mirabile, et stupende operationi delli demoni et de' malefici. Con li rimedii opportuni alle infermità corporali* (Macerata: Sebastiano Martellini, 1580), 297–300, on devout female exorcists. Just as a passing irony, readers may enjoy knowing that this publisher specialized in popular little editions of jokes and riddles, according to Ascarelli and Menato, *La tipografia del '500 in Italia,* 205. The earliest edition is Bologna, 1576; editions from 1582 onward are greatly expanded and feature the marginal content summaries typical of popular advice manuals. Burke, *The Historical Anthropology of Early Modern Italy,* 212, asserts that "only the clergy could exorcise," a theoretical prohibition I believe Menghi's readers violated freely, nor do I agree with Burke's assessment that Menghi was purposefully vague on "how to do it" (258, note 11). Mary R. O'Neil, "*Sacerdote*

ovvero strione: Ecclesiastical and Superstitious Remedies in Sixteenth-Century Italy," in Kaplan, ed., *Understanding Popular Culture,* 54–55, recognizes that Menghi aimed to reach several different audiences, ranging from "elevated intellects" to people who resorted to unauthorized practitioners of the magical arts. For her fuller assessment, see Mary R. O'Neil, "Discerning Superstition: Popular Errors and Orthodox Response in Late Sixteenth-Century Italy," PhD dissertation (Stanford University, 1981), esp. 304–77, for which reference I thank Jeffrey Chajes. For biographical material on Menghi, see A. Vacant and E. Mangenot, eds., *Dictionnaire de Théologie Catholique,* vol. 10, part 1 (Paris, 1928), 550–51, but note that some of the bibliographic details given therein are incorrect. On exorcism more generally, see Lyndal Roper, *Oedipus and the Devil: Witchcraft, Sexuality, and Religion in Early Modern Europe* (London, 1994), esp. 188–92, on exorcism and sexual dysfunctions in men, and the magisterial Stuart Clark, *Thinking with Demons: The Idea of Witchcraft in Early Modern Europe* (Oxford, 1997).

69. Menghi, *Compendio,* 121–26.

70. Menghi, *Compendio,* 263–67.

71. Marinello, *Delle medicine,* 4; Mercurio, *La commare,* bk. 2, chap. 25 (Biagi, et al., 109–10).

72. Lodovico Dolce, *Dialogo piacevole di Messer Lodovico Dolce. Nel quale Messer Pietro Aretino parla in difesa d'i male aventurati mariti* ([Venice]: Curzio Troiano Navò, 1542), 19 octavo leaves. Unlike Boccaccio's *Decameron* stories, this work is very hostile to women, who are characterized as being by nature unfaithful and covetous.

73. Gioberti, *Errori popolari,* 75–79. De Rocher's translation, *Popular Errors* (299, note), examines just what Joubert originally meant by *"un quarton de son,"* but for our purposes it is sufficient to note that he clearly meant an amount easy to lift.

74. Prospero Borgarucci, *Della contemplatione anatomica, sopra tutte le parti del corpo humano, libri cinque. Composti in lingua italiana dall' eccellente medico Prospero Borgarucci. Ne' quali ciascuno potrà facilmente apprendere l'ordine, et il vero modo di far l'anatomia. Et di conoscere tutte l'infermità, che ne' nostri corpi per diversi accidenti possono avvenire. Co' nomi di ciascuna parte dichiarati, per commune utile, in dodici linguaggi. Con molte altre cose, da altri anatomici, per avanti non più trattate* (Venice: Vincenzo Valgrisi, 1564). The quotation on conscious diffusion of knowledge is from Luigi Firpo's article on the Borgaruccis in *Dizionario biografico degli Italiani,* vol. 12: 566. Katharine Park, *Doctors and Medicine in Early Renaissance Florence* (Princeton, 1985), 193–94, notes that even before the printing press, books in merchants' libraries were mostly in Italian, whereas physicians collected Latin medical texts almost exclusively. Felice La Torre, *L'utero attraverso i secoli,* 279, comments that Borgarucci, even though he conducted anatomical research, did so without perspicacity and that he wrote in an infantile manner, describing trivial things in great detail and not dealing with truly consequential matters. All quite true I think, and very telling for assessing how Borgarucci thought laypersons should be informed about their anatomies.

75. Borgarucci, *Della contemplatione anatomica,* 120–26.

76. Giuseppe Liceti, *Il Ceva, overo dell' eccellenza, et uso de' genitali. Dialogo di Gioseppe Liceti, medico chirugo genovese. Nel quale si tratta dell' essenza, & generatione del seme humano; delle somiglianze dell' huomo, e lor cagioni; della differenza del sesso; della generatione de' mostri, e d'altre cose non meno utili; che dilettevoli* (Bologna: Giovanni Rossi [per] Simon Parlasca, 1598). The earlier work is his *La nobiltà de' principali membri dell' huomo. Dialogo . . . cavato da Aristotele, Platone, e Galeno . . .* (Bologna: Giovanni Rossi [per] Paolo Meietto, 1590).

77. See Jean Delumeau and Daniel Roche, *Histoire des pères et de la paternité* (Paris, 1990), 71–89, for evidence that male impotence increasingly became a subject of ridicule in the seventeenth century.

78. Gioberti, *Errori popolari*, 73, on tenderness after lovemaking, and 84, on "chaos."

79. Gioberti, *Errori popolari*, 82; the original wording is *"che si dicano calde come cagne,"* so I believe I have not resorted to excessive rhetorical flourish in this translation. Certainly de Rocher's translation in *Popular Errors*, 122, shows that the original French was even more offensive than the Tuscan version.

80. Ortensio Lando, *Paradossi cioe sentencie fuori del comun parere, novellamente venute in luce. Opra non men dotta che piacevole, e in due parti separata* (Venice: [Bernardino Bindoni?], 1544), 32–37.

81. Savonarola, *Ad mulieres ferrarienses*, 44–45.

82. Marinello, *Delle medicine*, 55–85. On fumigation tests for fertility, see Forbes, *The Midwife and the Witch*, 43–45.

83. Borgarucci, *Della contemplatione anatomica*, 127–32. For further commentary on this especially misogynous point, see Biagi et al. ed., *Medicina per le donne*, 28, who take it indirectly from Borgarucci through Felice La Torre, *L'utero attraverso i secoli*, 275. The "hidden" genitalia argument found in Borgarucci and others is a variant of the pro-woman stance taken by Agrippa in praising the "marvelous decency" of women whose sexual parts are "concealed in a secret and secure place"; see Agrippa, *On the Nobility and Preeminence of the Female Sex*, 54.

84. Giovanni Valverde, *Anatomia del corpo umano* (Rome: Antonio Salamanca & Antoine Lafréry, 1560), 91. This book of 154 folio-sized, illustrated pages clearly was more of a medical text than an advice manual, and its influence was through physicians rather than directly to the reading public. It is a translation by Antonio Tabo, made under the author's personal supervision, of his *Historia de la composicion del cuerpo humano* which had appeared in 1556. Italian translations also appeared in 1558 and 1559, followed by several Latin translations. The work plagiarizes most of the illustrations and much of the text of the 1543 classic by Andreas Vesalius, *De humani corporis fabrica*. Both Borgarucci and Valverde are included in the sweeping survey of Julia O'Faolain and Lauro Martines, *Not in God's Image* (London, 1973), 121–22.

85. Gabriele Falloppio, *Secreti diversi e miracolosi . . . raccolti dal Falloppia e approbati da altri medici di gran fama* (Venice: Vincenzo Valgrisi, 1570), 1–149, on ointments; 150–212, on waters and wines; and 213–366, on alchemy. Eamon, *Science and the Secrets of Nature*, 166–67, suggests that Fioravanti may have been the author of a preceding work with a similar title published in 1563. I have

not had an opportunity to examine the 1563 work, but if the two are essentially the same, then our Agato was both a ghostwriter and a plagiarist, not at all unlikely.

86. Anonymous, *Secreti naturali et medicinali per il rimedio di molte infermità. De i quali lo autore ne ha fatto più volte experienze. Nuovamente pale fati à benefizio del corpo humano. Dal M.R.* (Florence, n.d., ca. 1600), BNF shelf mark Palat. (14) X.4.1.67.

87. Estienne, *L'agricoltura,* 70, 157, 178, 190.

88. Mattioli, *Discorsi,* section on the *Matrice.* Renaissance people who preferred a more explanatory approach than Mattioli's listings could have consulted Marinello, *Delle medicine,* 123–234, for more than a hundred leaves on uterine disturbances.

89. Marinello, *Delle medicine,* 97, 113. See John M. Riddle, "Oral Contraceptives and Early-Term Abortifacients during Classical Antiquity and the Middle Ages," *Past and Present* 132 (1991): 3–32, for a pharmacological assessment showing the efficacy in terminating pregnancy of medicinals made from plants such as ferule, pomegranate, juniper, rue, pennyroyal, and wild carrot, all of which appear prominently in popular-advice manuals on herbals. The full story is told in Riddle's *Contraception and Abortion,* 144–57, for the Renaissance period. Also see Wolfgang Jöchle, "Menses-Inducing Drugs: Their Role in Antique, Medieval, and Renaissance Gynecology and Birth Control," *Contraception* 10 (October 1974): 425–39.

90. Ida Magli, *Gesù di Nazaret: Tabù e trasgressione* (Milan, 1982), 87–91.

91. Camporesi, *Juice of Life,* 111–21, provides interesting background on traditions concerning the powers of menstrual blood and includes the quotation from Innocent III. Popular menstrual taboos also are treated in Jacques Gélis, *History of Childbirth: Fertility, Pregnancy, and Birth in Early Modern Europe,* trans. Rosemary Morris (Boston, 1991), 13–14. I highly recommend this book for its treatment from an anthropological perspective of a wide range of childbirth issues.

92. Agrippa, *On the Nobility and Preeminence of the Female Sex,* 59.

93. Savonarola, *Ad mulieres ferrarienses,* 9; Marinello, *Delle medicine,* 97.

94. Marinello, *Delle medicine,* 56, 67; Savonarola, *Ad mulieres ferrarienses,* 24. See Ottavia Niccoli, "'Menstruum quasi monstruum': Parti mostrousi e tabù menstruali nel '500," *Quaderni Storici* 44 (1980): 402–28, available in English translation by Mary M. Gallucci in Edward Muir and Guido Ruggiero, eds., *Sex and Gender in Historical Perspective* (Baltimore, 1990), 1–25. On male menstruation, see Gianna Pomata, "Uomini mestruanti: Somiglianza e differenza fra i sessi in Europa in età moderna," *Quaderni Storici* (1992): 51–103.

95. Mercurio, *La commare,* bk. 1, chap. 16, 72–76.

96. Mattioli, *Discorsi,* 1,489, in either the 1568 edition (published when Mattioli was still alive) or the posthumous 1585 edition.

97. Marinello, *Delle medicine,* 3, 96.

98. Fioravanti, *La cirugia,* bk. 3, chap. 67 (Furfaro, 77); Estienne, *L'agricoltura,* 130, 144, 151, 158, 165, 173, 175, 206, 320, 321.

99. Marinello, *Delle medicine,* 97–99.

100. Marinello, *Delle medicine,* 99, 107–8, 122.

101. Palmieri, *Della vita civile*, 17.

102. Savonarola, *Ad mulieres ferrarienses*, 47–49.

103. Savonarola, *Ad mulieres ferrarienses*, 50–52; Gioberti, *Errori popolari*, 108–12.

104. Mercurio, *La commare*, bk. 1, chap. 10, 55.

105. Marinello, *Delle medicine*, 241–42.

106. Marinello, *Delle medicine*, 53.

Chapter Three

1. Marinello, *Delle medicine*, 241.

2. Marinello, *Delle medicine*, 235–40; Savonarola, *Ad mulieres ferrarienses*, 61.

3. Lorenzo Cantini, *Legislazione toscana*, vol. 2 (Florence, 1800), 171, for the legislation. On infanticide, see Richard C. Trexler, "Infanticide in Florence: New Sources and First Results," *History of Childhood Quarterly* 1 (summer 1973): 98–116.

4. Anonymous, *Thesoro di secreti naturali*, no pagination; Anonymous, *Segreti bellissimi non piu dati in luce. Ritrovati da me Carlo detto Il Franzolino* (Viterbo: Girolamo Discepolo, 1603), no pagination; Savonarola, *Ad mulieres ferrarienses*, 59–60. According to Forbes, *The Midwife and the Witch*, 38, the aristolochia and honey test appears in the authoritative printed Latin medical text by Antonio Guainerio, *De egritudinibus matricis* (1500).

5. Palmieri, *Della vita civile*, 17.

6. Gioberti, *Errori popolari*, 113–15. See Forbes, *The Midwife and the Witch*, 54–58.

7. Marinello, *Delle medicine*, 243–45. The baking test is reported in a seventeenth-century-Irish manuscript as well; see Patrick Logan, *Irish Country Cures* (New York, 1994, rpt. of 1981 ed.), 12–13, for which reference I thank Mary DeMeo.

8. Mercurio, *La commare*, bk. 1, chaps. 9–11, 46–58. Mercurio speculates that the mother's imagination may cause her child to be male or female, and he further allows that the Galenic two-seed theory that he thinks may be correct also must somehow affect the child's sex, but he admits to some uncertainty about how these factors might relate to each another.

9. Jacopo Berengario, *Carpi commentaria cum amplissimis additionibus super Anatomia Mundini* (Bologna, 1521); see also the readily available L. R. Lind, ed. and trans., *Jacopo Berengario da Carpi, A Short Introduction to Anatomy* (Chicago, 1959), 3–29, for biographical and bibliographical information, and 76–83, for Carpi's treatment of the uterus, including the illustration shown here, in *Isagogae breves* (1523 and 1525). The illustration is included in Harold Speert, *Iconographia Gyniatrica: A Pictorial History of Gynecology and Obstetrics* (Philadelphia, 1973), 11, along with the reference to Berengario's "*Tamen est purum mendatium dicere quod matrix habeat septem cellulas*" dismissal of prior scholarship. In addition, see Felice La Torre, *L'utero attraverso i secoli*, 199, which also discusses Mondino dei Luzzi (165–75). An Italian version of Mondino dei Luzzi's *Anatomia* first appeared in 1494, and may be found in a modern edition by Luigi

Firpo, *Medicina medievale* (Turin, 1972). More recently, on Berengario, see R. K. French, "Berengario da Carpi and the Use of Commentary in Anatomical Teaching," in Wear et al., *The Medical Renaissance of the Sixteenth Century*, 42–74. Also see Nancy Siraisi, *Medieval and Early Renaissance Medicine: An Introduction to Knowledge and Practice* (Chicago, 1990), 95–96. Laqueur, *Making Sex*, 79, includes this illustration but I think misses its original point, which was not primarily the inversion of male genitalia in the female but rather that the uterus was unified and did not have seven compartments; otherwise, stomping on the medical books makes no sense.

10. Marinello, *Delle medicine*, 249–50. Also see Gioberti, *Errori popolari*, 88–98, for a long discourse with exotic examples to show that women can carry up to nine children at once. Mercurio, *La commare*, bk. 1, chap. 14 (Biagi et al., 97–101), cites up to 366 children in one birth for Countess Margaret of Ireland, and several other exaggerated reports, starting with those given in Aristotle. The way Mercurio treats these reports leads me to believe that he does not trust them entirely.

11. Gioberti, *Errori popolari*, 99–107.

12. Mercurio, *La commare*, bk. 1, chaps. 7–8, 36–45.

13. Mercurio, *La commare*, bk. 1, chap. 6 (Biagi et al., 91).

14. Anonymous, *Thesoro di secreti naturali*. On classical writers who recommended lapidary amulets to prevent miscarriage or ease childbirth, see Forbes, *The Midwife and the Witch*, 64–79.

15. Marinello, *Delle medicine*, 259–66.

16. Savonarola, *Ad mulieres ferrarienses*, 82–87.

17. Mercurio, *La commare*, bk. 2, chap. 20 (Biagi et al., 34–35); also see bk. 1, chap. 19, 85–87. Mercurio again takes up the crusade against physicians who assist in abortions and in particular associates Jewish physicians with this practice in his *De gli errori popolari d'Italia*, 134–42, 159–62. In this work, he also rails against physicians who prescribe sexual intercourse and masturbation as medical cures for overcoming an imbalance of bodily humors due to sperm retention (579–82).

18. Savonarola, *Ad mulieres ferrarienses*, 62.

19. Savonarola, *Ad mulieres ferrarienses*, 125; Marinello, *Delle medicine*, 285–89.

20. Mercurio, *La commare*, bk. 2, chap. 27 (Biagi et al., 113–16).

21. Mercurio, *La commare*, bk. 2, chaps. 28–29 (Biagi et al., 116–24). Readers who wish to know more about this subject will find an outstanding scholarly treatment enhanced with illustrations in Renate Blumenfeld-Kosinski's *Not of Woman Born: Representations of Caesarean Birth in Medieval and Renaissance Culture* (Ithaca, 1990).

22. Gioberti, *Errori popolari*, 115–31.

23. Savonarola, *Ad mulieres ferrarienses*, 88–108.

24. Savonarola, *Ad mulieres ferrarienses*, 66–81, 118–19.

25. Marinello, *Delle medicine*, 250–58.

26. Girolamo Mercurio, *De gli errori popolari d'Italia* (Verona: Francesco Rossi, 1645), is the edition I used. To the best of my knowledge, this is the first reprint

of the 1603 original, so clearly it did not have the success of *La commare*. Another reprint followed in 1648, but again to the best of my knowledge, the work was not translated into other languages.

27. Mercurio, *La commare*, bk. 2, chap. 26 (Biagi et al., 110–12).

28. Mercurio, *La commare*, bk. 1, chaps. 2–3 (Biagi et al., 69–85). Among Aranzi's own publications, *De humano foetu libellus* (Bologna: Joannis Rubrii, 1564), went through several editions.

29. Biagi et al., *Medicine per le donne*, 25.

30. Biagi et al., *Medicine per le donne*, 23.

31. Gioberti, *Errori popolari*, 137. Notwithstanding his very influential work *La commare*, which was meant to educate midwives to do their job, Mercurio, *De gli errori popolari d'Italia*, 373–75, shares Gioberti's negative opinions about midwives. The disparagement with which physicians in western Europe looked upon midwifery, at least until men fully took over this profession in the eighteenth century, is shown convincingly in Jean Donnison, *Midwives and Medical Men: A History of Inter-Professional Rivalries and Women's Rights* (New York, 1977), 1–21. For popular attitudes toward the midwife, see Gélis, *History of Childbirth*, 103–11. Also see Merry E. Wiesner, "Early Modern Midwifery: A Case Study," in Barbara A. Hanawalt, ed., *Women and Work in Preindustrial Europe* (Bloomington, 1986), 94–113, and all the essays in Hilary Marland, ed., *The Art of Midwifery: Early Modern Midwives in Europe* (London, 1993); see also Forbes, *The Midwife and the Witch*.

32. Mercurio, *La commare*, bk. 2, chap. 18 (Biagi et al., 100–1). Donnison, *Midwives and Medical Men*, 7–8, concedes that printed books may have assisted midwives with advice but believes this would have been more likely in the city than in the countryside. Yet even the 1545 preface of a translation of Rösslin that she quotes claims that gentlewomen carried the book with them and read it, presumably to less literate and certainly less wealthy midwives, a means of dissemination applicable in rural areas no less than in cities.

33. During stays in four Italian villages while doing research for my *Fate and Honor, Family and Village* (Chicago, 1979), as well as during many summers spent in the Istrian village of Skvaranska, I witnessed firsthand as the local midwife lost her role in assisting at childbirth, since everyone now gives birth in the local hospital, but continued to practice as nurse and medical consultant of first resort, and in several places was the person called in to wash and dress the corpses of villagers who died at home. The midwife's role in preparation for burial is also attested to in John Henderson, *Piety and Charity in Late Medieval Florence* (Oxford, 1994), 158–59. On this side of the Atlantic, Laurel Ulrich's wonderful *A Midwife's Tale: The Life of Martha Ballard, based on her Diary, 1785–1812* (New York, 1991), recounts an equally wide variety of medical and social activities for the midwife. For present day functions of midwives, see Yvonne Lefèber, *Midwives Without Training: Practices and Beliefs of Traditional Birth Attendants in Africa, Asia, and Latin America* (Assen, 1994).

34. Mercurio, *La commare*, bk. 2, chap. 18 (Biagi et al., 100–105).

35. Mercurio, *De gli errori popolari d'Italia*, 390. On magical uses of the caul, see Forbes, *The Midwife and the Witch*, 94–111.

36. For an excellent introduction to the Latin medical literature, see Siraisi, *Medieval and Early Renaissance Medicine*, esp. 104–14, on the subject of procreation. Beryl Rowland, ed., *Medieval Woman's Guide to Health: The First English Gynecological Handbook* (Kent, 1981), provides both an easy-to-read modern edition of Trotula and an excellent general introduction to early vernacular works on gynecology. Trotula's *De mulierum possionibus ante in et post partum* was published in Venice as early as 1547, but I know of no sixteenth-century Italian translation.

37. The Spanish work is Damián Carbón, *Libro del arte de las comadres o madrinas, del regimiento de las preñadas y paridas, y de los niños* (Mallorca: Hernando de Cansoles, 1541), cited in Teresa Ortiz, "From Hegemony to Subordination: Midwives in Early Modern Spain," in Marland, ed., *The Art of Midwifery*, 95–114. It is readily available in a 1995 reprint from the Universidad de Alicante.

38. Figure 3.5 is an adaptation by Mercurio of the well-known and much-discussed drawing of the uterus in Vesalius, *De humani corporis fabrica* (1543). The story goes that Vesalius obtained the corpse from which it was extracted when a local monk's mistress died and he and his pupils snatched the body from its tomb. But the monk and the girl's parents complained of the outrage to the city magistrates; to hide their crime, the Vesalius group skinned the body to make it unrecognizable and carved out in very hasty fashion the female genitalia they most wished to study. What you see is what they thought they saw, *pace* Sigmund Freud. For further information, see J. B. de C. M. Saunders and Charles D. O'Malley, *The Illustrations from the Works of Andreas Vesalius of Brussels* (Cleveland, 1950). Also see Laqueur, *Making Sex*, 70–93.

39. Mercurio, *La commare*, bk. 1, chap. 2 (Biagi et al., 69–80).

40. The vituperative quality of Mercurio's attack on Rösslin is rather uncharitable considering how much the friar copied wholesale from Rösslin. Compare the treatment in Ozment, *When Fathers Ruled*, 101–21, with what I am presenting here. Rösslin himself also copied without acknowledgment from earlier writers, probably from Avicenna and Soranus and possibly from the Italian Michele Savonarola as well, again clearly evident in a comparison of Ozment's renderings of sources on childbearing and child rearing with mine in the following chapters. Coler's *Haussbuch*, also heavily cited by Ozment, was published only in 1604, years after every popular tract I discuss had been published, often in several languages, so one can assume Coler's familiarity with at least some of these works as well. The point here is not that one or another author was a plagiarist, since such a concept of intellectual property did not even exist, but how widely similar ideas were diffused both geographically and across class and religious divides. Hilda Smith, "Gynecology and Ideology in Seventeenth-Century England," in Berenice A. Carroll, *Liberating Women's History: Theoretical and Critical Essays* (Urbana, 1976), 97–114, provides an example of the pitfalls of particularism. The essay raises entirely sensible issues but except for the endnotes and a few details in the examples, it could as well be dealing with sixteenth-century Italy or third-century Rome.

41. Mercurio, *La commare*, bk. 1, chap. 3 (Biagi et al., 81–83).

42. Gioberti, *Errori popolari*, 139.

43. Mercurio, *De gli errori popolari d'Italia*, 382.

44. Savonarola, *Ad mulieres ferrarienses*, 120.

45. Gioberti, *Errori popolari*, 136.

46. Savonarola, *Ad mulieres ferrarienses*, 120; Biagi et al., *Medicine per le donne*, 17.

47. Savonarola, *Ad mulieres ferrarienses*, 109–10.

48. Savonarola, *Ad mulieres ferrarienses*, 120–24. For slight variations on what to do to ease a long labor, see Marinello *Delle medicine*, 268–69.

49. Savonarola, *Ad mulieres ferrarienses*, 112.

50. Savonarola, *Ad mulieres ferrarienses*, 126–27.

51. Donnison, *Midwives and Medical Men*, 21–22, who cites W. Radcliffe, *The Secret Instrument* (London, 1947), 38–39.

52. Savonarola, *Ad mulieres ferrarienses*, 113–16.

53. Marinello, *Delle medicine*, 270–80, 284–85. The incantation is identified by Forbes, *The Midwife and the Witch*, 80–81, as coming from Arnald of Villanova (ca. 1235–1311), the Spanish physician and theologian whose writings are specifically dismissed by Mrs. Isabella Cortese in her book of secrets.

54. Burke, "The Uses of Literacy in Early Modern Italy," 32, and note 51, cites the *Legenda et oratione di Santa Margherita* (Venice, ca. 1550).

55. Mercurio, *La commare*, bk. 2, chaps. 2–16, 125–55. By contrast, I believe herbal books, especially the carefully illustrated and indexed ones, were consulted on the spot as part of a good sales pitch by wholesale and retail merchants in herbs and spices.

56. Mercurio, *La commare*, bk. 2, chap. 25 (Biagi et al., 105–9).

57. Mercurio, *La commare*, bk. 2, chap. 26 (Biagi et al., 110–12).

58. Mercurio, *La commare*, bk. 1, chap. 1 (Biagi et al., 67–69); Biagi et al., *Medicine per le donne*, 68, supplies the offending quotation from Maffei da Solofra's work, *Scala naturale overo Fantasia dolcissima intorno alle cose occulte, e desiderate nella Filosofia* (Venice, n.d., dedicated 1564), chap. 21, c. 471: "Né vo' lasciar di dirvi, che generandosi la femina, come ben disse Aristotele, si genera il mostro perché la principale intentione della natura è di produrre sempre il maschio come cosa più perfetta."

59. Mercurio, *La commare*, bk. 1, chap. 1 (Biagi et al., 67–69).

60. Gioberti, *Errori popolari*, 132–59.

61. Marinello, *Delle medicine*, 248–49.

62. Gioberti, *Errori popolari*, 157ff.

63. Savonarola, *Ad mulieres ferrarienses*, 127–29; Marinello, *De medicine*, 289–96.

64. Marinello, *De medicine*, 279.

65. Marinello, *De medicine*, 296–311; Savonarola, *Ad mulieres ferrarienses*, 127–30.

66. Mercurio, *De gli errori popolari d'Italia*, 394–96.

67. The content here is primarily from Savonarola, whose ordering of tasks is followed by later writers; for similar advice, see, for example, Mercurio, *De gli errori popolari d'Italia*, 396–99, and *La commare*, bk. 1, chap. 26, 113–18.

68. Marinello, *Delle medicine,* 271.

69. Savonarola, *Ad mulieres ferrarienses,* 135–43.

Chapter Four

1. Plato, *The Republic,* bk. 5, 460d. This reference and a wealth of interesting material are found in Valerie A. Fildes, *Breasts, Bottles, and Babies: A History of Infant Feeding* (Edinburgh, 1986), 21, for the Plato reference. A more general survey is Valerie A. Fildes, *Wet Nursing: A History from Antiquity to the Present* (London, 1988), 15–30, for the classical background.

2. This is as good a place as any to note Jay E. Mechling's "Advice to Historians on Advice to Mothers," *Journal of Social History* (fall 1975): 44–63. His admonitions, although cast in a context of recent American social history in which the rhetoric of advice manuals can be tested against sociological survey data (equally unreliable in my judgment, although for different reasons), apply to historians of the sixteenth century as well. In a nutshell, he argues that people do not actually do what advice manuals tell them to do. In one sense, this argument hardly is new; we all know that laws forbidding certain behavior are a good indicator that the behavior occurred. Analogously, advice to do this or that probably means that people were not doing this or that, both before and after reading recommendations to the contrary. The problem is very complex, and there are no quick solutions. Certainly I have none.

3. Plutarch's most influential essays on questions of child rearing are *De liberis educandis,* which no one in the sixteenth century imagined to be the work of a pupil or close associate rather than of Plutarch himself, as modern scholars contend, and *De amore prolis,* both traditionally included in the *Moralia* and both published in Italian translations in the sixteenth century, as was Quintilian's *Institutio oratoria.*

4. Gioberti, *Errori popolari,* 160–73.

5. Mercurio, *La commare,* bk. 1, chap. 24, 104–8. He repeats the same arguments in *De gli errori popolari d'Italia,* 399–405.

6. Anonymous, *Indovinelli, riboboli, passerotti, et farfalloni. Nuovamente messi insieme, e la maggior parte non piu stampati, parte in prosa & parte in rima, & hora posti in luce per ordine d'alfabeto. Con alcune cicalate di donne di sententie, & proverbi posti nel fine. Opera molto piacevole, & bella da indovinare, & da far ridere nelle veghie per passar il tempo* (n.p., n.d., but certainly sixteenth-century Italy), BNF shelf mark Landau-Finaly 535.7. More graceful poetic works make the same general argument and carry all the venom of Mercurio's admonitions; see for example Luigi Tansillo, "La Balia" (Bologna, 1969 rpt.). Since this work remained unpublished between the time of its writing around 1565 until it was rediscovered and printed in 1767, we cannot say that it influenced anyone in the sixteenth century. Nevertheless the hostility toward use of wet nurses is typical of opinion throughout the Renaissance. For admonitions in domestic economy treatises, see Frigo, *Il padre di famiglia,* 117–18.

7. Savonarola, *Ad mulieres ferrarienses,* 147–48.

8. Palmieri, *Della vita civile*, 15.

9. Barbaro, "On Wifely Duties" in Kohl et al., *The Earthly Republic*, 221–23. According to Plutarch's life of Marcus Cato the Elder, his wife not only gave suck to their son but often to the infants of their servants so they would grow to love the little boy. The theory that the location of breasts in humans is designed to allow easy hugging and kissing during nursing comes from Plutarch's "De amore prolis" essay in the *Moralia*, bk. 6, 493A.

10. Savonarola, *Ad mulieres ferrarienses*, 147, 153–54.

11. Gioberti, *Errori popolari*, 176–81, 199–203.

12. Mercurio, *La commare*, bk. 1, chap. 25, 109–12. Most of his advice is repeated, although in a more scolding tone and with more classical references, in his *De gli errori popolari d'Italia*, 405–8. For a thorough summary table on the views of classic authors on breast-feeding and the qualities of wet nurses, see Fildes, *Breasts, Bottles, and Babies*, 60–68. The warning against baby talk is also found in Palmieri, *Della vita civile*, 16, and in Quintilian, *Institutio oratoria*, bk. 1, sec. 4–5; I used James J. Murphy, ed. and trans., *Quintilian on the Teaching of Speaking and Writing* (Carbondale, 1987).

13. Contrary evidence comes from James B. Ross, "The Middle-Class Child in Urban Italy, Fourteenth to Early Sixteenth Century," in Lloyd deMause, ed., *The History of Childhood* (New York, 1974), 183–228, and particularly note 42, on Paolo da Certaldo's admonition to visit infants put out to nurse. But as I have noted elsewhere, this author did not make it to a printed edition until the twentieth century. The experience of Florence's Innocenti hospital for foundlings, as reported in the thorough study by Philip Gavitt, *Charity and Children in Renaissance Florence: The Ospedale degli Innocenti, 1410–1536* (Ann Arbor, 1990), 230–31, is instructive: "Neighbors rather than inspectors discovered and reported the vast majority of deaths, mistreatment, and neglect. Neighbors often traveled long distances at their own expense to make personal representations to the prior about the activities of Innocenti wet nurses. The most common abuse was the wet nurse's failure to report the death of a child and to continue collecting payments." Gavitt readily concedes, and thoroughly documents, reports of a range of abuses by wet nurses, and yet his overall assessment of Florence's system of paid wet nurses is far more benign than anything suggested by Ross, even though Gavitt deals mostly with infants from the poorest classes.

14. Ross, "The Middle-Class Child in Urban Italy," 184–85.

15. The same is true of another work that features prominently in Ross's citations, the treatise of Giovanni Dominici, *"Regola del governo di cura familiare."* The powerful Dominican achieved the status of blessed, and some of his other writings were published, but this particular tract did not find a printer until 1860, except for a possible 1496 edition with no printer or place of publication identified. Therefore, even though the *Regola* was addressed to a woman explicitly as an advice manual on rearing her children and was written in Italian, its influence may have been primarily among a circle of elites engaged in the debate about humanist reliance on classical texts and whether proper Christian precepts were being abandoned. The published text is Donato Salvi, ed., *Regola del governo di*

cura familiare; compilata dal beato Giovanni Dominici, fiorentino (Florence, 1860); Arthur Coté, *On the Education of Children* (Washington, 1927), 9–30, provides a bio-bibliography and translates an excerpt.

16. Alessandro Perosa, ed., *Giovanni Rucellai ed il suo Zibaldone*, vol. 1 (London, 1960), 13, is cited by Ross, "The Middle-Class Child in Urban Italy," note 11, but the text says nothing about custom, only the following: *Ricordovi il modo abbiate a tenere nell'allevare e' vostri figluoli. Et prima, che la propria madre l'allatti quando fusse senza pericolo et sanza offensione della persona della madre; et se non è, togliete balia giovane, sana et lieta, di lungi dal marito e che non sia scilinguata.* One could force a reading of *"sanza offensione della persona della madre"* to imply custom, but then there is the injunction that the wet nurse should be away from her husband, which would not be the case if the child were put out in the countryside, so overall I take this brief reference, the only thing Rucellai has to say about breast-feeding, to be a routine statement that mothers should feed their own children but if they cannot or will not, then at least they should choose a healthy young nurse of good speaking habits. The reference certainly does not support Ross's conclusion, to which this notation is applied, that finding a wet nurse was a problem "which confronted most middle-class families."

17. Catherine Clinton, *The Plantation Mistress: Woman's World in the Old South* (New York, 1982), 155–56, reports that by the mid-nineteenth century, many elite southern women sought wet nurses, both white and black. It is interesting to see how little attention slaveholders paid to concerns about the biological and moral character of the wet nurse, which abound in biblical and Greco-Roman texts that surely were familiar to educated white American southerners, even if they did not read Italian advice manuals. For a thorough discussion of all aspects of wet nursing in the American South before the Civil War, see Sally G. McMillen, *Motherhood in the Old South: Pregnancy, Childbirth, and Infant Rearing* (Baton Rouge, 1990), 111–34. I also have learned from discussions on this matter with my colleagues Jennifer Morgan and Mia Bay.

18. Ross, "The Middle-Class Child in Urban Italy," 195, and note 64. Although I have not studied Florentine archival *ricordanze*, published selections reveal attitudes highly supportive of maternal care (e.g., Vittore Branca's edition of Giovanni di Pagolo Morelli, *Ricordi* [Florence, 1956], esp. 202, 207, 219–20) or indicative of close ongoing relations with the wet nurse (as in Giovanni Ciappelli's edition of Francesco di Matteo Castellani, *Ricordanze* [Florence, 1992], 113–14).

19. Charles Singleton, ed., *Canti carnascialeschi del Rinascimento* (Bari, 1936), 39–40. Ross's translation, not to mention interpretation, of this song is questionable. On page 190, she provides the following: "whoever has a baby, show him to us, / male or female, it doesn't matter." Then, on page 192, after much analysis, she resumes the quotation with, "We shall take good care of him." The original lines, however, are all within a single stanza: "Deh, chi n'ha si ce gli mostri: / maschio o femina che sia, / tanto ben tenuto sia." The three lines surely were meant to be sung together, not divided by two pages of academic prose, in which case they might be translated thus: "Well, show us what you have / male or female as it may be / very well treated it will be." So, what Ross renders as mercenary

indifference to gender, I see as a hearty promise to give equally good care whether the baby is a girl or a boy.

20. Christiane Klapisch-Zuber, *Women, Family, and Ritual in Renaissance Italy,* trans. Lydia G. Cochraine (Chicago, 1985), 132–64, examines the account books or diaries *(ricordanze)* of 84 Florentine couples who gave birth to 318 infants fed by 462 wet nurses from 1300 to 1530. Between 60 and 67 percent of these couples came from the city's governing circles, but among the others were artisans, doctors, jurists, and notaries. Exactly how many of the 84 couples were "artisans," Klapisch-Zuber does not say, and I must confess to some doubts about how many artisans had the time and knowledge to keep a diary or account book for posterity. Anyway, among babies put to a nurse other than the biological mother, she finds that a little more than half the boys and fully two thirds of the girls were sent to the countryside, about 13 percent of boys and girls stayed with a woman in town, and the remaining were fed by a live-in wet nurse.

According to Klapisch-Zuber, "the *ricordanze* never note, except in truly exceptional circumstances, that Florentine mothers nursed their children themselves," but in my view this is because the diaries are really annotated account books, not personal diaries, so no mention should be expected of items, such as maternal breast-feeding, that did not involve cash outlays. Notwithstanding the fragility of the evidence—account books from 84 couples, mostly elites, detailing payments for the feeding of 318 infants spread over 230 years in a total population during that span of more than 500,000 Florentine babies—Klapisch-Zuber concludes as follows: "We can state that in the large city of Florence, nursing by a salaried nurse or by a slave woman became the dominant practice, at least from the middle of the fifteenth century onward, even if we cannot for the moment trace the exact limits of the practice." Just what does "dominant" mean? I found buried in a footnote in Klapisch-Zuber's collaborative work with the late David Herlihy on the very detailed 1427 Tuscan tax census, covering both Florence and its environs, the fact that among 35,275 babies aged zero to three years enumerated in the census, only 234 were listed as being put out with wet nurses. By my reckoning, that comes to 1 baby out of each 150, clearly not a dominant practice no matter how you define dominance or quibble about defects in one source or another. It is not reasonable to assume that 149 out of every 150 families with a small baby forgot to tell the census taker that their infants were out to nurse and that the countryside nurses in turn forgot they had all those additional hungry mouths to feed. Nor was there any obvious economic gain in lying or being forgetful. The few whiners recorded in the census because they appealed for a tax reduction based on the high costs of paying a wet nurse point only to a perception of exceptional circumstances, not to normal practices. If dominance means at least 50.1 percent, and considering that weaning occurred between eighteen and twenty-four months, then among something like 20,000 eligible babies younger than age two enumerated in the 1427 census, about 10,000 would have been away from home competing for the breasts of another baby's mother. Surely some evidence beyond the unpublished memoirs of a few elite moralists would have survived to document so unusual a biological and cultural phenomenon.

324   NOTES TO PAGE 135

David Herlihy and Christiane Klapisch-Zuber, *Tuscans and Their Families: A Study of the Florentine Catasto of 1427* (New Haven, 1985), 147, report the census findings; the same numbers are reported in the French-language original (340, note 54). In fact, we know the kind of evidence that might be generated in a European culture in which a majority of children were nourished by a wet nurse if we consult George D. Sussman, *Selling Mothers' Milk: The Wet-Nursing Business in France 1715–1914* (Urbana, 1982). Certainly we have little such evidence for Florence and the surrounding Tuscan countryside, and we do know that the Florentines were very good record keepers.

Gavitt, *Charity and Children*, 225–26, finds that even the thoroughly documented number of children—2,567 in total—who passed through the Florence's Innocenti hospital for foundlings between 1445 and 1466, strained greatly the hospital's ability to find qualified wet nurses, a fact that suggests how difficult it would have been to locate anything like 10,000 wet nurses in the census year of 1427.

21. One might start with Lawrence Stone, *The Family, Sex, and Marriage in England, 1500–1800* (New York, 1977), 66–68, which reports mortality rates to the age of one in France at 15 to 30 percent, with an average of 21 percent, and suggests that actual rates were much higher due to underreporting of perinatal deaths. Similar figures are provided in André Burguière and François Lebrun, "The One Hundred and One Families of Europe," in André Burguière, Christiane Klapisch-Zuber, Martine Segalen, and François Zonabend, eds., *A History of the Family*, vol. 2, trans. Sarah Hanbury-Tenison, Rosemary Morris, and Andrew Wilson (Cambridge, 1996), 14. All other reports I know of also confirm that the 15 to 18 percent mortality rate calculated by Klapisch-Zuber for Florentine infants given to a wet nurse is a low number, one indicating good care and above-average health. No doubt Florentine patricians thought more about maternal beauty and convenience than infant health, in the process fashioning what Marilyn Yalom, *A History of the Breast* (New York, 1997), 49–104, so perceptively calls the shift from the sacred breast to the erotic breast, but this parental selfishness did babies no measurable harm as a health choice. On mothers abandoning their babies only to reclaim them as paid wet nurses, see Gavitt, *Charity and Children*, esp. 227. Infant mortality rates for foundlings in eighteenth-century Spain, where half of all boys and girls did not survive, were far higher than anything reported for fifteenth-century Florence; see Joan Sherwood, *Poverty in Eighteenth-Century Spain: The Women and Children of the Inclusa* (Toronto, 1988), 139.

22. On Machiavelli, see Hanna Pitkin, *Fortune Is a Woman: Gender and Politics in the Thought of Niccolò Machiavelli* (Berkeley, 1984), esp. 217–29. Also see Arlene W. Saxonhouse, *Women in the History of Political Thought: Ancient Greece to Machiavelli* (New York, 1985), 151–73. Bernardo Machiavelli, *Libro di ricordi*, ed. Cesare Olschki (Florence, 1954), details thousands of expenditures but makes no mention of wet nurses employed by Bernardo for Niccolò or any of his siblings.

23. Michael P. Carroll, *Veiled Threats: The Logic of Popular Catholicism in Italy* (Baltimore, 1996), 242–46.

24. The classic works are Philippe Ariès, *Centuries of Childhood: A Social History of Family Life*, trans. Robert Baldick (New York, 1962); Jean-Louis Flandrin, *Families in Former Times: Kinship, Household, and Sexuality*, trans. Richard Southern (Cambridge, 1979); David Hunt, *Parents and Children in History: The Psychology of Family Life in Early Modern France* (New York, 1970); and Stone, *The Family, Sex, and Marriage in England, 1500–1800*, esp. 85–119. A reasoned retreat from Ariès's view may be found in Henri Bresc, "Europe: Town and Country (Thirteenth–Fifteenth Century)," in André Burguière et al., eds., *A History of the Family*, vol. 1, 458–61. For a refreshingly iconoclastic review of this literature, see Linda Pollock, *Forgotten Children: Parent-Child Relations from 1500 to 1900* (Cambridge, 1983). Persuasive in an entirely different way is the conclusion by Steven Ozment in *Magdalena and Balthasar: An Intimate Portrait of Life in Sixteenth-Century Europe Revealed in the Letters of a Nuremberg Husband and Wife and Illuminated by Steven Ozment* (New York, 1986), 161–64. A balanced approach is Barbara Diefendorf, "Family Culture, Renaissance Culture," *Renaissance Quarterly* 40 (winter 1987): 661–81.

25. Both Boccaccio's introduction to the *Decameron*, with its description of the social disintegration caused by the plague, and Plutarch's "In Consolation to his Wife" (in Italian translation) were published on several occasions in the sixteenth century, just two examples to illustrate that maudlin sentimentality and grief over the deaths of young children were not invented in the eighteenth century. On painting, see Margaret R. Miles, "The Virgin's One Bare Breast: Female Nudity and Religious Meaning in Tuscan Early Renaissance Culture," in Susan R. Suleiman, ed., *The Female Body in Western Culture: Contemporary Perspectives* (Cambridge, 1986), 193–208.

26. Ozment, *When Fathers Ruled*, esp. 121, 126. Readers willing to sift through a fair amount of paternalistic cultural baggage also will find valuable nuggets in the classic study of Giovanni Tamassia, *La famiglia italiana nei secoli decimoquinto e decimosesto* (Milan, 1911), for example, 253–56, on maternal responsibility for breast-feeding and for their full participation in child rearing and discipline. Yalom, *A History of the Breast*, 75, states that 90 percent of European women functioned as milk bearers, while only 10 percent declined to breast-feed, although elsewhere she cites sources claiming a much higher percentage of children sent to wet nurses.

27. Mercurio, *La commare*, bk. 1, chap. 26, 113–14; also see his *De gli errori popolari d'Italia*, 408–11.

28. Gioberti, *Errori popolari*, 173, 204, 211–18.

29. I make no attempt here to introduce the complexities of Augustine's thought and the varieties of his influence over the centuries, on which topics one might begin with George Howie, *Educational Theory and Practice in St. Augustine* (New York, 1969), and his edition of relevant writings in *St. Augustine: On Education* (South Bend, 1969). As a quick refresher, however, allow me to insert here a quotation (translation by Howie) from Augustine's *Confessions*, bk. 1, sec. 6:

As a baby I learned how to suck, to lie peacefully when happy, to weep when I suffered physical distress. This was all there was.

Later I began to smile, at first while sleeping and later when awake.

326 NOTES TO PAGES 140–148

This has been reported to me, and I believe it because I see other babies doing the same thing. I cannot, of course, remember it for myself. Little by little, I began to know where I was, and I had the inclination to express my needs to those who had the means of satisfying them. But I failed because my needs were inside me whereas the people concerned were outside and were unable to enter into my mind by any of their faculties. So I would throw my limbs around and utter sounds, making the gestures of which I was capable, few in number and poor in quality as they were—for they were by no means accurate indications of my needs. And when people did not do what I wanted, either because they did not understand or because it might be bad for me to get what I wanted, I used to fly into tantrums with my elders because they were not my slaves, that is, because they were free people who would not do what I wanted. I avenged myself on them by screaming. That babies act like this I have understood from observing other babies. These others have unwittingly informed me of what I myself was like more accurately than the nurses who knew me.

30. Savonarola, *Ad mulieres ferrarienses*, 148–51.

31. Gioberti, *Errori popolari*, 58.

32. Falloppio, *Secreti diversi*, 140ff.; Estienne, *L'agricoltura*, 109, 177.

33. Fioravanti, *La cirugia*, chap. 79 (Furfaro, 78).

34. Durante, *Herbario*, 13, 22, 36.

35. Mattioli, *Discorsi*, section on *Mammelle*.

36. Mercurio, *La commare*, bk. 3, chap. 5, 248–52.

37. Mercurio, *La commare*, bk. 3, chap. 6, 252–55.

38. Mercurio, *La commare*, bk. 3, chap. 7, 255–57; similar advice on diet is found in Savonarola, *Ad mulieres ferrarienses*, 151–52.

39. Mercurio, *La commare*, bk. 3, chap. 8, 257–59. On becoming pregnant in the bath, see *La commare*, bk. 1, 51–55, wherein Mercurio makes it plain that, in his opinion, this is just another instance of women fooling gullible men by offering stories to cover their libidinous behavior, in this instance having sexual intercourse in the bathtub.

40. Savonarola, *Ad mulieres ferrarienses*, 161–64.

41. Savonarola, *Ad mulieres ferrarienses*, 144–58.

42. Savonarola, *Ad mulieres ferrarienses*, 159–61.

43. For an introduction to these Latin medical texts, see Arthur Abt and Fielding Garrison, *History of Pediatrics* (Philadelphia, 1965), esp. 60–68, and George Still, *The History of Paediatrics: The Progress of the Study of Diseases of Children up to the End of the XVIIIth Century* (London, 1965 rpt. of 1931 ed.), 94–180. Hull, *Women according to Men*, 117–19, discusses the paucity of vernacular guides on infant health and notes that the limited advice available tended to be appended to books on care during pregnancy rather than published in independent manuals (with the notable exception of Thomas Phaer's 1544 *Boke of Chyldren*). My understanding of sixteenth-century societal concerns about children is less pessimistic and condemnatory than Hull's, and takes more seriously the reasoning of writers such as Savonarola and Mercurio about

the risks of encouraging parents to treat their children's illnesses at home, at least once they became severe or persistent. But I also find that advice on infant care was included in books on pregnancy rather than published separately.

44. Savonarola, *Ad mulieres ferrarienses*, 166.

45. Mercurio, *De gli errori popolari d'Italia*, 420–22.

46. Mercurio, *La commare*, bk. 3, chaps. 23–60, 298–356; similar advice is found in Savonarola, *Ad mulieres ferrarienses*, 167–91.

47. Savonarola, *Ad mulieres ferrarienses*, 192–95.

48. Philip Greven, *Spare the Child: The Religious Roots of Punishment and the Psychological Impact of Physical Abuse* (New York, 1991).

49. See especially Quintilian, *Institutio oratoria*, bk. 1, sec. 3, 13–16. Also see bk. 2, sec. 2–4. Plutarch is also unequivocal, for example, in bk. 1, section 9A of *De liberis educandis:* "This also, I assert, that children ought to be led to honorable practices by means of encouragement and reasoning, and most certainly not by blows or ill-treatment, for it surely is agreed that these are fitting rather for slaves than for the freeborn; for so they grow numb and shudder at their tasks, partly from the pain of the blows, partly from the degradation. Praise and reproof are more helpful for the free-born than any sort of ill-usage, since the praise incites them toward what is honorable, and reproof keeps them from what is disgraceful."

50. For example, see the following works considered in Greven, *Spare the Child*, 60–72: Larry Christenson, *The Christian Family* (Minneapolis, 1970); James Dobson, *Dare to Discipline* (Wheaton, 1970); J. Richard Fugate, *What the Bible Says about . . . Child Training* (Garland, 1980); Jack Hyles, *How to Rear Children* (Hammond, 1972); Roy Lessin, *Spanking: Why When How?* (Minneapolis, 1979); and Larry Tomczak, *God, the Rod, and Your Child's Bod: The Art of Loving Correction for Christian Parents* (Old Tappan, NJ, 1982).

51. Vincent J. Horkan, *Educational Theories and Principles of Maffeo Vegio* (Washington, 1953), provides extensive selections and valuable commentary. See 11–13, on the intellectual setting, 66–71, on Vegio's admonitions against corporal punishment, and 73–74, on maternal indulgence. For a critical edition of the original text, see Maria Fanning, ed., *Maphei Vegii Laudensis de educatione liberorum et eorum claris moribus libri sex. A Critical Text of Books I–III* (Washington, 1933), and Anne Sullivan, ed., *Maphei Vegii Laudensis de educatione liberorum et eorum claris moribus libri sex. A Critical Text of Books IV–VI* (Washington, 1936), each of which also has useful notations and provides linkages to the classical texts used by Vegio. Nearly a century later, the renowned Erasmus gave vent to an interpretation similar to Vegio's on the Old Testament as possibly appropriate for ancient Jews but not for Christians; see J. K. Sowards, ed., *Collected Works of Erasmus*, vol. 26 (Toronto, 1985), 332.

52. Sowards, ed., *Collected Works of Erasmus*, vol. 26, 291–346, for the translation and annotation by Beert C. Verstraete of *De pueris statim ac liberaliter instituendis declamatio*. For the early publication history, see Jean-Claude Margolin, ed., *Erasme: Declamatio de pueris statim ac liberaliter instituendis* (Geneva 1966), 123–368, and esp. 238–66, for Italian translations. J. K. Sowards, "Erasmus and the Education of Women," *Sixteenth Century Journal* 14, no. 4 (1982): 86,

concludes as follows: "Erasmus was concerned, indeed almost obsessed with the problem of the abuse of children, whether by flogging schoolmasters, overbearing upper classmen at school, or brutal parents." Still useful is the interpretive work of William Harrison Woodward, *Desiderius Erasmus concerning the Aim and Method of Education* (New York, 1964 rpt. of 1904 ed., with a foreword by Craig R. Thompson). For the condemnation of Erasmus by a committee of high prelates instructed, in 1537, by Pope Paul III to recommend church reforms, see Elisabeth G. Gleason, ed. and trans., *Reform Thought in Sixteenth-Century Italy* (Ann Arbor, 1981), 96: "Because it is common nowadays to read to grammar school boys the *Colloquies* of Erasmus, which contain many things inciting uneducated minds to impiety, it should be forbidden to read them as well as other books of their kind in the schools."

Also relevant here is Erasmus's famous etiquette manual, *De civilitate morum puerilium,* published less than a year after *De pueris instituendis.* It is considered at length in the classic work by Norbert Elias, *The History of Manners,* trans. Edmund Jephcott (New York, 1978), 169–75, and in the recent Delumeau and Roche, *Histoire des pères,* 58–66. For an important critique of Elias, one that places greater emphasis on the religious origins of civility prescriptions than on their political, courtly context, see Dilwyn Knox, "*Disciplina.* The Monastic and Clerical Origins of European Civility," in John Monfasani and Ronald G. Musto, eds., *Renaissance Society and Culture: Essays in Honor of Eugene F. Rice, Jr.* (New York, 1991), 107–35. Also relevant are the Italian version of Knox's essay and the essay by Gabriella Zarri, "Disciplina regolare e pratica di coscienza: le virtù e i comportamenti sociali in comunità femminili (secc. xvi–xviii)," in Paolo Prodi, ed., *Disciplina dell' anima, disciplina del corpo e disciplina della società tra medioevo ed età moderna* (Bologna, 1994), 63–99, and 257–78, respectively. On the humanist contribution to Catholic Reformation ideas about child rearing and on the influence of Erasmus, see Ottavia Niccoli, *Il seme della violenza: putti, fanciulli e mammoli nell' Italia tra Cinque e Seicento* (Rome, 1995), 94–111, and "Creanza e disciplina: Buone maniere per i fanciulli nell' Italia della Controriforma," in Prodi, ed., *Disciplina dell' anima,* 929–63.

53. Ozment, *When Fathers Ruled,* 169–70.

54. Savonarola, *Ad mulieres ferrarienses,* 196–200.

55. Palmieri, *Della vita civile,* 18–20.

56. *Catechism of the Council of Trent,* 3.5.21–22.

57. William Harrison Woodward, *Vittorino da Feltre and Other Humanist Educators* (New York, 1973 rpt. of 1897 ed., with a useful introductory essay by Eugene Rice), 134–58, for an English selection from Piccolomini's treatise and generally for a good selection and overview of humanist writings on education. Equally valuable is Woodward's companion volume, *Studies in Education during the Age of the Renaissance, 1400–1600* (New York, 1967 rpt. of 1906 ed., with a foreword by Lawrence Stone). The most accessible complete Italian edition of Piccolomini's treatise is *L'educazione dei giovani: L'Umanesimo e i suoi problemi educativi,* ed. with critical commentary, Manfredi del Donno (Milan, 1960). Also see Eugenio Garin, ed., *Il pensiero pedagogico dello Umanesimo* (Florence, 1958), and for later humanists, Alessandro Dini, *La formazione intellettuale nel Cinquecento*

(Turin, 1978). Niccoli, *Il seme della violenza,* 116–20, shows the heavy reliance on Piccolomini by post-Tridentine pedagogue Andrea Ghetti da Volterra.

The prelates at Trent surely also knew of the sternly antihumanist views of Florentine Cardinal Giovanni Dominici. Even though these did not make it to a printed edition in the sixteenth century, they were influential in Dominican circles and their rejection is significant. Dominici believed that children should be beaten frequently, whether guilty or not, reasoning that, if they were guilty, let them be thankful for justice and if they were innocent, let them acquire merit by learning the virtue of patience.

58. To be sure, Cardinal Borromeo did much else as well. As a start, see Grendler, "Borromeo and the Schools of Christian Doctrine," in his *Books and Schools in the Italian Renaissance,* chap. 10; also see John Bossy, "The Counter-Reformation and the People of Catholic Europe," *Past and Present* 47 (1970): 51–70, who argues persuasively that the Counter Reformation church actively and successfully enforced uniform parochial practices and that in this drive Borromeo was the model for generations to come. The most comprehensive introduction is Luigi Secco, *La pedagogia della Controriforma* (Brescia, 1973), 43–68, 133–80, on the sections of Antoniano's book I focus on. Also see Luigi Volpicelli, ed., *Il pensiero pedagogico della Controriforma* (Florence, 1960), which provides less on Antoniano but gives entry to a wider range of Catholic Reformation authors.

59. On Catholic Reformation pedagogy more generally, see Giovanni Maria Bertin, *La pedagogia umanistica europea nei secoli XV e XVI* (Milan, 1961), 297–312. The quotation from Pope Pius XI is found in Mary Laurentana Zanfagna, *Educational Theories and Principles of Cardinal Silvio Antoniano* (Washington, 1940), 1. This work contains useful biographical information on Antoniano and on the publication history of his book (5–27). On the actual schools, see Paul F. Grendler, *Schooling in Renaissance Italy: Literacy and Learning, 1300–1600* (Baltimore, 1989), esp. 333–402, on the Catholic Reformation schools. See also Grendler's *Books and Schools in the Italian Renaissance,* in particular the essay "What Zuanne Read in School: Vernacular Texts in Sixteenth-Century Venetian Schools."

Long after recording my sense that Antoniano's book was rather tedious, I came across a reference (Niccoli, *Il seme della violenza,* 133–34) showing that the author himself regarded his work-in-progress with little enthusiasm, fearing that few people would be willing to read such a long work in an age when so many books were around.

60. Silvio Antoniano, *Tre libri dell' educatione christiana dei figliuoli* (Verona: Sebastiano Dalle Donne & Girolamo Stringari, 1584), 123–28, each of these being two-sided leaves.

61. Antoniano, *Tre libri dell' educatione christiana,* 129–45. On schooling for girls, see Grendler, *Schooling in Renaissance Italy,* 87–89. I agree with Ottavia Niccoli's assessment, *Il seme della violenza,* 135–39, that corporal discipline was central to Antoniano's model of how to mold good Christian boys and girls, but this discipline did not come with the rod. Indeed, precisely because Antoniano thoroughly believed in taming the flesh, his warnings against beating children take on added significance.

62. Bartolomeo de Medina, *Breve instruttione de' confessori*, 80, 154–55. Confessional manuals to advise both simple priests and laypersons were among the earliest printed books; see Schutte, "Printing, Piety, and the People in Italy," 15–16. On confession for children, see Trombetta, *La confessione della lussuria*, 81–83.

63. Frosino Lapini, *L'anassarcho del Lapino. Overo trattato de' costumi, e modi che si debbono tenere, o schifare nel dare opera a gli studii. Discorso utilissimo ad ogni virtuoso e nobile scolara* (Florence: Bartolomeo Sermartelli, 1571), 16–31, on schoolboys' characteristics, and 83–84, on teachers' obligations.

64. Tommasi, *Reggimento del padre*, 125–89.

65. Nicolò Vito di Gozze, *Governo della famiglia, di M. Nicolò Vito di Gozze, gentil'huomo Raguseo, Accademico Occulto: Nel quale brevemente, trattando la vera economia, s'insegna, non meno con facilità, che dottamente, il governo, non pure della casa tanto di città, quanto di contado; ma ancora il vero modo d'accrescere, & conservare le ricchezze* (Venice: Aldo [Manuzio], 1589), 86–88. Gozze also published a commentary on Aristotle and contemporary civic governance and a Platonic dialogue on beauty, both in the vernacular. Frigo, *Il padre di famiglia*, 37–38, provides background material on Gozze and concludes, as I do, that since this "dialogue" contains only one effective interlocutor, it should be seen as a closed instructional manual rather than an open discourse (for which Castiglione's *Courtier* is the obvious model).

66. Gozze, *Governo della famiglia*, 89, 99.

67. Gozze, *Governo della famiglia*, 58–65.

68. Paul F. Grendler, in "What Zuanne Read in School," and in his treatment of the vernacular curriculum in *Schooling in Renaissance Italy*, 275–332, begins to tap the richness of this subject and point to areas for further exploration. Especially intriguing is the evidence that parents sent books they had at home to school with their children so the instructor could teach the youngsters how to read them.

69. All material is taken from the English translation by Nicholas Fersin, which includes facsimiles of all original woodcuts, printed by the Library of Congress (1953) as *The Florentine Fior di Virtu of 1491*.

70. Anonymous, *El costume delle donne incomenzando da la pueritia per fin al maritar: La via el modo che se debbe tenere a costumarle e amaestrarle secondo la condition el grado suo, Et similmente de i fanciulli. Et e uno spechio che ogni persona doverebbe haverlo: I marime quelli che hanno figlie e figlioli over aspettano di havern. Con un capitolo de le trentatre cose che convien alla donna a esser bella* (Brescia: Damiano e Iacomo Philippo Turlini, 1536). Doglio, ed., *Galeazzo Flavio Capra*, 124, cites a Venice, 1525 edition.

71. Anonymous, *Il vanto e lamento della cortigiana ferrarese* (Siena, n.d., sixteenth century, perhaps 1540), BNF shelf mark Landau-Finaly 535.7.

72. Anonymous, *Barceletta nova qual tratta dil gioco, dil qual ne viene insuportabili vitii, & chi seguita ditto stile, gionge a inreparabile, e tristissima morte* (Venice, 1553), BNF shelf mark E.6.6.154.I.7.

73. Anonymous, *Frottola dun padre che haveva dua figliuoli, un buono chiamato Benedetto, & laltro cattivo chiamato Antonio* (n.p., n.d., but clearly sixteenth century), BNF shelf mark E.6.5.3.I.19.

74. Robert Darnton, *The Great Cat Massacre: And Other Episodes in French Cultural History* (New York, 1984), 215–56, 241, for the quotation.

Chapter Five

1. John R. Gillis, *Youth and History: Tradition and Change in European Age Relations 1770–Present* (New York, 1974), 95–183.

2. Barbara A. Hanawalt, "'The Childe of Bristowe' and the Making of Middle-Class Adolescence," in Barbara A. Hanawalt and David Wallace, eds., *Bodies and Disciplines: Intersections of Literature and History in Fifteenth-Century England* (Minneapolis, 1996), 155–78, puts a renewed emphasis on adolescence squarely in the fifteenth century for England, and this seems to be true for Italy as well. Ilana Krausman Ben-Amos, *Adolescence and Youth in Early Modern England* (New Haven, 1994), 10–38, shows how popular interpretations of classical authorities reinforced notions of adolescence in early modern Europe. Also see Paul Griffiths, *Youth and Authority: Formative Experiences in England, 1560–1640* (Oxford, 1996), esp. 17–61, on defining the age of youth and on youth as a "dangerous age."

3. Singleton, ed., *Canti carnascialeschi*, 240.

4. As a starting point on "ages of life" in Dante and on multiples of seven, see Klapisch-Zuber, *Women, Family, and Ritual in Renaissance Italy*, 94–97. More generally, see Elisabeth Crouzet-Pavan, "A Flower of Evil: Young Men in Medieval Italy," and Michel Pastoureau, "Emblems of Youth: Young People in Medieval Imagery," in Giovanni Levi and Jean-Claude Schmitt, eds., *A History of Young People in the West*, vol. 1., trans. Camille Naish (Cambridge, 1997), 173–83, 222–25, respectively. The authoritative work on Dante, which also delves into the relationship between ages of life and the balance of the four bodily humors, is Bruno Nardi, *Saggi di filosofia dantesca*, 2d ed. (Florence, 1967), 110–38. Humors theorists did not use divisions of the number seven, and generally posited a very lengthy adolescence, as long as thirty years beginning at birth, so their use of the term "adolescence" obviously does not convey the meaning intended by Palmieri. Also see Richard C. Trexler, *Public Life in Renaissance Florence* (Ithaca, 1991) 388–89, and Niccoli, *Il seme della violenza*, 7–22, for some of the ambiguities in designating stages in the life cycle. By contrast, an author who clearly viewed age seven as the beginning of the "age of discretion," defined as the ability to know right from wrong, is Gozze, *Governo della famiglia*, 63.

5. Palmieri, *Della vita civile*, 25, 28–30. For the same ideas in Quintilian, see *Institutio oratoria*, bk. 2, sec. 2.

6. Antoniano, *Tre libri dell'educatione christiana*, 158.

7. Antoniano, *Tre libri dell'educatione christiana*, 164–65.

8. Gozze, *Governo della famiglia*, 35–36.

9. Jacob Burckhardt, *The Civilization of the Renaissance in Italy* (New York, 1958 rpt. of 1929 ed.), 389–95.

10. Guido Biagi, *Men and Manners of Old Florence* (London, 1909), 148. Grendler, *Schooling in Renaissance Italy*, 94, curiously combines in a single paragraph on learned women both prostitutes such as Tullia d'Aragona and thoroughly

proper matrons like Moderata Fonte. Margaret F. Rosenthal, "Venetian Women Writers and Their Discontents," in James Grantham Turner, ed., *Sexuality and Gender in Early Modern Europe* (Cambridge, 1993), 107–32, chooses to bring together the writings of Fonte and the "honest courtesan" Veronica Franco. These pairings raise some problems. We may assume that Fonte's and Franco's lifestyles were very different, and I am certain that the individual qualities of their literary works, which I know firsthand, risk becoming obscured when joined in this way and viewed through an ultramodern prism. Rosenthal explicitly recognizes that Fonte surely knew of Franco's writings and made no reference to them in her own defense of women, nor are there any allusions in her writings or in those of her intellectual circle (such as Lucrezia Marinella), suggesting that "honest courtesans" provided anything for talented women to emulate or even to use as a tool in battle-of-the-sexes warfare. In the excellent introduction to her edition (Venice, 1988) of Moderata Fonte's *Il merito delle donne*, Adriana Chemello convincingly portrays the chasm separating Franco and Fonte (xii). Rosenthal's critical reading is one we moderns may find extraordinarily thought provoking, but I believe it was not the reading of Franco's contemporaries. Moreover, postmodern literary theory applied to Franco may unwittingly but inevitably bring us full circle back to the idealization of prostitution found in Burckhardt and Biagi. Should that be the case, the space enclosed by such a circle would include the territory of elitist eroticism covered by Lynne Lawner, *Lives of the Courtesans* (New York, 1987).

For a range of feminist scholarship on problems less intractable than the honest courtesan, see Margaret W. Ferguson, Maureen Quilligan, and Nancy J. Vickers, eds., *Rewriting the Renaissance: The Discourses of Sexual Difference in Early Modern Europe* (Chicago, 1986), and Marilyn Migiel and Juliana Schiesari, eds., *Refiguring Woman: Perspectives on Gender and the Italian Renaissance* (Ithaca, 1991).

11. Giovanni Antonio Massinoni, *Il flagello delle meretrici, et la nobiltà donnesca ne' figliuoli* (Venice: Giacomo Antonio Somascho, 1599), 8. I was not able to locate the earlier edition alluded to in this printing, nor any identification of Massinoni or other writings by him. The Somascho printing firm deemed the work important enough to bind it with a 1599 reprint of Giuseppe Passi's viciously misogynous *I donneschi difetti*.

Lawner, *Lives of the Courtesans*, 17, invokes the image of honest courtesans standing about on the Bridge of Tits, but I do not believe that was where Veronica Franco and other "sumptuous whores" (to use Venetian diarist Marin Sanudo's alternative phrase) composed their poetry and letters.

12. Anonymous, *I germini sopra quaranta meretrice della città di Fiorenza* (Florence: Michelangelo, figlio di Bartolomeo [de' Libri], 1553). Printed descriptive catalogs and prices for individually named prostitutes also exist for Venice, and these are discussed thoroughly in Rosenthal, *The Honest Courtesan*, 274–75, and, among sources not included by Rosenthal, in Fulvio Dittico, *Il catalogo delle principali e più onorate cortigiane di Venezia nel Cinquecento* (Venice, 1956), 7–8. For the full text of a 1566 catalog for Venice, see Antonio Barzaghi, *Donne o cortigiane? La prostituzione a Venezia: documenti di costume dal XVI al XVIII secolo* (Verona, 1980), 155–67, or Rita Casagrande di Villaviera, *Le cortigiane veneziane*

nel Cinquecento (Milan, 1968), 275–93, which also offers a thorough but romanticized view of the Venetian courtesan. See also Lawner, ed., *I modi*, 26–27. Rosenthal (40) asserts that Italian literary critics have seen these catalogs as "real" in the same way that analogous Flemish catalogs (with actual portraits) were real and served as practical guides for foreigners in selecting a prostitute according to their personal tastes, but I know of no historians or literary critics who make such a claim. Everyone agrees that their purpose was satirical.

13. Rosenthal, *The Honest Courtesan*, 127–35.

14. Moderata Fonte [Modesta Pozzo di Zorzi], *Il merito delle donne, scritto da Moderata Fonte in due giornate. Ove chiaramente si scuopre quanto siano elle degne, e piu perfette de gli huomini* (Venice: Domenico Imberti, 1600), 53. This work now is available in the modern Italian edition by Adriana Chemello cited earlier, and in an English translation (with an important introductory essay) by Virginia Cox (Chicago, 1997). Daria Martelli, *Moderata Fonte e Il merito delle donne: biografia e adattamento teatrale* (Venice, 1993), is a theatrical adaptation of the original work and also contains a biographical essay. Also see Cox's essay "The Single Self: Feminist Thought and the Marriage Market in Early Modern Venice," *Renaissance Quarterly* 48 (autumn 1995): 513–81. Under the same pseudonym, Fonte also wrote *Tredici canti del Floridoro, di Mad. Moderata Fonte. Alli Sereniss. Gran Duca, et Gran Duchessa di Thoscana* (1581), now available in a modern edition by Valeria Finucci (Modena, 1995). A good bio-bibliographical introduction may be found in Paola Malpezzi Price's entry on Moderata Fonte in Russell, ed., *Italian Women Writers*, 128–37.

On Venetian women writers more generally, see Grendler, *Schooling in Renaissance Italy*, 94–95, and Patricia Labalme, "Venetian Women on Women: Three Early Modern Feminists," *Archivio Veneto* 5, no. 117 (1981): 81–109. Fundamental is Adriana Chemello, "La donna, il modello, l'immaginario: Moderata Fonte e Lucrezia Marinella," in Marina Zancan, ed., *Nel cerchio della luna: Figure di donna in alcuni testi del XVI secolo* (Venice, 1983), 95–170. Also see Adriana Chemello, "Donna di palazzo, moglie, cortigiana: Ruoli e funzioni sociali della donna in alcuni trattati del Cinquecento," in Adriano Prosperi, ed., *La corte e il "Cortegiano"* (Rome, 1980), 113–32.

One of Moderata Fonte's main targets was the famous dialogue of Galeazzo Flavio Capra, *Della eccellenza e dignità delle donne* (Rome: Francesco Minizio Calvo, 1525). His defense of women was subtle enough to persuade the modern scholar Constance Jordan, *Renaissance Feminism*, 72–73, to classify his work as a "feminist critique," but Fonte knew better and explicitly refuted Capra (and Castiglione) concerning the female sex drive and any number of other matters. On the relationship between Fonte and Capra, see Chemello, "Donna di palazzo," and on Capra, see the excellent introduction in Maria Luisa Doglio, ed., *Galeazzo Flavio Capra: Della eccellenza e dignità delle donne* (Rome, 1985). Jordan describes Capra's treatise as telling readers "to see in the status quo the result of attempts by men to gain and retain power by limiting the field of choice for women," but Fonte certainly did not read things that way, and I doubt that sixteenth-century men did either. Capra's proof that women have more capacity for faith than men is in how many women had recently been burned as witches rather than recant; for proof of women's greater fortitude, he gives us Cleopatra putting an asp to her breast; and for proof of modesty, the fact that women's genitals are tucked invisibly in their bodies instead of hanging out, so that God won't see them when we all go naked to paradise. In my view Capra's book was popular because sixteenth-century men found it wickedly humorous, and probably so did quite a few (but absolutely not all) women. See Pamela J. Benson, *The Invention of the Renaissance Woman: The Challenge of Female Independence in the Literature and Thought of Italy and England* (University Park, 1992), 66–73, for an insightful analysis of this text.

My reading of Girolamo Ruscelli, *Lettura di Girolamo Ruscelli, sopra un sonetto dell' illustriss. signor marchese Della Terza alla divina signora marchesa del Vasto, ove con nuove et chiare ragioni si pruova la somma perfettione delle donne . . .* (Venice: Giovanni Griffio, 1552), similarly differs from Jordan's. Where she finds a philosophical position consciously in support of women (160–62), I see mostly a "professor of secrets" (to use William Eamon's apt phrase) and a professional writer out to entertain and sell books. Were it not rooted in their superior heads, Ruscelli reasons (20–21), women's hair would turn into serpents, like Medusa's did, and that is why women seldom go bald. Maybe there is logical insight in this explanation, but in my judgment what we have here is an attempt at clever humor in which the logic is incidental, the audience is male, and the target is female.

More generally, see Patricia Labalme, ed., *Beyond Their Sex: Learned Women of the European Past* (New York, 1984), especially the essays by Labalme and by Margaret King. For fifteenth-century works in a scribal culture, see Margaret King and Albert Rabil, eds., *Her Immaculate Hand: Selected Works by and about the Woman Humanists of Quattrocento Italy* (Binghamton, 1983). Also see Romeo De Maio, *Donna e Rinascimento* (Milan, 1987), 147–83. A good listing of relevant texts may be found in Conor Fahy, "Three Early Renaissance Treatises on Women," *Italian Studies* 11 (1956): 30–55, esp. 47–55, for forty-one titles on the equality or superiority of women that were written or published in the fifteenth and sixteenth centuries. Among these forty-one titles, only five are in Latin (two of them not published), suggesting that intended readers were women educated in Italian but perhaps not in Latin.

In what has been termed "battle-of-the-sexes" literature, bashing of women often takes place within the context of an advice manual, and shortly I shall consider several sixteenth-century spoofs. However, among books in defense of the equality or even the superiority of women, of which the total number surely is far less than the quantity of antifeminist popular texts, I have not come across any that use an advice-manual format. Pro-women texts tend to be vague and flowery, nothing one could pick up and act on; for example, see Nicolò Liburnio, *Le occorrenze humane* (Venice: De' figliuoli di Aldo [Manuzio], 1546), 33–36, on chastity and modesty. Nor does popular poetry in praise of the female sex include advice, in contrast to the equally bad verses that ridicule women. Typical examples of woman-on-a-pedestal poetry are Giacomo Beldando, *Lo specchio de le bellissime donne napoletane* (Naples: Giovanni Sultzbach, 1536), and Luigi Dardano, *La bella e dotta difesa delle donne in verso e prosa* (Venice: Bartolomeo

L'Imperatore, 1554). Cornelio Lanci, *Esempi della virtu delle donne. Ne' quali si vede la bellezza, prudenza, castità e fortezza delle vergini, maritate e vedove* (Florence: Francesco Tosi, 1590), is in the style of Plutarch's well-known essay "Concerning the Virtues of Women" (*Moralia*, bk. 3, 242E), and contains hundred of names and brief vignettes about classical Greco-Roman and early Christian women who preserved their virginity, forgave their philandering husbands, or offered insightful counsel, all of which might be useful in an elite salon debate, but none of which could be construed as a guide for proper daily behavior. The same must be said of Scipione Vasolo, *La gloriosa eccellenze delle donne, e d'amore* (Florence: Giorgio Marescotti, 1573), which extends the survey of outstanding women to some rather fabulous native North American examples. He also makes a brief foray into biology, asserting on page 11 that women have fewer teeth than men, because they are less biting and devouring. In sum, there is a pro-women literature here that merits close study, but I have reluctantly foregone the pleasure since it falls so far outside the advice-manual rubric.

For an excellent survey of battle-of-the-sexes literature in sixteenth-century England, see Katherine Henderson and Barbara McManus, *Half Humankind: Contexts and Texts of the Controversy about Women in England, 1540–1640* (Urbana, 1985), 3–46. Also see Francis Utley, *The Crooked Rib: An Analytic Index to the Argument about Women in English and Scots Literature to the End of the Year 1568* (Columbus, 1944). For the Italian scene, the best introduction is Francine Daenens, "Superiore perché inferiore: Il paradosso della superiorità della donna in alcuni trattati italiani del Cinquecento," in Vanna Gentili, ed., *Trasgressione tragica e norma domestica: Esemplari di tipologie femminili dalla letteratura europea* (Rome, 1983), 11–50, which has an especially useful bibliographical appendix. Also see the rich bibliography provided by Kelso, *Doctrine for the Lady of the Renaissance*, 326–462. Still, I agree with Virginia Cox's recent assessment that "there does not yet exist a comprehensive study of the debate on women in Italy" (514, note 4, of her *Renaissance Quarterly* article cited above). In the interim, a good starting point for placing Fonte and Marinella in context is Cox's translation of *The Worth of Women*, 12–17. Provocative insights on several aspects of *querelle des femmes* literature may be found in Juliana Schiesari, "In Praise of Virtuous Women? For a Genealogy of Gender Morals in Renaissance Italy," *Annali d'Italianistica* 7 (1989): 66–87.

15. The collection of women's lives, 104 in all, by Giovanni Boccaccio is readily available in a modern English translation with a useful introduction by Guido Guarino, *Concerning Famous Women* (New Brunswick, 1963). Also see the comments in Benson, *The Invention of the Renaissance Woman*, 9–31. Sixteenth-century readers had available an Italian translation by Vincenzo Bagli of the Latin original as early as 1506, and another by Giuseppe Betussi, in which the translator added material on famous women who postdated Boccaccio, titled *Libro di m. Gio. Boccaccio delle donne illustri / tradotto per messer Giuseppe Betussi; con una additione fatta dal medesimo delle donne famose dal te[m]po di m. Giovanni fino a i giorni nostri, & alcune altre state per inanzi; con la vita del Boccaccio* (Venice: Comin da Trino [per] Andrea Arrivabene, 1545). On the "illustrious-women" genre

more generally, see Beatrice Collina, "L'esemplarità delle donne illustri fra Umanesimo e Controriforma," in Zarri, ed., *Donna, disciplina, creanza cristiana,* 103–19.

16. Giovanni Michele Bruto, *The Necessarie, Fit, and Convenient Education of a Yong Gentlewoman* (London: Adam Islip, 1598), no pagination, also available in an Amsterdam, 1969 facsimile edition. For biographical information, see Domenico Caccamo's entry in *Dizionario biografico degli Italiani,* vol. 14 (Rome, 1972), 730–34. The Italian and French editions, (Antwerp: Chez I. Bellere [per] C. Plantain Anvers, 1555) and (Paris: Jean Ruelle, 1558), respectively, carried the title *La institutione di una fanciulla nata nobilmente = L'institution d'une fille de noble maison traduicte de langue tuscane en françois.* Thomas Salter, *A Mirrhor Mete for all Mothers, Matrones, and Maidens, Intituled the Mirrhor of Modestie, No Lesse Profitable and Pleasant, then Necessarie to bee Read and Practised* (London: Edward White, 1579), as Ruth Kelso determined, is a translation of Bruto's 1555/1558 work rather than the original it claims to be. On the reception of Salter in England, see Janis Butler Holm, "The Myth of a Feminist Humanism: Thomas Salter's *"The Mirrhor of Modestie,"* *Soundings* 67 (winter 1984): 443–52.

17. See Eric Cochrane, "The Renaissance Academies in their Italian and European Setting," in *The Fairest Flower: The Emergence of Linguistic National Consciousness in Renaissance Europe* (Florence, 1985), 21–39, for an excellent assessment of the place of these academies. Also see Thomas Crane, *Italian Social Customs of the Sixteenth Century and Their Influence on the Literatures of Europe* (New York, 1971 rpt. of 1920 ed.), 142–44, which reports that women occasionally participated in some academy activities.

18. Orazio Lombardelli, *Il giovane studente* (Venice: La Minima Compagnia, 1594), 38–39.

19. Nicoletta Maraschio, ed., *Trattati di fonetica del Cinquecento* (Florence, 1992), 81–90, presents all that is known about Lombardelli.

20. Orazio Lombardelli, *De gli ufizii e costumi de' giovani* (Florence: Giorgio Marescotti, 1579), 26–34, for the ten reasons why young men behave as they do, and 120, 124, for advice to converse with old people but not with women. Secco, *La pedagogia della controriforma,* 58–66, treats *Il giovane studente* as a straightforward, serious text, which is entirely reasonable, but he does the same for the 1579 book, a reading I do not share. The earlier work is unabashedly rhetorical and polemical, whereas the latter carries sobriety to the point of turgidity. Nevertheless, Secco pondered the same ten causes of youthful bad habits that I did and never cracked a smile, which may just reflect his clerical views versus my liberal skepticism, but I do believe the addition of a "What's the problem?" index in the revised edition unmasks a spoof. Volpicelli, ed., *Il pensiero pedagogico della controriforma,* 598–99, takes the same approach as Secco.

In *Il seme della violenza,* 129–33, and in "Creanza e disciplina," 956–60, Ottavia Niccoli offers a more complex reading. She shows persuasively Lombardelli's intellectual debt to Erasmus's *De civilitate morum puerilium* (see Sowards, *Collected Works of Erasmus,* vol. 25, 269–89, for the English translation and annotation by Brian McGregor), while pointing out the Italian's absurd expansion of detailed advice on trivia such as how to spit, sit, and position one's hands. With understandable exasperation, Niccoli concedes that reading all this stuff is "insupportable" to modern people, but she does not question how sixteenth-century men and women read the text. My sense, obviously beyond proof or disproof, is that even the Catholic Reformation did not suppress completely Italian peoples' legendary appreciation of humor. Reading Lombardelli as a spoof that mimicked Erasmus's own capacity for evoking the comic (as in the Eulalia/Xanthippe colloquy I consider in chapter 6) relieves the text of boredom. And for me, at least, allowed a few good laughs.

21. Artur Michel, "The Earliest Dance-Manuals," *Medievalia et Humanistica* 3 (April, 1945): 127, treats Zuccolo's book as a "polemical treatise against dancing" that nonetheless realistically portrays the sixteenth-century ballroom scene as well as the individual dances of the time.

22. Simeon Zuccolo, *La pazzia del ballo* (Padua: Giacomo Fabriano, 1549).

23. Alessandro Arcangeli, ed., *Rinaldo Corso: Dialogo del ballo* (Verona, 1987), provides the text from the Venice, 1555 original. In the introduction (20), he considers the relationship between the works of Zuccolo and Corso. Hostility to dancing flourished in some Protestant circles and found literary expression in Christopher Fetherstone, *A Dialogue agaynst Light, Lewde, and Lascivious Dauncing: Wherein are Refuted all those Reasons, which the Common People Use to Bring in Defence Thereof* (London, 1582), available in an Ibstock, 1973 reprint. Fetherstone also published an abridged translation of John Calvin's *Institution of Christian Religion* (1585), and *The Brutish Thunderbolt* (1586), an antipapal tract. Kelso, *Doctrine for the Lady of the Renaissance*, 420, also cites Pietro Vermigli (Peter Martyr), *A Briefe Treatise, Concerning the Use and Abuse of Dauncing* (London, 1580?), but I have not seen this work.

24. See Julia Sutton's edition and translation (Oxford, 1986) of the 1600, Venice printing (itself a revised edition of the 1581, Venice, *Il ballarino*) of Fabritio Caroso's *Nobiltà di dame*, esp. 134-50, for twenty-four notes on proper deportment at the ball.

25. Palmieri, *Della vita civile*, 30. On cross-dressing more generally, see Vern L. Bullough and Bonnie Bullough, *Cross Dressing, Sex, and Gender* (Philadelphia, 1993), 74-112.

26. Fausto Sebastiano da Longiano, *De lo istituire un figlio d'un Principe da li X in fino a gl'anni de la discretione* (Venice, 1542), no pagination.

27. Sabba da Castiglione, *Ricordi, overo ammaestramenti di Monsignor Sabba Castiglione, Cavalier Gierosolimitano, ne' quali con prudenti, e christiani discorsi si ragiona di tutte le materie honorate, che si ricercano à un vero gentil'huomo* (Venice: Giovanni Bonadio, 1565), 10. The earliest edition of the 1565 reprint is 1554, a substantial revision of the 1546 original. The two successive editions (1549 and 1554) became increasingly apocalyptic in tone according to Mario Pozzi, "I trattati di saper vivere fra Castiglione e Guazzo," in Alain Montandon, ed., *Traites de savoir-vivre en Italie* (Clermont-Ferrand, 1993), 157-58. On publication matters, see Claudio Scarpati, *Studi sul Cinquecento italiano* (Milan, 1982), 83-90. For biographical information, also see Franca Petrucci's entry in *Dizionario biografico degli Italiani*, vol 22 (Rome, 1979), 100-106.

28. Piccolomini, *L'educazione dei giovani*, 119.

29. Gozze, *Governo della famiglia*, 78–81.

30. Panfilo Fenario, *Discorsi di P. F. sopra i cinque sentimenti; ne i quali si dimostrano le varie lor potenze, e effetti e fin dove per lor menzo arriva l'intelletto humano* (Venice: Giovanni Battista Somascho, 1587), 89, on touching.

31. Gozze, *Governo della famiglia*, 82–85.

32. Sabba da Castiglione, *Ricordi*, 10–14.

33. Annibale Guasco, *Ragionamento del sig. Annibal Guasco a d. Lavinia sua figliuola, della maniera del governarsi ella in corte; andando per dama* (Turin: L'herede di [Nicolò] Bevilacqua, 1586), 11, 22. On conduct books for women at court, with specific attention to this text, see Ann Rosalind Jones, *The Currency of Eros: Women's Love Lyric in Europe, 1540–1620* (Bloomington, 1990), 15–20.

34. Innocentio Ringhieri, *Cento giuochi liberale, et d'ingegno* (Bologna: Anselmo Giaccarelli, 1551), 118, for a game in which the object is to match a classical or biblical defender of her chastity with the instrument or characteristic by which she protected her honor.

35. No further definition of sodomy is given. I surmise from the text as a whole that the author understood sodomy to include oral or anal sex between two males, possibly also between heterosexual couples, but probably not sexual relations between females, even though all these acts denied procreation. The reticence to write down the words here is noteworthy, since the manual's explicit purpose is to explain everything in plain language. Bestiality is not mentioned at all. On Mediterranean attitudes concerning sodomy and on silence concerning this sin, see Richard Trexler, *Sex and Conquest: Gendered Violence, Political Order, and the European Conquest of the Americas* (Ithaca, 1995), 38–60. Also see Michael Rocke, *Forbidden Friendships: Homosexuality and Male Culture in Renaissance Florence* (New York, 1996), 3–16, which acknowledges that sodomy was the unmentionable vice even as the book proceeds to explore in brilliant and thorough fashion just how clear it is that sodomy was talked about and practiced.

36. Lodovico Gabrielli da Ogobbio, *Methodo di confessione* (Venice: Gabriel Giolito De' Ferrari, 1572), 217–35.

37. Gaspar Loarte, *Avisi di sacerdoti et confessori* (Parma, 1584), BNF shelf mark Magliabechiana 12.N.9.214, 187–92.

38. *Catechism of the Council of Trent*, 2.8.33, for the admonition about using proper words, and 3.7.1, 3.7.5, for the injunctions not to say too much and to keep proscriptions general. For relevant theoretical insights, see Marjorie K. McIntosh, "Finding Language for Misconduct: Jurors in Fifteenth-Century Local Courts," in Hanawalt and Wallace, *Bodies and Disciplines* (Minneapolis, 1996), 87–122.

39. Bartolomeo de Medina, *Breve instruttione de' confessori*, 79, 144.

40. We all remember Boccaccio for his wonderfully salacious stories, which were widely read in the sixteenth century as well. What the friar probably had in mind, however, were items like the hugely popular and very wicked *barzellette* of Poggio Bracciolini, several about priests involved in ménages à trois with simple-minded parishioners, published in a variety of editions throughout the sixteenth century. For a selection, see Francesco Capriglione, ed., *Le facetiae di*

Poggio Bracciolini (Poggia, 1978), or Bernhardt J. Hurwood, ed. and trans., *The Facetiae of Giovanni Francesco Poggio Bracciolini* (New York, 1968); each contains a brief bio-bibliography on this apostolic writer at the Papal Curia who found sufficient creative energy in his old age to craft the book of jokes condemned a century later by the church on grounds of obscenity, insolence, and impertinence. Tale number 237 (English edition) or 239 (Italian edition) provides a sidesplitter on explaining incest in proper Tuscan dialect while confessing in Rome, one that highlights as only humor can the difficulties of recounting sins properly.

41. Cherubino da Firenze, *Confessionario*, 47–50. On the tension in confessional manuals between the traditional injunction to have every detail of desire drawn out in the penitent's discourse and the modern preference for modest vagueness, see Michel Foucault, *An Introduction*, vol. 1 of *The History of Sexuality*, trans. Robert Hurley (New York, 1980), 18–21.

42. Girolamo (Brother Silvano) Razzi, *Della economica christiana, e civile di don Silvano Razzi i due primi libri, ne i quali da una nobile brigata di donne, & huomini si ragiona della cura e governo famigliare: secondo la legge christiana, e vita civile* (Florence: Bartolomeo Sermartelli, 1568), 126–39, on mortal sin, 135, specifically on lust.

43. Daniela Frigo, "Dal caos all' ordine: Sulla questione del 'prender moglie' nella trattatistica del sedicesimo secolo," in Zancan, ed., *Nel cerchio della luna*, 57–93, surveys a wide range of literature on the "taking-a-wife" question, including not only advice manuals but also dialogues and courtesy books.

44. Giovanni Maria Bonardo, *Le ricchezze dell' agricoltura. Nelle quali sotto brevità si danno molti novi ammaestramenti, per accrescer le rendite de' campi, e insieme bellissimi secreti, si in materia di piantar, & inestare alberi, e viti, come di vini, & aceti, e come si sanno le colombaie col governo e l'augmento di quelle, e medesimamente alcuni ricordi per chi tiene fatori, castaldi, lavoratori. Cose per lo più non insegnate anchora d'alcuno scrittor di quest' arte antico, o moderno, mandate in luce da Luigi Groto cieco d'Hadria* (Venice: Fabio & Agostino Zoppini, 1589). Also by the same author, see *La minera del mondo nella qual si tratta delle cose piu secrete, e piu rare de' corpi semplici nel mondo elementare, e de' corpi composti, inanimati, & animati d'anima vegetativa, sensitiva, e ragionevole* (Venice: Fabio & Agostino Zoppini, 1585); *La grandezza, larghezza, e distanza di tutte le sfere ridotte a nostre miglia: cominciando dall' inferno fin' alla sfera, dove stani beati; e la grandezza delle stelle* (Venice: Francesco Rocca, All' insegna del Castello, 1563); and *Madrigali* (Venice: Fabio & Agostino Zoppini, 1587).

45. Giovanni Maria Bonardo, *Della miseria et eccellenza della vita humana, ragionamenti due, nel quale con infiniti essempi, cavati da piu famosi scrittori, s' impara quali siano i travagli, & quali siano le perfettioni di questo mondo* (Venice: Fabio & Agostino Zoppini, 1586), 35–37. For the opinions on Bonardo's discourse, see Giorgio Stabile's entry in *Dizionario biografico degli Italiani*, vol. 11 (Rome, 1969), 573–75.

46. Anonymous, *Della famosissima Compagnia della lesina: dialogo, capitoli, ragionamenti: Con l'assotigliamento in tredici punture della punta d'essa lesina*, 67, for the small-wife satire; this edition (Venice: L'Armanni, 1666) runs to over four hundred octodecimo pages. The earliest edition I have seen (Mantua, 1591),

BNF shelf mark Palat. 12.B.B.4.1.35, contained only sixty-three leaves and did not have the small-wife advice. On the publication of these chapbooks and the attribution of authorship to either Francesco Maria Vialardi or Tommaso Buoni, see the *National Union Catalog*, vol. 138, 216–17.

47. Angelo di Forte, *Dialogo de gli incantamenti e strigarie con le altre malefiche opre, quale tutta via tra le donne e huomini se esercitano, piacevole e molto utile a qualunque persona* (Venice: Agostino Bindoni, 1533), no pagination. Similar advice may be found in Bartolomeo Arnigio, *Le diece veglie di Bartolomeo Arnigio, de gli ammendati costumi dell' humana vita, nelle quali non sol si tratta di quelle vertù, ch' à viver nella luce de gli huomini, & di Dio bisognevoli sono* (Brescia: Francesco & Pietro Maria Marchetti, 1576), 231–32. After much discourse about the pitfalls of marrying a beautiful woman, however, Arnigio's interlocutor suddenly becomes aghast at the implications of what he is saying and assures his audience that he does not mean a man should flee from beauty. Being stuck with a truly ugly or deformed wife is like being half in hell, and it will make you nauseous for life. Arnigio seems to be a two-seed thinker, since he gives as a further excuse for seeking beauty in a wife that her offspring will be of her size, shape, look, and complexion.

48. Anonymous, *Stanze in lode della donna brutta* (Florence: Anton Francesco Doni, 1547), BNF shelf mark E.6.6.154.III.n.17.

49. Anonymous, *Giardino di virtu. Nel quale si contiene alcuni particolari, e maravigliosi secreti. Non più da persona alcuna dati in luce. E con diligenza, e spese di Zan Fritella ritrovati* (Florence, n.d., ca. 1600), BNF shelf mark Palat. (14) X.4.1.67. See Camporesi, *Juice of Life*, 43, 127–29, for background on this literary tradition. On standards of beauty, see Yalom, *A History of the Breast*, 52–55.

50. Ciro Spontone, *Hercole difensore d'Homero. Dialogo del Sig. Cavalliere Ciro Spontone; nel quale oltre ad alcune nobilissime materia, si tratta de'tiranni, delle congiure contro di loro, della magia naturale; & dell'officio donnesco* (Verona: Girolamo Discepolo, 1595), 192. Federico Luigini, *Il libro della bella donna* (Venice: Plinio Pietrasanta, 1554), now available in a Milan, 1974 reprint, covers much of the same ground but at far greater length, with more pseudoerudition and less humor. On this genre, see Naomi Yavneh, "The Ambiguity of Beauty in Tasso and Petrarch," in Turner, *Sexuality and Gender in Early Modern Europe*, 133–57. Now easily accessible in an excellent translation is Agnolo Firenzuola, *On the Beauty of Women* (Philadelphia, 1992, Konrad Eisenbichler and Jacqueline Murray, trans., of the original completed in 1541), which includes an informative introduction with an analysis of why Firenzuola should be read as a feminist.

51. Lando, *Paradossi*, 42–46. Stories of adulterous wives were very popular in this period; works that today are almost entirely forgotten were big sellers then, for example, the imitation of Boccaccio, with less literary talent exhibited but lots of sex, by Tommaso Costo, *Il fuggilozio. Diviso in otto giornate ove da otto gentilhuomini e due donne si ragiona delle malizie di femine e trascuragini di mariti* (Venice: Barezzo Barezzi, 1601).

52. Giuseppe Passi, *I donneschi difetti* (Venice, 1595), with reprintings in 1599, 1601, and 1618. The edition (Venice: Vincenzo Somascho, 1618) that I exam-

ined runs to nearly four hundred pages, and in the text I have translated only the chapter titles as an indication of the character of this work. The Aristotle reference and related historical examples begin on page 344. In this work, Passi proclaims himself *"Nell Illustrissima Academia de Signori Riccovrati di Padova, e Infermi di Ravenna l'Ardito."*

53. Lucrezia Marinella, *La nobiltà et l'eccellenze delle donne.* Labalme, "Venetian Women on Women," 91–93, sees some merit in this work but rightly implies that Marinella stooped to the polemical level of Passi. Chemello, "La donna, il modello, l'immaginario," 103, concludes that Marinella's work is an explicit and specific response to Passi. Beatrice Collina, "Moderata Fonte e *Il merito delle donne,*" *Annali d'Italianistica* 7 (1989): 142–43, makes the same point and adds that, had it not been for the market created by Passi's perverse tract, Fonte's work also might well have remained unpublished. I agree.

Jordan, *Renaissance Feminism,* 250–51, makes no connection between Passi and Marinella, possibly because she may have been unaware of the 1595 and 1599 editions of Passi when she cited the 1601 reprint that appeared after Marinella's tract apparently had boosted sales for both polemicists. The reliance on a later edition also may have affected Jordan's reading of Passi's subsequent work, *Dello stato maritale.* While she duly notes his continued adherence to misogynist stereotypes, Jordan tries valiantly to tease from Passi's warnings against marrying a woman who is richer than yourself some sort of concession to a woman's ability to use property to undermine natural male superiority. In a later essay, "Renaissance Women and the Question of Class," in Turner, ed., *Sexuality and Gender in Early Modern Europe,* 91, Jordan very consciously sets aside authorial intention and again credits Passi with the same insight or concession. My focus is more historical, I suppose, and my judgment is that no one living at the time Passi wrote could possibly have seen in his work any concession to anything feminist. He was a misogynist with a wicked sense of humor and a certain gift for words who deeply offended Lucrezia Marinella and other intellectual women of her time.

54. Giuseppe Passi, *Dello stato maritale. Trattato di Giuseppe Passi Ravennate Nell' Academia de' Signori Informi di Ravenna. L'Ardito. Nel quale con molti essempi antichi e moderni non solo si dimostra quello che una donna maritata deve schivare ma quello ancora che fare le convenga se compitamente desidera di satisfare all' ufficio suo. Opera non meno utile che dilettevole a ciascheduno* (Venice: Giacomo Antonio Somascho, 1602), 2, 81, 83, 123, 132, 144, for the particular bits of advice. Frigo, "Dal caos all' ordine," 73, accepts at face value Passi's statement that in this work he hopes to mitigate the harsh judgments of his previous tirade *(I donneschi difetti),* but in my view her reading is far too kind. His subsequent volume on male defects, *La monstruosa fucina delle sordidezze de gl' huomini* (Venice: Giacomo Antonio Somascho, 1603), which Frigo accepts as yet a further sign of remorse, I take as an attempt to cash in again on public interest in this genre by going one up on Marinella, all in good fun, of course. Equally, I ascribe the decision of his colleagues at the Accademia degli Informi to write poems in praise of women to appease public outrage over Passi's invectives more to condescension than contrition. And I certainly do not accept the conclusion that Passi's

decision to become a hermit had anything to do with penance over the furor stirred by his misogynous writings. Maria Fubini Leuzzi, "Vita coniugale e vita familiare nei trattati italiani fra XVI e XVII secolo," in Zarri, *Donna, disciplina, creanza cristiana,* 258–61, follows Frigo's charitable interpretation.

55. Anonymous, *Le malitie delle donne, con la superbia, e pompa, che usano. Et insegna alla gioventù a trovar buona moglie con un' essempio a maritati di attender a casa sua. Opera nuova, e piacevole, honesta, e da ridere* (Bassano, n.d., but surely sixteenth century), BNF shelf mark E.6.6.154.III.n.1; the title page indicates that there were earlier editions in Bologna, Venice, and Padua. For the publication history of this work, and the possibly related *Governo de fameglia,* see Salmore Morpurgo, "Il governo de famiglia e le malattie delle donne," *Miscellanea Rossi* 34, no. 14 (Florence, 1893): 5–57, esp. 55–57. Doglio, ed., *Galeazzo Flavio Capra,* 116–20, shows eleven editions published between 1487 and 1528.

56. Marcia Colish, "Cosmetic Theology: The Transformation of a Stoic Theme," *Assays* 1 (1981): 3–14, traces the shift by early Christian writers from Stoic condemnation of cosmetics for both genders to attacks on women almost exclusively, so Agnelli is traditional in his focus on women alone. On the gender imbalance in sumptuary legislation, see Ronald Rainey, "Dressing Down the Dressed-Up: Reproving Feminine Attire in Renaissance Florence," in Monfasani and Musto, eds., *Renaissance Society and Culture,* 217–37. Rocke, *Forbidden Friendships,* 38, mentions condemnation of male ostentation, but overall the evidence does not show this to have been a major concern. Episodes of transvestism also were reported only infrequently.

57. Peter Green, ed. and trans., *Ovid: The Erotic Poems* (Harmondsworth, 1982), 264–66, for "On Facial Treatment for Ladies." Ovid was widely available in vernacular translations in printed sixteenth-century editions, and his amorous poems appear prominently on lists of works women should not be reading. The same themes appear in humorous dialogues, such as Giuseppe Orologgi, *L'inganno* (Venice: Gabriel Giolito de' Ferrari, 1562), 131, for the presumed exchange between Lodovico Dolce and Girolamo Ruscelli, two prolific authors. Dolce complains that "women continuously apply polishes, white lead, fats, and alum to their faces, using infusions, masks, pastes, alembic waters, sublimations, and oils; all these disgusting things they plaster on at bedtime so that their poor husbands who think they have slept with a wife find themselves with a piece of stucco, having kissed a [facial] mask." And Ruscelli responds wisely that "the worst is that husbands wake up in the morning with their beards caked and discolored. Women don't realize that this falsification earns them cursing and hatred rather than affection or praise."

58. Cosmo Agnelli, *Amorevole aviso circa gli abusi delle donne vane. Utili per vergini, vedove, & maritate. Accioche ciascheduna viva honoratamente, secondo il grado loro* (Bologna: Giovanni Rossi [per] Giovanni Francesco Rasca & Gasparo Bindoni, 1592), 6–24.

My editor has given permission to include advice on walking in high heels that comes from a manual on dancing surely meant only for elites and therefore having no proper place in this book on popular manuals, but it is just too funny to resist as a contrast to Agnelli. The quote is from Caroso, *Nobiltà di dame,* 141.

Some ladies and gentlewomen slide their chopines along as they walk, so that the racket they make is enough to drive one crazy! More often they bang them so loudly with each step, that they remind us of Franciscan friars. Now in order to walk nicely, and to wear chopines properly on one's feet, so that they do not twist or go awry (for if one is ignorant of how to wear them, one may splinter them, or fall frequently, as has been and still is observed at parties and in church), it is better for [the lady] to raise the toe of the foot she moves first when she takes a step, by raising it thus, she straightens the knee of that foot, and this extension keeps her body attractive and erect, besides which her chopine will not fall off that foot. Also, by thus raising it she avoids sliding it along [the ground], nor does she make any unpleasant noise. Then she should put it down, and repeat the same thing with the other foot (which follows). In this way, and by observing [this rule], she may move entirely with grace, seemliness, and beauty, better than the way one walked before; for a natural step is one thing, but a well-ordered step is another. By walking this way, therefore, even if the lady's chopines are more than a handbreadth-and-a-half high, she will seem to be on chopines only three finger-breadths high, and will be able to dance *flourishes* and galliard variations at a ball, as I have just shown the world this day.

59. The quotation is from King and Rabil, eds., *Her Immaculate Hand*, 79–80. For an alternative translation, as well as a thorough introductory essay, which became available only after my book was in press, see Diana Robin, trans. and ed., *Laura Cereta: Collected Letters of a Renaissance Feminist* (Chicago, 1997), 84–85, for this passage. On Cereta's life and works, also see Albert Rabil Jr., *Laura Cereta, Quattrocento Humanist* (Binghamton, 1981), esp. 6, on her desire for eternal fame through her literary efforts, and 29, for an earlier letter conveying the same theme. Although Cereta's letters were not published in the sixteenth century, references to her correspondence do appear in various places, for example, Arnigio, *Le diece veglie*, 244. Also see Margaret L. King, "Book-Lined Cells: Women and Humanism in the Early Italian Renaissance," in Labalme, *Beyond Their Sex*, 71–73. Although Christine de Pisan's now famous *Treasure of the City of Ladies* did not obtain an Italian (or a French) printing in the sixteenth century, readers will note instantly the similarities between Cereta's condemnation of ostentatious dress and that by Christine de Pisan. For rejection of pomp and vanity by a female author with a dramatically different lifestyle, see the analysis of the honest courtesan Veronica Franco's writings by Rosenthal, in "Venetian Women Writers," 118–19, and *The Honest Courtesan*, 58–110.

All the more remarkable, then, is the vigorous defense of women's right to dress as they please found in Moderata Fonte's *Il merito delle donne*, a matter insightfully discussed in Cox, "The Single Self," 552–57.

60. *Catechism of the Council of Trent*, 2.8.13–14.

61. Fioravanti, *La cirugia*, bk. 2, chap. 24 (Furfaro, 63–64).

62. Tommasi, *Reggimento del padre*, 44–55. On domestic economy tracts more generally, see Manuela Doni Garfagnini, "Autorità maschili e ruoli femminili: le

fonti classiche degli 'economici'," in Zarri, ed., *Donna, disciplina, creanza cristiana,* 237-51.

63. Annibale Romei, *Discorsi del Conte Annibal Romei, gentilhuomo ferrarese. Divisi in cinque giornate* (Venice: Francesco Ziletti, 1585), 44-45. The book went through several editions, and the dialogue grew from five days to seven in an expanded version (Ferrara, 1586), so at least some readers must have enjoyed this book more than I did. It was translated into English in 1598.

64. Sabba da Castiglione, *Ricordi,* 214-23. The chart is my construction of the narrative in the original text. On the Catholic Reformation context of this work, and for bio-bibliographical matters, see Scarpati, *Studi sul Cinquecento italiano,* 27-121.

65. Leonardo Fioravanti, *Dello specchio di scientia universale, dell' eccellente medico, & cirugico M. Leonardo Fioravanti bolognese, libri tre* (Venice: Vincenzo Valgrisi, 1564), 209-16.

66. Gioberti, *Errori popolari,* 181. More generally, see O'Faolain and Martines, *Not in God's Image,* 142-43.

67. Anonymous, *Lamento de una gioveneta la quale fu volunterosa de esser presto maridata. Et una frottola del gallo. Et uno esordio sponsalitio* (n.p., n.d., but surely sixteenth century), BNF shelf mark E.6.5.3.II.2. Doglio, ed., *Galeazzo Flavio Capra,* 123, cites a Venice, 1524 edition. For the previously cited despairing commentary of Michele Savonarola, see his *Ad mulieres ferrarienses,* 192-95.

68. Marinello, *Delle medicine,* 1-2.

69. Gozze, *Governo della famiglia,* 24-26, 40.

70. Torquato Tasso, "The Father of the Family," in Carnes Lord and Dain Trafton, trans. and eds., *Tasso's Dialogues: A Selection with the Discourse on the Art of Dialogue* (Berkeley, 1982), 83-85. For a more playful variant on similar themes, see the dialogue between young Maddalena and the worldly wise Coppina in Bartolomeo Gottifredi, *Specchio d'amore* (Florence: Anton Francesco Doni, 1547), and in the more readily available Giuseppe Zonta, ed., *Trattati d'amore del Cinquecento* (Bari, 1968 rpt. of 1912 ed.), 249-302.

71. Domenico Bruni, *Difese delle donne, nella quale si contengono le difese loro* (Florence: Filippo & Jacopo Giunta, 1552), 80-85. My colleague William Connell provided me with a reference from Jacopo Maria Fioravanti, *Memorie storiche della città di Pistoja* (Bologna, 1986 rpt. of 1758 ed.), 430, stating that *Difese delle donne* goes by the name "Involatore," which would suggest that this eighteenth-century local expert surmised, or had evidence, that the book was used to seduce women with flattery. More conventional views may be found in Jordan, *Renaissance Feminism,* 167-70, and Cox, "The Single Self," 519.

72. Marinello, *Delle medicine,* 2.

73. Fioravanti, *Dello specchio di scientia universale,* 206.

74. Fioravanti, *Dello specchio di scientia universale,* 206-9.

75. *Enciclopedia italiana,* vol. 13 (Milan, 1932), 97.

76. Grendler, *Critics of the Italian World,* 65-69; the point is explored with even more explicit reference to market economics by Peter Burke, *Culture and Society in Renaissance Italy 1420-1540* (New York, 1972), 60-61, 104-5.

77. In fact, Marie-Françoise Piejus, "Venus Bifrons," in Josè Guidi, Marie-Françoise Piejus, and Adelin-Charles Fiorato, eds., *Images de la femme dans la littérature italienne de la Renaissance: Préjugés misogynes et aspirations nouvelles* (Paris, 1980), 154–55, notes a considerable increase during the decade from 1540 to 1550, of books in the genre of Dolce's and Vives's treatises on and for women. For Dolce's publication activities, see especially Bareggi, *Il mestiere di scrivere*, 285–90, and graph 33, which documents his extensive work for other printing firms as well.

78. In the notes that follow, the page references will be to Lodovico Dolce, *De gli ammaestramenti pregiatissimi, che appartengono alla educatione, & honorevole, e virtuosa vita virginale, maritale, e vedovile* (Venice: Barezzo Barezzi, 1622); included in the same volume is Agnolo Firenzuola, *Le bellezze le lodi, gli amori & costumi delle donne. Con lo discacciamento delle lettere di Agnolo Firenzuola, et di Alessandro Picolomini*. On Vives, I will use Juan Luis Vives, *De l'ufficio del marito, come si debba portare verso la moglie. De l'istitutione de la femina christiana, vergine, maritata, o vedova. De lo ammaestrare i fanciulli ne le arti liberali* (Venice: Vincenzo Valgrisi, 1546).

79. For extensive selections from Vives, see Foster Watson, ed., *Vives and the Renascence Education of Women* (New York, 1912); also see Foster Watson, ed., *Vives: On Education. A Translation of the De Tradendis Disciplinis of Juan Luis Vives* (Totowa, 1971 rpt. of 1913 ed. with a forward by Francesco Cordasco). For a more recent and sympathetic appraisal of Vives on women, along with brief samples of his writings, see Susan Groag Bell, ed., *Women from the Greeks to the French Revolution* (Belmont, 1973), 181–90; see also Melinda K. Blade, *Education of Italian Renaissance Women* (Mesquite, 1983).

Jordan, *Renaissance Feminism*, 117–19, is much harsher about Vives, but she fails to note the connection between Vives and Dolce; that may explain her ambiguous treatment of Dolce, 69–70. In my opinion, what Jordan sees as Dolce's "concession to feminist claims" that "woman is as intelligent as a man" is just a rhetorical device on his part to pave the way for even stricter control over women's lives. Gloria Kaufman, "Juan Luis Vives on the Education of Women," *Signs* 3 (summer 1978): 891–96, exposes Vives's antifeminist views. Also see Valerie Wayne, "Some Sad Sentence: Vives' *Instruction of a Christian Woman*," in Margaret Hannay, ed., *Silent but for the Word: Tudor Women as Patrons, Translators, and Writers of Religious Works* (Kent, 1985), 15–29, and Jones, *The Currency of Eros*, 22.

80. Dolce, *Ammaestramenti*, 7–49. On margins, see William W. E. Slights, "The Edifying Margins of Renaissance English Books," *Renaissance Quarterly* 42 (winter 1989): 682–716.

81. Henderson and McManus, *Half Humankind*, 73–74, make the important observation that English manuals on choosing a spouse, written somewhat later in the sixteenth century, are addressed directly to the young people making the choice, not to their parents.

82. Dolce, *Ammaestramenti*, 50–54.

83. Dolce, *Ammaestramenti*, 56–60.

Chapter Six

1. Jordan, *Renaissance Feminism*, 144, cites Nicolò Gozze, whom we have considered before, and Paolo Caggio; other writers easily could be added. The subtext in these familial-advice manuals is not political theory in defense of monarchy but a pervasive misogyny, exemplified nicely in Caggio, *Iconomica del Signor Paolo Caggio, gentil'huomo di Palermo. Nella quale s'insegna brevemente per modo di dialogo il governo famigliare, come di se stesso, della moglie, de' figliuoli, de' servi, delle case, delle robbe, & ogn'altra cosa a quella appartenente* (Venice: Al segno del pozzo [Andrea Arrivabene], 1552). A two-page table of contents promises answers to problems such as, "Why did nature make men robust and valorous and women weak and of little spirit," and further along gives advice on, "What damages are caused by wives who are pompous, proud, and domineering."

2. Joy Wiltenburg, *Disorderly Women and Female Power in the Street Literature of Early Modern England and Germany* (Charlottesville, 1992), 97-139, provides an excellent treatment of the marital-inversion literary genre. Works in Italian have not been as thoroughly considered, although my sense is that they were less common, at least in the sixteenth century. Still, the theme appears prominently in Italian art; see Anne Jacobson Schutte, "'Trionfo delle donne': Tematiche di rovesciamento dei ruoli nella Firenze rinascimentale," *Quaderni Storici* 44 (1980): 474-96.

3. Barbara B. Diefendorf, "Widowhood and Remarriage in Sixteenth-Century Paris," *Journal of Family History* 7 (winter 1982), 386, makes this very point: "The fact that widows as well as widowers could retain control over the estate of a deceased spouse is very important. It demonstrates that the basis for laws that subjected wives to the legal authority of their husbands lay less in the supposed incompetence of women than in the belief that each family should have one and only one head." The more conventional feminist view is expressed succinctly in Joan Kelly, "Early Feminist Theory and the *Querelle des Femmes*, 1400-1789," in her posthumously published book, *Women, History, and Theory: The Essays of Joan Kelly* (Chicago, 1984), 83: "To reduce women to subjection to husbands, however, and to deny them any other mode of life, women had to be, and were, regarded as rationally defective. They could not govern, nor could they be learned."

4. Giuseppe Falcone, *La nuova, vaga, e dilettevole villa* (Brescia: [Tommaso] Bozzola, 1599), 19. The earliest edition I know of is 1592; later editions followed in 1602, 1612, 1619, 1628, and 1691.

5. Camillo Fanucci, *Trattato di tutte le opere pie dell'alma città di Roma* (Rome: Lepido Faci & Stefano Paolini [per] Bastiano d' Franceschi, 1601), 173-75. More generally, see Sherrill Cohen, "Asylums for Women in Counter-Reformation Italy," in Sherrin Marshall, ed., *Women in Reformation and Counter-Reformation Europe* (Bloomington, 1989), 166-88; on Tuscany, see Sherrill Cohen, *The Evolution of Women's Asylums Since 1500: From Refuges for Ex-Prostitutes to Shelters for Battered Women* (New York, 1992). Evidence that battered women had at least limited access to legal redress may be found in the important recent article by Joanne M. Ferraro, "The Power to Decide: Battered

Wives in Early Modern Venice," *Renaissance Quarterly* 48 (autumn 1995), 492–512.

6. Arnigio, *Le diece veglie*, 256–57, makes the most extended use of the ship metaphor that I have come across.

7. King, *Women of the Renaissance*, 35–44, gives an excellent summary of the contemporary feminist view. Ruth Mohl, *The Three Estates in Medieval and Renaissance Literature* (New York, 1933), 351–52, notes a marked increase in misogynous literature toward the end of the thirteenth century, well before the period under primary consideration by Joan Kelly and the feminist scholars who expanded her challenge. R. Howard Bloch, *Medieval Misogyny and the Invention of Western Romantic Love* (Chicago, 1991), vigorously and astutely pushes the exploration of European misogyny back to its Judeo-Christian origins.

A powerful portrait of affectionate, trusting marriage among patriarchal Venetian patricians may be found in Stanley Chojnacki, "The Power of Love: Wives and Husbands in Late Medieval Venice," in Erler and Kowaleski, *Women and Power in the Middle Ages*, 126–48. On the substantial influence of women in the Venetian patriciate, see his "Patrician Women in Early Renaissance Venice," *Studies in the Renaissance* 21 (1974), 176–203. For a useful overview on patriarchal authority, see Barbara B. Diefendorf, "Give Us Back Our Children: Patriarchal Authority and Parental Consent to Religious Vocations in Early Counter-Reformation France," *Journal of Modern History* 68 (June 1996): 271–74. On the extent and limits of wifely subjection, see Sommerville, *Sex and Subjection*, 84–89.

8. I found this set of rules in Diane Bornstein, *The Lady in the Tower: Medieval Courtesy Literature for Women* (Hamden, 1983), 63, who translated them from Pietro Gori, ed., *Dodici avvertimenti che deve dare la madre alla figliuola quando la manda a marito* (Florence, 1885). How the original twelve rules of the title became thirteen in Bornstein's translation I am not sure. Especially incisive on the relationship between verbal expression and sexual freedom is Jones, *The Currency of Eros*, 15–35.

9. For an excellent introduction to the genre of parent-to-child advice in medieval literature, see Tauno F. Mustanoja, ed., *The Good Wife Taught Her Daughter & The Good Wyfe wold a Pylgremage & The Thewis of Gud Women* (Helsinki, 1948), esp. 161, for similar advice from a mother to her daughter:

> What man þe wedde schall befor God with a rynge,
> Honour hym and wurchipe him, and bowe ouer all þinge.
> Mekely hym answere and noght to haterlynge,
> And so þou schalt slake his mod and be his derlynge.
> > *Fayre wordes wratthe slakith,*
> > > *My der child*
> Swete of speche schalt þou be, glad, of myld
> Trewe in worde and in dede, in lyue and soule good.
> Kepe þe fro synne, fro vylenye, and schame,
> And loke þat þou bere þe so wele þat men seie þe no blame.
> > *Gode name fele wynneth*
> > > *My leue childe.*

Be þou of semblauntȝ sad, and euer of faire chere,
þat þi chere chaunge noght for noght þat þou maiste here.
Fare noght as a gygge for noght þat may betyde.
Laughe þou noght to lowde, ne ȝane þou noght to wyde.
> Lawchen þou maight and faire mought make,
> My der childe.

When þou goest be þe weie, goe þou noght to faste,
Wagge noght with þin hedde, þin schuldres awey to caste.
Be noght of many wordes; swere þou noght to grete.
Alle suche maners, my der child, þou muste lete.
> Euell lak, euell name,
> My leue child.

10. Plutarch, *Moralia*, bk. 2, 138–146A.

11. King, *Venetian Humanism*, 93. Also see King, "Caldiera and the Barbaros on Marriage and the Family," *Journal of Medieval and Renaissance Studies* 6 (1976): 19–50. In this article, King holds that, although "Francesco [Barbaro] relies heavily on classical sources, displaying his recently acquired knowledge of Greek, the *De re uxoria* is an original work" (32).

12. John Martin, "Out of the Shadow: Heretical and Catholic Women in Renaissance Venice," *Journal of Family History* 10 (spring 1985): 21–33, uses inquisition records to show that Venetian patriarchal ideology was widely diffused among artisans in the latter half of the sixteenth century. Style apparently mattered. Whereas Barbaro's treatise was translated and printed, that of his contemporary, Giovanni Caldiera, never found a publisher. On his thought, see Margaret King, "Personal, Domestic, and Republican Values in the Moral Philosophy of Giovanni Caldiera," *Renaissance Quarterly* 28 (winter 1975): 535–74.

13. King, "Caldiera and the Barbaros," 34, sees Francesco Barbaro as something of a defender of women: "Barbaro gives a lot of credit to women. See Gothein's discussion of the medieval antifeminist tradition and Barbaro's departure from it." Kohl et al., eds., *The Earthly Republic*, 179–87, share King's assessment of Barbaro and anticipate little of the feminist critique about to befall this humanist.

14. The translation is from Kohl et al., eds., *The Earthly Republic*, 202, 204. On Christian justifications for prescriptions on public behavior, which place great emphasis on the relationship between exterior appearances and interior reality, see Giovanni Pozzi, "Occhi bassi," in Edgar Marsch and Giovanni Pozzi, eds., *Thematologie des Kleinen: Petits thèmes littéraires* (Fribourg, 1986), 161–211.

15. Jordan, *Renaissance Feminism*, 41–47, 47, for the quotation; Kathleen Casey, "The Cheshire Cat: Reconstructing the Experience of Medieval Women," in Carroll, *Liberating Women's History*, 225–27; and Stanley Chojnacki, "'The Most Serious Duty': Motherhood, Gender, and Patrician Culture in Renaissance Venice," in Migiel and Schiesari, eds., *Refiguring Woman*, 133–54. Also see Ann Rosalind Jones, "Nets and Bridles: Early Modern Conduct Books and Sixteenth-Century Women's Lyrics," in Nancy Armstrong and Leonard Tennenhouse,

eds., *The Ideology of Conduct: Essays on Literature and the History of Sexuality* (New York, 1987), 52–63.

16. Kohl et al., eds., *The Earthly Republic*, 208–9.

17. Kelso, *Doctrine for the Lady of the Renaissance*, 78–135, is particularly relevant to "wifely duties" literature. The quotation concerning her restraint about imposing a comparative framework is found on page 280. Her bibliography of 891 items "for the lady" is found on pages 326–424. While not a complete listing, it certainly is a good start.

18. Palmieri, *Della vita civile*, 135. Sarah Pomeroy, *Goddesses, Whores, Wives, and Slaves* (New York 1975), 79–80, provides a glimpse of Xanthippe's relationship with Socrates, from which we may imagine that being married to the great man was not easy.

19. *Dialogo Erasmico di due donne maritate, in nel quale luna mal contenta del marito si duole, laltra la consiglia, e con esica ci esempi la induce a ben vivere, opera molto utile per le donne maritate. Tradotta per Andronico Collodio di latino in vulgare* (Venice: Ad instantia di Damonfido pastore detto il Peregrino, 1542). This edition—printed as a single "dialogue" or colloquy running to twenty-one octavo leaves—surely was meant as a nice little gift, not too expensive but very thoughtful, perhaps from a husband to his wife or perhaps among married women. It opens with a woodcut of two women engaged in dialogue, a powerful visual affirmation of the worth of women's talk.

20. The idea of sex as "medicine" to relieve male anxieties was ubiquitous; Marinello, *Delle medicine*, 34–35, even offers ointments to be rubbed on the genitals explicitly to reduce marital quarreling rather than solely for enhancement of physical performance.

21. Craig R. Thompson, ed. and trans., *The Colloquies of Erasmus* (Chicago, 1965), 114–27. For a convenient collection of Erasmus's writings most directly related to women, see Erika Rummel, ed., *Erasmus on Women* (Toronto, 1996).

22. Aldo Landi, ed., *Antonio Brucioli: Dialogi* (Naples, 1982), 553–88, provides excellent biographical and bibliographical information. In English, one might start with Paul F. Grendler, *The Roman Inquisition and the Venetian Press (1540–1605)* (Princeton, 1977).

23. De Bujanda, *Index de Rome 1557, 1559, 1564*, 155.

24. Landi, ed., *Antonio Brucioli: Dialogi*, 49–56.

25. Pietro Belmonte, *Institutione della sposa del cavalier Pietro Belmonte ariminese, fatta principalmente per Madonna Laudomia sua figliuola nelle sue nuove nozze* (Rome: Gl' heredi di Giovanni Osmarino Gigliotto, 1587), 14, 32, 39, 41, for the specific recommendations. Leuzzi, "Vita coniugale e vita familiare," 260–61, ignores unpleasantries such as the recommendation of live entombment in her benevolent treatment of Belmonte.

26. Orazio Lombardelli, *Dell' uffizio della donna maritata. Capi cento ottanta* (Florence: Giorgio Marescotti, 1583). The opening letter to Delia is dated October 6, 1574. The closing letter to his uncle is dated June 14, 1577. This work is extremely rare; I know of no copies in the United States, and the copy listed in the Biblioteca Nazionale Centrale di Firenze catalog was lost in the 1966 flood;

neither is it at the Riccardiana or any other reasonable place in Florence. The copy I used is from the British Library, shelf mark 524.b.12.(2.), bound with the unrelated Tommaso Buoni, *I problemi della bellezza, di tutti gli affetti humani* (Venice, 1605). The title page gives a publication year of 1584, but the back page clearly says 1583. Either way, his wife had been dead for at least six years, and the most likely occasion for publishing this work was in connection with Marescotti's reprinting of Lombardelli's *De gli ufizii e costumi de' giovani*. On reading between the lines, see Kelso, *Doctrine for the Lady of the Renaissance*, 95–96.

27. Anonymous, *Della famosissima Compagnia della lesina*, 74–76.

28. *Catechism of the Council of Trent*, 2.8.16–33. It is noteworthy that the catechism makes no parallel injunction against excessive female sexuality, obviously not because the clerics were protofeminists but because they did not accept the "daughters-of-Eve" view of women as creatures of insatiable lasciviousness. The catechism, as well as virtually all serious texts for laypersons, consistently identifies male lust as the drive that needs to be checked. Unlimited female sexual drive is a theme for humorous tracts, not for advice manuals and books presenting church teachings. Edmund Leites, "The Duty to Desire: Love, Friendship, and Sexuality in Some Puritan Theories of Marriage," *Journal of Social History* (spring 1982): 383–408, is excellent on the Tridentine background for Puritan emphasis on the sensuous pleasures of marriage.

29. *Catechism of the Council of Trent*, 2.8.2, 21, 27.

30. Bartolomeo de Medina, *Breve instruttione de' confessori*, 156–63.

31. Anonymous, *El costume delle donne*.

32. Tommasi, *Reggimento del padre*, 81–83, 102–7.

33. Sabba da Castiglione, *Ricordi*, 262–66. Martin, "Out of the Shadow," 25–26, emphasizes the importance of the confessional for Catholic women seeking counsel in dealing with brutish husbands.

34. Agostino Valerio, *Instruttione delle donne maritate* (Venice: Bolognino Zaltieri, 1575), 9–35. In the same year, 1575, the Zaltieri firm also published two other little vernacular works by him, *Ricordi lasciati alle monache nella sua visitatione fatta l'anno 1575*, and *Institutione d'ogni stato lodevole delle donne christiane*.

35. Agnelli, *Amorevole aviso*, 25–55.

36. Cherubino da Siena, *Regole*, 3–40.

37. Tommaso Garzoni, *Le vite delle donne illustri della scrittura sacra . . .* (Venice: Giovanni Domenico Imberti, 1588), 165, 173–74; this is a revised edition of the 1568 original. See Grendler, *Critics of the Italian World*, 191–93, for a brief general assessment of Garzoni and some specifics on his contribution to craniognomy. For a good introduction to Garzoni's most famous work, see John Martin, "The Imaginary Piazza: Tommaso Garzoni and the Late Italian Renaissance," in Samuel K. Cohn Jr. and Steven A. Epstein, *Portraits of Medieval and Renaissance Living: Essays in Memory of David Herlihy* (Ann Arbor, 1996), 439–54. The definitive Italian edition of several of Garzoni's works, with a useful commentary and thorough bibliography, is Paolo Cherchi, ed., *Tomaso Garzoni: Opere* (Ravenna, 1993), but this does not include *Le vite delle donne illustri*.

38. Hull, *Women according to Men*, 38, cites Francis Meres, *Gods Arithmeticke* (1597), D1 verso. He is better known as the author of a collection of apothegms

for use in grammar schools titled, *Wits Common Wealth.* On the Platonic and Aristotelian traditions, see Susan Moller Okin, *Women in Western Political Thought* (Princeton, 1979), 15–96, and Saxonhouse, *Women in the History of Political Thought,* esp. 37–91. On spiritual equality, see Sommerville, *Sex and Subjection,* 43–51.

39. Giacomo Lanteri, *Della economica trattato di m. Giacomo Lanteri gentilhuomo bresciano, nel quale si dimostrano le qualità, che all' huomo et alla donna separatamente convengono pel governo della casa* (Venice: Vincenzo Valgrisi, 1560), 111–49, for the section on *honestà feminile.* On Lanteri's career, see Frigo, *Il padre di famiglia,* 58. Jordan, *Renaissance Feminism,* 147, includes Lanteri's dialogue among those that served to undermine patriarchal structures, certainly an incidental and unintended consequence if, in fact, it had that consequence at all. More generally on the farmer's almanac genre, see Elide Casali, *Il villano dirozzato: Cultura società e potere nelle campagne romagnole della Controriforma* (Florence, 1982); it contains an excellent glossary of difficult agricultural terminology and good explorations among the primary sources.

40. Gozze, *Governo della famiglia,* 44–51.

41. Fioravanti, *Dello specchio di scientia universale,* bk. 3, chap. 24, 299–301. The facetiae of Poggio Bracciolini, published widely in the sixteenth century, were the sort of thing Fioravanti surely had in mind, along with Boccaccio's *Decameron.* I am persuaded by the horrified admonitions of writers such as Fioravanti that a fair number of honest matrons probably did enjoy reading this wicked, forbidden humor.

42. Sarah B. Pomeroy, ed. and trans., *Xenophon: Oeconomicus, A Social and Historical Commentary* (Oxford, 1994), 74–87; on Xenophon's popularity as a historian, see Peter Burke, "A Survey of the Popularity of Ancient Historians, 1450–1700," *History and Theory* 5 (1966): 135–52.

43. Pomeroy, ed. and trans., *Xenophon,* 87–90, for Pomeroy's commentary, and 139–63 (chaps. 7–10), for Xenophon's text. Also see Ruth H. Bloch, "Untangling the Roots of Modern Sex Roles: A Survey of Four Centuries of Change," *Signs* 4 (winter 1978): 237–52, esp. 238, for the finding that "traditional horizontal and qualitative sex distinctions, attributing to each sex a separate sphere of activity, were eclipsed by a vertical, hierarchical definition that stressed qualitative similarities. . . . Then, in the eighteenth and nineteenth centuries, with the rise of romantic evangelical Protestantism and industrialism, the cultural definition again shifted, with differences in kind subsuming differences in degree."

44. Falcone, *La nuova, vaga, e dilettevole villa,* 18–20.

45. See my *Fate and Honor, Family and Village,* especially the treatment of the village of Albareto in Emilia Romagna, and also my "Transformation of a Rural Village: Istria, 1870–1972," *Journal of Social History* (spring 1974): 243–70. Supporting observations abound in Patrizia Audenino, *Un mestiere per partire: Tradizione migratoria, lavoro e comunità in una vallata alpina* (Milan, 1990), passim.

46. Bonardo, *Le ricchezze dell' agricoltura,* 25–26.

47. Agostino Gallo, *Le vinti giornate dell' agricoltura. Et de' piaceri della villa. Di M. Agostino Gallo, nuovamente ristampate. Con le figure de gl' instrumenti pertinenti. Et con due tavole, una della dichiaratione di molti vocaboli, & l'altra delle cose*

notabili... (Venice: Camillo Borgominieri, 1584), 346–48. The *National Union Catalog* shows editions of the ten-day version in 1565 and 1566, the thirteen-day variant also in 1566, and then thirteen printings of the twenty-day version, eleven of them by 1629, one in 1674, and a straggler in 1775. There may well have been others that did not find their way to U.S. libraries, and there is a 1571 French translation.

48. Paolo Rigoli, "Pietanze in tavola," in Paola Marini, ed., *Cucine, cibi, e vini nell' età di Andrea Palladio (XVI sec)* (Vicenza, 1981), 27–28, cites G. A. Cibotto, *Teatro veneto* (Parma, 1960), 277, for this excerpt. The Venetian *mariazo* (*maritaggio* in Italian) was a type of popular farce, usually in rustic Padovan dialect, common in the repertoire of mountebanks and featuring the themes of love, matrimony, and domestic relations.

49. For a parallel conclusion, see Henderson and McManus, *Half Humankind,* 78–79.

50. Fonte, *Il merito delle donne,* 15–21. See Cox, "The Single Self," 529ff., for the suggestion that Venice's elite women in fact experienced a growing threat to their status and identity in the late sixteenth century and that *Il merito delle donne* should be read at least in part as a response to that threat. In addition to the previously cited works of Adriana Chemello, Beatrice Collina, and Patricia Labalme, see Paola Malpezzi Price, "A Woman's Discourse in the Italian Renaissance: Moderata Fonte's *Il merito delle donne,*" *Annali d'Italianistica* 7 (1989): 165–81, which is insightful in analyzing the garden where this discourse proceeds; and Constance Jordan, "Renaissance Women Defending Women: Arguments against Patriarchy," in Maria Ornella Marotti, ed., *Italian Women Writers from the Renaissance to the Present: Revising the Canon* (University Park, 1996), 55–67, which includes a brief commentary on Marinella as well. The significance of the garden, as well as several other important themes, are considered in Stephen D. Kolsky, "Wells of Knowledge: Moderata Fonte's *Il merito delle donne,*" *Italianist* 13 (1993): 57–96. These critics suggest that the protagonist in *Il merito delle donne* who is best seen as Fonte's alter ego is Corinna, the young interlocutor determined never to marry, who carries the intellectual burden of the dialogue. I would offer a different reading: Fonte as the polemical feminist Leonora—whose widowhood thereby transfers to her husband the impending death Fonte feared in real life—and the educated Lucrezia Marinella (in real life aged 21 and unmarried in 1592), or someone like her, as Corinna. This reading is congruent with what I believe were the publication circumstances surrounding Fonte's dialogue, to which I return in chapter 7.

Margaret Rosenthal, "Venetian Women Writers," 127, attributes the "I would rather drown" passage to the elder widow Adriana, rather than to Leonora, as I have it in my translation. Her version strikes me as contradictory to the sense of empowerment I believe Fonte intended in the text's sequence of words, kisses, and libations. Cox's translation, which became available only after I had done mine from the 1600 Italian original, shares my reading.

Rosenthal, *The Honest Courtesan,* 74–75, also provides some acute observations on inheritance practices among Venetian women, although the tantalizing suggestion that women more often than men designated inheritors beyond the family, so as to incorporate personal friends, cannot be pursued directly since the relevant endnote (39, on pp. 292–93) refers to an entirely different subject. Even Chojnacki's detailed studies, cited below, do not reveal a pattern of women making substantial bequests to friends. In any event, there is no hint in Fonte's dialogue that Leonora's acquaintances have any such hopes.

51. I want to thank this colleague, Martha Howell, for sharing with me early drafts of several chapters and the bibliography of her book, *The Marriage Exchange: Property, Social Place, and Gender in Cities of the Low Countries, 1300–1500* (Chicago, 1998).

52. For a general overview that is rather pessimistic in assessing the economic and social power of widows, see King, *Women of the Renaissance*, 56–62. By contrast, Diane Owen Hughes, "From Brideprice to Dowry in Mediterranean Europe," *Journal of Family History* 3 (fall 1978): 262–96, finds substantial legal protection for the control of wives and widows over their dowries (282). Nonetheless, daughters and younger brothers received less as property inheritance became more lineal in the sixteenth century, as shown in Diane Owen Hughes, "Representing the Family: Portraits and Purposes in Early Modern Italy," *Journal of Interdisciplinary History* 17 (summer 1986): 7–38. Also offering a positive assessment of women's ability to control property, in this instance in thirteenth-century Siena, is Eleanor S. Riemer, "Women, Dowries, and Capital Investment in Thirteenth-Century Siena," in Marion A. Kaplan, ed., *The Marriage Bargain: Women and Dowries in European History* (New York, 1985), 59–79.

Chojnacki, "The Power of Love," 136, details the formidable legal position of Venetian widows in the late fifteenth century. Further evidence on the power of Venetian widows, who appear prominently as testators and guarantors, may be found in the following essays by Stanley Chojnacki, "Dowries and Kinsmen in Early Renaissance Venice," *Journal of Interdisciplinary History* 5 (spring 1975): 571–600; "Kinship Ties and Young Patricians in Fifteenth-Century Venice," *Renaissance Quarterly* 38 (summer 1985): 240–70; and "Patrician Women in Early Renaissance Venice," 185–93. Dennis Romano, "Charity and Community in Early Renaissance Venice," *Journal of Urban History* 11 (November 1984): 63–81, ascribes the dominance of women among testators to wills made by pregnant women who feared for their survival (p. 66 and note 10), whereas I would place more emphasis on widows, but either way the evidence documents women exercising meaningful control over assets. Chojnacki's sample in the "Dowries and Kinsmen" essay shows 120 wills by wives and 76 by widows (p. 585). John C. Davis, *A Venetian Family and Its Fortune 1500–1900: The Donà and the Conservation of Their Wealth* (Philadelphia, 1975), 106–7, confirms that widows in this wealthy family sometimes left their dowry assets only to their daughters, presumably to offset the male linearity of their late husbands' bequests.

David Herlihy, *Medieval Households* (Cambridge, 1985), 154–55, explains the less favorable situation of a widow in Florence, where the law did not recognize her rights to conjugal property. Still, other evidence suggests that Florentine widows did cope; see David Herlihy, "Mapping Households in Medieval Italy," *Catholic Historical Review* 58 (1972): 17. Julius Kirshner, "Pursuing Honor While Avoiding Sin: The Monte Delle Doti of Florence," *Quaderni di "Studi Senesi"*

41 (1978): 7–8, esp. note 23, emphasizes limitations on widow's rights. The Florentine scene is thoroughly explored in the collected essays of Thomas Kuehn, *Law, Family, and Women: Toward a Legal Anthropology of Renaissance Italy* (Chicago, 1991), 238–57, on widows. Also see his "Law, Death, and Heirs in the Renaissance: Repudiation of Inheritance in Florence," *Renaissance Quarterly* 45 (autumn 1992): 484–516, on problems with estates carrying substantial liabilities. See Klapisch-Zuber, *Women, Family, and Ritual in Renaissance Italy*, 117–31, for the "Cruel Mother" essay, which uncompromisingly portrays male fights over female property. Ann Morton Crabb, "How Typical Was Alessandra Macinghi Strozzi of Fifteenth-Century Florentine Widows?" in Louise Mirrer, ed., *Upon My Husband's Death: Widows in the Literature and Histories of Medieval Europe* (Ann Arbor, 1992), 47–68, presents a nuanced account of a patrician widow's exercise of love and power. Recently available in English is the fine translation and commentary by Heather Gregory, ed. and trans., *Selected Letters of Alessandra Strozzi: Bilingual Edition* (Berkeley, 1997). Also see Francis Kent, *Household and Lineage in Renaissance Florence: The Family Life of the Capponi, Ginori, and Rucellai* (Princeton, 1977), 107–8, on how women divided their mass offerings between natal and conjugal kin. Sharon T. Strocchia, "Remembering the Family: Women, Kin, and Commemorative Masses in Renaissance Florence," *Renaissance Quarterly* 42 (winter 1989): 649–50, finds that women were "autonomous agents" who used the structural complexity of their familial situations to make meaningful choices about which family members would execute their wills and upon whom their blessings would be bestowed. A subtle balance is struck in Elaine G. Rosenthal, "The Position of Women in Renaissance Florence: Neither Autonomy nor Subjection," in Peter Denley and Caroline Elam, eds., *Florence and Italy: Renaissance Studies in Honour of Nicolai Rubinstein* (London, 1988), 369–81. On the plight of poor widows in Florence, where a welfare system encouraged them to care for their children, see Richard Trexler, "A Widows' Asylum of the Renaissance: The Orbatello of Florence," in Peter N. Stearns, ed., *Old Age in Preindustrial Society* (New York, 1982), 119–49. On the rituals of widowhood, see Isabelle Chabot, "'La sposa in nero.' La ritualizzazione del lutto delle vedove fiorentine (Secoli XIV–XV)," *Quaderni Storici* 86 (1994): 421–62.

James S. Grubb, *Provincial Families of the Renaissance: Private and Public Life in the Veneto* (Baltimore, 1996), 91–93, documents a complex reality in which at least some widows seem to have chosen to exercise less than the full rights accorded to them by law and in the intentions of their dead husbands. Grubb draws careful comparisons with both Florence and Venice, but his most suggestive insights come from the provincial records he has explored, which reveal tensions among male siblings who grappled against their mothers to exercise financial independence.

For an earlier period in Genoa we know that husbands, who themselves frequently remarried if their wives died, sometimes placed severe penalties meant to discourage their widows from taking second husbands, a pattern that may have continued into the sixteenth century. See Steven Epstein, *Wills and Wealth in Medieval Genoa, 1150–1250* (Cambridge, 1984), 108–117. Also see Diane Owen

Hughes, "Struttura familiare e sistemi di successione ereditaria nei testamenti dell' Europa medievale," *Quaderni Storici* 33 (1976): 929–52.

For England, see the excellent introduction in Merry E. Wiesner, *Women and Gender in Early Modern Europe* (Cambridge, 1993), 73–81, 103–9. Also see Judith M. Bennett, "Public Power and Authority in the Medieval English Countryside," in Erler and Kowaleski, eds., *Women and Power in the Middle Ages*, 18–29, esp. 23, describing the empowerment of widowhood for women. Also on England, see Michael M. Sheehan, *Marriage, Family, and Law in Medieval Europe: Collected Studies*, ed. James K. Farge (Toronto, 1996), especially the essay entitled, "The Wife of Bath and Her Four Sisters," 177–98; and see Sue Sheridan Walker, *Wife and Widow in Medieval England* (Ann Arbor, 1993), especially Barbara Hanawalt's essay, 141–64, for its treatment of remarriage as an "option," albeit a circumscribed option. Also see Cicely Howell, "Peasant Inheritance Customs in the Midlands 1280–1700," in Jack Goody, Joan Thirsk, and E. P. Thompson, eds., *Family and Inheritance: Rural Society in Western Europe, 1200–1800* (Cambridge, 1976), 141–45. Important essays by Barbara Hanawalt and by Judith Bennett on lower- and middle-class widows may be found in Mirrer, ed., *Upon My Husband's Death*, 21–46, 69–114, respectively. Barbara Hanawalt, "La debolezza del lignaggio. Vedove, orfani e corporazioni nella Londra tardo medievale," *Quaderni Storici* 86 (1994): 463–86, shows that generous dower provisions and preferences for appointing widows as guardians for their children gave surviving wives considerable power and respect.

For France, Natalie Zemon Davis, *The Return of Martin Guerre* (Cambridge, 1983), 30–31, provides an enlightening example or two on divergences between custom and contract for the Languedoc region. For comparative, theoretical perspectives on women and control over property, see Jack Goody, *Production and Reproduction: A Comparative Study of the Domestic Domain* (Cambridge, 1976). See his *Development of the Family and Marriage in Europe* (Cambridge, 1983), 60–68, for church teachings concerning widows. More generally, see the essays in Klapisch-Zuber, ed., *Silences of the Middle Ages*, esp. 308–11, of Claudia Opitz's "Life in the Late Middle Ages." Turning now to Germany, for problems and restrictions faced by widows who might have carried on their husbands' businesses, see Lyndal Roper, *The Holy Household: Women and Morals, in Reformation Augsburg* (Oxford, 1989), 49–54. For Poland, Hungary, and Russia, see various essays collected in Simonetta Cavaciocchi, *La donna nell'economia secc. XIII–XVIII* (Florence, 1990). The complexities of assessing remarriage strategies by widows are nicely introduced in David Sabean, *Property, Production, and Family in Neckarhausen, 1700–1870* (Cambridge, 1990), 233–34, 243–44. On the increased rights of widows to conjugal property in a French-speaking, Reformation district of Switzerland in the sixteenth century, see Jeffrey R. Watt, *The Making of Modern Marriage: Matrimonial Control and the Rise of Sentiment in Neuchâtel, 1550–1800* (Ithaca, 1992), 111–12. On the continued authority of widows over children who received some (but almost never all) of the familial property at the time of their father's death, see Sherrin Marshall Wyntjes, "Survivors and Status: Widowhood and Family in the Early Modern Netherlands," *Journal of Family*

History 7 (winter 1982): 396–405. On variations in the circumstances of widowhood shaped by production forces, see Martha Howell, "Women, the Family Economy, and the Structures of Market Production in Cities of Northern Europe during the Late Middle Ages," in Hanawalt, *Women and Work*, 198–222.

On reasons that society, more precisely men, might restrict a widow's freedom to remarry, see Alan Macfarlane, *Marriage and Love in England: Modes of Reproduction 1300–1840* (London, 1986), 231–37. Macfarlane then takes on the exceedingly difficult question of whether precipitous remarriage indicated lack of affection for the first spouse or perhaps exactly its opposite and concludes tentatively that the latter is more often true than the former. If this speculation has good foundation, then I suppose that the reluctance of widows to remarry should be taken as evidence that their first marriages were not all that happy, a notion fully in keeping with the thoughts of the ladies assembled in Moderata Fonte's dialogue.

Finally, and yet further afield, historians might broaden their concerns to consider questions such as those raised by anthropologist Julian Pitt-Rivers in "*La veuve andalouse,*" in Georges Ravis-Giordani, ed., *Femmes et patrimoine dans les sociétés rurales de l'Europe Méditerranéenne* (Paris, 1987), who argues that widows might either assume the authority formerly held by their husbands or, especially if they were indigent, suffer a dangerous fall in status and come under suspicion of deviancy and witchcraft.

53. Samuel K. Cohn Jr., *Death and Property in Siena, 1205–1800: Strategies for the Afterlife* (Baltimore, 1988), 198–209. Also see his *Women in the Streets: Essays on Sex and Power in Renaissance Italy* (Baltimore, 1996), for insightful analysis of issues ranging from the sexual behavior of widows to their plight in the Tuscan countryside.

54. Herlihy and Klapisch-Zuber, *Tuscans and Their Families*, 211–22, 217, for the quotation. Also see David Herlihy, "Vieillir à Florence au Quattrocento," *Annales E.S.C.* 24, no. 6 (1969): 1338–52. Anthony Molho, *Marriage Alliance in Late Medieval Florence* (Cambridge, 1994), 217–21, draws important comparisons between the Catasti of 1427 and 1480, but the reported drop in widows over time cannot be taken at face value, because the latter census omitted very poor families, thereby excluding a disproportionate number of widows. Also see 245–46, on other evidence of the pressure on widowers to remarry.

55. Giulia Calvi, *Il contratto morale: madri e figli nella Toscana moderna* (Rome, 1994), 16–19; also see her "Diritti e legami. Madri, figli, stato in Toscana (XVI–XVIII secolo)," *Quaderni Storici* 86 (1994): 487–510.

56. Vincenzo Maggi, *Un brieve trattato dell' eccellentia delle donne, composto dal prestantissimo philosopho (il Maggio) & di latina lingua, in italiana tradotto. Vi si e poi aggiunto un' essortatione a gli huomini perche non si lascino superar dalle donne, mostrandogli il gran danno che lor e per sopravenire* (Brescia: Damiano Turlino, 1545), 47–48.

57. A. Burguière, "Réticences théoriques et intégration pratique du remariage dans la France d'Ancien Régime—dix-septième—dix-huitième siècles," in J. Dupâquier, E. Hélin, P. Laslett, M. Livi-Bacci, and S. Sogner, eds., *Marriage*

and Remarriage in Populations of the Past (London, 1981), 41–48. In the same volume, see Louis Henry, "Le fonctionnement du marché matrimoniale," 191–98, for the preference of remarrying widowers for celibate women; Guy Carbourdin, "Le remariage en France sous l'Ancien Régime (seiziéme–dix-huitième siècles)," 273–86, for data on typical ages of widowhood; David Gaunt and Orvar Löfgren, "Remarriage in the Nordic Countries: The Cultural and Socio-economic Background," 49–60, for the emphasis on class, and Sune Åkerman, "The Importance of Remarriage in the Seventeenth and Eighteenth Centuries," 163–75, for an opposing conclusion; Roger Schofield and Edward A. Wrigley, "Remarriage Intervals and the Effect of Marriage Order on Fertility," 211–28, for the English parish findings; and Arthur E. Imhof, "Remarriage in Rural Populations and in Urban Middle and Upper Strata in Germany from the Sixteenth to the Twentieth Century," 335–46. On the village of Abingdon, see Barbara J. Todd, "The Remarrying Widow: A Stereotype Reconsidered," in Mary Prior, ed., *Women in English Society 1500–1800* (London, 1985), 54–92. Also see Alain Bideau, "A Demographic and Social Analysis of Widowhood and Remarriage: The Example of the Castellany of Thoissey-en-Dombes, 1670–1840," *Journal of Family History* 5 (spring 1980): 28–43, for more findings that widowers remarried sooner and more often than widows. On changes in residence by widows, see Annik Pardailhé-Galabrun, *The Birth of Intimacy: Privacy and Domestic Life in Early Modern Paris,* trans. Jocelyn Phelps (Philadelphia, 1991), 70.

58. Chilton Powell, *English Domestic Relations 1487–1653: A Study of Matrimony and Family Life in Theory and Practice as Revealed by the Literature, Law, and History of the Period* (New York, 1917), 158, on the specific point, and generally, for his sensible treatment of English writers on wifely duties.

59. Cicero, *On Old Age* and *On Friendship,* ed. and trans. Harry Edinger (Indianapolis, 1967), 3–39, is the modern edition I used. Cicero's writings were printed in several Italian translations in the sixteenth century.

60. Thucydides, *History of the Peloponnesian War,* trans. Charles Forster Smith (London, 1928), bk. 2, sec. 45, 341.

61. Agnelli, *Amorevole aviso,* 29.

62. Vives, *De l'istitutione de la femina christiana,* 184–95; Dolce, *De gli ammaestramenti,* 109–45. Selections from Vives, along with useful commentary, may be found in Joan Larsen Klein, *Daughters, Wives, and Widows: Writings by Men about Women and Marriage in England, 1500–1640* (Urbana, 1992), 97–100, 119–22. See also Kelso, *Doctrine for the Lady of the Renaissance,* 127–29.

63. Shulamith Shahar, *The Fourth Estate: A History of Women in the Middle Ages,* trans. Chaya Galai (London, 1983), 94–95.

64. *Select Letters of St. Jerome,* trans. F. A. Wright (Cambridge, 1963 rpt. of 1933 ed.), 161, for letter 38 to Marcella; 233, for letter 54 to Furia. Jerome's letters were published in a Tuscan translation in 1562, but this was a high-quality edition probably meant for reading by monks and nuns in their monasteries and convents rather than by laypersons in their homes.

65. Bernardo Trotto, *Dialoghi del matrimonio, e vita vedovile* (Turin: Francesco Dolce, 1578), 44–45; Jordan, *Renaissance Feminism,* 154–60; and Kelso, *Doc-*

trine for the Lady of the Renaissance, 100, 108. The 1583 edition published with Gl'Heredi del Bevilacqua (the same firm that did Guasco's letter to his daughter Lavinia) touts itself as greatly expanded and corrected.

66. Henderson and McManus, *Half Humankind,* 75–77, make parallel observations about the English scene.

67. Carlo Dionisotti, "L'Italia del Trissino," in Neri Pozza, ed., *Convegno di studi su Giangiorgio Trissino* (Vicenza, 1980), 11–22, agrees with the factual material presented here but reads the *Epistola* very differently than I do. He believes the text undermines the assertion by scholars who link Trissino's *Epistola* with Margarita Pia Sanseverina's decision to enter a convent. I see vindictive misogyny already in the *Epistola,* spurred by Margarita's rejection and years before Bianca had eaten into his fortune. Moreover, I see further hostility to women with whom he has been intimate in his exclusion of Bianca from his *I ritratti delle bellissime donne d'Italia* (Rome: Ludovico Degli Arrighi, 1524). Again, Dionisotti takes a more defensive line and suggests that the admitted exclusion only means than everyone already knew how beautiful Bianca was; he further speculates that she may have been included in an earlier manuscript version. To his credit, Dionisotti at least confronts the unhappy details of Trissino's life, which go unmentioned by virtually all other modern literary critics. For example, Beatrice Corrigan, ed., *Two Renaissance Plays* (Manchester, 1975), which includes the *Sofonisba,* tells only that he "survived two wives and all his children except a son by each marriage," and writes that "Trissino's literary activity continued throughout his life and may have hastened his death" (9).

68. Giovan Giorgio Trissino, *Epistola del Trissino de la vita, che dee tenere una donna vedova* (Rome: Ludovico Vicentino [Degli Arrighi] e Lautizio Perugino, 1524), BNF shelf mark Palat. 2.10.2.33.II, where this work is bound together with *I ritratti.* To the best of my knowledge, neither work is available in a modern edition, nor are they included in the 1729 edition of Trissino's works. Jordan, *Renaissance Feminism,* 71–72, is the only modern literary critic who discusses the *Epistola.*

69. Giulio Cesare Cabei, *Ornamenti della gentil donna vedova. Opera del signor Giulio Cesare Cabei, nella quale ordinatamente si tratta di tutte le cose necessarie allo stato vedovile, onde potrà farsi adorno d'ogni habito virtuoso, & honorato* (Venice: Cristoforo Zanetti, 1574), 43–45, on external appearances. Cabei's message, which runs to 133 dull octavo pages now available only in a few rare-book rooms, is amply captured in Kelso, *Doctrine for the Lady of the Renaissance,* 130–31.

70. Horatio Fusco Monfloreo D'Arimini, *La vedova del Fusco* (Rome: I Dorici, 1570), 30, for the quotation, and 31–39, for the characteristics of bad and good widows. I have been unable to locate any copies of this work in the United States or England. The shelf mark for the copy I used is BNF Palat. 7.5.1.59, and the author is cataloged as Fusco, Monflorio Orazio. Kelso, *Doctrine for the Lady of the Renaissance,* 367, lists the author as Fusco, Horatio. She recognized that Fusco's voice is very different from the ones heard in other texts on widows but did not examine the content deeply or explore the possibility that the author was a woman. Other scholars (for example, Benson, Jordan, King, and Rabil) make

absolutely no mention of Fusco, while Zarri et al. list the work but did not actually see it. The obscurity is undeserved.

My sense that the author is female, based on how the text reads, was reinforced when I subsequently learned that one Lucrezia Dorico was among the heirs who entered the Dorici publishing house, between 1566 and 1572, as *"stampatrice alli Coronari."* See Ascarelli and Menato, *La tipografia del '500 in Italia,* 107, and Francesco Barberi, "I Dorico, tipografi a Roma nel Cinquecento," *La Bibliofilia* 67, no. 2 (1965): 225.

71. Savonarola's *"lo amico de' pazzi diventa simile a loro"* is a lively rendition of the Vulgate original I assume he may have used: *qui cum sapientibus graditur sapiens erit amicus stultorum efficientur similis.*

72. Girolamo Savonarola, *Libro della vita viduale.* I used the edition in Mario Ferrara, ed., *Edizione nazionale delle opere di Girolamo Savonarola: Operette spirituali,* vol. 1 (Rome, 1973), 12–62. The publication history is on pages 299–317.

Chapter Seven

1. Fioravanti, *Dello specchio di scientia universale,* bk 1, chap. 25, 62. Eamon, *Science and the Secrets of Nature,* esp. 249–62, insightfully explores the issues raised by Fioravanti. Fioravanti was by no means unique in realizing the democratizing possibilities of the printing press; related ideas appear in Garzoni's *La piazza universale,* in Mercurio's epilogue to *De gli errori popolari d'Italia,* and in the prefaces to his *La commare* and to Marinello's *Delle medicine.* Cox, "The Single Self," 524, suggests that Moderata Fonte in *Il merito delle donne* also intended to convey "that women might one day be in a position to engage in the same kind of professional activities as men."

2. Peter Burke, *The Fortunes of the* Courtier: *The European Reception of Castiglione's* Cortegiano (University Park, 1995), esp. 43–45, for the quoted material, and 158–162, for the editions and translations.

3. Virginia Cox, *The Renaissance Dialogue: Literary Dialogue in Its Social and Political Contexts, Castiglione to Galileo* (Cambridge, 1992), 70–113. Also see Valerio Vianello, *Il "giardino" delle parole: Itinerari di scrittura e modelli letterari nel dialogo cinquecentesco* (Rome, 1993), 11–12. On the "courtesy-manual" genre more generally, see the insightful essay by Daniela Romagnoli, "Cortesia nella città: Un modello complesso. Note sull' etica medievale delle buone maniere," in her edited *La città e la corte: Buone e cattive maniere tra medioevo ed età moderna* (Milan, 1991), 21–70, as well as other contributions in this volume.

4. Jones, *The Currency of Eros,* 36.

5. See Burke, *Culture and Society in Renaissance Italy,* 60–61, 104–5, on Dolce and the rise of a market for books.

6. On China, see Dorothy Ko, *Teachers of the Inner Chambers: Women and Culture in Seventeenth-Century China* (Stanford, 1994), 29.

For an assertion that European publishers were ahead of their Chinese counterparts in exploiting the commercial and social possibilities of mass literacy, see

Chandra Mukerji, *From Graven Images: Patterns of Modern Materialism* (New York, 1983), 142.

7. Weaver, "Spiritual Fun," 173–76. More generally on cloistered women and artistic creativity, see the essays in Craig A. Monson, ed., *The Crannied Wall: Women, Religion, and the Arts in Early Modern Europe* (Ann Arbor, 1992). On the pressures against publication by nuns, see Francesca Medioli, *L' "Inferno monacale" di Arcangela Tarabotti* (Turin, 1990), 159–62.

8. Luciana Borsetto, "Narciso ed Eco. Figura e scrittura nella lirica femminile del Cinquecento: Esemplificazioni ed appunti," in Zancan, ed., *Nel cerchio della luna,* 171–264, esp. 254–64, for the listing of published Italian female authors.

9. On memorial volumes specifically and also more generally on female authors, see Anne Jacobson Schutte, "Irene di Spilimbergo: The Image of a Creative Woman in Late Renaissance Italy," *Renaissance Quarterly* 44 (spring 1991): 42–61. Also see De Maio, *Donna e Rinascimento,* 147–83. An English translation of Tullia d'Aragona, *Dialogue on the Infinity of Love* (Chicago, 1997), with a good introduction by Rinaldina Russell, makes this work readily available; a translation of selected writings by Veronica Franco also is forthcoming. Also see Fiora A. Bassanese, "Selling the Self; or, the Epistolary Production of Renaissance Courtesans," in Marotti, ed., *Italian Women Writers,* 69–82.

10. On the literary activities of religious women who were not saints, see Katherine Gill, "Women and the Production of Religious Literature in the Vernacular, 1300–1500," in E. Ann Matter and John Coakley, eds., *Creative Women in Medieval and Early Modern Italy: A Religious and Artistic Renaissance* (Philadelphia, 1994), 64–104. For the sixteenth century, see Elisabetta Graziosi, "Scrivere in convento: Devozione, encomio, persuasione nelle rime delle monache fra Cinque e Seicento," in Zarri, ed., *Donna, disciplina, creanza cristiana,* 303–31. In the same collection of essays, Tiziana Plebani, "Nascita e caratteristiche del pubblico di lettrici tra Medioevo e prima età Moderna," 27, makes the astute observation that women writers in the scribal culture generally "dictated" their works or wrote to family members, thus staying within the boundaries established for female discourse. On the significance of medieval women as owners of manuscript books, see Susan Groag Bell, "Medieval Book Owners: Arbiters of Lay Piety and Ambassadors of Culture," in Erler and Kowaleski, *Women and Power in the Middle Ages,* 149–87.

11. Fonte, *Tredici canti del Floridoro,* ix–xlvi, contains an excellent introduction by Valeria Finucci and lists the only two works Fonte published thereafter in her lifetime, one in 1581, and the other in 1582. I believe *La Resurrettione di Giesù Christo . . . ,* published in 1592, was posthumous.

12. Stephen D. Kolsky, "Wells of Knowledge: Moderata Fonte's *Il merito delle donne,*" 92, note 20, catches this phrase but suggests that it may result from Doglioni's revision, in 1600, of his original 1593 text. I am doubtful, if only because there are no other signs of attempts to bring the biographical material up-to-date, for example, to record Filippo's death or even the progress of her children. Indeed, the very next lines treat Fonte's devotion to housekeeping and child rearing with a tone of immediacy suggesting that her death was fresh. The addition to the published work of the brief pieces from two of Fonte's children

in my judgment only stresses her role as a mother, while leaving backstage the reality that she had also been a wife.

13. See earlier citations for bio-bibliographic details on Fonte, all of which rest primarily on Doglioni's 1593 biography. Modern critics Chemello, Collina, Cox, Labalme, and Malpezzi Price all mention the delay in publication but either make little of it or else emphasize only the enhanced market for *querelle des femmes* literature in the wake of Passi's misogynous *I donneschi difetti*. Cox, "The Single Self," 561–62, states that "the undesirability of marriage is a constant theme of *Il merito delle donne* . . . one of the elements in her argument [that] seems most clearly to derive from experience rather than literary tradition." Being in whole-hearted agreement, I am emboldened to suggest that Messer Zorzi also got the message and did what he could to make sure the world did not find out how it was to be his wife. Elsewhere, Cox suggests that Zorzi was sympathetic to his wife's writing (p. 4 of her translation, *The Worth of Women*), but I remain skeptical, at least once Fonte strayed from the subject of Christ's resurrection.

Doglioni's biographical sketch, written in 1593, may be found in the 1600 edition of *Il merito delle donne* (1–7) and in Cox's translation (31–40). Collina, "Moderata Fonte e *Il merito delle donne*," 142–43, highlights the importance of the twin publications by Marinella and Fonte but does not pursue reasons for the delay in publishing *Il merito delle donne*.

14. Bill Gates, with Nathan Myhrvold and Peter Rinearson, *The Road Ahead*, rev. ed. (New York, 1996).

INDEX

abortion. *See* miscarriage (and abortion)

academies (literary societies), 185, 336n. 17

Acosta, Christoforo (Christovan da Costa), 49

adolescents: and age of discretion, 177–78, 331n. 4; corporal punishment of, 178–79; historical issues concerning, 175–76, 331n. 2; lifestyle (diet, dress, exercise, sleep) of, 190–92; moral and spiritual growth of, 177–81, 184–85, 190–92; sins of, 179–81, 186–87, 191. *See also* chastity; children; daughters; sons; students, proper habits of

adultery, 189, 192, 224, 233, 236, 245, 340n. 51. *See also* cuckolds

advice manuals: characteristics of, 1–4, 9–11, 15, 18, 45–48, 81, 125–26, 148–51, 216–17, 225, 233–34, 284–85; and Greco-Roman antecedents, 22, 41, 76, 78–80, 97, 124–25, 143–44, 219, 223–24, 250 *(see also individuals by name)*; satires of, 29–30, 57, 58, 186–90, 197–208, 235; and sixteenth-

century printing and print culture, 5, 9, 13–20, 41–42, 84, 157; versus books of popular errors, 19–20, 94–95, 149–50, 302n. 5; versus books of secrets, 9–10, 45, 61, 62; versus confessionals, 165–66, 192–97; versus courtesy manuals, 282–83; versus dialogues, 213–14, 216–17, 225, 232, 283; versus farmers' almanacs, 251–52, 254–55; versus herbals, 45–49, 319n. 55. *See also* adolescents; babies; children; daughters; fathers; midwives; mothers; sons; widows

Agato, Pietro Angelo (pseudo-Falloppio), 61–62, 140, 313–14n. 85

Agnelli, Cosmo, 204–6, 241–42, 265

Agrippa (Henricus Cornelius Agrippa von Nettesheim), 26, 66

Alamanni, Antonio, 176–77

Albert the Great, 82, 105, 117, 308n. 46

Alberti, Leon Battista, 7, 294–95n. 6

Alciato, Andrea, 40

anatomy: denounced, 43; of female genitalia, 60–61, 77–80, 98, 101–6, 313n. 83 (illustrations, 103,

hair coloring and styling, 205; on
lust, 195, 197; on marital relations,
236–37, 239, 244; on menstruation, 66; on pain during parturition, 116–17; reading of, 185; on
widows, 266, 273; on women,
170–71, 246, 248
Biondo, Michelangelo, 148
bloodletting, 82, 141, 142, 143
Boccaccio, Giovanni, 54, 136, 185,
197–98, 218, 235, 335n. 15
bodily humors: in adolescents, 187;
in babies, 145, 151; and breast-
feeding, 126, 141–43, 145; imbalances of, 43, 154; and impotence,
50–51; and infertility, 58–59; and
pregnancy, 89–94, 117; and sexual
intercourse, 26–29, 54; theory of,
17–18; in widows, 267
Boethius, 38
Boldo, Bartolomeo, 28, 34
Bonardo, Count Giovanni Maria:
bio-bibliographical details, 198;
on whether to marry, 198–99; on
wives as household managers in
rural settings, 254–55
Bonaventure, Saint, 52
Borgarucci, Prospero: on female genitalia, 60–61; on male genitalia,
55–57
Borromeo, Charles (archbishop of Milan), Saint, 162, 329n. 58
Borsetto, Luciana, 286
Botticelli, Sandro, 13
Bottini, Albertini, 66
boys. See sons
breast-feeding: and abstinence from
sexual intercourse, 134, 139–40,
141, 152; and benefits of maternal
milk, 126, 128–29, 138, 139, 217,
321n. 9, 325n. 26; and conception,
128; and deviltry, 144–45; joys of,
127–28; and menstruation, menstrual blood, 67, 128–29, 140–42;
and problems with milk —of coagulation, 143–44, —of excess,

120, 142; —of insufficiency, 140–
41; —of quality, 139, 140, 142–
43; technique and timing of, 137–
39; weaning from, 138, 139, 145
Brucioli, Antonio, 230–32
Bruni da Pistoia, Domenico, 214
Bruto, Giovanni Michele, 183–85,
336n. 16
Burke, Peter, 282–83, 284
Burkhardt, Jacob, 181

Cabei, Giulio Cesare, 270
Caggio, Paolo, 346n. 1
Cappello, Bianca, 287
Capra, Galeazzo Flavio, 333–34n. 14
carnal desire. See lust
Carnegie, Dale, 4
Caroso, Fabritio, 190
Carpi, Berengario (da), Jacopo. See
Berengario da Carpi, Jacopo
Carroll, Michael P., 135
Casey, Kathleen, 222, 226
Castiglione, Count Baldassare, 183,
213, 282–83
Catechism of the Council of Trent: on
the conjugal debt, 32; on corporal
punishment of children, 155, 161–
62; on lust, 196–97; on marital relations, 208, 236–38; on proper
words concerning sex, 194–95
Catherine of Aragon (queen of England), 216
Catholic Reformation: and child rearing, 168–70; and exorcism, 52;
and printed books, 5–6, 8–9, 35–
36, 162, 231, 283; and widows,
261, 266; and women, 237, 246–
47, 257, 286. See also individuals by
name
Cereta, Laura, 207–8, 285–86,
343n. 59
cesarean section, birth by, 86, 98
Chartier, Roger, 11, 297n. 13
chastity: and beauty, 180–81; and
confession, 192–97; preserving in
daughters, 168, 184, 192; teaching

150; —at parturition, 111–16,
118; —as physicians' assistants,
98–99; —in postpartum care,
119–23; —in removal of a dead
fetus, 85–88 (illustrations, 87, 88)
miscarriage (and abortion), 82–86,
314n. 89. *See also* fetus; menstruation and menstrual blood; pregnancy
misogyny, 57–60, 67, 197–98, 201–
4, 213, 232. See also *querelle des
femmes* literature; women: and Renaissance patriarchy
Mondino dei Luzzi, 78–80
Monica (mother of Saint Augustine),
Saint, 156
mothers: as indulgent, 157, 184, 187,
189; responsibilities in rearing
daughters, 180, 218, 237, 241,
347–48n. 9; as teachers, 158–60,
240. *See also* adolescents; babies;
breast-feeding; chastity; children;
pregnancy; wives
music: as sinful, 185, 189; as soothing, 169, 192
Muzio, Girolamo, 282

Nenni, Giovambattista of Bari, 282
nursing. *See* breast-feeding; wet
nurses

obesity: in babies, 138; in children,
168; in pregnant women, 115–16
opium, 49
orgasm, 34–35, 49, 59, 70
Ovid: amorous writings of; cited in
children's books, 171; on cosmetics, 205–6
Ozment, Steven, 9, 137, 158, 295n.
8

Palmieri, Matteo: on adolescence,
177–79, 190; bio-bibliographical
details, 35, 179; on breast-feeding
and wet nurses, 128–29; on child
rearing, 160–61, 162; on concep-

tion, 35; on intractable wives, 229;
on the life cycle, 295–96n. 11; on
signs of fetus's sex, 76; on signs of
pregnancy, 70
Paolo da Certaldo, 7–8, 132, 294n. 6
parents. *See* fathers; mothers
parturition: fetal position during,
106, 108, 112, 114–15; (illustration, 109); and husband's assistance, 108, 110; and midwife's
duties, 111–16 (illustration, 113);
mother's position during, 110–11;
by obese women, 115–16 (illustration, 116); reasons for pain during,
115, 117–18; supernatural aids in,
101, 108, 110, 112, 114, 319n. 53;
superstitions about, 118; of twins,
114–15; and use of herbals and
unctions, 110–12, 114, 115, 118.
See also postpartum care
Passi, Giuseppe: bio-bibliographical
details, 201–2, 341–42n. 54; on
governing wives, 203; and response
by Lucrezia Marinella, 202
patriarchy. *See* women: and Renaissance patriarchy
Paul, Saint, 30–31, 208
perfumes. *See* cosmetics
Pericles, 265
physicians: as abortionists, condemned, 84–85, 316n. 17; and
advice manuals, 18–20, 56, 150,
279–80, 309n. 53; and bodily humors theory, 17–18; and children's
illnesses, 148–49; as cross-dressers,
98–99; *onestà* (modesty) of, 97–98;
training of, 55–56, 61
Piccolomini, Alessandro, 7, 217, 250
Piccolomini, Enea Silvio. *See* Pius II,
Pope
Pisanelli, Baldasar, 28
Pitkin, Hanna, 135
Pius II, Pope (Enea Silvio Piccolomini), 162, 190
Pius XI, Pope, 162
placenta, removal of, 119

teachers *(continued)*
158–59, 163–67. *See also* children:
schooling of; students, proper habits of
Tertullian, 144
Thesoro di secreti naturali, 41, 75, 82
Tommasi, Francesco: bio-bibliographical details, 302n. 9; on child rearing, 166–68; on choosing a wife,
209; on conception, 23; on frequent sexual intercourse, 30; on
marital relations, 238–39; on pil-
low talk, 32;
Trexler, Richard, 176
Trissino, Giovan Giorgio, 267–70,
358n. 67
Trotto, Bernardo, 34, 266–67, 306n.
35
Trotula of Salerno, 82, 102, 318n.
36
Trunconius, Jacobus, 148
Tuscany, marital status in, 262–63
twins: conception of, 77–80, 316n.
10; parturition of, 114–15

umbilical cord, tying of, 121
uroscopy, 59, 71–72
uterus: anatomy of, 60–61, 71, 73–
76, 77–80, 93–94, 98, 101–8,
315–16n. 9 (illustration, 79); and
conception, 20–22, 24, 55, 57,
58–60; cures for various ailments
of, 59, 61–63, 314n. 88; and miscarriage, 82–84. *See also* infertility;
parturition; postpartum care

Valiero (misspelled as Valerio),
Cardinal Agostino, 240–41
Valverde, Juan, 60–61, 313n. 84
Vegio, Maffeo, 156–57, 162
Venice, printing in, 8, 11–13, 298n.
15
Vergerio, Pier Paolo, 156
vernacular, use in: confessionals,
165–66, 192–97, 338–39nn. 40,
41; herbals, 45; medical advice

manuals, 14–15, 19–20, 23–24,
55–56, 60–61, 143, 301n. 23; pornographic books, 33–34, 57;
schools, 170–74. *See also* reading:
and the vernacular
Vesalius, Andreas, 60–61, 78, 144,
318n. 38
virginity, signs of, 20, 105, 211–12
Vittori, Leonello, 148
Vives, Juan Luis, 216–17, 222, 265,
345n. 79

weaning. *See* breast-feeding: weaning
from
Weaver, Elissa, 285
wet nurses: disparagements of, 127,
129, 130–31, 149, 169, 320n. 6;
duties and qualities of, 129–31,
144, 167, 321n. 12; and economic
arrangements, 133–34; historical
debate over the extent and consequences of using, 131–37, 271,
321n. 13, 322–24nn. 18–20; and
survival rates of infants, 134–35,
324n. 21; in various cultures, 124–
25, 132, 322n. 17
widowers, 262, 265
widows: burial choices by, 261; com-
petence of, 221, 228–29, 260–63,
269, 271–72, 278, 346n. 3, 353–
56n. 52; paucity of advice manuals
for, 265; proper behavior of, 267,
269–71, 273–76; remarriage by,
245, 259, 262–67, 271, 272–74,
356n. 54, 356–57n. 57; spiritual
perfection in, 274, 276–77; as wet
nurses, 129
wives: choosing of, 50, 199–201,
203, 210–11, 213, 215, 219, 272;
and the conjugal debt, 30–31; governance of, 36, 203, 213–14, 220–
23, 226–27, 239; as household
managers generally, 15–16, 221–
23, 244–45; as household managers in rural settings, 249–57; and
obeying, pleasing, soothing, and